JOB STRESS
INTERVENTIONS

EDITED BY

LAWRENCE R. MURPHY,

JOSEPH J. HURRELL, JR.,

STEVEN L. SAUTER, AND

GWENDOLYN PURYEAR KEITA

AMERICAN PSYCHOLOGICAL ASSOCIATION

WASHINGTON, DC

First Printing November 1995
Second Printing December 1996

Published by
American Psychological Association
750 First Street, NE
Washington, DC 20002

Copies may be ordered from
American Psychological Association
Order Department
P.O. Box 92984
Washington, DC 20090-2984

In the United Kingdom and Europe, copies may be ordered from
American Psychological Association
3 Henrietta Street
Covent Garden, London
WC2E 8LU England

Typeset in Century Schoolbook by Easton Publishing Services, Inc., Easton, MD

Cover designer: Minker Design, Bethesda, MD
Printer: Kirby Lithographic Company, Inc., Arlington, VA
Technical/production editor: Valerie Montenegro

Library of Congress Cataloging-in-Publication Data
Job stress interventions / edited by Lawrence R. Murphy . . . [et al.].
    p. cm.
    Derived from the 1992 conference, Stress in the 90s: a changing workforce in a changing workplace.
    Includes bibliographical references and index.
    ISBN 1-55798-281-3 (acid-free paper)
    1. Job stress—Congresses. 2. Stress management—Study and teaching—Congresses. 3. Employees—Training of—Congresses. 4. Employees—Counseling of—Congresses. 5. Employee health promotion—Congresses. 6. Employees—Health risk assessment—Congresses. I. Murphy, Lawrence R. II. American Psychological Association.
HF5548.85.J655 1995
158.7—dc20   95-37647
                                                       CIP

British Library Cataloguing-in-Publication Data
A CIP record is available from the British Library.

Printed in the United States of America

Contents

Contributors

Alexis D. Abernethy, *Department of Psychiatry, University of Rochester Medical Center, Rochester, NY*

Robert J. Biersner, *Division of Occupational Safety and Health, U.S. Department of Labor, Washington, DC*

Robert D. Caplan, *Department of Psychology, George Washington University, Washington, DC*

Sue Cartwright, *Manchester School of Management, University of Manchester Institute of Science and Technology, Manchester, England*

Cary L. Cooper, *Manchester School of Management, University of Manchester Institute of Science and Technology, Manchester, England*

Wayne Corneil, *Employee Assistance Services, Health and Welfare Canada, Ottawa, Ontario, Canada*

Carol A. Craft, *Saint Louis Continuing Education Center, Department of Veterans Affairs, Washington, DC*

Joan Curran, *Human Resource Development, University of Michigan, Ann Arbor*

Erik de Gier, *Consumentenbond, the Hague, the Netherlands*

Stewart I. Donaldson, *Center for Organizational and Behavioral Sciences, The Claremont Graduate School, Claremont, CA*

Donald Elisburg, *Donald Elisburg Law Offices, Potomac, MD*

George S. Everly, Jr., *International Critical Incident Stress Foundation, Inc., Ellicott City, MD*

Georgina J. Flannery, *Newton Free Library, Newton, MA*

Raymond B. Flannery, Jr., *Department of Psychiatry, Harvard Medical School, Boston, MA*

David Foster, *Department of Psychology, George Washington University, Washington, DC*

Charles Gallagher, *Massachusetts Department of Mental Health, Boston, MA*

Daniel C. Ganster, *Department of Management, University of Arkansas, Fayetteville*

James E. Green, *Justin Industries, Inc., Ft. Worth, TX*

M. Annette Hanson, *Department of Psychiatry, Harvard Medical School, Boston, MA*

Catherine A. Heaney, *School of Public Health, Ohio State University, Columbus*

Irene L. D. Houtman, *TNO Institute of Preventive Health Care, Leiden, the Netherlands*

George W. Howe, *Department of Psychiatry and Behavioral Sciences, George Washington University Medical Center, Washington, DC*

Timothy J. Huelsman, *Department of Psychology, Saint Louis University, St. Louis, MO*

Barbara A. Israel, *Department of Health Behavior and Health Education, University of Michigan, Ann Arbor*

Janice R. W. Joplin, *Department of Management, Southern Illinois University at Edwardsville*

Joseph B. Keyes, *Division of Mental Retardation, Delaware Health and Social Services, Georgetown, DE*

Richard M. Kolbell, *Northwest Occupational Medicine Center, Portland, OR*

Michiel A. J. Kompier, *TNO Institute of Preventive Health Care, Leiden, the Netherlands*

Kari Lindström, *Department of Psychology, Finnish Institute of Occupational Health, Helsinki, Finland*

Mindy Lockshin, *Department of Psychology, George Washington University, Washington, DC*

Miya Maysent, *Drake Beam Morin, Inc., Jacksonville, FL*

Claire McGrath, *Department of Psychology, George Washington University, Washington, DC*

Jeffrey T. Mitchell, *Department of Emergency Health Services, University of Maryland–Baltimore County, Baltimore*

Stacey Kohler Moran, *St. Paul Fire and Marine Insurance Co., Ocean Springs, MS*

David C. Munz, *Department of Psychology, Saint Louis University, St. Louis, MO*

Lawrence R. Murphy, *Robert A. Taft Laboratories, National Institute for Occupational Safety and Health, Cincinnati, OH*

Debra L. Nelson, *Department of Management, Oklahoma State University, Stillwater*

Walter E. Penk, *Department of Psychiatry, Harvard Medical School, Boston, MA*

Samuel B. Pond III, *Department of Psychology, North Carolina State University, Raleigh*

Richard H. Price, *Institute for Social Research, University of Michigan, Ann Arbor*

James Campbell Quick, *Department of Management, University of Texas at Arlington*

Jane Rafferty, *Institute for Social Research, University of Michigan, Ann Arbor*

Andrew E. Scharlach, *School of Social Welfare, University of California, Berkeley*

Susan J. Schurman, *Department of Labor Studies and Employment Relations, Rutgers–The State University of New Jersey, New Brunswick*

Carlla S. Smith, *Department of Psychology, Bowling Green State University, Bowling Green, OH*

Stefanie Spera, *Drake Beam Morin, Inc., Phoenix, AZ*

Lorne M. Sulsky, *Department of Psychology, University of Calgary, Alberta, Canada*

Nico Terra, *Stichting Arbeid en Nieuwe Technologie, Amsterdam, the Netherlands*

John A. Thomason, *Organizational Behavior Consultants, Lillington, NC*

Judy C. Turner, *Basic Military Training, Lackland Air Force Base, TX*

Michelle van Ryn, *School of Public Health, State University of New York at Albany*

Amiram D. Vinokur, *Institute for Social Research, University of Michigan, Ann Arbor*

Jack G. Wiggins, Jr., *Psychological Development Center, Inc., Cleveland, OH*

Shelly C. Wolff, *General Electric Co., Health Care Management Programs, Fairfield, CT*

Preface

The pages of the popular press testify to the growing levels of work-related stress felt by many Americans and to the price paid by individuals and organizations in terms of personal well-being and productivity. What is the best approach for managing or controlling stress on the job? Is intervention at the individual level the best way to handle stress, or are organizational interventions such as job redesign or joint worker–management stress committees more effective? Evidence to answer these and other crucial questions is contained in this book.

The purpose of this book is to present new research on the effectiveness of a variety of job stress intervention programs and applications. The findings suggest ways in which individuals, organizations, and policymakers can help prevent stress before it affects mental health and job performance or, when this is not possible, alleviate the effects of existing job stress. Collectively, the authors draw attention to new issues that demand further exploration and identify important gaps in the existing knowledge. In this way, we hope that the book will initiate a new generation of research and discussion.

This book owes its existence to a long and fruitful collaboration between the National Institute for Occupational Safety and Health (NIOSH) and the American Psychological Association (APA) that began in the late 1980s. At that time, the two organizations joined forces to refine and implement NIOSH-proposed strategies for the prevention of work-related psychological disorders.[1] The first product of the partnership was a jointly sponsored national conference in 1990 titled Work and Well-Being: An Agenda for the 1990s. Its proceedings were subsequently published in two books. The first contained action plans for improving the organization (design) of work, the surveillance of psychosocial risk factors and stress disorders, and mental health delivery systems.[2] The second book contained a series of international reports on occupational mental health risks and interventions.[3] The conference also served as an impetus for the initiation of a graduate fellowship program in occupational health psychology; the start-up of a new journal, the *Journal of Occupational Health Psychology*; and a subsequent conference on job stress in 1992.

The 1992 conference, Stress in the '90s: A Changing Workforce in a Changing Workplace, drew more than 800 international participants and covered a broad range of topics. This book is the third of three books derived from that

---

[1] Sauter, S. L., Murphy, L. R., & Hurrell, J. J., Jr. (1990). Prevention of work-related psychological disorders: A national strategy proposed by the National Institute for Occupational Safety and Health (NIOSH). *American Psychologist, 45,* 1146–1158.

[2] Keita, G. P., & Sauter, S. L. (Eds.). (1992). *Work and well-being: An agenda for the 1990s.* Washington, DC: American Psychological Association.

[3] Quick, J. C., Murphy, L. R., & Hurrell, J. J., Jr. (Eds.). (1992). *Stress and well-being at work: Assessments and interventions for occupational mental health.* Washington, DC: American Psychological Association.

conference. The first book[4] concentrated on factors that may predispose the individual worker to stress. It explored the shifting demographics of the work-force, work—family dynamics, and implications for job stress. The second book[5] focused on organizational risk factors for job stress. It investigated changes in job demands and associated stress risks in today's workplace, as well as new ways of conceptualizing and assessing organizational risk factors. This present book draws on the findings of both previous books and examines interventions at the individual, organizational, and policy levels.

We thank Judy Nemes of the American Psychological Association for her extensive editorial support in preparation of this book, Lynn Letourneau for her assistance with administrative details, and several anonymous reviewers for their valuable suggestions for chapter revisions. Finally, we thank each of the chapter authors for their patience and hard work during the longer-than-expected process of preparing this book for publication.

Lawrence R. Murphy
Joseph J. Hurrell, Jr.
Steven L. Sauter
Gwendolyn Puryear Keita

---

[4]Keita, G. P., & Hurrell, J. J., Jr. (Eds.). (1994). *Job stress in a changing workforce: Investigating gender, diversity, and family issues*. Washington, DC: American Psychological Association.

[5]Sauter, S. L., & Murphy, L. R. (Eds.). (1995). *Organizational risk factors for job stress*. Washington, DC: American Psychological Association.

Introduction

The workplace and the work experience are changing at breakneck speed. Global competition, corporate downsizing and reorganization, new management philosophies, increased workforce diversity, new technologies, and—particularly in the health care field—fear of HIV and AIDS and multidrug-resistant tuberculoses are all elements that contribute to the change. The rate of change also has increased. Technological developments in the computer field are so rapid that state-of-the-art equipment purchased 6 months ago already is outdated. Application packages are upgraded so frequently that one is in a seemingly constant state of training. Thus, as soon as one masters a word processing program, a new version appears, and the learning process begins anew.

Twenty-five years ago, Alvin Toffler (1970) coined the term *future shock* to describe "the shattering stress and disorientation that we induce in individuals by subjecting them to too much change in too short a time" (p. 2). In the modern workplace, future shock has become reality. The changing workplace is a breeding ground for stress and associated mental and physical health disorders. As never before, there is a need for effective interventions to prevent, reduce, and manage job stress.

Although there is general agreement that stress is a growing problem in the modern workplace, there is less agreement on the optimal strategy for reducing or controlling stress. Historically, three distinct approaches have been used, each with a distinct focus and preferred interventions. In medical terminology, these approaches can be classified as primary, secondary, and tertiary prevention.

Primary prevention seeks to alter the source of stress at work and is the most fundamental approach to the problem of work stress. This approach can be reactive (i.e., changing the work conditions that produce stress) or proactive (i.e., preventing work conditions from becoming stressful). In both cases, the focus is on the sources of stress, not the symptoms or outcomes of stress. Primary prevention requires an assessment of job and work organization factors to identify the stress "hot spots" in the organization. Examples of primary prevention strategies are job or task redesign, participative management, and job enlargement. Despite their advantages, these strategies are expensive to implement and often disruptive to production schedules; thus, they have tended to be less acceptable to management than secondary or tertiary strategies. Scientific evaluations of primary prevention strategies for reducing work stress are rare in the published literature (see Ivancevich, Matteson, Freedman, & Phillips, 1990; Murphy, 1988, for reviews), and there is little practical guidance for companies on how best to reduce employee stress at this level. Because primary prevention is often more difficult to implement, chapters describing this approach appear in the second main section of this book, after chapters describing more widely used interventions focusing on the individual worker.

Section II of this book (The Work Setting) contains seven chapters that address primary prevention strategies for reducing work stress. Three of the chapters take a broad overview of stress and offer general guiding principles for designing stress interventions. The remaining five chapters describe and evaluate specific job and organizational change programs for relieving stressful working conditions. Taken together, these chapters provide the necessary conceptual background for planning stress interventions and offer concrete examples of specific worksite interventions.

Secondary prevention aims to reduce the severity of stress symptoms before they lead to more serious health consequences. Stress management programs are good examples of secondary prevention. These programs seek to educate workers about the causes and consequences of stress and teach them relaxation and coping skills for managing the physiological and psychological symptoms of stress. The most common types of stress management strategies are progressive muscle relaxation, cognitive–behavioral skills training, and meditation. These strategies became popular in the 1980s, riding on the coattails of the worksite health promotion movement (Murphy, 1988). Such strategies are easy to design, implement, and evaluate and are generally well received by workers.

The first main section of this book (The Worker) contains 11 chapters that describe secondary prevention strategies. These strategies are divided into two parts, one focusing on stress management training and the other on coping strategies. It is significant that three of the five chapters on coping strategies specifically deal with job loss and unemployment. This is not coincidental but reflects the trend toward company downsizing and reorganization that began in the late 1980s and accelerated in the 1990s. The chapters describing stress management training, on the other hand, are more generic in nature and involve teaching workers somatic and cognitive relaxation skills instead of specific coping skills for specific stressors (e.g., job loss). The studies described present evidence that secondary prevention strategies are effective in helping workers deal with the symptoms of stress and therefore have a place in worksite stress reduction programs. However, most authors recommend that secondary strategies be linked with primary prevention efforts to achieve more comprehensive programs.

Tertiary prevention involves the treatment of health conditions, regardless of the source. Tertiary prevention is reactive, inasmuch as the health problem already exists, and the main effort involves treating the health disorder, not eliminating the sources of stress at work. Stress-related disorders (whether identified as such) traditionally have been dealt with by the company medical department, often through an employee assistance program (EAP). EAPs see a wide spectrum of stress problems, some of which have their root causes in the work environment. However, the typical EAP provides limited feedback to management, usually in the form of information about how many employees were seen in the EAP and the types of health problems encountered. EAPs generally focus on characteristics of the employee, not on characteristics of the work environment, which may be causing the employee's stress. The third part of The Worker section describes tertiary prevention programs, and all have a single focus: posttraumatic stress disorder (PTSD). PTSD is perhaps the most severe form of work stress and certainly has one of the most debilitating outcomes (Everly, 1989). Although once restricted primarily to first responders and emergency response personnel, PTSD is being seen more and more often among workers in other occupational groups (e.g., taxi drivers, convenience store workers, bank employees) who are exposed to physical assaults and other forms of violence at work. Increasingly, occupational health providers are called on to treat employees exposed to traumatic events and to assist workers in dealing with the emotional and physical ramifications of such exposure.

Collectively, these chapters suggest that stress interventions must address both individual worker and job and organizational factors, and be sensitive to the dynamic nature of stress, to be effective for long-term stress prevention and reduction. Provisions for worker participation in all aspects of stress interventions promote greater worker involvement and ultimately should increase the odds of success (Sauter, Murphy, & Hurrell, 1990). Beyond the organizational level, policy and legislative actions at the national level can have important influences on workplace stress. For example, occupational safety and health policies and standards can be used to prevent or reduce the impact of large-scale stressors such as involuntary layoffs and discrimination in employment due to disability. The third and final section of this book is devoted to an examination of some key policy and legislative issues.

It is hoped that this book will both stimulate new research in the area of job stress interventions and make a contribution toward reducing stress at work and improving worker well-being and organizational effectiveness. The limited, narrow focus of much of the stress management research literature will not be adequate to address the nature and types of stressors that workers currently face and emergent stressors that workers may be required to face in the decade to come.

References

Everly, G. (1989). *A clinical guide to the treatment of the human stress response*. New York: Plenum Press.

Ivancevich, J. M., Matteson, M. T., Freedman, S. M., & Phillips, J. S. (1990). Worksite stress management interventions. *American Psychologist, 45*, 252–261.

Murphy, L. R. (1988). Workplace interventions for stress reduction and prevention. In C. L. Cooper & R. Payne (Eds.), *Causes, coping, and consequences of stress at work*. Chichester, England: Wiley.

Sauter, S. L., Murphy, L. R., & Hurrell, J. J., Jr. (1990). A national strategy for the prevention of work-related psychological disorders. *American Psychologist, 45*, 1146–1158.

Toffler, A. (1970). *Future shock*. New York: Random House.

THE WORKER

Introduction

The chapters in this section of the book are concerned with job stress interventions at the individual level, that is, those interventions dealing with secondary and tertiary prevention. We have divided the chapters into three parts. Part I, entitled "Stress Management Training," includes chapters that discuss a variety of types of worker training aimed at teaching workers the skills necessary to manage their responses to stressful situations. Part II, "Coping With Job Stress and Unemployment," concerns intervention efforts aimed at increasing workers' abilities to cope with job-related stress. Part III, "Understanding and Treating Posttraumatic Stress," contains chapters that focus on the sequelae of acutely stressful events.

The chapters in Part I provide a description of a broad range of stress management interventions that involve attempts to train employees either to modify or control their appraisal of stressful situations (secondary prevention) or to cope more effectively with stress reactions (tertiary prevention). Thomason and Pond describe an experiment that evaluated the effects of a stress management program composed of cognitive restructuring, positive self-talk, muscle relaxation, autogenic exercises, and imagery exercises on psychological and physiological outcomes. In the second chapter, Abernethy examines the efficacy of anger management training in reducing reported stress among a group of police officers. Kolbell, in the third chapter, describes the effects of relaxation training on the health and cognitive performance of a group of social service employees. In the fourth chapter, Keys examines the effects of stress inoculation training on measures of anger and staff turnover. Munz and Craft, in the next chapter, discuss a stress management program that has been ongoing for more than 13 years. The authors elaborate not only features of the program but also factors that they consider "critical" to the overall success of the program. In the final chapter, Donaldson provides a theoretical yet engaging discussion of the role of worksite health promotion in reducing stress and enhancing health and job performance.

Augmenting workers' abilities to cope with work-related stress is the focus of chapters in Part II. Heaney, Price, and Rafferty in the leading chapter describe a field experiment aimed at examining the efficacy of a program intended to increase social support and participation in work-related decisions. This program involved specific skills training and clearly resulted in enhanced mental health and job satisfaction. The following chapter, by Smith and Sulsky, examines the stress coping process. The results of their study suggest that workers may not need to be trained in more active coping but may benefit from training aimed at how to effectively use active coping to manage stress related to unsuccessful coping attempts.

The final three chapters in Part II examine coping with job loss. Vinokur, Price, Caplan, van Ryn, and Curran describe a field experiment designed to examine the effects of increased social support and improved skills and cognition relevant to coping with job loss. The results of the experiment suggest that such interventions can provide net benefits to the unemployed individual as well as the community. Howe, Caplan, Foster, Lockshin, and McGrath discuss how to design and evaluate family-focused preventive interventions aimed at reducing the risk of emotional disorders and family dysfunction following job loss. In the final chapter of Part II, Maysent, Spera, and Morin evaluate a stress reduction intervention for unemployed workers. The intervention involved stress education, training in recognition of individual stress response, techniques to minimize the effects of stress, providing the opportunity to use these techniques, and helping workers to plan for future stressors.

For many years, it has been recognized that after experiencing an extreme event or events outside the range of normal human experience, a person may develop characteristic symptoms that are not linked to any clearly defined somatic pathology. Such symptoms, now recognized as posttraumatic stress disorder (PTSD), have become increasingly linked to traumatic stress that occurs at the workplace. The chapters in Part III provide an understanding of the nature of this disorder and discuss new approaches to treatment. Everly and Mitchell in the initial chapter describe the use of critical incident stress debriefing (CISD) and traumatic stress defusing techniques for the prevention of PTSD. This chapter emphasizes the importance of pretrauma education as a preventive tactic. In the following chapter, Corneil describes a study of PTSD among firefighters, who, many think, have an excessive risk for developing such disorders. His results emphasize the importance of social support and organizational context in the development of PTSD and suggest important avenues of intervention. The final chapter in Part III, by Flannery, Hanson, and Gallagher, describes and evaluates a voluntary, peer-help, crisis-intervention systems approach for dealing with the psychological consequences of assaults by patients in state mental hospitals.

Part I

Stress Management Training

1

Effects of Instruction on Stress Management Skills and Self-Management Skills Among Blue-Collar Employees

John A. Thomason and Samuel B. Pond III

Authorities have long acknowledged the existence of work-related job stress in organizations (Brodsky, 1982; Ivancevich & Matteson, 1980). Numerous approaches have been advocated to manage stress (e.g., Benson, 1975; Ellis, 1963; Jacobson, 1970). Practitioners advocating stress management instruction often claim significant benefits for organizational members and for organizations as a direct result of this instruction (Quick & Quick, 1984). Despite these claims, several review articles have noted that there has been only limited methodologically sound research conducted in organizational settings on the effects of instruction in the generally accepted approaches to managing stress (Ivancevich & Matteson, 1987; Ivancevich, Matteson, Freedman, & Phillips, 1990; Murphy, 1984, 1987; Newman & Beehr, 1979).

In this study we examined many of the methodological deficiencies of previous studies on stress management training (SMT) in organizational settings to isolate the effects of the instruction. Claims of success made by some trainers of stress management skills have meager empirical support. The purpose of our study was to substantiate or disprove the claims describing the benefits of SMT.

In addition, we assessed whether self-management would augment the effects of SMT. By including training in stress management and self-management to one group of research participants, this study is yet another application of self-management in an organizational setting. Second, we studied whether training in self-management skills would augment training outcomes. Finally, self-management was investigated as a tool to decrease posttraining decay.

Self-management is an important extension of social learning theory (Bandura, 1986). Self-management typically involves self-monitoring, specifying goals, evaluating monitored behavior against goals, and self-reinforcement (Kanfer & Karoly, 1982). Several authors have encouraged organizations to adopt self-management (e.g., Hackman, 1986; Luthans & Davis, 1979; Manz & Sims, 1980; Mills, 1983); despite the recommendations, only isolated research on self-management in organizational settings has been conducted (Frayne & Latham, 1987).

Method

Sample

The custody staff of a large prison in the southeastern United States served as research participants for the study. McGrath (1976) noted that field studies on job stress have more external validity than do laboratory studies. Also, the training program was offered to custody staff, thus addressing a need for research on groups other than white-collar workers (Murphy, 1984).

While soliciting volunteers at preshift roll calls, all staff ($N = 148$) were asked to complete a demographics questionnaire constructed to obtain background information relevant to this study. Of those surveyed, 83 volunteered to participate in the study; 54 participants completed the entire study. Participants were predominately male; the modal ages were 36–40 and 41–45.

Analysis of the information obtained from the initial screening revealed that the participants did not differ from nonparticipants and that the participants who dropped out of the study did not differ from the participants who completed the study.

Participants were randomly assigned to one of four groups: (a) a group receiving training on stress management skills and self-management skills (the SMTSM group); (b) a group receiving training only on stress management skills (the SMT group); (c) a placebo group receiving training on personal development skills (the PD group); and (d) a no-treatment control group (the NTC group). Twenty-one participants were initially assigned to all groups, with the exception of the NTC group; the remaining 20 participants were assigned to the NTC group. At the end of data collection, 14 participants remained in the SMTSM and the PD groups; 13 participants remained in the SMT and the NTC groups.

Participants in the NTC group were informed that the demand for training had exceeded immediate capabilities and that their names had been placed on a waiting list to receive training at a later date.

Measures

The training programs were evaluated on the following criteria: reaction, learning, and outcomes (Kirkpatrick, 1959a, 1959b, 1960).

Reaction measure. A 10-item questionnaire was constructed to gauge the participants' reactions to the training. The questionnaire contained 5-point Likert-type items. Items tapped reaction to the content of training and the trainer (e.g., "The training you received helped you to feel more confident about your ability to control your own behavior. If you were given the opportunity, would you take another course with this instructor?"). The questionnaire was administered to participants during the last training session.

Learning measure. Measures of the amount of material learned during training consisted of an 18-item multiple-choice quiz constructed for this study. Each question had four distractor alternatives along with the correct alternative. Test items addressed knowledge of the sources of personal stress and knowledge of cognitive restructuring and relaxation techniques. The quiz was administered during the first and last training sessions.

Outcome measures. We examined three classes of responses to stress: physiological, somatic, and psychological symptoms.

The physiological measure of stress was blood pressure, which was measured with an automated sphygmomanometer (i.e., Sharp Model MB 550). This device is considered accurate to within 3 mm Hg or within 2% of the reading, whichever is greater.

Blood pressure has been recommended as a physiological index of experienced stress (Murphy, 1984). Several researchers have concluded that training in progressive relaxation, an element of SMT, lowers blood pressure (Jacobson, 1940; Paul, 1969; Paul & Trimble, 1970). Quick and Quick (1984) stated that "blood pressure control is a valid objective of stress management training as well as a measure of stress" (p. 128).

The SCL-90-R was used to assess somatic symptoms (Derogatis, 1977). This 90-item, multidimensional self-report symptom inventory has been used to evaluate stress management research examining the effects of meditation and other relaxation techniques (e.g., Carrington et al., 1980; Shapiro & Lehrer, 1980). The psychometrically sound SCL-90-R yields three global measures of distress and nine primary symptom dimensions.

Psychological measures for the study included measures of anxiety and job satisfaction. The State-Trait Anxiety Inventory-Form Y (STAI) was used to assess levels of state anxiety (Spielberger, 1983). Two types of anxiety are measured with this scale: state and trait. State anxiety reflects transitory feelings of fear or worry that vary from one situation to another. Trait anxiety reflects a more stable tendency to respond anxiously to stressful situations (Spielberger, 1975). The internal consistency of the STAI ranges from .86 to .95 (Katkin, 1978).

The effect of SMT on employee job satisfaction has never been investigated (Ivancevich & Matteson, 1987; Murphy, 1987). The Job In General (JIG) scale was used to establish levels of employee satisfaction. The JIG scale measures overall evaluation of the job and reflects the respondent's weighting of several of the components of job satisfaction that are usually considered to be relevant to the respondent (Ironson, Smith, Brannick, Gibson, & Paul, 1989). The internal consistency of the JIG averages .91 (The Revised JDI, 1987).

Procedure

Study design. The study design consisted of a true experiment (Cook & Campbell, 1979) with two treatment groups (i.e., the SMT and the SMTSM groups) and two control groups (i.e., the PD and the NTC groups). Data on all outcome measures were recorded prior to engaging in any training (i.e., pre-training), after the training had been completed (i.e., posttraining), 3 months after the training had been completed (i.e., a 3-month follow-up), and again 6 months after the training had been completed (i.e., a 6-month follow-up). After the 6-month follow-up data were collected from participants in the NTC group, they received instruction on stress management skills.

When data were collected at more than one observation period, we conducted an analysis of covariance (ANCOVA) for the initial analysis. Pretraining data served as the covariate. If a main effect or the interaction effect was statistically significant, simple main effects were then examined.

Training sessions. The training exercises we used were highly similar to the SMT used by Ganster, Mayes, Sime, and Tharp (1982). A multimodal approach to SMT has been recommended (Murphy, 1984); therefore, participants were exposed to several stress management techniques (i.e., cognitive restructuring, positive self-talk, deep muscle relaxation, autogenic instructions, and imagery exercises). The training in self-management skills that we used corresponded closely to the training outlined by Frayne (1986).

Participants in the SMT and SMTSM groups received 9 hr of instruction in stress management techniques evenly distributed over six training sessions. At the end of each SMT session, participants in the SMTSM group received an additional 30 min of training in self-management skills (i.e., a total of 3 hr of instruction evenly distributed over six training sessions). Participants in the PD group received 9 hr of instruction in PD techniques that were not expected to affect the indexes of stress; this training also was evenly distributed over six training sessions.

Training sessions for all groups were videotaped prior to meetings. These training tapes were used to ensure that all SMTSM and SMT participants received identical instruction on stress management skills. The training tapes were occasionally interrupted at selected points to allow for questions or responses from the participants.

Results

Measures

Reaction measure. The reaction questionnaire was administered to all participants in the SMTSM, PD, and SMT groups during the final training session. The means and standard deviations of the scores from this questionnaire are shown in Table 1.

Table 1. Means and Standard Deviations of the Total Score on the Reaction Questionnaire

Group	M	SD
Posttraining SMTSM	46.33	3.68
PD	37.20	6.49
SMT	46.60	7.16

Note. SMTSM = stress management + self-management training; PD = personal development training; SMT = stress management training.

A one-way analysis of variance (ANOVA) was conducted comparing total scores on the reaction questionnaire for the groups. Results reveal a statistically significant difference between the groups, $F(2, 41) = 12.05, p < .01$.

Learning measure. The learning questionnaire was administered to all participants at pretraining and again at posttraining. We hypothesized that the treatment groups that received training on stress management skills (i.e., the SMTSM and the SMT groups) would score higher than the other groups on the posttraining administration of the learning questionnaire and that their posttraining score would be higher than their pretraining score. The means and standard deviations of the scores on the learning questionnaire are shown in Table 2.

A repeated measures ANCOVA was conducted on the total learning questionnaire score for all groups; results of these statistical analyses are shown in Table 3.

The time effect, the group effect, and the Time × Group interaction were significant. Although there was no statistically significant difference between groups at pretraining, the difference between groups was statistically significant at posttraining, $F(3, 55) = 7.35, p < .01$. Inspection of the data indicates that the groups that received training on stress management skills had higher posttraining scores on the learning questionnaire.

Table 2. Means and Standard Deviations of the Total Score on the Learning Questionnaire

Group	M	SD
Pretraining SMTSM	7.80	2.70
PD	9.13	1.92
SMT	7.60	2.03
NTC	7.43	2.10
Posttraining SMTSM	11.33	2.85
PD	8.53	1.46
SMT	8.47	4.02
NTC	5.93	3.52

Note. STMSM = stress management + self-management training; PD = personal development training; SMT = stress management training; NTC = no-treatment control.

Table 3. Statistical Analyses of the Total Score on the Learning Questionnaire

Repeated measures ANCOVA source	F	dfs	MS
Error	54	0.46	—
Pretest (covariate)	1, 54	0.04	0.09
Group	3, 54	9.10	19.85*
Error	54	0.25	—
Pretest (covariate)	1, 54	0.07	0.29
Time	1, 54	14.00	55.39*
Group × Time	3, 54	5.71	22.58*

Note. ANCOVA = analysis of covariance.
*$p < .01$.

Follow-up comparisons across the groups revealed statistically significant differences for both the SMTSM and the NTC groups. The total score on the learning questionnaire improved substantially between pretraining and post-training for the SMTSM group, $F(1, 14) = 28.58$, $p < .01$, although the total score decreased significantly for the NTC group, $F(1, 13) = 4.79$, $p < .05$. Although there was a slight increase between pretraining and posttraining for the SMT group and a slight decrease between pretraining and posttraining for the PD group, neither difference approached statistical significance.

Outcome measures. Outcome measures were collected during every data collection period. Outcome measures were categorized as follows: physiological (i.e., blood pressure), somatic symptoms (i.e., the SCL-90-R), and psychological symptoms (i.e., the STAI and the JIG).

For the physiological measure, we hypothesized that the treatment groups that received instruction on stress management skills would have lower blood pressure on the posttraining measures than on the pretraining measure. The mean scores and standard deviations of blood pressure readings are shown in Table 4.

A repeated measures ANCOVA was conducted on the blood pressure data; results of these analyses are presented in Table 5. These analyses revealed statistically significant group and time main effects, as well as a significant Group × Time interaction.

Comparisons within the SMTSM data revealed that the pretraining data were significantly different from an average of all of the later data collection periods (i.e., pretraining, posttraining, 3-month, and 6-month follow-ups), $F(1, 12) = 76.77$, $p < .01$.

A follow-up comparison across the separate groups revealed that only the SMTSM group exhibited a statistically significant difference across time, $F(3, 36) = 12.11$, $p < .05$.

For the somatic measure, we hypothesized that scores on the global scale of the SCL-90-R (i.e., the Grand Total scale) would decrease following instruction on stress management skills.

The means and standard deviations from this global scale on the SCL-90-

Table 4. Means and Standard Deviations of Blood Pressure Readings

Group	M	SD
Pretraining		
SMTSM	94.15	11.15
PD	81.58	9.52
SMT	91.17	9.15
NTC	91.08	14.01
3 month		
SMTSM	81.92	7.48
PD	78.58	9.69
SMT	86.00	4.26
NTC	93.92	11.03
Posttraining		
SMTSM	85.33	9.32
PD	82.00	13.29
SMT	88.83	6.91
NTC	88.92	9.23
6 month		
SMTSM	84.39	14.27
PD	85.67	5.26
SMT	91.00	8.20
NTC	93.83	11.42

Note. SMTSM = stress management + self-management training; PD = personal development training; SMT = stress management training; NTC = no-treatment control.

R are shown in Table 6. Results of the statistical analyses of the SCL-90-R are presented in Table 7.

A repeated measures ANCOVA of the Grand Total scale indicated significant group and time main effects; the interaction effect also was significant.

Follow-up comparisons for the separate groups revealed that only the SMTSM group exhibited statistically significant differences across time, $F(3, 36) = 3.98$, $p < .05$. The data also indicate that an average of all of the posttraining measures were significantly different from the pretraining measure, $F(1, 13) = 7.93$, $p < .05$.

The psychological measures included the STAI and the JIG scale. Follow-

Table 5. Statistical Analyses of the Blood Pressure Ratings

Repeated measures ANCOVA source	F	dfs	MS
Error	44	2.51	—
Pretest (covariate)	1, 44	0.01	0.00
Group	3, 44	40.56	16.17*
Error	42	1.10	—
Pretest (covariate)	3, 42	0.01	0.01
Time	1, 42	46.94	42.84*
Group × Time	3, 42	15.65	14.29*

Note. ANCOVA = analysis of covariance.
*$p < .01$.

Table 6. Means and Standard Deviations of the Grand Total Scale of the SCL-90-R

Group	M	SD
Pretraining		
SMTSM	88.36	64.93
PD	45.46	32.53
SMT	80.62	46.30
NTC	47.58	31.39
3 month		
SMTSM	66.29	46.26
PD	31.77	24.31
SMT	69.62	32.16
NTC	46.67	38.27
Posttraining		
SMTSM	62.07	44.78
PD	39.00	29.62
SMT	68.23	36.39
NTC	49.25	42.09
6 month		
SMTSM	57.07	44.58
PD	32.54	23.28
SMT	56.62	37.26
NTC	43.92	27.79

Note. SMTSM = stress management + self-management training; PD = personal development training; SMT = stress management training; NTC = no-treatment control.

ing instruction on stress management skills, decreases on the State scale of the STAI were anticipated.

The means and standard deviations for the groups on the State scale of the STAI are shown in Table 8. Results of the statistical analyses of the STAI are presented in Table 9.

The repeated measures ANCOVA of the State scale indicated that the group main effect, the time main effect, and the Group × Time interaction effect were significant.

Follow-up comparisons for the separate groups revealed that only the SMTSM group differed significantly across time, $F(3, 39) = 7.05$, $p < .01$.

Table 7. Statistical Analyses of the Grand Total Scale of the SCL-90-R

Repeated measures ANCOVA source	F	dfs	MS
Error	47	9.72	—
Pretest (covariate)	1, 47	0.00	0.00
Group	3, 47	166.14	17.09*
Error	143	2.08	—
Pretest (covariate)	1, 143	167.62	80.76*
Time	3, 143	103.70	49.97*
Group × Time	9, 143	33.76	16.27*

Note. ANCOVA = analysis of covariance.
*$p < .01$.

Table 8. Means and Standard Deviations of the State Scale on the STAI

Group	M	SD
Pretraining		
SMTSM	40.77	13.25
PD	29.00	7.32
SMT	40.17	14.80
NTC	35.33	13.49
3 month		
SMTSM	35.07	7.25
PD	37.14	16.23
SMT	37.50	8.44
NTC	40.08	6.33
Posttraining		
SMTSM	30.21	8.30
PD	35.64	20.06
SMT	35.17	13.34
NTC	35.92	9.04
6 month		
SMTSM	31.21	7.49
PD	32.64	8.32
SMT	41.08	11.19
NTC	41.00	5.56

Note. STAI = State-Trait Anxiety Inventory; SMTSM = stress management + self-management training; PD = personal development training; SMT = stress management training; NTC = no-treatment control.

We hypothesized that there would be no differences between groups on job satisfaction, as assessed by the JIG scale. Table 10 contains means and standard deviations for the JIG scale. Statistical analyses of the JIG scale data are shown in Table 11.

The repeated measures ANCOVA of the JIG scale indicated that the group, time, and the Group × Time interaction effect were significant.

Additional analyses revealed that there were no significant differences between groups at any observation period and that only the NTC group exhibited significant change over time, $F(3, 32) = 3.08$, $p < .05$.

Table 9. Statistical Analyses of the State Scale of the STAI

Repeated measures ANCOVA source	F	dfs	MS
Error	47	2.51	—
Pretest (covariate)	1, 47	0.01	0.00
Group	3, 47	40.70	16.21*
Error	143	0.74	—
Pretest (covariate)	1, 143	59.77	80.74*
Time	3, 143	35.73	48.27*
Group × Time	9, 143	12.66	17.11*

Note. STAI = State-Trait Anxiety Inventory; ANCOVA = analysis of covariance.
*$p < .01$.

Table 10. Means and Standard Deviations of the JIG Scale

Group	M	SD
Pretraining		
SMTSM	33.64	8.90
PD	37.93	11.61
SMT	30.08	16.65
NTC	37.75	9.58
3 month		
SMTSM	37.21	10.18
PD	37.07	11.66
SMT	29.42	13.69
NTC	31.83	7.54
Posttraining		
SMTSM	33.57	12.81
PD	38.79	9.42
SMT	28.08	12.49
NTC	34.83	8.17
6 month		
SMTSM	35.93	8.32
PD	38.43	7.60
SMT	32.25	10.98
NTC	30.50	6.80

Note. JIG = Job In General scale; SMTSM = stress management + self-management training; PD = personal development training; SMT = stress management training; NTC = no-treatment control.

Discussion

This study was designed to examine the effects of instruction on stress management skills and self-management skills among blue-collar employees.

Measures

Reaction measure. The statistical analyses of the responses to the reaction questionnaire revealed that the two groups that received instruction on stress

Table 11. Statistical Analyses of the JIG Scale

Repeated measures ANCOVA source	F	dfs	MS
Error	47	2.40	—
Pretest (covariate)	1, 47	0.01	0.00
Group	3, 47	40.14	16.70*
Error	143	0.67	—
Pretest (covariate)	1, 143	53.81	80.63*
Time	3, 143	31.87	47.76*
Group × Time	9, 143	10.96	16.42*

Note. JIG = Job In General scale; ANCOVA = analysis of covariance.
*$p < .01$.

management skills (i.e., the SMTSM and the SMT groups) had a more favorable reaction to the training that they received than did the PD group.

Kirkpatrick (1959a) stated that "the first step in the evaluation process is to measure the reactions to the training program" (p. 8). Kirkpatrick emphasized that participants must rate an instruction program positively to obtain maximum benefits; because all groups rated the instruction programs as being above average, the requirements of this premise were met.

Learning measure. As expected, both of the groups that received instruction on stress management techniques had higher total scores on the learning questionnaire at posttraining. However, only the difference between pretraining and posttraining for the group receiving training on stress management and self-management skills was statistically significant.

Kirkpatrick (1959b) noted that "it is important to recognize that a favorable reaction to a program does not assure learning" (p. 21). He emphasized the importance of objectively determining the amount of learning that had occurred. Because questions on the learning questionnaire tapped knowledge about SMT, and scores increased from pretraining to posttraining for the groups' receiving SMT (although the difference for the SMT group was not statistically significant), an argument could be made that learning had occurred.

Outcome measures. The physiological data indicate that training on stress management skills reduced blood pressure, although the difference between the pretraining measure and an average of the posttraining measures was statistically significant only for the SMTSM group. The data also indicate that a slight decrease in blood pressure for the SMT group continued after training until the 3-month follow-up; however, the decrease was not statistically significant.

As was the case for the physiological measure, the somatic data indicate that the instruction on stress management skills resulted in decreases on the global dimension score of the SCL-90-R, although the difference was statistically significant only for the SMTSM group.

Posttraining scores on the State scale of the STAI were significantly lower than were pretraining scores for the SMTSM group. Although State scores for the SMT group were lower than the pretraining score at the posttraining measure and at the 3-month follow-up, State scores for this group at the 6-month follow-up were slightly higher than at pretraining. However, the differences between pretraining and posttraining measures were never significant for the SMT group.

The job satisfaction data show that there were no statistically significant changes on the JIG scale between pretraining and any of the posttraining administrations for either the SMTSM or the SMT group. Moreover, the differences between groups on scores on the JIG scale were never statistically significant.

Our results suggest that instruction on stress management skills does not affect global satisfaction with one's job as measured by the JIG scale.

Summary of the outcome measures. Kirkpatrick (1960) emphasized that an additional criterion to be considered when evaluating training programs is whether there are actual changes in behavior.

To summarize, it would seem that training in stress management skills affected several outcome variables, but not to the extent that the differences were statistically significant. Training on stress management skills appeared to have had at least some impact on the physiological measure, the measure of somatic symptoms, and on anxiety.

Self-Management

The additional training on self-management skills seemed to augment the instructional program on stress management. Specifically, the group that received stress management and self-management training exhibited significant differences across time on blood pressure, somatic symptoms, and state anxiety. Because there were no significant differences between groups on the reaction measure or the job satisfaction scale, and because there were no significant differences across time for other groups, it would seem that the differences between the SMTSM and the SMT groups were likely the result of the additional training on self-management skills that was presented to the SMTSM group. Finally, the additional training on self-management skills appeared to reduce posttraining decay.

Summary and Conclusions

This study was designed to assess the effects of instruction on stress management skills among blue-collar workers. In addition, the study was designed to assess whether instruction on self-management would augment the effects of stress management training.

Ganster et al. (1982) noted that the effects of training on stress management were not dramatic. The changes noted on the dependent variables used in the current study were also usually fairly small. Although there were changes in the predicted direction for the group that received SMT on the learning questionnaire, blood pressure, and somatic symptoms, these differences were not statistically significant across time. Nevertheless, these slight changes in the predicted direction suggest that the stress management instruction was helpful.

Frayne (1986) concluded that training in self-management skills had positive effects on attendance among blue-collar workers; positive results were also noted in the current study addressing employee stress. The additional training in self-management skills, coupled with the training on stress management, was associated with significant changes on the learning questionnaire, blood pressure, somatic symptoms, and state anxiety. Overall, these findings suggest that the additional training on self-management skills enhanced the results of the training on stress management skills.

Finally, our results indicate that training on stress management skills did not affect job satisfaction as measured by the JIG scale. These findings contradict prior anecdotal claims that instruction on stress management skills would improve job satisfaction.

In conclusion, it would appear that self-management training augmented instructional programs and that the effects of stress management instruction also were modest for blue-collar workers.

References

Bandura, A. (1986). *Social foundations of thought and action: A social cognitive theory.* Englewood Cliffs, NJ: Prentice Hall.

Benson, H. (1975). *The relaxation response.* New York: William Morrow.

Brodsky, C. M. (1982). Work stress in correctional institutions. *Journal of Prison and Jail Health, 2,* 74–102.

Carrington, P., Collings, G. H., Benson, H., Robinson, H., Wood, L. W., Lehrer, P. M., Woolfolk, R. L., & Cole, J. W. (1980). The use of meditation-relaxation techniques for the management of stress in a working population. *Journal of Occupational Medicine, 22,* 221–231.

Cook, T. D., & Campbell, D. T. (1979). *Quasi-experimentation design and analysis issues for field settings.* Boston: Houghton Mifflin.

Derogatis, L. R. (1977). *SCL-90: Administration, scoring and procedures manual for the revised version.* Baltimore: Clinical Psychometric Research.

Ellis, A. (1963). *Reason and emotion in psychotherapy.* New York: Lyle Stuart.

Frayne, C. A. (1986). *The application of social learning theory to employee self-management of attendance.* Unpublished doctoral dissertation, University of Washington, Seattle, WA.

Frayne, C. A., & Latham, G. P. (1987). Application of social learning theory to employee self-management of attendance. *Journal of Applied Psychology, 72,* 387–392.

Ganster, D. C., Mayes, B. T., Sime, W. E., & Tharp, G. D. (1982). Managing organizational stress: A field experiment. *Journal of Applied Psychology, 67,* 533–542.

Hackman, J. R. (1986). The psychology of self-management in organizations. In M. S. Pollack & R. O. Perloff (Eds.), *Psychology and work: Productivity change and employment* (pp. 85–136). Washington, DC: American Psychological Association.

Ironson, G. H., Smith, P. C., Brannick, M. T., Gibson, W. M., & Paul, K. B. (1989). Construction of a Job In General scale: A comparison of global, composite, and specific measures. *Journal of Applied Psychology, 74,* 193–200.

Ivancevich, J. M., & Matteson, M. T. (1980). *Stress and work.* Glenview, IL: Scott Foresman.

Ivancevich, J. M., & Matteson, M. T. (1987). Organizational level stress management intervention: A review and recommendation. *Journal of Organizational Behavior Management, 8,* 229–247.

Ivancevich, J. M., & Matteson, M. T., Freedman, S. M., & Phillips, J. S. (1990). Worksite stress management interventions. *American Psychologist, 45,* 252–261.

Jacobson, E. (1940). Variation of blood pressure with skeletal muscle tension and relaxation. *Annals of Internal Medicine, 13,* 1619–1625.

Jacobson, E. (1970). *You must relax.* New York: McGraw-Hill.

Kanfer, F. H., & Karoly, P. (1982). The psychology of self management: Abiding issues and tentative directions. In P. Karoly & F. H. Kanfer (Eds.), *Self management and behavior change: From theory to practice* (pp. 571–599). Elmsford, NY: Pergamon Press.

Katkin, E. S. (1978). State-Trait Anxiety Inventory review. In O. K. Buros (Ed.), *The eighth mental measurements yearbook* (pp. 1095–1096). Highland Park, NJ: Gryphon Press.

Kirkpatrick, D. T. (1959a). Techniques for evaluating training programs. *American Society of Training Directors Journal, 13,* 3–9.

Kirkpatrick, D. T. (1959b). Techniques for evaluating training programs: 2. Learning. *American Society of Training Directors Journal, 13*(12), 21–26.

Kirkpatrick, D. T. (1960). Techniques for evaluating training programs: 3. Behavior. *American Society of Training Directors Journal, 14*(1), 13–18.

Luthans, F., & Davis, T. R. V. (1979). Behavioral self management: The missing link in managerial effectiveness. *Organizational Dynamics, 8*, 41–60.

Manz, C. C., & Sims, H. P., Jr. (1980). Self management as a substitute for leadership. *Academy of Management Review, 5*, 361–367.

McGrath, J. E. (1976). Stress and behavior in organizations. In M. Dunnette (Ed.), *Handbook of industrial and organizational psychology* (pp. 1351–1395). Chicago: Rand McNally.

Mills, P. K. (1983). Self management: Its control and relationship to other organizational properties. *Academy of Management Review, 8*, 445–453.

Murphy, L. R. (1984). Occupational stress management: A review and appraisal. *Journal of Occupational Psychology, 57*, 1–15.

Murphy, L. R. (1987). A review of organizational stress management research: Methodological considerations. *Journal of Organizational Behavior Management, 8*, 215–227.

Newman, J. E., & Beehr, T. A. (1979). Personal and organizational strategies for handling job stress: A review of research and opinion. *Personnel Psychology, 32*, 1–43.

Paul, G. (1969). Psychophysiological effects of relaxation training and hypnotic suggestion. *Journal of Abnormal Psychology, 74*, 423–427.

Paul, G., & Trimble, R. (1970). Recorded vs. "live" relaxation training and hypnotic suggestion: Comparative effectiveness for reducing physiological arousal and inhibiting stress response. *Behavior Therapy, 1*, 285–302.

Quick, J. C., & Quick, J. D. (1984). *Organizational stress and preventive management.* New York: McGraw-Hill.

The Revised JDI: A facelift for an old friend. (1987, August). *The Industrial Organizational Psychologist*, p. 31.

Shapiro, S., & Lehrer, P. M. (1980). Psychophysiological effects of autogenic training and progressive relaxation. *Biofeedback and Self Regulation, 5*, 249–255.

Spielberger, C. D. (1975). The measurement of state and trait anxiety: Conceptual and methodological issues. In L. Levi (Ed.), *Emotions: Their parameters and measurement* (pp. 718–719). New York: Raven Press.

Spielberger, C. D. (1983). *Manual for the State-Trait Anxiety Inventory (Form Y) (Self-Evaluation Questionnaire).* Palo Alto, CA: Consulting Psychologists Press.

2

The Development of an Anger Management Training Program for Law Enforcement Personnel

Alexis D. Abernethy

Law enforcement personnel experience unique anger-provoking stressors because of the demands of a paramilitarylike organization and conflictual interactions with citizens. The inability to manage recurrent anger-provoking situations has been associated with impulsive behavior, aggression (Hecker & Lunde, 1985), and cardiovascular disease (Rosenman, 1985). For example, the use of excessive force by police officers has gained increased attention and represents an undesirable behavioral outcome that may be related to uncontrolled aggression and unresolved anger (Titchener, 1986). Although anger management training programs have been developed to address this important source of law enforcement stress (Lester, Leitner, & Posner, 1984; Novaco, 1977; Sarason, Johnson, Berberich, & Siegel, 1979), evaluation of these programs has been hampered by methodological problems. In this chapter, I discuss the Rochester training module and implications for future training and research.

Law Enforcement, Stress, and Anger Management

Law Enforcement Stress

Psychological disorders are considered one of the 10 leading occupational diseases (Millar, 1984). Sauter, Murphy, and Hurrell (1990) identified major psychosocial risk factors that threaten workers' psychological well-being: workload, work schedule, role stressors, career security, interpersonal relations, job content, and intervening variables. Hurrell, Pate, and Kliesmet (1984) found that organizational stressors were a major source of police stress. Rochester police officers who received anger management training experienced situations that involved promotions and transfer assignments, conflicts in relationships with coworkers and supervisors, and role conflict as the most anger provoking.

Karasek and Theorell's (1990) model of job stress provided a useful framework for considering the effects of psychological stress on the worker. They proposed that jobs with high psychological demands and low decision latitude caused the greatest strain. Role conflict and role confusion contributed to increased distress and might evoke anger. For example, law enforcement personnel are frequently exposed to life-threatening situations that are physically and psychologically demanding. Their role mandates that they serve and protect others who may verbally and physically attack them. These personnel have less emotional latitude than do citizens because a response of fear or retaliation to these volatile encounters is not appropriate. Although officers are instructed to use their judgment in selecting the minimum amount of force necessary to control suspects, their decision latitude is narrowed by frequent second-guessing and departmental regulations (Desmedt, 1984). In addition, substantial role confusion may arise for some law enforcement personnel who recognize that retaliation is practiced, despite regulations that prohibit it.

Anger Management

Anger, hostility, and aggression have been considered distinct but related concepts. *Anger* has been defined generally as an emotional state that includes feelings of irritation, annoyance, and rage. *Hostility* refers to negative attitudes that motivate aggressive behavior. *Aggression* is a destructive behavioral response that is directed at others. Megargee (1985) identified two types of motivation for aggression: intrinsic (angry) and extrinsic instigation. Intrinsic instigation arises from the angry or hostile person's conscious or unconscious desire to hurt or to injure another person. Extrinsic aggression arises from other needs such as a desire for power, excitement, or property.

I studied anger management for the following reasons: Anger often motivates aggressive behavior (e.g., intrinsic aggression); officers identified anger-provoking events as a major source of stress; and consultation with officers revealed the inability to manage anger effectively or unresolved anger as a common focus of treatment. Although hostility has been linked more strongly to aggression than has anger, the selection procedures for most police departments screen out individuals who may be predisposed toward hostility and aggression. The perspective offered here was that although individual variables strongly influence the development of personality characteristics, the work environment may also contribute to the development of negative or positive characteristics. For example, Beutler, Nussbaum, and Meredith (1988) found that police officers developed maladaptive coping patterns (e.g., an increased tendency toward substance abuse) during the first 5 years of service. I hypothesized that if officers received early intervention in anger management, the deleterious consequences (e.g., hostility, aggression, and brutality) of failing to manage recurrent anger-provoking work situations could be appropriately minimized.

Definitions of healthy anger management have evolved over the years. Psychosomatic theorists viewed suppressed anger as a sign of an individual's internal conflict between aggression and dependency. Suppressed anger was viewed as maladaptive and associated with cardiovascular difficulties (Gentry,

Chesney, Hall, & Harburg, 1981). Spielberger, Jacobs, Russell, and Crane (1983) made a distinction between anger as an emotional state, as a trait (i.e., the frequency of angry feelings), and as a behavioral response to angry feelings. They refined the conceptualization of anger and proposed that extreme Anger-In or Anger-Out scores coupled with strong trait or state tendencies indicated maladaptation.

Anger Management Studies

The methodological problems that hampered anger intervention studies in general also hindered intervention studies with police officers. Most studies were uncontrolled or had a generalized focus on stress management instead of anger management. Lester et al. (1984) conducted stress management training with a group of 55 police officers who reported increased job satisfaction following training, but there was no control group. Sarason et al. (1979) conducted stress management training that had an anger management component. They used a pretest–posttest design and randomly assigned officers to a control group or training group. Scores on psychological measures did not change after training, but observer ratings and self-ratings made of "mock scenes" of police work were supportive of the treatment effectiveness.

Novaco (1977) developed stress inoculation training for anger control and organized it into three components: (a) cognitive preparation, in which the functions and determinants of anger were addressed; (b) skill acquisition, in which cognitive control, relaxation, and communication techniques were learned, and (c) application training, in which skills were practiced through role playing. Probation counselors reported decreased anger following the training, but an outcome study was not conducted for police officers (Novaco, 1980).

Efforts to conduct and evaluate anger management training programs have been hampered by organizational barriers. Ivancevich, Matteson, Freedman, and Phillips (1990) identified a lack of support in collecting adequate samples and in using control groups as two major barriers. They listed several needs that should be addressed in conducting intervention research in organizations: (a) asking the right questions (e.g., Were the goals, design, and outcomes valued by top management?); (b) theory building and application (e.g., Did the research and reported results emerge from a theoretical context?); (c) methodological and design issues (e.g., Was a solid research design used?); (d) relapse prevention (e.g., Have steps been taken to minimize the resumption of maladaptive behaviors?); (e) targeting situational stressors (e.g., Were organizational factors that contribute to stress targeted for intervention?); and (f) the role of individual differences (e.g., Have gender, racial, and personality differences been considered?). I examine these questions next.

Development of the Rochester Training Module

Background

The Rochester Police Department (RPD) has provided stress management training to its officers for a number of years, but the interest in anger management stemmed from unique concerns. First, the training unit of the RPD, the Professional Development Section, had genuine concern about the well-being of its officers. This unit recognized that work-related situations exposed officers to a number of anger-provoking interactions and that all officers would benefit from specialized instruction in anger management. Second, increased national publicity concerning alleged police brutality provided the political pressure and funds to develop interventions that would reduce these occurrences. Third, the RPD wanted to develop an anger management training program that had empirical data that supported its effectiveness so that this program could be adopted by other police departments nationwide. Consequently, key areas of support outlined by Ivancevich et al. (1990) were obtained because management valued this area of training and supported the use of a research design. Although some objections arose in the implementation of a controlled design, these negotiations were facilitated by the RPD's commitment to establish objective indicators of the program's effectiveness and the assurance that control officers would eventually receive the training. The use of a control intervention (instruction on how to handle citizens with mental illness), which all officers eventually would receive, was essential in justifying the cost of including control officers.

Although top management supported this research and training, cooperation was more difficult to achieve at lower levels of management as standard procedures for sample selection were instituted, such as descriptive data on patrol officers and randomization. Negotiations were successful to the extent that management was persuaded, using practical examples, that the research design was the best tool for them to accomplish their goals (objective validation of the program's effectiveness) and the strong recommendation of the investigator. An invaluable asset was the support and cooperation of the Professional Development Section staff and their commitment to persistently present these arguments at all levels of management where resistance might emerge. The selection of outcome measures was limited by the type of data already collected on the officers, time constraints, and the use of measures that were valued by the RPD.

Anger was conceptualized using Biaggio's (1987) extension of Leventhal's (1984) *perceptual theory of emotion*. Anger was viewed as a subjective perceptual experience that was mediated by expressive–motor processes (i.e., a response to anger-provoking stimuli), memories of past emotional experiences (i.e., a record of past anger-provoking events), and conceptual processes (i.e., developed rules about emotive responding). Workers exposed to recurrent anger-provoking stimuli would be required to use anger management strategies more frequently. Useful interventions included the following: limiting the number of anger-provoking stimuli, reorganizing memories of past experiences, and altering attitudes about anger-provoking situations (Biaggio, 1987). Similar to Spielberger's (1988) view, neither anger-in nor anger-out was considered maladaptive; however, a tendency to become easily provoked (high trait anger) or to be constantly angry (high state anger) combined with a tendency to express or to suppress anger was considered maladaptive.

Exhibit 1.   Anger Management Training Outline

Introduction
Overview of stress
Barriers to acknowledging anger
Defining and recognizing anger
Managing anger: Exercising choices
Relaxation and meditation exercises
Dysfunctional styles of adaptation
Alcohol, nutrition, and fitness
Defense mechanisms
Anger-resolution process
Providing feedback
Anger-provoking scenarios

Anger Management Training Module (AMTM)

The AMTM was developed by members of the Professional Development Section of the RPD in consultation with me. The 6-hr training module in anger management was taught during a single day by two male trainers (a civilian stress management counselor and a lieutenant) who were certified by the New York State Bureau of Municipal Police.

The training was introduced as a specialized component of stress management training. The potential difficulty of expressing anger in an officer's personal and professional life was discussed. Training goals were shared: to increase officers' awareness of their anger (antecedents, response, and consequences) and to improve their anger management skills. Officers were asked to reflect on their own anger experiences; identify themes that elicit anger; understand how anger affects their body and behavior; understand the effect of these physical and psychological responses to anger on their relationships with their family, fellow officers, supervisors, and citizens; explore how they express and avoid anger; understand how anger may be used negatively or constructively; and practice effective methods of anger management (e.g., relaxation, making better choices, giving feedback). Officers completed structured exercises in their personal workbooks, and volunteers shared their responses in a group-discussion format. Instruction also covered dysfunctional styles that may develop as a result of inadequate anger management: uncontrolled aggression, abusive behavior, alcoholism, poor dietary habits, conflictual interpersonal relationships, and withdrawal. Officers responded to video presentations of angry encounters, rated their degree of anger, and discussed ways of resolving these situations. Exhibit 1 provides a training outline.

Study Design

One hundred thirty patrol officers were randomly selected from a pool of 234 officers who were representative of the RPD. Officers were randomly assigned to a training or a control group. Scheduling conflicts or work-related emergencies prevented 33 officers from participating. Ninety-seven officers began the study; 5 were excluded because of significant changes in their work assignment or retirement.

Psychological measures included the following: (a) the Profile of Mood States (POMS), a 65-item adjective checklist designed to assess feelings and mood changes in response to therapeutic intervention; and (b) Spielberger's (1988) State-Trait Anger Expression Inventory (STAXI), a 40-item measure that is composed of five scales: State Anger, Trait Anger, Anger-In, Anger-Out, and Anger Expression.

Frequency distributions for all performance data collected by the RPD in 1987 were examined. Seven of the 33 variables that were deemed to be related to difficulties in anger management and that had an adequate range of values were selected for individual analyses: the number of misdemeanor arrests, felony arrests, violation arrests, traffic arrests, disorderly conduct arrests, appearance tickets, and use of force arrests (less than deadly). Performance variables were compared across three measurement periods: pretest (January–April), posttest (August–November), and follow-up (January–April).

The control group received instruction in a mental health course. This general curriculum was presented in a lecture format and provided an overview of psychological theory, psychopathology, and instructions on how to handle citizens with mental illness. This curriculum was offered exclusively to control officers and included the same number of instructional hours as did the training (6 hr). Only one of the instructors, the stress management counselor, taught this course.

The procedure for the training and control officers was similar. Forty-eight officers were assigned to one of five groups of 9–12 individuals for 1 day of training. After a brief introduction, the officers were asked to complete several psychological inventories (20–35 min). After a short break, 3 hr of instruction were followed by lunch and another 3-hr instructional period. At the end of training, officers completed the inventories and returned 4–6 months later to complete the psychological measures. Forty-four officers in the control group were assigned to one of five groups of 8–12 individuals. They participated in a mental health course according to the same time schedule as the AMTM.

Statistical Analyses

Chi-square tests and t tests were conducted to test for demographic differences between the treatment and control groups. An analysis of variance (ANOVA) with repeated measures was used to test for overall differences between the treatment and control group on performance and psychological variables. To determine whether assignment to the treatment or control group as well as various covariates would influence changes on the outcome measures between posttest and pretest (PO-PR) and follow-up and pretest (FO-PR), regression analyses were performed using difference scores calculated from these two time periods. Independent variables of race (African American, Hispanic), years of service, age, sex, shift (day, evening, and night), and assignment (the Clinton and Highland sections) were used to predict angry mood, trait anger, misdemeanor, violation, traffic and disorderly conduct arrests, appearance tickets, and use-of-force arrests.

Results

The control and training groups were compared on age, gender, race, years of service, shift, and assignment. Significant differences were obtained on age, $t(90) = 2.23$, $p = .03$, and assignment, $t(5) = 11.25$, $p = .05$. The mean age of the officers who received training was 29.8 years ($SD = 5.7$). The mean age of the control officers was 32.6 years ($SD = 6.2$). The most marked assignment differences were related to only two of six assignment sections in which one assignment area was overrepresented and the other was underrepresented.

Using 30 years of age as a cutoff, the ANOVA results with repeated measures (2 [group] $\times$ 2 [age] $\times$ 3 [time]) indicated an age effect, $F(1, 72) = 5.91$, $p = .02$, but no overall differences were found on the performance variables. Orthogonal comparisons indicated a second-degree treatment effect on angry mood, $F(1, 72) = 4.41$, $p = .04$; control and trained officers differed on angry mood.

Regression analyses revealed that control officers had larger difference scores on angry mood than did trained officers, $t(77) = 2.70$, $p = .009$. Trained officers showed little variation in angry mood, whereas control officers reported less anger between pretest and posttest. Treatment group also predicted changes in the number of use of force arrests between pretest and posttest $t(76) = -1.70$, $p = .09$; officers who received training had smaller increases in the use-of-force than did control officers. Seventy-two percent of the trained officers reported that the training had increased their awareness of anger. They described the training as valuable and wished that it had been available earlier in their careers. Officers also indicated that they had used some of the techniques.

Gender predicted angry mood and trait anger. Female officers experienced increased anger, $t(77) = 2.98$, $p = .004$, between pretest and posttest, whereas male officers reported less anger. Gender, $t(76) = 2.24$, $p = .03$, also predicted trait anger: Female officers' scores increased and male officers' scores decreased on trait anger between pretest and posttest.

Summary and Conclusions

These results provide limited support for the effectiveness of this training module in anger management; treatment differences were found for the use-of-force arrests and angry mood, but other treatment differences on anger and performance variables were not found. The findings on use of force were in the hypothesized direction, such that trained officers had smaller increases than did control officers.

Although more extended training with greater opportunity for practice might have had a more powerful effect on the officers, management made an initial commitment to a brief pilot training. The successful execution of this program coupled with the positive subjective reports of officers provided more internal support for this program and led to a commitment to extend the training to 21 hr of instruction over 3 days. In addition, the department made a commitment to provide this training to all of its sworn personnel and provided resources to train peer counselors to become course instructors.

The theoretical implications of this research in clarifying the relation between ineffective anger management and maladaptive outcomes were limited because of the absence of high scores on Spielberger's measures. However, the differences on mood scores have implications for future interventions. Angry mood corresponded to the expressive–motor dimension of Biaggio's (1987) conceptualization of anger. The reduction in angry mood for control officers contrasted by the absence of change for officers in the training group on the day of instruction was an unexpected finding. Reduced anger has been reported as an indicator of treatment effectiveness in anger intervention studies (O'Donnell & Worell, 1973), but decreased anger was not necessarily viewed as a favorable outcome in the current study. If anger was reduced in response to effective anger management strategies that regulated the stimulation or the response, this would be viewed as a positive outcome; however, if this anger reduction reflected an overuse of certain maladaptive strategies (i.e., denial or suppression), this outcome would not be considered favorable. Because Hecker and Lunde (1985) proposed tailored interventions for chronically hostile individuals, initial assessment of anger management preferences might be an important step in tailoring certain interventions so that individuals adopt new methods of anger management or strengthen less effective ones. This screening was not conducted here, so the implications of reduced mood for control officers was unclear; however, screening anger management tendencies would be an important feature of future anger management training (Biaggio, 1987).

Although a randomized, controlled design was used, problems in implementing this research design interfered with sample selection. Pretreatment differences on age and assignment between the training and control group complicated the interpretation of these data and might have suppressed a stronger treatment effect. Adjustments have been made so that in future studies, sampling and randomization procedures would be under my control. Assessment of anger management has continued to be a challenge. Despite the conceptual clarity of Spielberger's measure, the absence of a wide range of scores in this study limited my ability to assess a treatment effect. Spielberger (1988) added a new dimension to his scale, anger control, which addresses the capacity for anger regulation. In subsequent studies with the RPD, this revised scale has been used in conjunction with behavioral measures of anger. In addition, assessments of alcohol intake, diet, and exercise have been included.

The research design allowed for comparisons of individual differences including race, gender, and age. Reductions in angry mood for female officers was unexpected because little variance by sex has been reported for normal participants on the POMS. When sex differences have been obtained in outpatient samples, anger has been the sole subscale that has not yielded significant differences (McNair, Lorr, & Droppleman, 1971). Similarly, increased trait anger for female officers was an unexpected finding; with the exception of Anger-In and State Anger scores for college students, minimal-to-no sex differences have been reported on Spielberger's scale (Stoner & Spencer, 1986; Spielberger, 1988). These results point to the importance of further research on female police officers. Although differences were not obtained on race, this variable should be considered in future studies.

In summary, the AMTM was developed to increase officers' awareness of anger and to improve their ability to manage their anger. An initial 6-hr module was pilot tested. Subjective and limited objective findings supported this module. The module has been expanded to 21 hr and is under revision. Additional self-report, objective, and behavioral measures have been added. A second evaluation study will be conducted on the basis of these results and lessons learned from this organization-based research.

References

Beutler, L. E., Nussbaum, P. D., & Meredith, K. E. (1988). Changing personality patterns of police officers. *Professional Psychology: Research and Practice, 19*, 503–507.

Biaggio, M. K. (1987). Clinical diagnosis of anger management. *American Journal of Psychotherapy, 41*, 417–427.

Desmedt, J. C. (1984). Use of force paradigm for law enforcement. *Journal of Police Science and Administration, 12*, 170–176.

Gentry, W. D., Chesney, A. P., Hall, R. P., & Harburg, E. (1981). Effect of habitual anger-coping pattern on blood pressure in black/white, high/low stress area respondents. *Psychosomatic Medicine, 43*, 83.

Hecker, H. L., & Lunde, D. T. (1985). On the diagnosis and treatment of chronically hostile individuals. In M. A. Chesney & R. H. Rosenman (Eds.), *Anger and hostility in cardiovascular and behavioral disorders* (pp. 227–240). Washington, DC: Taylor & Francis.

Hurrell, J. J., Pate, A., & Kliesmet, R. (1984). *Stress among police officers* (DHHS [NIOSH] Pub. No. 84-108). Washington, DC: U.S. Government Printing Office.

Ivancevich, J. M., Matteson, M. T., Freedman, S. M., & Phillips, J. S. (1990). Worksite stress management interventions. *American Psychologist, 45*, 252–261.

Karasek, R., & Theorell, T. (1990). *Healthy work: Stress, productivity, and the reconstruction of working life.* New York: Basic Books.

Lester, D., Leitner, L. A., & Posner, I. (1984). The effects of a stress management training program on police officers. *International Review of Applied Psychology, 33*, 25–31.

Leventhal, H. (1984). A perceptual-motor theory of emotion. *Advances in Experimental Social Psychology, 17*, 117–182.

McNair, D. M., Lorr, M., & Droppleman, L. F. (1971). *Profile of Mood States.* San Diego, CA: EDITS.

Megargee, E. I. (1985). The dynamics of aggression and their application to cardiovascular disorders. In M. A. Chesney & R. H. Rosenman (Eds.), *Anger and hostility in cardiovascular and behavioral disorders* (pp. 31–58). Washington, DC: Taylor & Francis.

Millar, J. D. (1984). The NIOSH-suggested list of the ten leading work-related diseases and injuries. *Journal of Occupational Medicine, 26*, 340–341.

Novaco, R. W. (1977). A stress inoculation approach to anger management in the training of law enforcement officers. *American Journal of Community Psychology, 5*, 327–346.

Novaco, R. W. (1980). Training of probation counselors for anger problems. *Journal of Counseling Psychology, 27*, 385–390.

O'Donnell, C. R., & Worell, L. (1973). Motor and cognitive relaxation in the desensitization of anger. *Behavior Research and Therapy, 11*, 473–481.

Rosenman, R. H. (1985). Health consequences of anger and implications for treatment. In M. A. Chesney & R. H. Rosenman (Eds.), *Anger and hostility in cardiovascular and behavioral disorders* (pp. 103–125). Washington, DC: Taylor & Francis.

Sarason, I. G., Johnson, J. H., Berberich, J. P., & Siegel, J. M. (1979). Helping police officers to cope with stress: A cognitive-behavioral approach. *American Journal of Community Psychology, 7*, 593–603.

Sauter, S. L., Murphy, L. R., & Hurrell, J. J. (1990). Prevention of work-related psychological disorders: A national strategy proposed by the National Institute for Occupational Safety and Health. *American Psychologist, 45*, 1146–1158.

Spielberger, C. D. (1988). *State-Trait Anger Expression Inventory: Research edition.* Odessa, FL: Psychological Assessment Resources.

Spielberger, C. D., Jacobs, G. A., Russell, S., & Crane, R. S. (1983). Assessment of anger: The State-Trait Anger Scale. In J. N. Butcher & C. D. Spielberger (Eds.), *Advances in personality assessment* (Vol. 2). Hillsdale, NJ: Erlbaum.

Stoner, S. B., & Spencer, W. B. (1986). Age and sex differences on the State-Trait Personality Inventory. *Psychological Reports, 59*, 1315–1319.

Titchener, J. L. (1986). Post-traumatic decline: A consequence of unresolved destructive drives. In C. R. Figley (Ed.), *Trauma and its wake* (Vol. 2, pp. 5–10). New York: Brunner/Mazel.

3

When Relaxation Is Not Enough

Richard M. Kolbell

Stress is a construct that has been used to define a stimulus, response, or the interaction between the two. Most often, the term is used to identify a particular response of an organism to an identified demand stimulus, termed a *stressor*. For a stimulus to elicit a stress response, thus earning its name, it must be perceived by the organism as exceeding its ability to cope with the demand (Lazarus, 1967; Novaco, 1979). In this chapter, I define the term *stress* as a condition that arises when an individual experiences a demand that exceeds his or her real or perceived abilities to successfully cope with the demand, resulting in disturbance to his or her physiological or psychological equilibrium.

The role of psychosocial stress in the development of physical illness has interested scientists and philosophers for more than 2,000 years. Research efforts during the past 15 years have provided increasing support for the consideration of stress as a risk factor in the etiology of illness and disease. The physiology of the stress response is becoming increasingly identified and provides an understanding of the mechanisms by which stress may influence illness (Britton & Koob, 1988; Jemmott & Magliore, 1988; Kennedy, Kiecolt-Glaser, & Glaser, 1988).

One area in which this is significant is the workplace; in response to stressors in the workplace, perturbations in the physical and psychological functioning of employees can be expected. This notion is logically consistent and also has received empirical support (House, 1981; Kahill, 1988; McGee, 1989; Spector, Dwyer, & Jex, 1988). By its very nature, work will place coping demands on employees, perhaps more consistently than any other context. Stress in the workplace may ultimately affect productivity and therefore the economic, political, and social correlates of employee output. This last item may be of particular significance when one considers that the estimates of the costs of stress exceed $150 billion annually (Donatelle & Hawkins, 1989).

In addition to the physiological events, psychological events such as cognitive functioning form a part of the stress response. This is consistent with the Yerkes–Dodson "inverted U function" (1908, cited in Sanford, 1985), which states that there is an optimal level of arousal outside of which attention and performance diminish. There is empirical evidence to support this (Buckelew & Hannay, 1986; Hockey, 1979). Following this, memory (Everly & Horton, 1984), academic performance (Spiegal, Smolen, & Jonas, 1986), decision making (McGee, 1989), and problem-solving skills (Fehrenbach & Peterson, 1989) may be compromised during periods of excessive arousal, or stress. Thus, in response to stressors in the workplace, perturbations in the physical and psychological functioning of employees can be expected. This notion is logically consistent and also has received empirical support (House, 1981; Kahill, 1988; McGee, 1988; Spector et al., 1988). Research and observation of these events, coupled with the rising costs associated with health care and health-related problems, has prompted industry to seek remedies.

Worksite Stress Management Interventions

Several worksite-based stress management interventions (SMIs) have been developed and investigated. A sizable literature has developed, much of it concluding that SMIs may be effective in attenuating the negative aspects of the stress responses (Carrington et al., 1980; Charlesworth & Dempsey, 1982; Girdano & Everly, 1979; Pelletier & Lutz, 1988; Wertkin, 1985). The benefits to an employer of implementing an SMI in the workplace have been argued by many (Adams, 1988; Cole, Tucker, & Friedman, 1987; Golembiewski & Munzenrider, 1987; Jaffe, Scott, & Orioloi, 1986; Pelletier & Lutz, 1988).

There are methodological problems in the stress management literature that make it difficult to be certain about these conclusions. For example, the absence of control groups in many designs, the lack of randomization, and the confounding effects of social support are considerable threats to internal validity in much of the research. Nevertheless, stress management programs have become increasingly visible components of employee health programs (Hillenberg & DiLorenzo, 1987). A wide variety of approaches have been developed, including meditation and various other forms of relaxation training, biofeedback, cognitive–behavioral approaches, massage, and education. As business managers seek to contain health-related expenses and improve the performance of workers, programs that tout their effectiveness in affecting these areas become appealing. Caveat emptor!

Evaluation of an SMI

The effectiveness of meditation as a brief, inexpensive approach to stress management has been investigated and found effective (Bruning & Frew, 1987; Carrington et al., 1980; Dilbeck & Orme-Johnson, 1987; English & Baker, 1983; Jevning, Wells, Wilson, & Guich, 1987). This approach may be attractive as a relaxation technique because it is easily taught, can generally be practiced with little difficulty at the worksite, and can be implemented with little expense to the employer.

In a recent experimental study, Kolbell (1992) investigated the effectiveness of meditation as a workplace-based SMI. The purpose of current study was to determine whether meditation as an SMI could significantly affect employee health and cognitive function in an at-risk population while controlling for the effects of social support.

Method

I examined the effects of a worksite SMI on health and cognitive functioning among employees of a children's services division. Thirty-eight participants were randomly assigned to a treatment group, a social support group, or a no-treatment control group. Individuals in the treatment condition participated in a relaxation group that consisted of training and practice in insight meditation. Each group met at the workplace for 20 min each work day for 4 weeks. Training was provided using prerecorded audiotapes with instructions on how to meditate. Each participant was given an audiotape to facilitate their learning and instructed to practice at least once per month after the training period. Participants in the social support condition participated in a social support group that met daily for 20 min at the workplace for 4 weeks. Group direction was provided by prerecorded audiotapes that encouraged open discussion of stress, empathic listening, development of skills in providing support, and encouragement to use these skills outside the training situation. Each participant was provided with an audiotape of the instructions and was instructed to practice his or her skills after the training period. The control group received no intervention.

Maslach Burnout Inventory (MBI; Maslach & Folkman) scores were obtained for all participants as a measure of stress before and after treatment. Measures of cognitive functioning—the Arithmetic and Digit Symbols subtests of the Wechsler Adult Intelligence Scale–Revised (WAIS-R; Wechsler, 1981) and the Verbal Reasoning Test (Corsini & Renck, 1958)—were obtained after treatment. The Problem Solving Inventory was administered after treatment as a measure of perceived problem-solving ability and style. Pretreatment measures of health functioning were obtained using self-report of physical symptoms and sick days for the 5 months before treatment. Posttreatment measures included sick days, self-reports of symptoms, and physician visits for the 5-month period after treatment. Scores on the Somatization scale of the Brief Symptom Inventory were obtained after treatment.

Results

Stress was evaluated before and after treatment using the MBI (see Table 1). I used a multivariate analysis of covariance (MANCOVA) because of the intercorrelations between the subscales of the MBI. Between-groups differences on scores obtained on the MBI were evaluated, with pretest scores used as the covariate. There was no significant effect for group, $F(6, 64) = 0.788, p < .250$, as determined by Wilks's lambda.

Health functioning was evaluated using four measures of theoretically correlated variables. Total sick days for the 5-month period before and after

Table 1. Means and Standard Deviations on the Maslach Burnout Inventory Subscale Scores by Treatment Group

Group and subscale score	Pretreatment		Posttreatment	
	M	SD	M	SD
Meditation				
Personal Achievement	36.66	7.67	36.74	6.56
Emotional Exhaustion	28.40	9.26	27.27	11.01
Depersonalization	12.67	7.92	11.07	7.17
Social support				
Personal Achievement	34.57	5.83	34.79	6.53
Emotional Exhaustion	29.14	7.25	27.57	6.30
Depersonalization	10.64	5.08	9.43	4.96
Control				
Personal Achievement	31.55	11.14	35.70	5.31
Emotional Exhaustion	24.91	11.78	29.63	10.90
Depersonalization	8.10	6.18	11.82	5.08

treatment, average monthly visits to a physician for 5 months after treatment, scores on the Somatization scale of the Brief Symptom Inventory, and the self-report measure of six different physical symptoms were used to evaluate health functioning (see Tables 2 and 3). A MANCOVA was used to test for between-groups differences on all health measures, with pretreatment sick days and pretreatment symptom reports used as the covariates. No significant effects of group were found for any of the variables related to health outcomes, $F(18, 38) = 0.393$, $p < .270$, as determined by Wilks's lambda.

Cognitive functioning was examined in two dimensions: actual performance on tests of mental ability and self-perceptions of problem-solving style (see Tables 4 and 5). Performance was evaluated on three separate tests of mental ability that assess functioning in three conceptually and practically different domains: concentration and ability to compute arithmetic functions mentally (the Arithmetic subtest of the WAIS-R); a timed task of attention, concentration, and visuomotor speed and integration (the Digit Symbols subtest of the WAIS-R); and a test of verbal reasoning abilities (the Verbal Reasoning Test). A one-way analysis of variance was used to analyze the data generated by each of these measures of cognitive functioning. No significant between-groups differences were found on Digit Symbols, $F(2, 37) = 0.11$, $p < .899$, Arithmetic, $F(2, 37) = 1.27$, $p < .293$), or Verbal Reasoning, $F(2, 37) = 0.31$, $p < .734$.

Table 2. Means and Standard Deviations for Health Variables by Treatment Group

Group	Somatization scale		Physician visits		Sick days	
	M	SD	M	SD	M	SD
Meditation	0.53	0.52	3.8	0.18	5.07	3.89
Social support	0.65	0.35	3.6	0.17	6.15	7.38
Control	0.39	0.61	1.6	0.17	6.18	4.09

Table 3. Means and Standard Deviations for Health Symptoms by
Treatment Group

Symptom group	Pretreatment		Posttreatment	
	M	SD	M	SD
Headaches				
Meditation	7.53	1.55	7.10	1.51
Social support	7.64	1.22	6.51	1.42
Control	7.91	1.58	7.18	1.33
Muscle pain				
Meditation	9.33	1.68	8.53	1.66
Social support	9.14	1.24	7.35	2.01
Control	10.27	2.15	8.27	2.35
Gastrointestinal				
Meditation	7.47	1.73	7.05	1.45
Social support	7.00	1.24	6.21	1.74
Control	7.73	1.49	6.73	1.31
Cardiac				
Meditation	4.80	1.15	4.49	1.00
Social support	5.00	0.96	4.22	1.14
Control	4.27	0.47	3.86	0.69
Temperature				
Meditation	5.20	1.21	4.68	1.11
Social support	5.00	0.96	4.22	0.81
Control	4.82	0.87	4.58	1.25
Mental status				
Meditation	12.20	2.01	11.31	2.07
Social support	12.21	1.76	10.74	2.02
Control	12.50	2.17	11.01	2.44

Discussion

These findings can be conceptualized as falling into one of three basic categories: organizational, individual, or those relating to the intervention.

Organizational Factors

Organizational factors are those aspects of the worksite that may be stressful
in and of themselves, regardless of the nature and type of work performed.

Table 4. Means and Standard Deviations on Measures of Cognitive Functioning by
Treatment Group

Group	Digit Symbols		Arithmetic		Verbal Reasoning	
	M	SD	M	SD	M	SD
Meditation	60.33	10.96	8.80	1.97	48.53	10.36
Social support	58.74	16.22	9.36	1.95	50.21	11.40
Control	58.27	8.93	10.00	1.73	51.63	7.06

Table 5. Means and Standard Deviations on Problem-Solving Inventory Subscales by Treatment Group

Group	Confidence		Approach–Avoidance		Personal Control	
	M	SD	M	SD	M	SD
Meditation	29.87	5.93	53.93	5.86	18.7	3.41
Social support	29.43	6.82	55.14	5.68	16.9	6.14
Control	29.64	6.77	54.27	7.44	20.45	5.33

Within this conceptualization, organizational structure, the stability of management, the availability of resources and workload, the stability of the employee's role, the nature of the work environment, the efficiency of operation, and the availability of supervision are all potential stressors (Heaney & van Ryan, 1990; Ivancevich, Matteson, Freedman, & Phillips, 1990; Parasuraman & Alutto, 1984). Conceptualizing stress as an interactional process between environmental factors (stressors) and individual response suggests that the magnitude and nature of environmental factors may modulate the stress response: Stress increases as the demands for coping increase (Lazarus & Folkman, 1984).

The history of the children's services division during the past 5 years suggests that there are several organizational factors that may cause stress. These include four different administrators, decreasing administrative support, frequent changes in role expectations, a reconfiguration of service provision, increased public scrutiny and criticism, and interagency conflict (K. Leahy & P. Bowman, personal communication, 1992). Additionally, socioeconomic forces such as decreased funding to service providers and an increased need for services have led to layoffs, hiring freezes, and an imbalance in the supply:demand ratio, which the organization's existing policies and procedures are neither designed nor equipped to handle (P. Bowman, personal communication, 1992). On a broader scale, the agency has gone from a decentralized approach to service delivery to a centralized approach and back again, which has required changes in policy and procedures and caused a disruption in work routine and physical relocation of offices, workers, and equipment. The most recent occasion for this change occurred during the 2nd and 3rd weeks of the intervention.

It may be that interventions directed at changing the individual's response to stressors is an insufficient measure when there is significant and persistent organizational disequilibrium. Heaney and van Ryan (1990) suggested that because organizational factors are beyond the individual employee's ability to effect change, individually focused interventions are unlikely to be successful. Rather, what may be necessary is a stress management program that combines elements of an individually focused approach with efforts directed at organizational change. Indeed, researchers who have used organizationally based strategies or combined organizational with individual approaches have found support for this hypothesis (Ganster, Mayes, Tharp, & Sime, 1988; Jackson, 1983; Jones et al., 1988). The costs of implementation, the inability to gain commitment from management for organizationally based interventions, and the ease of implementation of individually based programs have contributed to the relative paucity of organizationally based interventions (Handy, 1986). In the current study, because of the extent of organizational disruption and the focus on testing a brief, inexpensive treatment, intervention at this level was not feasible.

Individual Factors

Although the influence of organizational factors on participants' responses to treatment may be central to understanding the results of this study, consideration of individual factors also may contribute.

It was apparent early in the treatment process that participants found daily attendance at the meditation and social support groups to be another responsibility that interfered with the time available to handle their workload. Although these data were not systematically gathered, informal and unsolicited comments from the respondents suggested that the intervention was partly viewed as yet another demand with which they had to cope. Thus, any potential benefits inherent in the interventions might have been offset by the perception of the intervention as a stressor.

It may be the case that only employees who were experiencing high levels of stress volunteered for the study. In fact, according to the scores on the MBI, respondents typically scored in the high-average to high range for burnout. However, according to the normative sample for the MBI, the mean subscale scores for the respondents in this study fell within 1 *SD* of the mean scores for the normative sample of social workers. Because there are no available norms for the MBI on workers in industries other than helping professions, comparisons of stress levels as measured by this instrument are not possible. Given epidemiological data and theoretical assumptions regarding burnout, it may be that these individuals experience higher levels of burnout than do employees in other fields and thus may require a more potent intervention, a "stronger medicine" than a brief instruction in meditation. The stress-reducing benefits of meditation may be effective with more moderate populations (Carrington et al., 1980) or may require a longer, more intensive training and practice schedule.

Finally, given the weak nature of the intervention, as reflected by the health and cognitive function outcomes, a substantially larger number of respondents would have been required to detect a significant effect.

Intervention-Related Factors

Heaney and van Ryan (1990) pointed out that some individual interventions may have adverse side effects, such as increased psychophysiological reactivity to stressors among meditators (Sawada & Steptoe, 1988). In the case of the meditation intervention, a prominent feature of the training is developing awareness of physical states. It is conceivable that as one's awareness of one's body increases, so does recognition of physical distress and complaints of somatic symptoms; this may in turn act as a stressor and may result in a greater incidence of sick days and health care utilization. Similarly, in the social support condition, because respondents focused on stress in their discussions, they might have increased their sensitivity to stressors in the workplace and thus perceived more of the daily demands as exceeding their ability to cope.

As suggested earlier, meditation may not be enough to reduce stress in this high-risk population. In a similar study undertaken by Carrington et al. (1980), meditation was found to be effective in reducing stress among a group of telephone company employees. Because social service employees are at higher risk for developing stress-related disorders (Clower, 1990), it can be argued that the stress levels experienced by this population are greater than those experienced by telephone company employees. Thus, they may require a different level and type of intervention, perhaps one that combines meditation with interventions targeted at the organizational level.

Comparison With Other Studies

As discussed earlier, previous research on the effectiveness of worksite SMIs has methodological flaws. Bearing in mind the problems with the research, the findings do suggest potential benefits to employees in the areas of health and job performance. The wide variety of approaches to stress management, and differences among dependent variables, has made comparisons across studies difficult.

The current study is unique in that a meditation technique was used and global health and cognitive functioning were the dependent variables; thus, strict comparison with other studies is not possible. The effects of meditation on cognitive functioning among employees has not been evaluated previously. However, the use of meditation and its effects on health-related variables (e.g., cardiovascular stress response) has been studied. This allows a comparison of one type of intervention (meditation) across other studies that argue for the potential health benefits of meditation training for employees.

English and Baker (1983) examined the effects of meditation versus relaxation in a group of volunteers from the community at large in Madison, Wisconsin. Stressors included exposure to a cold-pressor test and a reaction time task; measures included blood pressure and heart rate and were taken during and after exposure to the stressor. Both the meditation and relaxation groups showed significant decreases in systolic and diastolic blood pressure relative to a control group in the period following exposure to the stressor. However, measurement during the exposure to the stressors indicated no significant differences in blood pressure or heart rate. Thus, in the presence of a stressor the potentially health-related benefits of meditation were not apparent, suggesting that individuals who are exposed to continuous stressors may not benefit from these techniques. In the current study, many of the stressors were continuous, and measurement was taken during exposure to these stressors; this may explain the lack of significant effects. The type and duration of stressors obviously were different in the current study and in English and Baker's study; it also can be argued that the participants were different. English and Baker conducted a brief laboratory investigation without follow-up; results obtained from a laboratory may be different from those obtained in the field. Finally, it may be that the change in blood pressure among respondents in English and Baker's study represents change that is significant statistically but not clinically, thus raising questions about the effect of these techniques on clinical health status.

Bruning and Frew (1987) applied meditation training in a field experiment, using employees in a hospital equipment manufacturing company as participants. Participants were assigned to either a cognitive stress management group, a meditation group, an exercise group, or a control group. Participants in the experimental conditions received training for 8–10 hr in 1 week and were instructed to practice their skills during the 13 weeks that followed; meditators were instructed to practice their techniques for 15–20 min, once or twice per day. Dependent variables included pulse, blood pressure, and galvanic skin response (GSR). Significant and equivalent effects for all treatments were found on pulse and blood pressure, but not GSR. On the basis of these findings, Bruning and Frew suggested that these interventions may have some beneficial effects in modulating negative consequences of stress among workers. The extent of stress among the participants was not clear; pretreatment measures were within normal limits for pulse, blood pressure, and GSR, suggesting that the participants might not have been under significant stress at the time of measurement. Thus, in addition to the obvious occupational differences, the nature of the stressors among respondents in the study by Bruning and Frew might have been much different from those experienced by the social service employees who served as participants in the current study. Also, Bruning and Frew did not control for the effects of social support; thus, their conclusion that these interventions contributed to decreasing pulse and blood pressure may be confounded with the effects of social support. Finally, the relatively low pulse rates observed before treatment (average pulse = 74) reflects a healthy population to begin with; posttreatment pulse rates declined by an average of 6 points. The significance of this decline in terms of health outcomes is unclear, especially in the absence of clinical data.

In a widely cited, well-controlled study, Carrington et al. (1980) assigned 154 telephone company employees to a relaxation group, one of two meditation groups, or a control group. Training was provided by prerecorded audiocassette tape. Respondents learned the techniques in their homes and were instructed to practice for 15–20 min twice daily. Two weeks following the instruction period, they met as a group and received instructions from a psychologist in the use of these techniques in managing stress. Measures were obtained pretreatment, 6 weeks posttreatment, and 5.5 months posttreatment and included a personality inventory and the SCL-90-R (Derogatis, 1977), which is a self-report symptom checklist from which the Brief Symptom Inventory is derived. The control and treatment groups showed significant differences pre- and posttreatment on the Somatization scale of the SCL-90-R; at the 5.5-month measurement, significant between-groups differences were found between the meditation and relaxation groups and the control groups. There was no significant difference between meditation and relaxation groups. Differences between that study and the current investigation may explain some of the variance between the respective results. The subject groups were different; there is evidence to suggest that stress levels among social service workers are higher than in non-helping professions (Clower, 1990). Therefore, an intervention that is successful with a population in which stress levels are lower may not be as effective in another high-stress population. Second, respondents received the treatments at their leisure in their home, where the training did not interfere with their work time and did not appear as another work-related demand. Also, the home environment is more conducive to learning these techniques than the workplace, where contextual cues for responses to occupational stressors are omnipresent. Third, respondents received specific instructions in the clinical use of these techniques, which might have facilitated application of the techniques more regularly in the management of daily stress. The finding that the control group in the Carrington et al. (1980) study showed a significant difference on posttreatment measures is interesting. Seamonds (1982) demonstrated that simply interviewing employees about stress and providing referrals for stress management had a significant effect on absenteeism. This suggests that among some populations, a limited intervention may be sufficient to affect health functioning. Thus, it may be that the brief lecture about stress provided to all respondents prior to treatment and the process of measurement had a similar positive effect in the Carrington et al. study. That no such effect was observed in the current study suggests that this effect may be specific to organizations in which the nature and degree of stress are different. Finally, no direct health outcomes were measured by Carrington et al.; the correlation between scores on the SCL-R-90 and health status is not known.

Implications

The findings of the current study have implications for the practical application of SMIs as well as for future research. In terms of the practical application of SMIs, it may be important to consider both the source of the stressors and the individual responses to those stressors. As is the case with psychotherapy and behavior change, intervention is based on a careful evaluation of the patient relative to contextual factors, or stressors. Applying a palliative treatment without considering or addressing the etiology of the patient's complaint (stress) may result in the failure to achieve treatment goals (reducing stress and stress-related health or cognitive problems). In the current study, because the magnitude of organizational factors that contributed to the employee stress levels required an intervention directed at changing those factors, perhaps teaching employees different coping strategies should also be done. This implies that an approach to stress management should consist of an evaluation process that determines the source and nature of the stressors as well as assessing the individual's response. Following this, development of an appropriate intervention strategy that will achieve the desired goals becomes more likely. This approach is consistent with the transactional perspective of stress defined at the outset of this chapter, and has been suggested elsewhere (Hillenberg & DiLorenzo, 1987).

As the results of my study show, interventions that have demonstrated efficacy in one setting or with one population of workers may not have the same success in another situation. Although a number of researchers have suggested the potential health benefits of practicing meditation, methodological problems render those claims tentative at best. Also, as discussed earlier, changes recorded in physiological measures do not necessarily translate into changes in health outcomes. Thus, the selection of an intervention and the expectations for that intervention should be carefully evaluated prior to initiating a worksite SMI.

Because the findings in the general area of stress management are inconsistent, additional well-controlled research in this area is warranted. The relationships among the type and severity of stressors, populations, and types of interventions can be examined in future research, which may provide useful information regarding the design and selection of interventions. Because evaluation is an essential precursor to the development of an appropriate intervention, the development of sound protocols for evaluating organizational and individual components of occupational stress is necessary. Finally, the use of health outcome variables as opposed to more reductionist physiological variables is necessary to determine the practical value of these technologies in affecting health functioning.

Conclusions

The primary conclusion that can be drawn from the current study is that a brief training in meditation was no different from social support or no-treatment controls on measures of health and cognitive functioning among social service workers. These findings are inconsistent with previous studies that have shown significant effects of relaxation training, meditation, and other individually focused interventions among other populations using different measures of health functioning. I suggest that the predominantly physiological measures used in previous studies may not predict outcomes that are more directly related to health and illness. I did not use objective measures of physiological functioning, so the effects of meditation on this type of variable in this population cannot be discerned.

The organization in which the study was conducted has a recent history significant for its organizational stressors. I did not assess the organizational factors because intervention was not targeted at organizational change. It is hypothesized that a meditation strategy that seeks to modulate the stress response of individuals is insufficient in the face of these organizational factors and that intervention targeted at organizational change might have been warranted. Careful evaluation of stressors may be necessary to develop an intervention strategy appropriate to the needs of each situation.

References

Adams, J. D. (1988, August). A healthy cut in costs. *Personnel Administrator*, 42–47.

Britton, K. T., & Koob, G. F. (1988). Behavioral effects of corticotrophin releasing factors. In A. Schatzberg & C. Nemeroff (Eds.), *The hypothalamic-pituitary-adrenal axis: Physiology, pathophysiology, and psychiatric implications* (pp. 55–66). New York: Raven Press.

Bruning, N. S., & Frew, D. R. (1987). Effects of exercise, relaxation and management skills training on physiological stress indicators: A field experiment. *Journal of Applied Psychology, 72*, 515–521.

Buckelew, S. P., & Hannay, H. J. (1986). Relationship among anxiety, defensiveness, sex, task difficulty, and performance on various neuropsychological tests. *Perceptual and Motor Skills, 68*, 807–810.

Carrington, P., Collings, G. H., Benson, H., Robinson, H., Wood, L., Lehrer, P., Woolfolk, R., & Cole, J. (1980). The use of meditation-relaxation techniques for the management of stress in a working population. *Journal of Occupational Medicine, 22*, 221–231.

Charlesworth, E., & Dempsey, G. (1982). Trait anxiety reduction in a substance abuse population trained in stress management. *Journal of Clinical Psychology, 38*, 754–758.

Clower, I. (1990, September). *Mental stress claims in Oregon, 1984–1988.* (Report to Oregon Department of Insurance and Finance.) Salem, OR: State of Oregon.

Cole, G. E., Tucker, L. A., & Friedman, G. M. (1987, Spring). Absenteeism data as a measure of cost effectiveness in stress management programs. *American Journal of Health Promotion*, 12–15.

Corsini, R., & Renck, R. (1958). *The Verbal Reasoning Test.* Chicago: Industrial Relations Center, University of Chicago.

Derogatis, L. (1977). *SCL-90-R manual.* Towson, MD: Clinical Psychometric Research.

Dilbeck, M. C., & Orme-Johnson, D. W. (1987). Physiological differences between Transcendental Meditation and rest. *American Psychologist, 42*, 879–881.

Donatelle, R., & Hawkins, M. (1989). Employee stress claims: Increasing implications for health promotion programming. *American Journal of Health Promotion, 3*, 19–25.

English, E. H., & Baker, T. B. (1983). Relaxation training and cardiovascular response to experimental stressors. *Health Psychology, 2*, 239–259.

Everly, G. S., & Horton, A. M. (1984). Neuropsychology of post-traumatic-stress-disorder: A pilot study. *Perceptual and Motor Skills, 68*, 807–810.

Fehrenbach, A. M., & Peterson, L. (1989). Parental problem-solving skills, stress, and dietary compliance in phenylketonuria. *Journal of Consulting and Clinical Psychology, 57*, 237–241.

Ganster, D. C., Mayes, B. T., Tharp, G. D., & Sime, W. E. (1988). Managing occupational stress: A field experiment. *Journal of Applied Psychology, 72*, 515–521.

Girdano, D. A., & Everly, G. S. (1979). *Controlling stress and tension.* Englewood Cliffs, NJ: Prentice Hall.

Golembewski, R. T., & Munzenrider, R. (1987, Winter). Social support and burnout as covariants of physical symptoms: Where to put marginal dollars. *Organizational Development Journal*, 92–96.

Handy, J. (1986). Considering organizations in organizational stress research: A rejoinder to Glowinkowski and Cooper, and to Duckworth. *Bulletin of the British Psychological Society, 39*, 205–210.

Heaney, C. A., & van Ryn, M. (1990). Broadening the scope of worksite stress programs. *Academy of Management Journal, 4*, 413–420.

Hillenberg, J. B., & DiLorenzo, T. M. (1987). Stress management training in health psychology practice: Critical clinical issues. *Professional Practice: Research and Practice, 18*, 402–404.

Hockey, R. (1979). Stress and cognitive components of skilled performance. In V. Hamilton & G. Warburton (Eds.), *Human stress and cognition* (pp. 141–178). New York: Wiley.

House, J. S. (1981). *Work stress and social support.* Reading, MA: Addison-Wesley.

Ivancevich, J. M., Matteson, M. T., Freedman, S. M., & Phillips, J. S. (1990). Worksite stress management interventions. *American Psychologist, 45*, 252–261.

Jackson, S. E. (1983). Participation in decision making as a strategy for reducing job-related strain. *Journal of Applied Psychology, 68*, 3–19.

Jaffe, D. T., Scott, C. D., & Orioli, E. S. (1986). Stress management: Programs and prospects. *American Journal of Health Promotion*, *1*, 29–37.

Jemmott, J. B., & Magliore, K. (1988). Academic stress, social support, and secretory IgA. *Journal of Personality and Social Psychology*, *55*, 803–810.

Jevning, R., Wells, I., Wilson, A. F., & Guich, S. (1987). Plasma thyroid hormones, thyroid stimulating hormone, and insulin during acute hypometabolic states in man. *Physiology & Behavior*, *40*, 603–606.

Jones, J. W., Barge, B. N., Steffy, B. D., Fay, L. M., Kuntz, L. K., & Wuebeka, L. J. (1988). Stress and medical malpractice: Organizational risk assessment and intervention. *Journal of Applied Psychology*, *73*, 727–735.

Kahill, S. (1988). Symptoms of professional burnout: A review of the empirical evidence. *Canadian Psychologist*, *29*, 284–297.

Kennedy, S., Kiecolt-Glaser, J. K., & Glaser, R. (1988). Immunological consequences of acute and chronic stressors: Mediating role of interpersonal relationships. *British Journal of Medical Psychology*, *61*, 77–85.

Kolbell, R. (1992, November). *Stress, health, and cognitive function: When relaxation is not enough.* Paper presented at APA/NIOSH conference, Washington, DC.

Lazarus, R. S. (1967). Cognitive and personality factors underlying threat and coping. In M. Appley & R. Trumbull (Eds.), *Psychological stress* (pp. 151–181). New York: Appleton-Century-Crofts.

Lazarus, R. S., & Folkman, S. (1984). *Stress, appraisal and coping.* New York: Springer-Verlag.

Maslach, C., & Folkman, S. E. (1981). *Maslach Burnout Inventory.* Palo Alto, CA: Consulting Psychologists Press, Inc.

McGee, R. (1989). Burnout and professional decision making. *Journal of Counseling Psychology*, *36*, 345–351.

Novaco, R. W. (1979). The cognitive regulation of anger and stress. In P. Kendall & S. Hollon (Eds.), *Cognitive–Behavioral Interventions* (pp. 241–286). New York: Academic Press.

Parasuraman, S., & Alutto, J. A. (1984). Sources and outcomes of stress in organizational settings: Towards the development of a structural model. *Academy of Management Journal*, *27*, 330–350.

Pelletier, K. R., & Lutz, R. (1988). Healthy people—healthy business: A critical review of stress management programs in the workplace. *American Journal of Health Promotion*, *3*, 5–12.

Sanford, A. J. (1985). *Cognition and cognitive psychology.* New York: Basic Books.

Sawada, Y., & Steptoe, A. (1988). The effects of brief meditation training on cardiovascular stress responses. *Journal of Psychophysiology*, *2*, 249–257.

Seamonds, B. C. (1982). Stress factors and their effect on absenteeism in a corporate employee group. *Journal of Occupational Medicine*, *24*, 393–397.

Spector, P. E., Dwyer, D. J., & Jex, S. M. (1988). Relation of job stressors to affective, health and performance outcomes: A comparison of multiple data sources. *Journal of Applied Psychology*, *73*, 11–19.

Spiegal, D. A., Smolen, R. C., & Jonas, C. K. (1986). An examination of the relationships among interpersonal relationship stress, morale, and academic performance in female medical students. *Social Science and Medicine*, *23*, 1157–1161.

Wechsler, D. (1981). *WAIS-R Manual.* New York: Psychological Corporation.

Wertkin, R. A. (1985). Stress-inoculation training: Principles and applications. *Social Casework*, *12*, 611–616.

4

Stress Inoculation Training for Staff Working With Persons With Mental Retardation: A Model Program

Joseph B. Keyes

The growth of organizationally sponsored stress reduction and prevention programs and workshops has accelerated rapidly during the past decade. The Medical Literature Analysis and Retrieval System database indicates that more than 1,200 articles on stress were published between 1976 and 1985 (Vingerhoets & Marcelissen, 1988). However, in a recent review of worksite stress management interventions, Ivancevich, Matteson, Freedman, and Phillips (1990) noted that the current understanding of the effectiveness of various intervention strategies is severely limited.

The purpose of this chapter is to present a research-based model of a work-related stress reduction program for a specific type of organization: the social service agency working with clients with special needs. The model was developed by analyzing the type and source of work-related stressors for staff and designing procedures to directly reduce and prevent maladaptive stress reactions. It is based on research conducted with organizations serving individuals with mental retardation and developmental disabilities. The program developed fits within the theoretical framework of cognitive–behavioral procedures termed *stress inoculation training* (SIT; Meichenbaum, 1985).

Stress Analysis

It has been noted that, as a group, individuals with mental retardation exhibit more behavior problems and emotional disturbances than is observed in the general population (Borthwick-Duffy & Eyman, 1990; Iverson & Fox, 1989). Parsons, May, and Manolascino (1984) estimated the prevalence rate of emotional problems in people with mental retardation to be 20–35%. It is obvious that professional and paraprofessional staff are faced at various times with highly disturbed and agitated individuals. This is typical for organizations that deal with special-needs populations such as juvenile delinquency, traumatic brain injury, emotional disorders, and so on.

Browner et al. (1986) found aggressive behavior to be a significant source

45

of stress for direct-contact workers. This was the only aspect of their work with clients that staff reported to be stressful. In studying abuse-provoking characteristics of individuals with mental retardation, researchers have found that aggression is the most significant distinguishing characteristic between individuals with mental retardation who were abused by staff and those who were not (Marchetti & McCartney, 1990; Rusch, Hall, & Griffin, 1986). These researchers have suggested that direct-contact staff working with aggressive individuals may benefit from specialized training, sensitizing them to the possibility that the person's aggression may provoke abusive responses. In addition, Lakin, Bruininks, Hill, and Hauber (1982) noted that high staff turnover is a chronic problem facing large public facilities and private community-based facilities. Occupational stress may play a role in this turnover rate because there is a direct relation between job-related stress and turnover (Rosen, 1986).

It is therefore important to train staff to be effective in conflict management or crisis management. The majority of states and service agencies provide in-service training for dealing with aggressive behavior (Knowles & Landesman, 1986). This training has focused predominantly on the management of conflict external to the staff member (i.e., techniques that staff should use to diffuse or deescalate the anger and agitation of the client). A second aspect of training that has not been adequately or systematically addressed centers on intrapersonal stress or anger (i.e., the stress experienced by the staff person as a result of the conflict situation). Staff can experience high intrapersonal conflict when trying to manage a situation with a disturbed or agitated individual (Browner et al., 1986; Rusch et al., 1986). This is especially true when staff members become the target of hostile abuse from the client. Staff members often must absorb the individual's frustration and hostility. Interpersonal crisis intervention skills are designed to enable the staff member to respond to the individual's anger and agitation with effective intervention and deescalation techniques. However, the individual's displaced anger and hostility may produce anger and agitation among staff. If staff are agitated and angry, it is less likely that they will be able to carry out the intervention procedures effectively and systematically (Novaco, 1975).

Therefore, the potential negative effects of stress in this type of work for staff are numerous and may include increased stress, increased client abuse, increased staff turnover, and ineffective application of intervention procedures. One approach to training (Meichenbaum, 1977, 1985) is a set of specific procedures to reduce and prevent maladaptive stress reactions. It can be compared to a medical inoculation in which an individual's resistance is enhanced by graduated exposure to stress stimuli.

SIT has been shown to be effective with a wide variety of disorders and occupational groups for whom the management of intrapersonal stress and anger is important to functioning. It has been used as treatment and a prevention. Nomelini and Katz (1983) found that SIT is effective in reducing anger and abusive behaviors in parents who abused their children. It also has been effective with urban schoolteachers (Forman, 1982), police officers (Novaco,

1977), probation officers (Novaco, 1980), nurses (West, Horan, & Games, 1984), and military recruit trainees (Novaco, Cook, & Savason, 1983).

Stress Inoculation Training

We have recently developed SIT procedures for staff working with people with mental retardation and developmental disabilities. The training package is based on Meichenbaum's (1977, 1985) stress inoculation treatment paradigm and is designed specifically to address the needs of people working with individuals with mental retardation and other social service organizations working with similar special-needs populations (e.g., psychiatric disturbance, juvenile delinquency, traumatic brain injury, substance abuse, etc.).

The treatment paradigm has three phases: conceptualization, skills acquisition and rehearsal, and application and follow-through. The primary focus of the conceptualization stage is on helping staff to better understand the nature of stress and anger, understand its effect on emotion and performance, and reconceptualize it in transactional terms (i.e., interactions between the individual and the environment). A cognitive model of stress and the arousal of anger based on Beck's (1984) and Meichenbaum's (1985) analyses is presented. This model posits that emotions (anger arousal) are largely determined or mediated by the individual's thinking or interpretation of the situation. An analysis is made of cognitive interpretations of various stress-provoking situations. The individual's stress is recast in terms that are specific and amenable to solutions. This phase proposes that the individual's stress goes through stages and is at least partially under the person's control.

During the skills acquisition and rehearsal phase, staff members develop and rehearse a variety of coping skills, including self-instruction training or guided self-dialogue, cognitive restructuring, problem-solving training, and relaxation training. Self-instruction training and guided self-dialogue teach statements that stressed individuals can say to themselves while preparing for a stressor, when confronting and handling a stressful event, when feeling overwhelmed by stress, and when reflecting on their coping efforts. Relaxation training involves teaching muscle relaxation, breathing exercises, and cognitive cue-controlling procedures. Cognitive restructuring includes teaching the individuals to be aware of automatic thoughts, images, behavioral expectations, and cognitive distortions and to use thought-catching strategies and reinterpretation for behavioral expectations and cognitive distortions. Problem-solving training is a cognitive therapy strategy that views a stressful event as a definable problem to be solved. It involves assessment, generating possible alternative courses of action, decision making, and implementation of a set of skills and methods for the self-regulation of anger and stress within the individual. The coping skills trained emerge from the reconceptualization process.

The application and follow-through phase involves the practicing of the techniques learned in the first two phases. Role-playing methods are used for this purpose. Each individual is given an opportunity to test his or her proficiency in anger and stress management in a controlled situation. The provocative impact of the role-play situation is graduated in intensity and complexity. The closer the training sessions are to the criterion situation, the greater the generalization.

The training is best conducted in at least a 1-day workshop with 12–16 staff people per workshop. The extensiveness and intensity of training may be increased by additional workshop time. A sample workshop outline can be found in the Appendix.

Effects of Stress Inoculation Training

Two recent studies have examined the effects that SIT procedures (Keyes, 1989; Keyes & Dean, 1988) have on direct-contact staff behavior and performance.

Study 1 (Keyes & Dean, 1988)

Participants

The participants were 100 direct-contact staff working at three medium-sized intermediate care facilities for the mentally retarded (ICF/MR) with censuses of 32, 150, and 85 clients. Each facility was licensed under Title XIX licensing regulations and served clients with all levels of mental retardation. Facilities 1, 2, and 3 had 45, 148, and 85 direct-contact staff, respectively. Staff participating in the study had a mean age of 30.84 years and a mean of 5.1 years of experience. Seventy-one of the staff were women and 29 were men. Ninety-two percent of staff had a high school diploma, 7% had some college, and 1% a college degree. Staff were randomly selected to participate in the study, and the training was conducted as part of the facility's staff development program.

Procedure

Attention-control group. Fifty staff members from Facilities 1 and 2 participated in the attention-control procedure consisting of a small-group (3–4 staff) lecture and discussion regarding stress and anger. A cognitive–behavioral (Beck, 1984) approach to stress, anger, and emotion was used. The relationship of stress and anger to crisis intervention was discussed. The information provided was that of the conceptualization phase, described earlier. The small-group discussion lasted 1–2 hr.

Stress inoculation training group. Fifty staff members from Facility 3 participated in SIT. The training package was developed from Meichenbaum's (1977, 1985) stress inoculation treatment paradigm, described earlier. The

Table 1. Means and Standard Deviations on Anger Inventory by Sex

Group	Prescores	SD	Postscores	SD
SIT				
Male (n = 14)	291.43	47.17	223.64	55.64
Female (n = 36)	272.08	54.47	226.58	51.05
Control				
Male (n = 15)	270.53	69.06	266.93	70.18
Female (n = 35)	279.71	45.12	275.74	44.37

Note. SIT = stress inoculation training.

training was conducted in a 1-day workshop with 12–16 staff members per workshop.

Data collection. The Anger Inventory (Novaco, 1975) was administered to all participants before and after treatment. This inventory has been used widely as a self-report measure of anger reactions to 90 provocations. Respondents rate the degree to which the incident described would anger or provoke them on a scale ranging from 1 *(not at all)* to 5 *(very much).*

A workshop six-item evaluation questionnaire was completed by all participants in the SIT group at the completion of the workshop. A follow-up six-item evaluation questionnaire on the usefulness of the training was administered to the SIT participants approximately 3.5 months following the completion of training.

Participant evaluations are limited by their very nature in their ability to measure behavioral change. Therefore, an outcome measure of behavioral change was necessary. The frequency of the use of emergency restraint was monitored prior to and after SIT. Data were collected for two 5-month periods in succeeding years (January to May) to control for any seasonal trends in the area. Data were not analyzed from the two facilities participating in the attention-control procedure because the proportion of staff trained at the three facilities varied. It was expected that as staff became more proficient in managing their own stress in crisis situations, there would be a reduction in the frequency of physical confrontations (emergency restraints).

Results

Table 1 shows the mean pre- and postscores on the Anger Inventory. An analysis of variance (ANOVA) on pretest–posttest difference scores indicated significant main effects for treatment, $F(1, 96) = 119.80$, $p < .001$, and sex, $F(1, 96) = 4.91$, $p < .05$. The SIT group had lower Anger Inventory scores than did the attention-control group. The sex main effect and Treatment × Sex interaction was due to men scoring slightly higher on the pretest ($Ms = 280.62$ and 275.85 for men and women, respectively) and the higher male prescores in the SIT group. The difference scores decreased more for the men in the SIT group than for the women in the SIT group. The decrease for both sexes was the same in the attention-control group.

Table 2. Frequency of Emergency Restraint by Month Prior to and Following Training

	Pre-SIT					Post-SIT			
Mo 1	Mo 2	Mo 3	Mo 4	Mo 5	Mo 1	Mo 2	Mo 3	Mo 4	Mo 5
16	15	17	16	16	7	6	13	6	5

Note. SIT = stress inoculation training; Mo = month.

Participants in the SIT group rated the overall quality of the workshop at its completion on a 5-point scale (5 = *excellent*, 1 = *poor*). The mean rating of the participants was 4.43, and 87% of them rated the overall quality of the workshop as 5 or 4.

Approximately 3.5 months after the workshop, participants were asked to complete a survey on the usefulness of the training. This was done to determine the participants' evaluations after having been able to use the training in actual work situations. A 5-point scale (5 = very much, 3 = some, and 1 = none) was used to rate the usefulness of the techniques in working with clients. The mean rating score was 3.8, with 71% of the participants rating the training as 5 or 4. Only 17% of the participants rated the training usefulness as 2 or 1.

Agency policy and procedure requires the completion of a restraint report form by all staff participating in or observing a restraint. The restraint report form and the observer restraint form are completed immediately after the restraint and are reviewed by administrative and clinical staff daily. Because this was a retrospective analysis of records, there was no way to independently verify the reliability of the data. However, the facility was licensed under federal government Title XIX regulations and has a strict internal audit and review system to ensure the completeness and accuracy of required paperwork. During the course of the study, the residential census remained steady, averaging between 83 and 85.

Table 2 shows the frequency of emergency restraints for a 5-month period prior to workshop training and 5 months after the training.

A chi-square one-sample test conducted on the overall emergency restraint rates before and after SIT shows that rates were significantly lower following training, $\chi^2(1, N = 117) = 18.56, p < .01$.

Study 2 (Keyes, 1989)

Participants

The participants in this retrospective investigation consisted of all residents and direct-contact staff of an 85-bed licensed (ICF/MR) residential facility during two successive 12-month periods. The facility served individuals with all levels of mental retardation according to American Association on Mental

Table 3. Effects of SIT on Client Abuse and Staff Turnover

Variable	Pretraining (12 months)	Posttraining (12 months)
Cases of suspected abuse	28	15 $\chi^2 = ns$
Substantiated cases of abuse	13	4 $\chi^2(1, N = 17) = 4.76$*
Direct-care turnover unadjusted	60%	35% $\chi^2(1, 72) = 5.06$*
Direct-care turnover adjusted for abuse terminations	51%	33% $\chi^2 = ns$

Note. SIT = stress inoculation training.
*$p < .05$.

Retardation criteria, and all were ambulatory. The staff had a mean age of 30.84 years, 71% were women, and 29% were male.

Procedure

During the last month of the first 12-month period, all currently employed direct-contact staff participated in SIT conducted as part of the agency's in-service training program. The training was also added to the 1-week orientation in-service training that all newly hired direct-contact staff are required to attend the first week of employment. The SIT package was identical to that described previously.

Data Collection

Data were collected on the number of verified cases of physical and verbal abuse. As a Title XIX certified facility, the agency has a strict policy prohibiting abuse. All staff receive in-service training regarding human rights and client abuse. Information was also obtained on the direct-contact staff turnover rate during the 2-year course of this study. These records were maintained by the personnel department of the agency for all departments and staff. The turnover rate was determined by dividing the number of separations by the average number of direct-contact staff employed during a 12-month period and multiplying by 100.

Data from both of these sources were extracted for the first 12-month period, including the last month during which SIT was conducted for all direct-contact staff. Data were also extracted from these sources for the subsequent 12 months. The selection of two identical 12-month periods balanced the data for any seasonal trends.

Results

The results of this study are shown in Table 3. During the prestress inoculation training 12-month period, there were 28 cases of suspected abuse, and during the 12 months following the training, there were 15 cases. A chi-square one-sample test analysis was not significant. There were 13 confirmed or substantiated cases of abuse during the first 12-month period and four substantiated cases during the second 12-month period. A chi-square one-sample test showed a significant reduction in the confirmed cases of abuse following SIT, $\chi^2(1, N = 17) = 4.76, p < .05$.

The direct-contact annual staff turnover rate was 60.0% during the 12-month period prior to SIT. A turnover rate of 35.0% occurred during the 12 months following SIT. A significant chi-square value, $\chi^2(1, N = 72) = 5.06, p < .05$, indicated that the turnover rate for direct-contact staff was reduced after SIT. When the turnover rates were adjusted to exclude individuals terminated because of substantiated abuse, the rates for the two 12-month periods were 51% and 33%, respectively. A chi-square one-sample test of these data approached significance, $\chi^2(1, N = 64) = 3.18$, but it was not significant at the .05 level.

General Discussion

Overall, the results of these studies suggest that SIT can be effective in reducing the intrapersonal aspect of stress for direct-contact staff working with individuals with mental retardation and developmental disabilities. These results are consistent with other studies that showed that SIT is effective for managing intrapersonal stress in a variety of occupational groups (Forman, 1982; Novaco, 1977, 1980; Novaco et al., 1983).

The finding that Anger Inventory scores were significantly reduced in the SIT group is consistent with other studies in which this scale was used to measure effects of SIT on a variety of subject populations (Levenkron, Cohen, Mueller, & Fisher, 1983; Moon & Eisler, 1983; Novaco, 1975). The participant evaluation data indicate that the training was viewed as useful by most of the participants (84%) immediately after completing training. More important, a follow-up scale, administered approximately 3.5 months after the training, showed that nearly three fourths (71%) of the participants continued to rate the training techniques useful. This shows that SIT was found useful by staff members after they had an opportunity to apply the procedures in their actual work setting for a period of time.

The finding that the use of emergency restraint significantly decreased following SIT suggests that a resultant change in staff behavior occurred. The training produced a clinically meaningful change in the outcome of client crisis situations. The finding suggests that staff were more effective in managing an agitated individual and that fewer crisis situations resulted in physical confrontations (emergency restraints). By being able to manage their own stress, staff might have been better able to systematically direct their behavior at resolving the individual's crisis and agitation. This interpretation must be made cautiously because it was not possible to directly measure staff behavior in actual crisis situations, nor was it possible to compare the frequency of emergency restraint before and after administration of the attention-control procedure.

The results of Study 2 indicate that SIT for direct-contact staff members produced a decrease in client abuse. This finding is consistent with Nomelini and Katz's (1983) study, in which SIT was found to be effective in reducing abusive behavior in parents who abused their children. The results also support the Rusch et al. (1986) suggestion that staff working with aggressive individuals may benefit from specialized training sensitizing them to the possibility that the individual's aggression may provoke abusive responses.

The effects of SIT on overall turnover are less clear. Although annual turnover rates decreased significantly following training, the rates were not significantly reduced when separations caused by abuse were removed. This may suggest that the stress reduction effects found are specific to client–staff interaction-based stress. Other occupational stress aspects of the job are most likely not significantly affected by this particular kind of training. Further research should explore the application of SIT to other aspects of job stress.

Conclusions

Several conclusions and recommendations can be made regarding the use of SIT procedures with staff and organizations working with special-needs client populations:

1. SIT reduces the intrapersonal stress experienced by staff.
2. Staff members have found SIT to be useful in their actual work with aggressive, agitated, and disturbed clients.
3. When staff are trained to manage their intrapersonal stress during crisis situations with agitated individuals, there is a resulting decrease in the use of physical confrontation procedures such as restraint.
4. SIT is effective in reducing staff abusive behavior.
5. The effects of SIT are specific to client–staff interaction-based stress, not to general or nonspecific stress.
6. Incorporating SIT into an agency's overall staff training program, especially for staff working with aggressive individuals, is recommended.
7. Meichenbaum (1985) discussed the use of follow-up and booster sessions with SIT for fine-tuning coping skills and troubleshooting any specific difficulties. However, there are few data to suggest the timing or effects of such sessions. It is recommended that retraining be conducted at least annually. SIT should be extended beyond the initial workshop and incorporated as part of the on-the-job experience with debriefing and booster sessions for individuals as indicated.

References

Beck, A. (1984). Cognitive approaches to stress. In R. Woolfolk & P. Lehrer (Eds.), *Principles and practices of stress management* (pp. 91–110). New York: Guilford Press.

Borthwick-Duffy, S., & Eyman, R. K. (1990). Who are the dually diagnosed? *American Journal on Mental Retardation, 94,* 586–595.

Browner, C. H., Ellis, K. D., Ford, T., Silsby, J., Tampoya, J., & Yee, C. (1986). Stress, social support and health of psychiatric techniques in a state facility. *Mental Retardation, 25,* 31–38.

Forman, S. (1982). Stress management for teachers: A cognitive-behavioral program. *Journal of School Psychology, 20,* 180–187.

Ivancevich, J. M., Matteson, M. T., Freedman, S. M., & Phillips, J. S. (1990). Worksite stress management intervention. *American Psychologist, 45,* 252–261.

Iverson, J. C., & Fox, R. A. (1989). Prevalence of psychopathology among mentally retarded adults. *Research in Developmental Disabilities, 10,* 77–83.

Keyes, J. B. (1989). Stress inoculation training for direct contact staff: Effect on turnover and abuse. *Disabilities and Impairments, 3,* 15–21.

Keyes, J. B., & Dean, S. F. (1988). Stress inoculation training for direct contact staff working with mentally retarded persons. *Behavioral Residential Treatment, 3,* 315–323.

Knowles, M., & Landesman, S. (1986). National survey of state-sponsored training for residential direct care staff. *Mental Retardation, 25,* 293–300.

Lakin, K. C., Bruininks, R. H., Hill, R. K., & Hauber, F. A. (1982). Turnover of direct-care staff in a national sample of residential facilities for mentally retarded persons. *American Journal of Mental Deficiency, 87,* 64–72.

Levenkron, J. C., Cohen, J. S., Mueller, H. S., & Fisher, E. B. (1983). Modifying the Type A coronary-prone behavior pattern. *Journal of Consulting and Clinical Psychology, 51,* 192–204.

Marchetti, A. G., & McCartney, J. R. (1990). Abuse of persons with mental retardation: Characteristics of the abused, the abusers, and the informers. *Mental Retardation, 28,* 367–371.

Meichenbaum, D. (1977). *Cognitive-behavior modification: An integrative approach.* New York: Plenum.

Meichenbaum, D. (1985). *Stress inoculation training.* Elmsford, NY: Pergamon Press.

Moon, J. R., & Eisler, R. M. (1983). Effects of anger control training on abusive parents. *Cognitive Therapy and Research, 7,* 57–68.

Nomelini, S., & Katz, R. C. (1983). Effects of anger control training on abusive parents. *Cognitive Therapy and Research, 7,* 57–68.

Novaco, R. W. (1975). *Anger control: The development and evaluation of an experimental treatment.* Lexington, MA: Heath.

Novaco, R. (1977). A stress inoculation approach to anger management in the training of law enforcement officers. *American Journal of Community Psychology, 5,* 327–346.

Novaco, R. (1980). Training of probation officers for anger problems. *Journal of Counseling Psychology, 27,* 385–390.

Novaco, R., Cook, T., & Sarason, I. (1983). Military recruit training: An arena for stress-coping skills. In D. Meichenbaum & M. Jarenko (Eds.), *Stress reduction and prevention* (pp. 175–191). New York: Plenum.

Parsons, J. A., May, J. G., & Menolascino, F. J. (1984). The nature and incidence of mental illness in mentally retarded individuals. In F. J. Manolascino & J. A. Stock (Eds.), *Handbook of mental illness in the mentally retarded* (pp. 3–44). New York: Plenum.

Rosen, R. H. (1986). *Healthy companies: A human resources approach.* New York: American Management Association.

Rusch, R. S., Hall, J. C., & Griffin, H. C. (1986). Abuse-provoking characteristics of institutionalized mentally retarded individuals. *American Journal of Mental Deficiency, 90,* 618–624.

Vingerhoets, A. J. J. M., & Marcelissen, F. H. G. (1988). Stress research: Its present status and issues for future developments. *Social Sciences and Medicine, 26,* 279–291.

West, D., Horan, J., & Games, P. (1984). Component analysis of occupational stress inoculation applied to registered nurses in an acute care hospital setting. *Journal of Counseling Psychology, 31,* 209–218.

Appendix

Course Outline
I. Introduction
  A. Overview of course
  B. Objectives of course
  C. Cognitive–behavior modification and stress inoculation training (SIT) approaches
    1. Definitions
    2. Phases of SIT
    3. Crisis intervention: Explanation of interpersonal and intrapersonal crisis (stress) management
II. Conceptualization Phase
  A. Cognitive theory of emotion (anger and stress; Beck, 1984)
  B. Emotions mediated by the individual's thinking interpretation of the situation
  C. Anger and stress arousal: Cognitive mediation
  D. Types of provocations (discussion and examples from participants) and cognitive mediation
    1. Annoyances
    2. Frustrations
    3. Harassments
    4. Assaults
  E. Transactional nature of provocational sequence (stress and coping)
  F. Development of reconceptualization of the individual's stress–anger reactions
III. Skills Acquisition and Rehearsal Phase
  A. Small-group exercises designed to develop a variety of coping skills
  B. Relaxation training
  C. Cognitive strategies that emphasize cognitive self-control skills
    1. Cognitive restructuring
    2. Cognitive errors
  D. Problem-solving training
    1. Assessment
    2. Generation of alternatives
    3. Decision making
    4. Implementation
    5. Evaluation
  E. Self-instructional training (guided self-dialogue)
    1. Preparing for stressor
      a. Focus on specific preparation for task
      b. Combat negative thinking
      c. Emphasize planning and preparation
    2. Impact and confrontation
      a. Control stress reaction
      b. Reassure the person that he or she can handle the situation
      c. Reminder to use coping responses

        d. Remain focused on task
    3. Coping with arousal
        a. Set up contingency plans
        b. Prepare to deal with worst situation
    4. Evaluation of Coping Efforts and Self-Rewards
        a. Evaluation attempt
        b. Review experiences
        c. Praise self
        d. What should have been done differently
IV. Application and Follow-Through Phase
    A. Imagery rehearsal
    B. Behavioral rehearsal, role-playing, and modeling
    C. Graduated intensity and complexity
    D. Individual tests his or her proficiency in anger management
 V. Evaluation and Discussion
    A. Presentation of data related to application of SIT with staff working
        with individuals with mental retardation (Keyes, 1989; Keyes & Dean,
        1988)
    B. Evaluating SIT outcomes and follow-up
    C. Integration with other in-service programs
    D. Training instructors.

5

A Worksite Stress Management Program: Theory, Application, and Outcomes

David C. Munz, Timothy J. Huelsman,
and Carol A. Craft

Organizational life is stressful, and the more job stress employees experience, the more there are problems for everyone—employees, families, organizations, and society at large (Burke & Greenglass, 1987; Cooper & Payne, 1988). Typically, attempts to lessen the adverse effects of occupational stress have consisted of organizational interventions designed to reduce the sources of stress (stressors) or individual stress management training to minimize the negative outcomes of exposure to worksite stressors. Stress research, although currently popular, has not resolved the disagreements about how to manage work stress (Ivancevich, Matteson, Freedman, & Phillips, 1990). In our view, there is an abundance of individual and organizational stress interventions (Landy, 1992; Lehrer & Woolfolk, 1993; Newman & Beehr, 1979). What is lacking is a synthesis of theory, application, and evaluation carried out within an action-research framework over a sustained period of time. Using such an approach would allow cost-effective worksite stress programs to evolve gradually. In this chapter we present the outcomes of our action-research approach to designing and evaluating an individual stress management program.

The opportunity to develop a stress program arose in 1979 when Saint Louis University Medical Center established a Department of Health Promotion under the direction of David C. Munz. The purpose of the department was to offer local organizations a full complement of health promotion and disease prevention services. A comprehensive worksite stress management program was created as one of the department's numerous offerings. The stress program remains part of the medical center's expanded corporate health services initiative. Also, hospitals in numerous cities use the stress program as part of their outreach wellness programming. In 1990, the program underwent an extensive revision.

One of the first organizations to use the program, in 1981, was the Veterans Health Administration (VHA) within the Department of Veterans Affairs (VA). The program was disseminated throughout VHA using a training-of-trainers model, and it is now used by more than 65 VA medical centers. The national and regional continuing education centers within VHA provide the coordination and support the ongoing evaluative research of the program's effectiveness. VHA is the research population from which data were collected for this chapter.

Our focus is on the theory, application, and outcomes of worksite stress management training in VA medical centers. In terms of theory, we present the revised stress program with its theoretical underpinnings and intervention methodologies. Fourteen years of application have generated specific delivery tactics that contribute to program viability. Last, and most important, we identify the outcomes of delivery of this type of worksite intervention. Our research suggests that the program makes a difference at the individual level. Studies in progress are evaluating whether the difference leads to positive effects for the organization.

Theory: Assumptions and Program Features

Assumptions

As the stress management program was being developed, a number of assumptions were adopted concerning the nature of stress and how stress management should be delivered at the worksite. Assumptions about the nature of occupational stress were derived from the stress research literature. Delivery assumptions, however, were influenced by the general literature on what constitutes successful worksite health promotion.

Four assumptions about the nature of occupational stress guided program design. Each assumption had certain implications. For example, we adopted the *eclectic* view of the nature of stress and how it affects an individual. This allowed us to combine compatible features from diverse sources in the development of the intervention model. Adoption of the *transactional* view of the person–organization interaction allowed us to place equal responsibility for ownership of stress management on the organization and its members. The *cybernetic* assumption was the basis for emphasizing the value of feedback and self-regulatory systems. *Self-management* provided the integrating theme (i.e., individuals were assumed to be capable of actively intervening to influence their physical and psychological systems to minimize wear and tear caused by environmental demands).

The assumptions made about the effective delivery of worksite stress management had a strong influence on the program content and format. Our intent was to design a program that was of low cost to the organization and could be delivered at the worksite in a group environment by nonprofessional trainers (training-of-trainers concept). We adopted a skill enhancement approach rather than a remedial intervention approach with the belief that skill training would be used if reinforced by a strong organizational commitment to the program. *Organizational commitment* was defined as a cultural shift toward acknowledging the value of stress management training for all employees. Also, commitment was to be evidenced by management's attendance at programs, use of the worksite for delivery, and delivery within the normal workday. A recent indicator of this cultural shift is the opening of the program by organizations to spouses and significant others. Finally, we believed that successful program content and formatting would evolve over time if we remained committed to an action-research approach to evaluation. Our hope was that ongoing program development would come from the trainers and our efforts to be open to their feedback.

Program Features

The current program, 14 years later, is an outgrowth of numerous contributors to its development. The recent revision took 2 years (1989–1990). More than 50 trainers had input into the revision. The program's key features are in four areas: nature of stress, assessment, self-management, and format.

Concerning the nature of stress, there are three important conceptual inputs presented at the beginning of the program. First, stress management training, along with organizational stress reduction and an employee assistance program (EAP), are positioned as the components of a comprehensive worksite intervention program. The hope is that participants will become aware of their contribution (stress management training) and that of the organization (stressor reduction and EAP) to a comprehensive effort to manage stress in their organization.

Second, as shown in Figure 1, the dynamic stress model is used to illustrate the transactional and cybernetic nature of stress (Edwards, 1992; Lazarus & Folkman, 1984; Selye, 1950, 1976). The intent is to develop participant understanding of (a) the interactive influence of environmental demands and personal characteristics on the initial reaction to demands and how this reaction affects the various systems of the individual (specifically, the central and autonomic nervous systems, as well as the musculoskeletal system; Lacy, 1950); (b) the stress response as an early warning indicator of excessive wear and tear in those systems; (c) the escalating nature of the stress response and stress outcomes as they influence environmental demands; and (d) the value of self-management of the physical and psychological systems to minimize the negative nature of the stress response and to maximize the potential of a positive contribution to the adaptive system (initial reaction). Consistent with the eclectic view, the model incorporates a number of theoretical positions. However, for the purpose of helping participants understand the dynamic nature of stress, we use an oversimplified model.

The third conceptual input is a detailed presentation of the participants' responsibilities for program success. We want participants to know early in the program that a long-term commitment is necessary if stress management is to become a natural part of their response repertoire to environmental demands. Specific behavioral responsibilities are presented for each stage of the program. For example, early in the program, self-motivation and skill-learning behaviors are necessary, whereas later in the program conscious practice outside of the classroom is required. Nine behavioral requirements

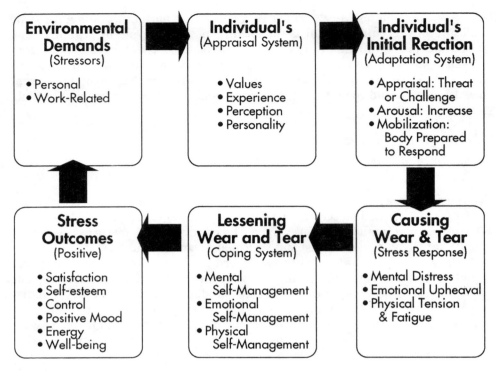

Figure 1. The dynamic stress model.

are presented, covering the three stages of the program (skill development, refinement, and application).

Self-assessments, the second key feature, are presented throughout the program as awareness-building tools to help participants personalize the components of the dynamic stress model. For example, the stress response indicator helps participants recognize the early warning signs of mental, physical, and emotional wear and tear. Other self-assessments address personality characteristics such as locus of control, hardiness, optimism, negative affectivity, and coping style. These assessments help participants identify potential mediating or buffering personal dispositions. A general well-being indicator is used to show the connection between stress and wellbeing. The goal is to develop participant understanding of the interaction between personal characteristics and the stressors of daily living and to expand self-monitoring capability.

Strategies for self-management, the third key feature, are identified in the matrix shown in Table 1. The strategies are based on three self-regulatory counters to mental, physical, and emotional reactions to stressors. For example, the reframing response counters the mental reaction and minimizes mental wear and tear (distress). The three reframing strategies are cognitive reprogramming, shifting mental states, and mental imaging. Within each of these strategies are specific activities, or "tools," that help to develop greater control of the mental processes. Underlying the movement response to counter physical

Table 1.   Self-Management Strategies

Self-manage-ment level	Mental (reframing)	Physical (movement)	Emotional (relaxation)
Situational	Cognitive reprogramming	Complex movement	Receptive state
Renewal	Shifting mental states	Physical tension re-duction	Relaxation
Preventive	Mental imaging	Total movement se-quence	Inner silencing

strain is our belief that the body becomes tense and fatigued when under demands to perform. Replenishing the body's flexibility, energy, and responsiveness requires teaching participants conscious deployment of three movement strategies: complex movement exercises, physical tension reduction, and the total movement sequence. Each of these strategies has highly specific activities that can be used to replenish physical energy, stamina, endurance, and flexibility. The relaxation response is the counter to emotional upheaval. Our belief is that for each situation (demand) there is an optimal level of arousal to perform at potential and that after the demand there should be a short recovery (lowering of arousal). Too much or too little arousal is not good for performance or for emotional well-being. The relaxation response, as the counter to emotional upheaval (or too much arousal), can be mastered through the use of three strategies: receptive state, relaxation, and inner silencing.

Self-management strategies are taught at three levels: situational, renewal, and preventive. At the situational level, strategies work on the initial stress reaction (adaptive system). Renewal strategies are used to recover from excessive wear and tear by returning to a positive mental, emotional, and physical state. Preventive strategies are used to strengthen the adaptation system and decrease the chances of an excessive stress response in the face of environmental demands. Strategies build on each other as the participant progresses from the situational to renewal to preventive levels. Some renewal strategies may be used situationally, and some preventive strategies are also potential renewal strategies. The matrix presented in Table 1 is somewhat arbitrary in design. Its primary purpose is pedagogical. By the end of the program, participants develop their own framework for organizing and using the 60 specific self-management interventions taught under the matrix's headings.

In terms of delivery format, the program consists of 12 modules and a total of 18 hr of training. Flexibility of delivery is increased because of its modular format. The program can be delivered once a week for 12 weeks, 3 hr a week every other week for 12 weeks, and once a month (6 hr) over 3 months, but other variations are possible. Spreading out the program across a 3-month period allows for gradual skill development, refinement, and natural application. The training approach to maximize learning follows the theory (tell), demonstrate (show), practice (do), and action (commit) model. Support materials consist of a participant manual (167 pages), trainer manual (250 pages), and films and training tapes.

Application: Critical Factors and Issues

In 1981, the VA, through one of its regional continuing education centers, began the implementation of this stress management program for its employees. The initial phase consisted of the delivery of the 18-hr stress management program to a critical mass of employees within a medical center, the selection of potential trainers from the "graduating" group of participants, the preparation of trainers in a week-long training program, and the monitoring of the new trainers as they began their program delivery at their respective medical centers.

The program was offered to multidisciplinary groups of participants, usually in three 1-day sessions separated by 2–3 weeks. The initial implementation of the program occurred over a 3-year period; 25 VA medical centers engaged in the program and established their own training teams and facility-based implementation. The first author delivered the program in the initial year; subsequently, a core group of VA master trainers was prepared to deliver the program to new sites. From 1981 to 1988, approximately 7,000 employees participated in these programs. In 1984, the program spread to another of the VA's regional continuing education centers; since that date, the program has expanded farther to all of the regional continuing education units servicing the VA's system of 165 medical centers. To date, approximately 400 trainers have been prepared to deliver the program, and more than 10,000 VA employees have participated in the program. Sixty-five VA medical centers currently are active in delivering the program on more than an annual basis.

During the 14-year history of the VA's experience with the stress management program, a number of critical factors and issues emerged. In the medical centers whose programs incorporated the critical factors and addressed the issues, the program has enjoyed success and longevity.

Critical Factors

1. *Resources.* Adequate resources to initiate a program are perhaps the first critical factor. Resources included various print and video products, but more important, they were defined in terms of the individuals who would commit to training, coordinating, and supporting the program within each medical center. Often, the significance of the human involvement is not included in initial program planning. Yet, typically in organizations without training departments, individuals who become trainers add this role to their regular job. Planners need to be cognizant of this reality and ensure that other resources (e.g., additional numbers of trainers, greater number of print and video materials) are available to support the most critical of resources, the individual responsible for the program's implementation.

2. *Cascading approach.* A cascading program (i.e., one that is recurring on a local level with in-house trainers who have been prepared by master trainers) lends support to the environment of change that the program intends. It provides the opportunity for regularly scheduled programs

throughout the year, which eventually yields a critical mass of participants. It occasions ongoing announcements about the program and informal conversations with current participants, all of which help to remind previous participants about the program's content and their intent to practice it. Postgraduation "brown bag" lunches or other brief sessions also are helpful in sustaining the support of the program and are facilitated by the cascading nature of the program.

3. *Administrative support.* Support from top levels of administration is critical for the initiation and continuance of the program. Up-front commitment, an early seminar for top management, and presence at the beginning and end of the program to kick it off are ways of sustaining involvement at the top. One medical center's director regularly appeared on the first day of the program to listen to participants' discussion of organizational stressors. On the program's last day, he would return to report proposed ideas or action for resolving some of those stressors. Keeping decision makers informed and involved yields resources, time, and satisfied participants.

4. *Expert trainers.* The VA found that a variety of disciplines could be accessed for trainers. They had success with psychologists, nurses, social workers, and other types of health care and administrative professionals. More important criteria than background discipline were intense commitment to the program, competency in its content, ease in teaching, and the schedule flexibility to create time to regularly deliver the program.

The development of expertise necessitated time, particularly for those individuals who were not professional trainers. The "trainer" program involved two distinct but interconnected dimensions. Trainers had to master the content and the process of delivering that content. The preparation of trainers evolved from a 3- to 5-day program so as to develop trainer skills in both these dimensions. A variety of teaching approaches was used, with the most successful being the microteaching of program modules with learner feedback from colleagues and master trainers.

Posttraining activities also facilitated a program's success. As new trainers began their program delivery, master trainers visited them, serving as observers and consultants. The use of training teams within a medical center, usually composed of 4–8 individuals depending on the institution's size, lent support to the program, deterred trainer fatigue, and eased the training burden.

5. *Evaluation and celebration.* Collecting information from the participants about the program, guiding their use of the self-management tools, and follow-up evaluations showed the VA's commitment to making the program work, helped in making improvements, and provided feedback to medical center management. Also, finding ways to celebrate the success of the program with participants, trainers, and management helped the program become part of the organization's culture. Certificates of program completion to participants and letters of commendation to trainers sent through the medical center director accomplished the goal of individual recognition and kept the program visible to the administration.

Issues

Some issues have evolved over the course of the program's extension and expansion, each of which represents a decision point. The VA's response to each issue offers one set of strategies that may be useful to others.

1. *Program maintenance.* Once a program is initiated in an organization, resources to maintain it are critical if the program is to endure. Resources include the preparation of new trainers, the updating of "old" trainers, and the modification of training materials. Budgetary considerations of these maintenance resources must be accomplished in the initial program planning, not included as an afterthought.

2. *Audience type.* The majority of programs within the VA were offered to mixed audiences, both in terms of disciplines and levels, and these were found to be successful more often than not. The mixture of types of roles represented and the casual, comfortable dress requested of program participants tended to have a "leveling" force in creating a more homogenous audience and was effective in extricating them from their usual organizational roles.

3. *Cost.* The value of the dollars expended always must be weighed against the benefits obtained. Some of the benefits obtained (e.g., changes in health behavior, weight reduction, decreased tension, and depression) were difficult to measure in terms of real dollars invested. However, in terms of dollars invested in this program, its cost-effectiveness was clear and attributed primarily to the cascading nature of the program. Through 1987, with 6,050 participants having completed the program, the cost was $2.61 per contact hour, or $36.66 per participant for the 18-hr program.

4. *Program formatting.* The program is intense in its need to experience, or practice, the techniques. Although the program can be offered in a variety of formats, care must be taken to avoid too concentrated a session at any one time. Three sequential 1-day sessions were hazardous, in the VA's experience, because participants became overwhelmed with the sheer number of techniques possible to use and had no time to experience the potential applicability of any of them. On the other hand, scheduling too infrequent sessions runs the risk of participants forgetting the conceptual threads that bind the program.

5. *Trainer aids.* How much is enough to provide accurate direction but not too much so as to inhibit creativity? Program materials included a trainer manual, but they were not constructed in "cookbook" fashion. In the domain of physical techniques, some trainers had difficulty providing accurate demonstrations. The VA remedied this problem by preparing a videotape for all training teams that demonstrated all of the physical techniques. This enhanced continuity among trainers and provided an in-house resource for trainer and participant practice.

6. *Program coordination.* Centralized coordination of the program, complete with an information tracking mechanism, is important. This becomes more important when a program starts expanding beyond the scope originally intended. Centralized coordination assists in ensuring a continued "quality control" of the program and serves as the visible and formal link within the

organization for the maintenance, support, and responsible execution of the program.

7. *Participant mentality.* Just as the effects of stressors have not occurred overnight, neither will the successful management of stressors become immediately evident. Participants in the stress management program needed to be reminded regularly that the program was not a quick fix. Exposure to new content and the practice of stress management techniques within the confines of the classroom were necessary but not sufficient conditions for the incorporation of new behaviors into their lifestyles.

Outcomes: Past, Present, and Future Research

Past

Since its inception, end-of-program evaluations and anecdotal evidence have been collected that attest to the effectiveness of the VA's stress management program. In addition, the thousands of VA employees who have voluntarily participated, the hundreds who have graduated from the program to continue their involvement as trainers, and the dozens who have risen through the ranks to become master trainers provide testimony to the program's popularity and success.

This evidence is encouraging, but more objective assessments of impact are desirable. Past research conducted at the VA (Wheeler & Munz, 1985) showed that participants completing the 18-hr program over a 3-month period showed a significant improvement in psychological well-being; participants became less anxious, tense, depressed, fatigued, and confused and more satisfied with their jobs. These participants showed continued improvement at a follow-up assessment 3 months after completion of the program.

The fact that VA employees attend the program, speak highly of it, use its tools and information, and show improvements in psychological well-being may warrant its continuation. However, the question still remains as to whether the program affects work-related behaviors and organizational outcomes. To this end, a research plan was developed to study the effects of the program on employee work perceptions and mood.

Present

The first phase of the research plan was to investigate the relationships among training in stress management and work environment perceptions and the mood disposition of program participants. The intent was to design the study so that the results could guide the development of further research studies assessing job behaviors and organizational outcomes.

Eight VA facilities volunteered to participate in the study. Each facility has been offering the stress management training program on-site for at least 6 years. Few facilities offered the full 18-hr program but delivered a 6-hr (Level

1) or 12-hr (Levels 1 and 2) version. A random sample of the eight facilities provided 567 usable responses from employees (approximately 1,500 were sent; 38% were usable). Research participants were asked to respond to three questionnaires and a short instrument to determine their level of participation in the program.

Work environment perceptions were measured by a version of the Organizational Climate Questionnaire (James & James, 1989). The questionnaire's 60 self-report items have been empirically divided into four categories that seem to exhaust the "climate" domain: leader facilitation and support, role stress and lack of harmony, job challenge and variety, and work-group cooperation. In addition, most categories are further divided into a number of subcategories (see Figures 2 and 3). Job satisfaction was measured by the 20-item short form of the Minnesota Satisfaction Questionnaire (Weiss, Dawis, England, & Lofquist, 1967). Mood was measured by the Positive and Negative Affect Schedule (PANAS; Watson, Clark, & Tellegen, 1988). The PANAS is an adjective checklist on which the respondent indicates how he or she generally feels. The scale measures two stable but independent dimensions: positive affectively (zest for life, feeling "up" versus "down") and negative affectivity (unpleasant arousal, feeling "upset" versus "peaceful").

The level of participation was assessed with a 9-item scale that classified each respondent on items ranging from "I attended classes when they were scheduled" to "I spontaneously use the stress management skills to lessen the wear and tear of daily living and to increase my general well-being." If respondents had not attended stress management training, they were asked if they were likely to participate in the future.

This study was designed to answer several key questions. These questions are posed and then answered.

1. What percentage of VA employees have participated in stress management training? Of those who have not participated, what percentage plan to attend? Of the 567 responding employees, 207 (37%) attended some stress management training. Of the 360 who did not attend the program, 215 (60%) planned to attend and 145 (40%) did not plan to attend. Assuming representative sampling of facilities and employees within facilities, approximately 60% of the employees within a VA facility were likely to volunteer for stress management training if they had not already had such training. Approximately 40% of the employees of a facility did not intend to attend and could be identified as unlikely to volunteer. Almost 40% of the employees probably already had participated if the program was offered at their facility as in our sample of eight facilities (as mentioned in the Application section, availability of programs varies from facility to facility throughout the country). Whether these percentages are representative of other types of organizations is an empirical question.

2. How does the "likely to volunteer" subgroup compare with the "unlikely to volunteer" subgroup in terms of environment perceptions, mood at work, and job satisfaction? As shown in Figure 2, a profile analysis revealed that those likely to volunteer (plan to attend) were generally more negative about their work environment, had more negative mood, and were less satisfied with

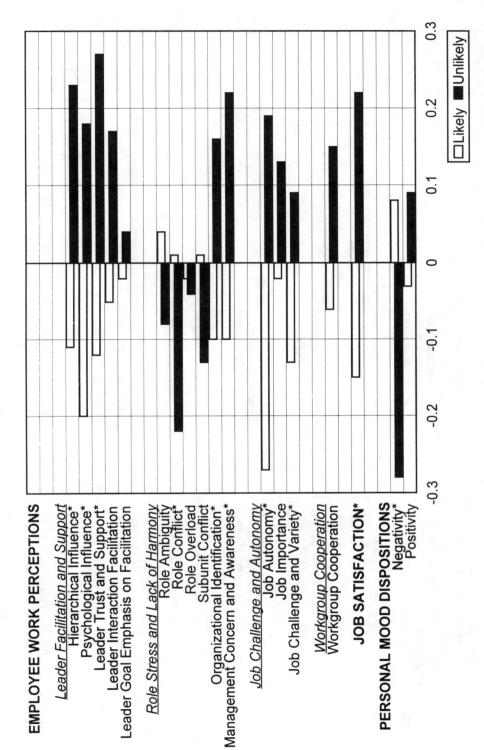

Figure 2. Profile analysis of likely versus unlikely to volunteer, $F(17, 332) = 2.40, p < .005$. Post hoc analyses revealed significant differences on scales marked with an asterisk. All scale values are standardized scores.

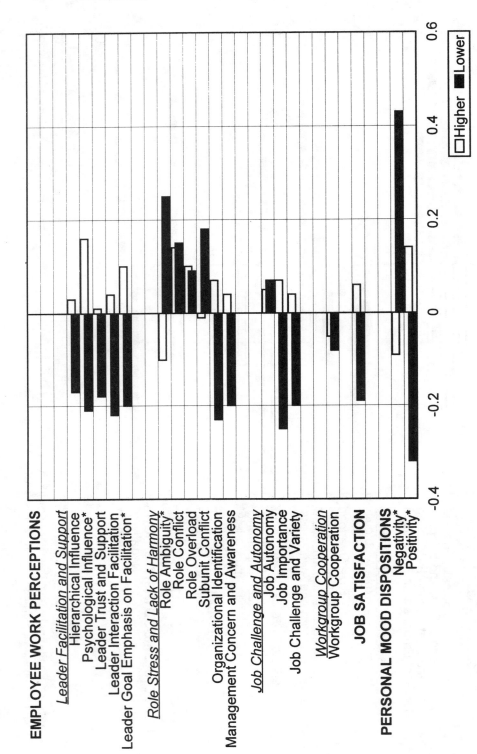

Figure 3. Profile analysis of higher versus lower impact participants, $F(17, 187) = 2.10$, $p < .01$. Post hoc analyses revealed significant differences scales marked with an asterisk. All scale values are standardized scores.

their job than those unlikely to volunteer (planned not to attend a program) $F(17, 332) = 2.40$, $p = .002$. The figure also presents the variables on which the two groups were not significantly different (note that even these variables, although not statistically significant, are in the right direction).

These findings suggest that employees who planned to attend might have intended to do so because of a felt need. Also, the reason 40% of the employees planned not to attend was that they did not have the same felt need. Whether their intention to attend is driven by perceptions and mood is a question for future research. What is clear is that the two groups represent different "employees" in terms of work perceptions and mood.

3. What percentage of participants invested in learning the stress management "techniques"? Of the 207 stress management program participants, 119 (58%) reported that they "continued to use the skills," "searched for new skills," and "spontaneously used the tools." These respondents were called "higher impact" particpants as compared with the 88 (42%) of the respondents who reported that they merely "attended classes when scheduled," were "open to the program," and "refined some of the skills so that they would become a regular part of (their) life." This latter subgroup was labeled the "lower impact" subgroup. These findings suggest that approximately 60% of the participants of a program invested in the program, whereas for whatever reason approximately 40% of the participants did not take the step of further refinement of their skills.

4. How do the higher impact participants compare with the lower impact participants in terms of work environment perceptions, mood at work, and job satisfaction? As shown in Figure 3, a profile analysis revealed that the higher impact group reported more positive work perceptions and a more positive mood than those reporting lower impact for the program, $F(17, 187) = 2.10$, $p = .009$, (again, note that nonsignificant variables are in the right direction). These findings suggest that stress management participants who reported that they invested in skill refinement had a different (more positive) perception of their work environment (in certain areas) and a less negative—more positive work mood than those participants who attended the program and were less affected.

5. Are the work perceptions and mood of those who attended stress management more positive than those who did not? And are there specific variables accounting for this difference? The answer to this question is not straightforward because within the control group, there were already differences in perceptions and mood between those likely and those unlikely to volunteer. Also, within the participant group, there were differences between the higher impact participants and the lower impact participants. Contrasting the control group with the participant group may not be the best comparison, because we know that within the control group the likely-to-volunteer subgroup was significantly more negative than the less-likely-to-volunteer subgroup. Also, the program for the participant group has been shown to have a differential effect for the lower impact subgroup, who was more negative than the higher impact subgroup.

One way to answer this question is to assume that the program participants came from the likely-to-volunteer subgroup and to hypothesize that the lower impact program participants should report work perceptions and mood states similar to the likely-to-volunteer subgroup. In other words, they were less affected by the program. Following this logic, the higher impact program participants would report work perceptions and mood states similar to the less-likely-to-volunteer subgroup because they were more affected. If this were supported by the results, it would mean that the higher impact participants became more positive and therefore were more like those less likely to volunteer, whereas those lower impact participants remained the same—like the more negative likely-to-volunteer participants. Only those perceptions and mood states that show differences between higher and lower impact participants would be used to test this hypothesis.

The results appear to support this hypothesis. On three of the work perception factors on which the higher impact subgroup was more positive than the lower impact subgroup, the higher impact participants were similar to the less-likely-to-volunteer participants, and lower impact participants were similar to those in the likely-to-volunteer subgroup. On the mood dimensions, the results show a different pattern. For negative mood, higher impact participants were slightly less negative than those less likely to volunteer. However, both of these groups were less negative than the lower impact and likely-to-volunteer subgroups. There were differences here as well with the lower impact subgroup responding more negatively than the less-likely-to-volunteer subgroup. For positive mood, the lower impact subgroup was less positive than the other groups. This suggests that the program may influence mood by decreasing the negative state for those affected but that those less affected may actually become more negative after the program. Although the program does not seem to increase positive mood, it may decrease it for the lower impact participants.

Future

Completion of the first phase of the research plan generated a number of interesting findings and questions to be addressed in the next research phase. The findings that those who planned to volunteer for a stress program were more negative about their work environment, had more negative mood, and were less satisfied with their job (compared with those unlikely to volunteer) are counter to the myth that those who attend stress management are not those who really need it. Of course, whether those who say they plan to attend actually do awaits further research. For motivational and program evaluation reasons, researchers need to learn more about these two types of employees. For now, intent to volunteer for a stress management program appears to be a relevant research variable.

The finding that the program had a differential impact on its participants suggests that research is needed to uncover the reasons for the differential effect. Clearly, 40% of the participants classified as lower impact is unacceptable. Future research of the program will build the impact variable into its designs. As already mentioned, a prospective longitudinal study is necessary to support the causal relationships among stress management, work perceptions, and mood.

The apparent relationship between stress management and mood suggests that those job behaviors having been demonstrated to be correlates of mood may be worthy of investigation. George and Brief (1992) made the case for the contribution of positive mood at work to organizational spontaneity (i.e., extrarole behaviors that are performed voluntarily and that contribute to organizational effectiveness, such as helping coworkers, developing oneself, protecting the organization, making constructive suggestions, and spreading goodwill). Because the stress management program appears to contribute to positive mood at work, we plan to experimentally investigate the stress management–mood–spontaneity behavior relationship.

The stress management program in the VA has achieved a life of its own. Trainers are excited to deliver the program, the VA medical centers support its offering, and participants show up. That is the good news. The program is alive and well. Now the tough work: to demonstrate its effectiveness at the individual and organizational levels. Progress is being made, but much more remains to be done.

References

Burke, R. J., & Greenglass, E. R. (1987). Work and family. In C. L. Cooper & I. T. Robertson (Eds.), *International review of industrial and organizational psychology* (pp. 273–320). New York: Wiley.

Cooper, C. L., & Payne, R. (1988). *Causes, coping and consequences of stress at work.* New York: Wiley.

Edwards, J. R. (1992). A cybernetic theory of stress, coping, and well-being in organizations. *Academy of Management Review, 17,* 238–274.

George, J. M., & Brief, A. P. (1992). Feeling good–doing good: A conceptual analysis of the mood at work–organizational spontaneity relationship. *Psychological Bulletin, 112,* 310–329.

Ivancevich, J. M., Matteson, M. T., Freedman, S. M., & Phillips, J. S. (1990). Worksite stress management interventions. *American Psychologist, 45,* 252–261.

James, L. A., & James, L. R. (1989). Integrating work perceptions: Explorations into the measurement of meaning. *Journal of Applied Psychology, 74,* 739–751.

Lacy, J. L. (1950). Individual differences on somatic response pattern. *Journal of Comparative and Physiological Psychology, 43,* 338–350.

Landy, F. J. (1992). Work design and stress panel. In G. P. Keita & S. L. Sauter (Eds.), *Work and well-being* (pp. 115–196). Washington, DC: American Psychological Association.

Lazarus, R. S., & Folkman, S. (1984). *Stress, appraisal, and coping.* New York: Springer-Verlag.

Lehrer, P. M., & Woolfolk, R. L. (Eds.). (1993). *Principles and practice of stress management (2nd ed.).* New York: Guilford Press.

Newman, J. E., & Beehr, T. A. (1979). Personal and organizational strategies for handling job stress: A review of research and opinion. *Personnel Psychology, 32,* 1–43.

Selye, H. (1950). *The physiology and pathology of exposure to stress: A treatise based on the concepts of general-adaptation-syndrome and the disease of adaptation.* Montreal: ACTA Insurance Medical Publishers.

Selye, H. (1976). *The stress of life* (2nd ed.). New York: McGraw-Hill.

Watson, D., Clark, L. A., & Tellegen, A. (1988). Development and validation of brief measures of positive and negative affect: The PANAS scales. *Journal of Personality and Social Psychology, 54,* 1063–1070.

Weiss, D. J., Dawis, R. V., England, G. W., & Lofquist, L. H. (1967). *Manual for the Minnesota Satisfaction Questionnaire*. Minneapolis: Industrial Relations Center, University of Minnesota.

Wheeler, R., & Munz, D. C. (1985, August). *Psychological and physiological effects of a stress management program*. Paper presented at the 93rd Annual Convention of the American Psychological Association, Los Angeles.

6

Worksite Health Promotion: A Theory-Driven, Empirically Based Perspective

Stewart I. Donaldson

The most remarkable aspect of the 10 leading causes of death in the United States today is the disproportionately high number of controllable "lifestyle," or behavioral risk, factors (see U.S. Department of Health and Human Services [DHHS], 1991). The prevalence and importance of health-damaging behavior has led the way for behavioral scientists to work collaboratively with various branches of medicine and biology to understand the linkages between behavior and health. For example, a 20-member panel of physicians and scientists constituting the U.S. Prevention Services Task Force concluded that influencing health-related behavior is more likely to reduce morbidity and mortality than any other category of clinical intervention (U.S. Preventive Services Task Force, 1989).

New etiologies of morbidity and mortality have forced health scientists to reconceptualize the nature of health and well-being in modern societies. Several recent trends are notable. First, many health researchers have moved beyond the traditional medical model of health and illness and have adopted the biopsychosocial model as a framework for their research activities (see Matarazzo, Weiss, Herd, Miller, & Weiss, 1984; Taylor, 1990). Second, many scientists are beginning to recognize the need for addressing issues concerning the grossly neglected upper reaches of the illness–wellness continuum. For example, theorists such as Seeman (1989) have proposed models of positive health dealing explicitly with the upper end of the health continuum as a way of furthering the conceptualization of wellness and effective human functioning. Third, Antonovsky (1987) suggested the need for a timely paradigm shift to what he called "salutogenesis inquiry." The central themes of salutogenesis inquiry are that research efforts should not concentrate strictly on the minority

This work was funded in part by a grant from the John Randolph Haynes and Dora Haynes Foundation. Portions of this work were part of my doctoral dissertation, submitted to the Claremont Graduate School. Portions of this chapter were presented at the American Psychological Association and the National Institute for Occupational Safety and Health Conference on Stress in the '90s: A Changing Workforce in a Changing Workplace held in Washington, DC, in November 1992. Special thanks to Andrea Piccinin, Robert Gable, and the anonymous reviewers for their insightful comments.

but on the majority of living people (those who are healthy, not ill, at any given time) and that research should address the issue of why so many people remain healthy despite the ubiquitous pathogens in their bodies and the environment. These rising trends and challenges have facilitated a rapid expansion of programmatic efforts to influence behavior patterns associated with mortality, morbidity, and wellness.

The purpose of this chapter is to review conceptual, methodological, and practical issues relevant to systematically promoting health at work. Ways to construct and evaluate theoretical or conceptual frameworks including both employee behavior and working conditions are explored. The value of moving away from "mindless monistic" research strategies and toward "planned critical multiplism" is discussed. Finally, practical implications of a theory-driven, empirically based perspective, such as being able to reach traditionally underserved employee populations, are outlined.

Worksite Health Promotion

Historically, employee health has been addressed from a secondary prevention, or treatment and compensation, perspective. For example, employee assistance programs (EAPs) that identify, treat, and rehabilitate employees whose job performance has deteriorated because of alcohol or drug abuse are commonplace (see Sonnenstuhl & Trice, 1986). In the past decade, however, there has been a dramatic increase in the number of employers concerned with addressing employee health issues before they become problems (Fielding & Piserchia, 1989). Many human resource systems now incorporate policies, programs, and procedures designed to promote health and prevent illness (i.e., a primary prevention and health promotion orientation). In fact, the worksite has become one of the most popular venues for delivering health promotion services.

Worksite health promotion (WHP)[1] programs traditionally consist of a combination of diagnostic, educational, and behavior modification activities— initiated, endorsed, and supported by an employing organization—designed to support the attainment and maintenance of health and well-being (Matteson & Ivancevich, 1988). Although WHP programs can be classified into three general content areas (i.e., screening, education, and behavior change programs; Terborg, 1986), the programs now being implemented in the workplace vary widely in content and scope. This diversity in program content and scope makes it extremely difficult to compare programs and their outcomes (Terborg, 1988).

Presumed Benefits

A long list of presumed benefits is used to sell the idea of WHP to both private and public organizations. A partial listing of the presumed benefits of WHP

---

[1]The term *worksite health promotion* is used to refer to any health promotion of wellness-oriented intervention delivered in the workplace. Although there are definitional distinctions (e.g., see Terborg, 1986), I use the terms *worksite health promotion, occupational health promotion, wellness in the workplace*, and so on, interchangeably.

Exhibit 1.   Presumed Benefits of Worksite Health Promotion

Direct Cost Savings

- Reductions in costs due to reduced absenteeism
- Reductions in costs due to reduced tardiness
- Reductions in costs due to reduced voluntary turnover
- Reduced medical costs
- Reduced use of medical facilities
- Reductions in disability and workman's compensation
- Reduced insurance premiums

Indirect Benefits

- Improved employee physical health
- Improved employee mental health
- Increased employee job performance
- Lower levels of stress and burnout
- Increased employee job satisfaction
- Increased organizational commitment and loyalty
- Improved employee self-image and greater employee creativity
- Reductions in employee strikes and grievances
- Improved corporate image
- Improved labor relations
- Improved recruiting

programs is displayed in Exhibit 1. Unfortunately, many of the claims about the benefits of WHP are based largely on testimonials and anecdotal evidence presented in trade magazines, government publications, and the mainstream press (Matteson & Ivancevich, 1988; Terborg, 1986; Warner, 1987).

Pelletier (1991) reviewed findings from 26 WHP programs implemented in major corporations and concluded that there is a growing body of evidence indicating that comprehensive WHP programs are both health and cost-effective. However, most reviewers of the WHP literature have been highly critical. For example, Conrad, Conrad, and Walcott-McQuigg (1991) contended that "a careful examination of the literature reveals that claims about the effectiveness of WHP are, in general, based on flawed studies containing serious threats to the validity of their conclusions" (p. 112). Other reviewers of the WHP literature also have concluded that scientifically sound data are sparse (e.g., Falkenberg, 1987; Fielding, 1991; Matteson & Ivancevich, 1988; Terborg, 1986; Warner, 1987; Warner, Wickizer, Wolfe, Schildroth, & Samuelson, 1988).

Lack of Theory

Not only is there uncertainty about the empirical evidence related to the outcomes of WHP interventions, but empirically based theoretical or conceptual frameworks explaining the processes that link a WHP program with its objectives are virtually nonexistent. The absence of guiding conceptual frameworks is evidenced by the lack of consistency across programs with respect to which behavior patterns or aspects of an employee's "lifestyle" are promoted, the methods used to accomplish positive health, and the amount of service administered to the participants. Furthermore, standard experimental research defining WHP interventions as simple molar treatments (i.e., comparing outcome measures of employees from an organization with a WHP program with employees from a similar organization without WHP activities) fails to capture the multidimensional complexity of most WHP programs and consequently contributes little to the understanding of how to consistently design and implement effective WHP programs (see Lipsey, 1988).

Research Dilemmas

Except for some of the large-scale comprehensive WHP programs (e.g., Live for Life, Staywell), sophisticated program evaluation activities are seldom a substantial component of WHP (Ilgen, 1990; Terborg, 1986). For example, Davis, Rosenberg, Iverson, Vernon, and Bauer (1984) found that only one third of the companies with WHP programs they surveyed kept records on absenteeism or turnover and that only 7% looked at changes in job performance. If any evaluation was done, it was limited to internal criteria such as participation rates and user satisfaction with health promotion activities.

Several factors have been identified as inhibitors of informative WHP outcome research. First, because it is often difficult (sometimes impossible) to maintain experimental control, to standardize data collection procedures, and to uphold the strength and integrity of WHP interventions, evaluators using approaches that rely solely on experimental or quasi-experimental designs often fail to rule out plausible rival hypotheses. For example, many have suggested that "Hawthorne effects," self-selection, attrition, maturation, statistical regression to the mean, testing, history, diffusion of treatment effects, compensatory rivalry, small sample sizes (often due to low participation rates or using the organization as the unit of assignment), and noncomparability of treatments across sites and across time threaten the validity of previous WHP research (e.g., see Conrad et al., 1991; Warner et al., 1988). In addition, there are a number of common practical problems associated with evaluating an ongoing WHP program. These problems include severe time and resource restrictions, lack of organizational cooperation with research requirements, and biases of involved personnel who need to view WHP as effective (Matteson & Ivancevich, 1988; Terborg, 1986).

Issues From a Theory-Driven, Empirically Based Perspective

> Nothing is as practical as a good theory.
>
> *Kurt Lewin (1945, p. 129)*

The dearth of empirical evidence supporting the presumed benefits of WHP and the lack of theory development suggest that the fundamental assumptions of WHP need to be examined carefully. It is now crucial that researchers attempt to understand if and how promoting "healthful employee lifestyles"

Exhibit 2.   Advantages of Using Program Theory in Evaluation Research

- It is a basis for informed choices about method.
- It enables the researcher to distinguish between the validity of program imple-
  mentation ("action theory") and the validity of program theory ("conceptual the-
  ory").
- It makes possible careful definition and operationalization of the independent
  (program) variables.
- It helps identify pertinent variables and how, when (e.g., dose–response and treat-
  ment-decay functions), and on whom they should be measured.
- It permits sources of extraneous variance to be identified and controlled.
- It alerts the researcher to potentially important or intrusive interactions (e.g.,
  differential participant response to treatment).
- It dictates the proper statistical model for data analysis and the tenability of the
  assumptions required in that model.
- It makes it possible to make a thoughtful and probing analysis of the validity of
  evaluation research in a specific context.
- It helps develop a cumulative wisdom about how programs work and when they
  work.

Note. Derived from Bickman (1987), Chen (1990), Lipsey (1993), and Lipsey and Pollard (1989).

affects desired health and work performance outcomes. Most important, empirically based theoretical frameworks suggesting how to simultaneously maximize employee health and organizational effectiveness are essential for the
future development of cost and health effective WHP interventions.

In recent years, there has been much discussion about moving beyond
traditional "black-box" program evaluations to theory-oriented approaches (see
Bickman, 1987; Chen, 1990; Lipsey, 1993). The advantages of using program
theory in evaluation research are numerous. Program theory can help (a)
identify pertinent variables and how, when, and on whom they should be
measured; (b) distinguish between the validity of program implementation and
the validity of program theory; and (c) develop a cumulative knowledge base
about how and when programs work (Chen, 1990; Lipsey & Pollard, 1989).
Exhibit 2 is a summary of the advantages of using program theory in evaluation research.

Many factors may interact to make a particular application of WHP effective. For example, organizational benefits derived from WHP programs may
be the result of Hawthorne effects, development of goodwill, initial employee
lifestyles (i.e., unhealthful lifestyles have plenty of room for improvement),
increased social interaction, and so forth. However, these factors may be influenced by a wide variety of situations and workplace interventions. Traditional atheoretical, or black-box, evaluations run a high risk of allowing the
influence of this menagerie of potential factors to masquerade as program
effects. Conversely, theory-oriented WHP research and program evaluation
have enormous potential for identifying and controlling extraneous sources of
variance and for isolating the effects of the factors that WHP programs specifically attempt to change (i.e., the presumed "active" ingredients).

The screening and educational components of WHP serve important functions (e.g., early disease detection, treatment compliance, and motivating be-havior change). However, establishing and maintaining health-promoting be-havior, or "healthful employee lifestyles," are the main objectives of most comprehensive WHP programs and policies. I illustrate the role of theory in WHP research by discussing issues related to the short-term effects of healthful employee lifestyles and by exploring the potential value of expanding the emphasis of WHP to include improvements in employee working conditions.

Employee Lifestyle

The term *health-related lifestyle* has been conceptualized and defined in nu-merous ways. For example, Breslow (1990) suggested that an individual's lifestyle is made up of the behaviors the person adopts from among those available in the context of his or her life circumstances. A similar definition of lifestyle was offered by Bouchard, Shephard, Stephens, Sutton, and Mc-Pherson (1990): "Lifestyle is the aggregate of an individual's behaviors, actions, and habits which can affect personal health" (p. 7).

The most common WHP activities are designed to affect an employee's "health practices" or "physical lifestyle" (e.g., see Breslow & Breslow, 1993; Donaldson & Blanchard, 1995). These include activities that aim to improve exercise regimens, eating habits, sleep patterns, weight control, and the pre-vention and termination of excessive alcohol use, cigarette smoking, and other substance abuse.

Some health promotion programs also include activities intended to im-prove psychological aspects of an individual's lifestyle such as social relations, intellectual activity, and occupational conditions (Hettler, 1984). This is usu-ally referred to as the "wellness lifestyle approach" and is a multidimensional strategy for realizing a person's potential for optimal health and well-being. For example, the worksite wellness program developed by Adolph Coors com-pany offers classes in anger management, parenting skills, and family oriented fitness programs, in addition to traditional WHP activities (Terborg, 1988). However WHP programs designed to influence psychosocial factors are prob-ably still the exception rather than the rule.

Much research has demonstrated that psychosocial factors play a large role in determining health and well-being (e.g., see Jammott & Locke, 1984; Pelletier, 1992). Reviewers of the relatively new field of health psychology suggest that substantial theoretical and empirical contributions have been made toward understanding the role of psychosocial factors in health and illness (Rodin & Salovey, 1989; Taylor, 1987, 1990). The recent alliance be-tween the American Psychological Association (APA) and the National Insti-tute of Occupational Safety and Health (NIOSH) has produced important work emphasizing psychosocial issues related to worksite health research (see Keita & Sauter, 1992; Quick, Murphy, & Hurrell, 1992) and an agenda for occupa-tional mental health promotion (APA/NIOSH Health Promotion Panel, 1992).

Examining the interactions among the various facets of employee lifestyle (both physical and psychosocial) in relation to employee health, well-being, and performance at work may yield valuable insights into the practice of lifestyle modification and WHP programming. After all, it takes considerable time, effort, and resources to live a healthful lifestyle. It may be that employees who live a well-balanced lifestyle receive the greatest health benefits, whereas those who invest a disproportionate amount of time and energy in one or two facets such as exercising, preparing nutritious meals, or developing and maintaining a complex social network may not benefit as much. Given that optimizing each lifestyle facet may be virtually impossible, it may be more beneficial to teach effective allocation of time and resources so that employees can attend to all important health-related aspects of their lifestyles rather than focusing on just one or two facets. Similarly, WHP practitioners who target their interventions at only a limited number of facets may produce unintended consequences (e.g., employees who are obsessed with managing their body weight, exercise routines, cholesterol levels, etc.). Future basic research efforts investigating these issues and evaluating WHP programs with these issues in mind may lead to a better understanding of how to achieve optimal health and well-being through lifestyle modification and WHP programming.

One potential drawback of the traditional lifestyle-oriented approach to WHP programming and research is that it runs the risk of leading researchers and program developers to focus solely on employee behaviors or the role that employees have in their own health. Another direction for WHP theory, research, and programming is to understand the impact of (and improve) the quality of working conditions (generally the employers' responsibility) in combination with employee personal behaviors or health-related lifestyle.

Working Conditions

In 1989, the *American Journal of Health Promotion* revised its definition of health promotion to reflect the importance of health promotive environments:

> Health promotion is the science and art of helping people change their lifestyle to move toward a state of optimal health. Optimal health is defined as a balance of physical, emotional, social, spiritual and intellectual health. Lifestyle change can be facilitated through a combination of efforts to enhance awareness, change behavior, and create environments that support good health practices. Of the three, supportive environments will probably have the greatest impact in producing lasting changes. (O'Donnell, 1989, p. 5)

This definition stresses the importance of the environment for influencing an individual's lifestyle. This perspective suggests that organizations involved in WHP should develop cultures or working environments that are highly supportive of healthful lifestyle practices. Although this perspective adds another important dimension to the practice of WHP, it does not go far enough.

Sloan (1987) pointed out that the current dominant paradigm of WHP research, which focuses on employee personal behaviors, severely limits the understanding of larger issues in the field (e.g., how best to promote healthy and effective functioning in the workplace). One of the main criticisms of the current paradigm is that most WHP efforts fail to consider the system of work in which employee behavior is embedded. Recent work suggests that WHP programs may achieve substantial health and work-related benefits by promoting favorable employee working conditions, in addition to providing health-related behavior change activities and environments that support these activities (see Karasek & Theorell, 1990; Stokols, 1992).

Designing and implementing interventions to improve working conditions is not new to the field of organizational psychology. For example, quality of worklife (QWL) programs designed to improve employee productivity and well-being have similar objectives to WHP programs (Sonnenstuhl, 1988). Unlike traditional WHP programs, which often presume that an employee's personal behavior (lifestyle) is primarily responsible for health, well-being, and performance at work, QWL programs focus on what an employer can do to improve employee working conditions. QWL approaches that included team building, quality circles, job enrichment, survey feedback, flextime, shared decision making, and open-door policies have been reported to be effective for improving employee well-being and productivity (e.g., see Greenberg & Baron, 1993). Multidisciplinary WHP efforts that target aspects of the working environment, in addition to employee behavior, may prove to be a powerful strategy for promoting health, well-being, and performance at work (see Stokols, 1992).

Short-Term Outcomes

Explaining processes through which employee lifestyle and working conditions affect relatively immediate work outcomes (e.g., job performance, absenteeism, and health care costs) is essential for establishing WHP as a viable human resource management strategy, in contrast to another management fad. For example, there is considerable evidence to suggest that lifestyle factors reduce the risk of disease, promote longevity, and compress morbidity (DHHS, 1991). However, the long-term benefits of leading a healthful lifestyle are not as important to employers (usually the funding source for WHP programs) as are the relatively immediate effects that presumably influence an organization's profitability (Warner et al., 1988). In fact, some reviewers of the WHP literature have argued that promoting healthful employee lifestyles saves money for future employers, not necessarily current employers, and that employees who live longer cost employers more in pensions funds and health care costs later in life (e.g., see Warner, 1987).

The subsequent discussion of using theory-driven research to understand the short-term benefits of healthful employee lifestyles and working conditions is not intended to be exhaustive. Rather, its purpose is to illustrate ways in which WHP researchers might use theory to gain a richer understanding of the value of WHP. I discuss potential short-term outcomes such as increased job performance, lower absenteeism, and reductions in employee stress to show how basic multidisciplinary research at the worksite might inform WHP program developers and evaluators of the processes through which WHP programs may affect their intended outcomes (i.e., small treatment theories; Lipsey, 1993).

Job performance. One of the primary reasons organizations attempt to improve employee lifestyles through WHP is to increase job performance. Increases in employee health are presumed to be related to increases in qualitative and quantitative improvements in job performance. Several explanations such as the following are commonly given for this relationship: Healthy workers perform better than their less healthy counterparts because of higher energy levels, and increased physical work capacity will increase clear thinking, improve alertness, and lessen productivity decrements resulting from fatigue (see Donaldson, 1991; Matteson & Ivancevich, 1988; Terborg, 1986).

Although the presumed link between employee lifestyle and job performance remains intuitively attractive, the few studies that have been conducted offer no clear evidence of its validity (see Donaldson, 1993; Gebhardt & Crump, 1990; Terborg, 1988). For example, the National Aeronautics and Space Administration (NASA), the Campbell Soup Company, and the Tenneco Organization reported that participation in WHP was associated with high levels of employee job performance (Bernaki & Baun, 1984; Durbeck et al., 1972; Rudman, 1987). However, findings from the NASA and Campbell Soup Company studies are limited because they relied on employee self-reports of job performance. Although supervisor job performance ratings were related to health promotion adherence in the Tenneco study, job performance did not change as a result of the health promotion intervention.

The contingency approach for studying organizational behavior (the hallmark of modern organizational behavior) assumes that behavior in work settings is a complex result of many interacting factors (Greenberg & Baron, 1993). There is substantial literature that suggests that job performance is determined by several individual beliefs and characteristics, as well as by the nature of one's job and working conditions. For example, expectancy theory predicts that motivation is the product of three employee beliefs: (a) Effort will result in performance, (b) performance will result in rewards, and (c) the rewards are perceived as valuable to the employee (see Miller & Grush, 1988). Expectancy theory emphasizes that motivation is not synonymous with job performance; rather, an employee's motivation in combination with his or her skills and abilities, role perceptions (i.e., what he or she believes is expected), and opportunities to perform determine job performance. (For a general discussion of employee job performance, see Greenberg & Baron, 1993.)

Considering this theoretical framework, it seems naive to assume that employee lifestyle or traditional WHP programs would necessarily lead directly to improved job performance. It is likely, however, that employee fitness and well-being enhance factors (e.g., skills and abilities) that lead to high levels of job performance. The challenge for WHP researchers is to develop and rigorously test theoretical models that explain under what conditions WHP or healthful employee lifestyle factors lead to relatively immediate organizational benefits such as improved employee job performance.

Absenteeism. The most plausible explanation for reductions in absenteeism is that employees who lead a healthful lifestyle are absent less often because they experience fewer and less severe illnesses. There are a number of reports that seem to indirectly substantiate this claim. Gebhardt and Crump (1990) reported that absenteeism has been shown to drop anywhere from 20% to 55% as a result of WHP programs ranging in lengths from 1 to 5 years. However, some reviewers of the WHP literature caution against the overinterpretation of this relationship because many of the reports suffer from poor or no controls, record keeping is suspect, and research design is poor overall (e.g., Matteson & Ivancevich, 1988).

Stress. Frequent and intense stressors have become an inescapable aspect of many occupations. High levels of stress can have a dramatic impact on employee health and organizational profitability (see Ivancevich, Matteson, Freedman, & Phillips, 1990). For example, considerable research has demonstrated that occupational stressors such as role ambiguity, quantitative work overload or underload, qualitative work overload or underload, responsibility for others, and hazardous physical environments can have deleterious effects on employee health and well-being (see Kahn & Byosiere, 1992). Other research suggests that personal sources of stress such as life changes and daily hassles can also lead to adverse health consequences (see Smith, 1993).

Although most researchers of stress focus on personal and job stress in isolation, combining personal and job stress into one construct (total negative life stress) predicts negative organizational outcomes better than does either personal or work stressors alone (Baghat, McQuaid, Lindolm, & Segovis, 1985). A recent study showed that total negative life stress predicted unique variance in employee vitality, positive well-being, anxiety, depression, physician visits, somatic complaints, illness absences, and supervisory ratings of job performance, absenteeism, and tardiness (Donaldson, 1993). That is, employees who reported high levels of negative life stress tended to have the poorest health and work performance characteristics.

More important for understanding the value of WHP and employee lifestyle, research suggests that leading a healthful lifestyle may buffer some of the adverse effects of stress (Brown, 1991). In fact, Donaldson (1993) found that employee physical lifestyle buffered the adverse consequences of total negative life stress on anxiety, depression, physician visits, and company records of health care costs. Although that study was somewhat exploratory and needs replication, it suggests a potentially fruitful direction for future WHP theory, research, and programming. For example, developing and examining the effects of WHP programs that directly reduce job stressors (i.e., improve working conditions) and promote a healthful lifestyle (a buffer of stress) may show dramatic reductions in an employee's total negative life stress and its deleterious consequences.

The prior discussion illustrates some ways in which basic multidisciplinary research at the worksite might inform WHP program developers and evaluators about program theory. Another approach for developing program theory is to extract implicit program theory from WHP program developers and other WHP personnel who may be familiar the way a WHP program seems to operate (see Chen, 1990; Lipsey & Pollard, 1989).

Testing Program Theory

Although WHP program theory might take a variety of forms, it is probably most common to think in terms of "variable-oriented" mediation models or intervening mechanism theories (Chen, 1990; Lipsey & Pollard, 1989). However, the prior example of employee lifestyle buffering the negative effects of total life stress (Donaldson, 1993) illustrates the importance of conceptualizing and examining moderator as well as mediation effects (see Baron & Kenny, 1986). In fact, ruling out plausible moderators (e.g., employee characteristics, type of job, organizational context, etc.) of key paths in a mediation model is one way of demonstrating the generalizability of intervening mechanism theories (Donaldson, Graham, & Hansen, 1994). Regardless of the specific program theory form or conceptual model used to represent how a WHP presumably achieves its objectives, designing rigorous empirical evaluations to test a priori program theory should be a priority. Accumulation of theory-driven, empirically based research promises to produce a generalizable knowledge base that will enable WHP program developers to consistently design effective programs.

Once a priori program theory has been specified, researchers should attempt to design evaluations that specifically test program theory as rigorously as possible given the practical constraints of the evaluation context. Chen and Rossi (1987) pointed out that evaluation researchers have traditionally focused on maximizing internal validity at the cost of compromising other validity issues. They suggested a more flexible approach using model specification in addition to (ideally), or in place of (if necessary), traditional randomized experimental designs. This approach requires using program theory to identify and control for potential threats to internal, statistical conclusion, construct, and external validity. Lipsey (1993) also described how to use program theory to design rigorous theory-driven program evaluations.

Critical Multiplism

Traditionally, WHP researchers have generally followed the conventional dictums of the "experimental paradigm" (Conrad et al., 1991; Lipsey, 1988), which has also been recently referred to as "mindless monism" (Shadish, 1993). A general research strategy more consistent with theory-driven, empirically based WHP is "postpositivist critical multiplism" (Cook, 1985) or "planned critical multiplism" (Shadish, 1993).

Critical multiplism concedes that no single study or evaluation is free of bias or is a completely accurate representation of reality (even randomized experiments). Therefore, the key to developing a useful knowledge base is to triangulate on research issues by using multiple methodological strategies with different strengths and weaknesses. For example, critical multiplism calls for (a) the use of multiple stakeholders to formulate research questions, (b) multiple operations of constructs, (c) multitrait–multimethod research, (d) multivariate causal models instead of simple univariate ones, (e) the competitive testing of multiple rival hypotheses rather than testing a single hypothesis, and (f) the use of multiple theoretical and value frameworks to interpret research questions and findings (Cook, 1985; Shadish, 1993). Also, using multiple strategies for addressing often-unavoidable problems such as attrition (Graham & Donaldson, 1993), for interpreting effects at multiple levels of analysis (e.g., organization, worksite, department, employee; see Bryk & Raudenbush, 1987; Graham, Donaldson, Hansen, Rohrbach, & Unger, 1995; Koepke & Flay, 1989), for honestly examining potential harmful effects or unintended outcomes (e.g., Donaldson, Graham, Piccinin, & Hansen, 1995), and for systematically synthesizing multiple evaluations or studies related to each other in an unpredictable fashion (see Cooper & Hedges, 1993) will increase confidence in the validity of empirical evidence related to the benefits of WHP. Although a detailed discussion of how to improve the quality of empirical research related to WHP is beyond the scope of this chapter, others have devoted entire articles to this issue (e.g., Conrad et al., 1991).

Construct Validity

One methodological issue in WHP research that has not received adequate attention elsewhere is construct validity. Measurement of employee health and work-related behavior is central to understanding the efficacy and effectiveness of WHP programs. Despite its importance, measurement has been one of the main shortcomings of health behavior research (see D'Onofrio, 1989). The problem is that researchers must rely greatly on self-reports because they are relatively easy to obtain and are often the only feasible way to assess the constructs of interest. The disadvantages of self-reports are well documented; they are prone to many kinds of response bias. In general, research participants want to respond in a way that makes them look as good as possible. Thus, they tend to underreport behaviors deemed inappropriate by researchers or other observers, and they tend to overreport behaviors viewed as appropriate. This limitation seriously brings into question the validity of much of the prior research related to WHP.

Recent developments in the analysis of multitrait–multimethod data are beginning to show some of the practical value initially foreseen by Campbell and Fiske (1959). In short, by collecting WHP data from multiple sources (e.g., employees, coworkers, supervisors, or even from company records) on constructs that are likely to be influenced by the same biases (e.g., social desirability bias), the researchers can establish convergent and discriminant validity (Campbell & Fiske, 1959) and understand and control for some of the biases in the data (Graham & Collins, 1991; Graham, Collins, Donaldson, & Hansen, 1993). It is important to collect WHP data in ways that minimize the influence of response bias. However, in the context of WHP research, it may be virtually impossible to completely prevent response bias. Collecting data on the same variables from different perspectives (e.g., employee, coworker, supervisor, company records, etc.) may dramatically increase understanding about construct validity in WHP research.

Practical Implications

There are important practical implications of a theory-driven, empirically based perspective of WHP. First, it suggests that organizations must be wary of WHP zealots. Decisions about program development (or adoption) and implementation should be anchored in theory and sound science. That is, science, not ideology, should drive WHP (Evans, 1988).

For example, almost without exception, WHP practitioners are specialists designed to address a specific lifestyle facet (Ilgen, 1990). Naturally, their version of WHP will reflect their specialties. Health educators promote employee health by educating employees about beneficial health habits, dietitians promote employee health with nutrition, fitness specialists promote employee health with exercise regimens, training and development specialists are likely to promote employee health by expanding knowledge and skills, counseling psychologists may promote employee health by improving employee social relationships, and so forth. Under some (or many) conditions, theory-driven, empirically based research may show that multifaceted approaches to lifestyle improvement are more effective than simply focusing on a limited number of aspects of an employee's lifestyle. If this is the case, science will suggest that WHP programs that are structured to integrate and coordinate the services of specialists, versus programs managed by specialists committed to one discipline of lifestyle improvement, will be more likely to achieve employee health and organizational benefits. The important point is that objective empirical evidence, not just the ideologies of WHP personnel or specialists, should be used to develop WHP programs.

Second, organizational decision makers must demand that WHP program developers explain how and why their WHP program will produce health and organizational benefits in their specific workplace. Several questions should be addressed before an organization decides to invest in a WHP program including:

1. What is the current state of affairs in our organization with respect to employee lifestyle, working conditions, health, and relevant organizational behaviors?
   - Conducting a needs analysis is essential for identifying the specific aspects of employee health, lifestyle, and working conditions that could be substantially improved with WHP activities and those areas that are already being maintained at desired levels. Needs-analysis strategies often provide insights about the determinants of problem areas.
2. What types of interventions are most likely to meet our present needs and future goals?
   - This issue should be evaluated by considering the empirical evidence on the effects of a wide variety of interventions related to the organization's specific needs and future goals.
3. When considering the WHP option, organizational decision makers should address the following questions:

- Who will participate?
- Is it feasible to deliver this type of intervention successfully in our particular workplace?
- What unintended consequences may result?
- What are the expected costs and benefits?
- Is this the most economical method for addressing our particular employee health concerns (i.e., economic efficiency issues)?
- What are the ethical issues that pertain to our organization's right to influence our employees' personal lives?
- What are the ethical issues that pertain to our organization's failure to provide health promotive activities and favorable working conditions?

4. How will we determine whether WHP (or any other strategy) is effective?
   - An evaluation system should be a permanent component of WHP programs. Constant empirical feedback to organizational decision makers about the implementation, processes, outcomes, and economics of their particular WHP program is vital. For example, formative evaluation techniques can be used to refine and hone interventions, theory-driven summative evaluations can be used to determine if and why a program is effective or ineffective, and cost–benefit and cost-effectiveness analyses should be performed to estimate both the short- and long-term returns on investment (see Fielding, 1991).

Finally, a theory-driven, empirically based perspective of WHP promises to promote an inclusive, rather than exclusive, strategy for enhancing health and well-being at work. That is, by specifically tailoring WHP interventions to worksite needs and goals, most employers, not just large organizations with the resources to make substantial long-term investments in WHP, can potentially benefit from WHP (see Donaldson & Blanchard, 1995). This is particularly important considering that most reports about the effects of WHP programs deal with worksites of 500–5,000 employees, whereas the majority of the workforce is employed in worksites with 50 or fewer employees (Fielding, 1991). In addition to reaching underserved employee populations, employees who are the most vulnerable with respect to leading an unhealthful lifestyle and working in unfavorable conditions may gain more access to WHP services.

Conclusions

The cost of human failings due to the absence of health promotion, or the presence of well-intended but misdirected health promotion efforts, is enormous to modern societies. These consistently increasing costs to individuals and society at large are reflected in restorative treatments implemented directly in hospitals, clinics, residential living settings, community mental health centers, EAPs, the practice of psychotherapy, and more indirectly in society's delinquency, criminal justice, substance abuse, and legal systems (Cowen, 1991).

Many employers are currently investing considerable resources in WHP with the expectation that it will produce substantial organizational dividends. This presents an important window of opportunity for health and organizational scientists to develop WHP programs that are based on sound scientific principles that will meet both public health goals and organizational objectives. If WHP programs are designed and implemented with an empirically based understanding of why past interventions have produced or failed to produce desired outcomes, they will be much more likely to realize their potential.

References

APA/NIOSH Health Promotion Panel. (1992). Occupational mental health promotion: A prevention agenda based on education and treatment. *American Journal of Health Promotion, 7,* 37–44.

Antonovsky, A. (1987). *Unraveling the mystery of health: How people manage stress and stay well.* San Francisco: Jossey-Bass.

Baghat, R. S., McQuaid, S. J., Lindholm, H., & Segovis, J. (1985). Total life stress: A multimethod validation of the construct and its effects on organizationally valued outcomes and withdrawal behaviors. *Journal of Applied Psychology, 70,* 202–214.

Baron, R. M., & Kenny, D. A. (1986). The moderator–mediator variable distinction in social psychological research: Conceptual, strategic, and statistical considerations. *Journal of Personality and Social Psychology, 51,* 1173–1182.

Bernacki, E. J., & Baun, W. B. (1984). The relationship of job performance to exercise adherence in a corporate fitness program. *Journal of Occupational Medicine, 26,* 529–531.

Bickman, L. (1987). The functions of program theory. *New Directions for Program Evaluation, 33,* 5–18.

Bouchard, C., Shephard, R. J., Stephens, T., Sutton, J. R., & McPherson, B. D. (Eds.). (1990). *Exercise, fitness, and health: A consensus of current knowledge.* Champaign, IL: Human Kinetics.

Breslow, L. (1990). Lifestyle, fitness, and health. In C. Bouchard, R. J. Shepard, T. Stephens, J. R. Sutton, & B. D. McPherson (Eds.), *Exercise, fitness, and health: A consensus of current knowledge* (pp. 153–163). Champaign, IL: Human Kinetics.

Breslow, L., & Breslow, N. (1993). Health practices and disability: Some evidence from Alameda County. *Preventive Medicine, 22,* 86–95.

Brown, J. D. (1991). Staying fit studying well: Physical fitness as a moderator of life stress. *Journal of Personality and Social Psychology, 60,* 555–561.

Bryk, A. S., & Raudenbush, S. W. (1987). Applying the hierarchical linear model to measurement of change problems. *Psychological Bulletin, 101,* 147–158.

Campbell, D. T., & Fiske, D. W. (1959). Convergent and discriminant validation by the multitrait-multimethod matrix. *Psychological Bulletin, 56,* 81–105.

Chen, H. T. (1990). *Theory-driven evaluations.* Newbury Park, CA: Sage.

Chen, H. T., & Rossi, P. H. (1987). The theory-driven approach to validity. *Evaluation and Program Planning, 10,* 95–103.

Conrad, K. M., Conrad, K. J., & Walcott-McQuigg, J. (1991). Threats to internal validity in worksite health promotion program research: Common problems and possible solutions. *American Journal of Health Promotion, 6,* 112–122.

Cook, T. D. (1985). Post-positivist critical multiplism. In L. Shotland & M. M. Marks (Eds.), *Social science and social policy* (pp. 21–61). Beverly Hills, CA: Sage.

Cooper, H., & Hedges, L. V. (1993). *The handbook of research synthesis.* New York: Russell Sage Foundation.

Cowen, E. L. (1991). In pursuit of wellness. *American Psychologist, 46,* 404–408.

Davis, M. F., Rosenberg, K., Iverson, D. C., Vernon, T. M., & Bauer, J. (1984). Worksite health promotion in Colorado. *Public Health Reports, 99,* 538–543.

Donaldson, S. I. (1991). Employee lifestyle, health, and organizational behavior: Implications for occupational health promotion (Doctoral dissertation, The Claremont Graduate School, 1991). *Dissertation Abstracts International, 52*(3-B), 1761.

Donaldson, S. I. (1993). Effects of lifestyle and stress on the employee and organization: Implications for promoting health at work. *Anxiety, Stress, and Coping, 6,* 155–177.

Donaldson, S. I., & Blanchard, A. L. (1995). The seven health practices, well-being, and performance at work: Evidence for the value of reaching small and underserved worksites. *Preventive Medicine, 24,* 270–277.

Donaldson, S. I., Graham, J. W., & Hansen, W. B. (1994). Testing the generalizability of intervening mechanism theories: Understanding the effects of adolescent drug use prevention interventions. *Journal of Behavioral Medicine, 17,* 195–216.

Donaldson, S. I., Graham, J. W., Piccinin, A. M., & Hansen, W. B. (1995). Resistance skills training and alcohol use onset: Evidence for beneficial and potentially harmful effects in public and private Catholic schools. *Health Psychology, 14,* 291–300.

D'Onofrio, C. N. (1989). The use of self-reports on sensitive behaviors in health promotion evaluation. *New Directions for Program Evaluation, 43,* 59–74.

Durbeck, D. C., Heinzelmann, F., Schacter, J., Haskell, W. L., Payne, G. H., Moxley, R. T., Nemiroff, M., Limoncelli, D. D., Arnoldi, L. B., & Fox, S. M. (1972). The National Aeronautics and Space Administration–U.S. Public Health Service evaluation and enhancement program. *American Journal of Cardiology, 30,* 784–790.

Evans, R. I. (1988). Health promotion: Science or ideology? *Health Psychology, 7,* 203–219.

Falkenberg, L. E. (1987). Employee fitness programs: Their impact on the employee and the organization. *Academy of Management Review, 12,* 511–522.

Fielding, J. E. (1991). The challenges of work-place health promotion. In S. M. Weiss, J. E. Fielding, & A. Baum (Eds.), *Perspectives in behavioral medicine: Health at work* (pp. 13–28). Hillsdale, NJ: Erlbaum.

Fielding, J. E., & Piserchia, P. V. (1989). Frequency of worksite health promotion activities. *American Journal of Public Health, 79,* 16–20.

Gebhardt, D. L., & Crump, C. E. (1990). Employee fitness and wellness programs in the workplace. *American Psychologist, 45,* 262–272.

Graham, J. W., & Collins, N. L. (1991). Controlling correlational bias via confirmatory factor analysis of MTMM data. *Multivariate Behavioral Research, 26,* 501–523.

Graham, J. W., Collins, N. L., Donaldson, S. I., & Hansen, W. B. (1993). Understanding and controlling for response bias: Confirmatory factor analysis of multitrait-multimethod data. In R. Steyer, K. F. Wender, & K. F. Widamen (Eds.), *Psychometric methodology: Proceedings of the 7th European Meeting of the Psychometric Society in Trier* (pp. 585–590). Stuttgart: Gustav Fisher Verlag.

Graham, J. W., & Donaldson, S. I. (1993). Evaluating interventions with differential attrition: The importance of nonresponse mechanisms and use of follow-up data. *Journal of Applied Psychology, 78,* 119–128.

Graham, J. W., & Donaldson, S. I., Hansen, W. B., Rohrbach, L. A., & Unger, J. (1995). *Tracing the process of longitudinal prevention program effects with hierarchical data and complex missing data patterns.* Manuscript submitted for publication.

Greenberg, J., & Baron, R. A. (1993). *Behavior in organizations.* Needham Heights, MA: Allyn & Bacon.

Hettler, W. (1984). Wellness: The lifetime goal of a university experience. In J. D. Matarazzo, S. M. Weiss, J. A. Herd, N. E. Miller, & S. M. Weiss (Eds.), *Behavioral health: A handbook of health enhancement and disease prevention* (pp. 1117–1124). New York: Wiley.

Ilgen, D. R. (1990). Health issues at work: Opportunities for industrial/organizational psychology. *American Psychologist, 45,* 273–283.

Ivancevich, J. M., Matteson, M. T., Freedman, S. M., & Phillips, J. S. (1990). Worksite stress management interventions. *American Psychologist, 45,* 252–261.

Jammott, J., & Locke, S. (1984). Psychosocial factors, immunologic mediation, and human susceptibility to infectious disease: How much do we know? *Psychological Bulletin, 95,* 78–108.

Kahn, R. L., & Byosiere, P. (1992). Stress in organizations. In M. D. Dunnette & L. M. Hough (Eds.), *Handbook of industrial organizational psychology* (Vol. 3, 2nd ed., pp. 571–650). Palo Alto, CA: Consulting Psychologists Press.

Karasek, R., & Theorell, T. (1990). *Healthy work: Stress, productivity, and the reconstruction of working life.* New York: Basic Books.

Keita, G. P., & Sauter, S. L. (Eds.). (1992). *Work and well-being: An agenda for the 1990s.* Washington, DC: American Psychological Association.

Koepke, D., & Flay, B. R. (1989). Levels of analysis. *New Directions for Program Evaluation, 43,* 75–88.

Lewin, K. (1945). The Research Center for Group Dynamics at Massachusetts Institute of Technology. *Sociometry, 2,* 126–136.

Lipsey, M. W. (1988). Practice and malpractice in evaluation research. *Evaluation Practice, 9,* 5–24.

Lipsey, M. W. (1993). Theory as method: Small theories of treatments. *New Directions for Program Evaluation, 57,* 5–38.

Lipsey, M. W., & Pollard, J. A. (1989). Driving toward theory in program evaluation: More models to choose from. *Evaluation and Program Planning, 12,* 317–328.

Matarazzo, J. D., Weiss, S. M., Herd, J. A., Miller, N. E., & Weiss, S. M. (Eds.). (1984). *Behavioral health: A handbook of health enhancement and disease prevention.* New York: Wiley.

Matteson, M. T., & Ivancevich, J. M. (1988). Health promotion at work. In C. L. Cooper & I. T. Robertson (Eds.), *International review of industrial and organizational psychology* (pp. 279–306). New York: Wiley.

Miller, L. E., & Grush, J. E. (1988). Improving predictions in expectancy theory research: Effects of personality, expectancies, and norms. *Academy of Management Journal, 31,* 424–433.

O'Donnell, M. P. (1989). Definition of health promotion: 3. Expanding the definition. *American Journal of Health Promotion, 3,* 5–6.

Pelletier, K. R. (1991). A review and analysis of the health and cost-effective outcome studies of comprehensive health promotion and disease prevention programs. *American Journal of Health Promotion, 5,* 311–315.

Pelletier, K. R. (1992). Mind-body health: Research, clinical, and policy applications. *American Journal of Health Promotion, 6,* 345–358.

Quick, J. C., Murphy, L. R., & Hurrell, J. J. (Eds.). (1992). *Stress and well-being at work: Assessments and interventions for occupational mental health.* Washington, DC: American Psychological Association.

Rodin, J., & Salovey, P. (1989). Health psychology. *Annual Review of Psychology, 40,* 533–579.

Rudman, W. J. (1987). Do onsite health and fitness programs affect worker productivity? *Fitness in Business, 2,* 2–8.

Seeman, J. (1989). Toward a model of positive health. *American Psychologist, 44,* 1099–1109.

Shadish, W. R. (1993). Critical multiplism: A research strategy and its attendant tactics. *New Directions for Program Evaluation, 60,* 13–57.

Sloan, R. P. (1987). Workplace health promotion: A commentary on the evolution of a paradigm. *Health Education Quarterly, 14,* 181–194.

Smith, J. C. (1993). *Understanding stress and coping.* New York: Macmillan.

Sonnenstuhl, W. J. (1988). Contrasting employee assistance, health promotion, and quality of worklife programs, and their effects on alcohol abuse and dependence. *Journal of Applied Behavioral Science, 24,* 347–363.

Sonnenstuhl, W. J., & Trice, H. M. (1986). *Strategies for employee assistance programs: The crucial balance.* Ithaca, NY: ILR Press.

Stokols, D. (1992). Establishing and maintaining healthy environments: Toward a social ecology of health promotion. *American Psychologist, 47,* 6–22.

Taylor, S. E. (1987). The progress and prospects of health psychology: Tasks of a maturing discipline. *Health Psychology, 6,* 73–87.

Taylor, S. E. (1990). Health psychology: The science of the field. *American Psychologist, 45,* 40–50.

Terborg, J. R. (1986). Health promotion at the worksite: A research challenge for personnel and human resources management. In K. M. Rowland & G. R. Ferris (Eds.), *Research in personnel and human resources management* (pp. 225–267). Greenwich, CT: JAI Press.

Terborg, J. R. (1988). The organization as a context for health promotion. In S. Spacapan & S. Oskamp (Eds.), *The social psychology of health* (pp. 119–127). Newbury Park, CA: Sage.

U.S. Department of Health and Human Services. (1991). *Healthy people 2000: National health promotion and disease prevention objectives* (DHHS Publication No. PHS 91-50212). Washington, DC: U.S. Government Printing Office.

U.S. Preventive Services Task Force. (1989). *Guide to clinical preventive services*. Baltimore: Williams & Wilkins.

Warner, K. E. (1987). Selling health promotion to corporate America: Uses and abuses of the economic argument. *Health Education Quarterly, 14*, 39–55.

Warner, K. E., Wickizer, T. M., Wolfe, R. A., Schildroth, J. E., & Samuelson, M. H. (1988). Economic implications of workplace health promotion programs: Review of the literature. *Journal of Occupational Medicine, 30*, 106–112.

Part II ——————————————————

Coping With Job Stress
and Unemployment

7

The Caregiver Support Program: An Intervention to Increase Employee Coping Resources and Enhance Mental Health

Catherine A. Heaney, Richard H. Price, and Jane Rafferty

Numerous worksite sources of stress have been identified and linked to adverse effects on employee well-being, particularly in the human services sector (Cherniss, 1980; Edelwich & Brodsky, 1980; Shinn, Rosario, March, & Chestnut, 1984). These sources of stress include work overload, interpersonal conflicts with other staff, role conflict (i.e., conflicts between competing priorities or between an employee's values and a supervisor's instructions), lack of recognition, and emotional demands from clients.

As occupational stress has come to be viewed as a transactional process whereby employees appraise and react to potential sources of stress in the work environment, researchers have become increasingly interested in understanding the coping resources from which employees can draw when faced with problems at work. Stress management and stress reduction practitioners also have focused on employee coping resources. Because some of the stressors in the worksite cannot be reduced or modified (e.g., dealing with clients may be inherently unpredictable and emotionally demanding), practitioners have attempted to increase employee coping resources so that resistance to the ill-effects engendered by exposure to stressors is maximized.

The workplace has become the locus of many stress management and stress reduction programs. A 1985 national survey of worksites with 50 or more employees indicated that 27% of the sites offered some stress management activity to their employees (U.S. Department of Health and Human Services [DHHS], 1987). By 1992, that figure had risen to 37% (DHHS, 1993). However, few of the existing worksite stress programs have been rigorously evaluated. Thus, this proliferation of programs has not resulted in a significant increase in the understanding of how best to intervene in the stress processes of em-

This research was supported in part by a grant from the National Institute of Mental Health (5P50MH38330) to the Michigan Prevention Research Center (Richard H. Price, principal investigator).

ployees (Heaney & van Ryn, 1990; Ivancevich, Matteson, Freedman, & Phillips, 1990; Murphy, 1988).

In this chapter, we attempt to enhance the understanding of how to effectively increase important employee coping resources and thus improve employee mental health. First, we define coping resources and briefly review the evidence linking them to mental health. We then describe a theory-based program designed to increase employees' coping resources. Finally, we report the results of a field experiment conducted to evaluate the program.

Coping Resources

Worksite coping behavior is determined partly by the amount and the quality of resources that the employee can draw on when faced with a problem or potentially stressful situation. Coping resources have usually been defined as personal attributes and skills that are considered adaptive or advantageous across many situations (Menaghan, 1983) and are associated with effective coping behavior. Thus, self-esteem (Fleishman, 1984), mastery (Pearlin & Schooler, 1978), a sense of coherence (Antonovsky, 1979), and problem-solving skills (Cox, 1987) have been identified as coping resources.

However, coping resources also can include characteristics of the social and organizational environment that facilitate effective coping behavior or broaden the range of potential coping behaviors available to employees. For example, Thoits (1986) conceptualized social support as a coping resource because it can help a person to modify a stressful situation, to change the meaning of the situation, or to decrease the emotional upset associated with the problematic situation. By receiving tangible aid, instrumental aid, or information from others, employees are no longer constrained by their own abilities and personal resources when solving problems or dealing with difficult situations. By receiving emotional support, understanding, or affirmation, employees may suffer less distress when faced with difficult situations. Thus, the availability of support from others broadens an employee's repertoire of coping strategies.

Organizational factors also can affect an individual's ability to cope effectively with stressful aspects of the job. For example, the extent to which employees are able to exert control over their work is associated with decreased perceived work stress and buffers the negative impact of work stress on health (Spector, 1986). Specifically, employees who suffer high job demands and have little control over decisions regarding their jobs are the most likely to suffer adverse stress-related mental and physical health symptoms (Karasek, 1979).

The organizational context can either support feelings of control or undermine them. For instance, organizations can enhance an employee's perceived control by providing a climate in which employees can meaningfully participate in decision-making processes. Participation in decision making has been associated with greater job satisfaction, lower perceived stress, the use of active problem-solving coping strategies, and better mental health (Cherniss & Egnatios, 1978; Jackson, 1983; Morris, Steers, & Koch, 1979). If employees are able to influence decisions at the workplace, their perceptions of their abilities to exercise control over specific worksite stressors may be enhanced (Ganster, 1988).

Description of the Caregiver Support Program

This intervention for human services workers, called the Caregiver Support Program (CSP), was intended to increase social support and participation in work-related decisions. Specifically, the program was designed with two primary goals in mind: (a) to teach employees about the helping potential of support systems and to build skills in mobilizing available support from others at work and (b) to teach employees about participatory problem-solving approaches and to build skills in implementing such approaches in work team meetings. Because managers were included in the training, we expected that changes in managers' attitudes toward participation and skills in facilitating employee participation would create an organizational context amenable to employees participating in and having influence over decision making. We also expected that these changes in individual skills and organizational decision-making processes would enhance employees' perceptions of their ability to cope and result in improved employee mental health.

The CSP involved six training sessions. Each session was 4–5 hr long and was held in convenient community sites. The first three sessions were held a week apart, and the fourth through sixth sessions were held 2 weeks apart. The participants were direct-care staff and home managers who worked in group homes that provided residential care for adults with developmental disabilities or mental illness in 11 counties in Michigan. Each training group consisted of approximately 10 home managers and 10 direct-care staff. Training sessions were led by two facilitators who were chosen because of their expertise in managing group processes and for their knowledge of the caregiving profession.

Content

The first session focused on understanding existing helping networks, and the second focused on strengthening those networks. In these sessions, participants were introduced to the various types of social support exchanged between people: emotional, instrumental, informational, and appraisal (House, 1981). They then explored how social support from others might help solve problems and reduce distress at work, using a brainstorming activity to list specific ways that others might aid in dealing with specific common job stressors. Next, participants mapped and diagnosed the strengths and weaknesses of their social networks at work. Finally, participants refined the interpersonal skills associated with exchanging social support with others, including clarifying misunderstandings, providing constructive feedback, and asking others for help. This latter skill was addressed because caregivers are known to feel uncomfortable about seeking aid for themselves (Cherniss, 1980) and because beliefs about help seeking are associated with increased support mobilization, independent of the number of potential supporters available (Eckenrode, 1983).

Researchers have not yet validated particular techniques for improving the exchange of social support at the worksite (Gottlieb, 1988). Therefore, although the skill areas were chosen on the basis of prior research during the program development process, we decided that the actual strategies for improvement should be generated by the participants themselves in relation to problems they had experienced. Thus, participants were not instructed how to behave; instead, with the guidance of the trainers, they gleaned suggestions for change from the stories of others' effective, supportive social interactions at work.

Session 3 involved teaching individuals how to develop and lead effective training activities. The home manager and one direct-care staff person from each home attended the CSP sessions. They were expected to train the rest of the staff on CSP concepts and skills. Thus, in this session, participants developed a training activity that addressed one of the social network skills covered in the first two sessions and that they thought would be useful and appropriate in their group homes. Participants then practiced facilitating the activity, discussed their experiences, and brainstormed strategies for overcoming obstacles to the implementation of the activities in the group homes.

Sessions 4 and 5 dealt with increasing worker participation in decision making. Caregivers discussed the pros and cons of encouraging all workers in the home to participate in important policy and client decisions. The trainers highlighted the advantages of such a process for both supervisors and subordinates (Van de Ven, 1982) and then presented a group problem-solving process that could be used in staff meetings (Johnson & Johnson, 1982). Next, caregivers practiced using this group process to prioritize and solve problems. They also planned how these procedures could be adapted for use in staff meetings at their worksites.

The final session was dedicated to techniques for maintaining new skills over the long term and enhancing occupational self-esteem. This session underscored the importance of following up on any new initiatives tried out in the group homes. An initial qualitative assessment of the stressors in the group homes had indicated that many new programs were instituted in the homes but that few of them survived setbacks or waning enthusiasm on the part of the initiator. Participants discussed the costs of not following up and then developed strategies that could be used in the homes to aid in maintaining new programs and initiatives over time.

Learning Processes

The learning processes of the CSP were structured according to the principles of social learning theory (Bandura, 1977), which suggests that modeling and rehearsal of new behaviors are crucial to a successful learning process. Trainers were therefore instructed to model new skills and then allow participants to rehearse the new behaviors in the relative safety of the training group. Only after developing a feeling of mastery were participants encouraged to try out new behaviors at their workplaces. Positive reinforcement was given throughout the learning process to keep motivation and self-efficacy high.

The learning processes were also shaped by Janis's (1983) work on effective short-term counseling techniques. He suggested that trainers are most effective in bringing about participants' changes in attitudes and behaviors if the trainers are perceived to be knowledgeable, likable, admirable, and accepting. To develop this image, trainers provided unconditional positive regard for the participants, offered specific and contingent praise for behavior change efforts, and made moderate self-disclosures about their own attempts at behavior change (Janis, 1983).

In spite of this careful preparation, we expected that some participants might experience setbacks when trying out new behaviors. Consequently, Meichenbaum's (1985) procedure for inoculation against setbacks was incorporated after each new set of behaviors was learned. Participants were asked to think about possible setbacks that might occur, to anticipate constructive responses to them, and to imagine themselves using these constructive responses in their workplaces.

Transfer of Training

For any worksite training effort, it is important that the knowledge and skills taught in the training sessions be transferred to the work setting. Studies have shown that the transfer of skills from the training context to the actual worksite often does not occur (Baldwin & Ford, 1980), thus wasting the time and resources spent on the training.

The transfer process can be enhanced in several ways (Baldwin & Ford, 1980; Goldstein, Lopez, & Greenleaf, 1979). First, transfer is facilitated by providing the learner with general principles that guide successful performance. Second, the problems and situations used as examples should be similar to those encountered regularly in the workplace. Third, the training should provide a wide range of examples so that the likelihood is increased that participants will be able to generalize a skill to a wide variety of situations and settings. These three processes, along with the social learning theory concepts described earlier, were incorporated into the CSP learning activities in order to facilitate the transfer of knowledge and skills to the worksite.

There are two transfer processes that must occur for the CSP to be effective. First, participants in the training sessions have to use their newly learned knowledge and skills back in the group homes. Second, the participants have to train the rest of the staff in the group home (who did not have an opportunity to attend the CSP sessions) in the concepts and skills of the CSP.

Method

Sample, Recruitment, and Data Collection

A multistage recruitment procedure was used to recruit employees into the study. First, provider agency administrators from 73 nonprofit corporations who operated group homes were invited to orientation sessions. During these sessions, project objectives were outlined; the advantages of participating were detailed; assurances of confidentiality were provided; the importance of evaluating training was emphasized; and the necessity of random assignment to experimental condition was discussed. Fifty-five of the 73 agencies agreed to participate and to recruit staff members working in their eligible group homes.

Half of the group homes within each participating agency were then randomly assigned to receive the CSP (the experimental group), and the other half were not (the control group). If an agency had an odd number of homes, the extra home was assigned to the experimental group. Managers in all of the homes were invited to participate in the study and asked to recruit their staff to participate. Managers in the experimental homes were invited to participate in the CSP training and to invite one person from their direct-care staff to attend as well.

Data were collected from employees in group homes using self-administered surveys. Surveys were sent to each staff member at the group home where he or she was employed. Five dollars were enclosed with each survey as remuneration for the time needed to fill it out. Data were collected from both control and experimental group members 1 month prior to the beginning of the training program and 5 weeks after training ended. Thus, the time interval between data collection points was approximately 4 months.

Figure 1 shows the sample sizes, response rates, and quit rates for both the experimental and control groups. Response rates and turnover rates did not significantly differ between the two groups. For this study, employees who responded to the survey at Times 1 and 2 were included in the analyses ($N = 1,375$). The mean age for this sample was 31.5 years ($SD = 10.1$), with employees ranging in age from 18 to 79 years. Eighty-one percent of the employees were female, and 80% were White. Average tenure in the job was 1 year 4 months. Employees earned an average hourly wage of $5.69, with some employees earning minimum wage ($3.35) and others earning as much as $11.00 an hour. Forty-one percent of the sample had never married, and 39% were currently married.

Measures

The CSP was expected to have an impact on interpersonal skill-related outcomes, group problem solving, and overall mental health and job satisfaction. We describe the measures in each of these categories.

Interpersonal skill-related outcomes. Outcomes in this category included social support and appraisals of strategies for coping with interpersonal stressors. Two outcome measures of social support were assessed. Supervisor support was measured by five items asking how much ($1 = none$, $5 = a\ great\ deal$) the respondent received of each of the following from his or her immediate supervisor in the past 4 weeks: useful information; care and concern; help in thinking through problems; help in getting materials, supplies, and services; and praise and appreciation (Cronbach's $\alpha = .89$). The measure was based on

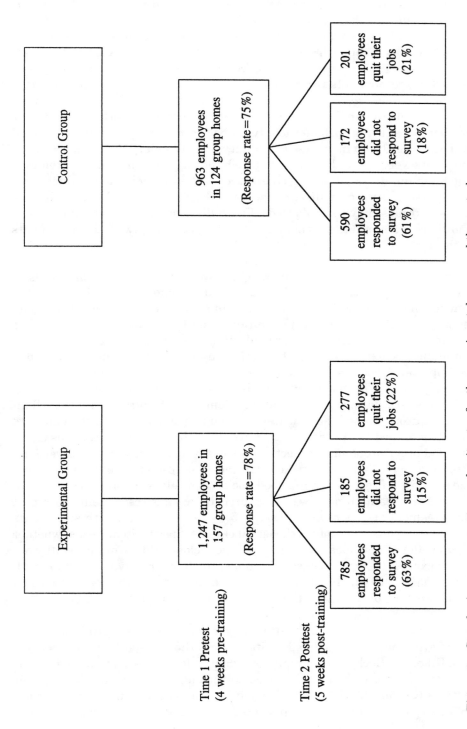

Figure 1. Sample size, response rates, and quit rates for the experimental group and the control group.

an index developed by Abbey, Abramis, and Caplan (1985). Supportive feed-back was measured using a two-item scale that asked how often (1 = *never*, 7 = *almost always*) the respondent had been told he or she "did a good job on a task" and had "received feedback that was helpful and constructive" during the past 4 weeks (Cronbach's α = .74). This index was also based on the work of Abbey et al. (1985). Self-appraisal of coping behavior was measured by four items asking respondents the extent to which they agreed (1 = *strongly dis-agree*, 5 = *strongly agree*) with statements that they had been trained with special methods to handle disagreements and overload at work and that they were effective at using such methods (Cronbach's α = .86). Items were adapted from Lazarus's (1966) measures of primary and secondary appraisal. Finally, respondents were asked the extent to which they agreed with three statements about handling disagreements. These items asked the extent to which they felt they had control over disagreements, the extent to which they felt they had lots of things they could do to deal with disagreements, and the extent to which there were others to whom they could go for help with disagreements (Cronbach's α = .67).

Group problem-solving outcomes. There were three outcome measures in this domain. Group problem solving addressed respondents' perceptions of the extent to which staff were given a chance to suggest problems for discussion, to help set priorities, to generate solutions, and to develop action plans. The extent to which the house manager made decisions without seeking input from the staff and the extent to which the staff focused on minor issues and avoided more important problems also were included in this six-item measure (Cron-bach's α = .83). The measure of positive work team functioning assessed respondents' evaluations of how well problems and disagreements were han-dled in the group home. The four items asked respondents about the extent to which they agreed (1 = *strongly disagree*, 5 = *strongly agree*) that disagree-ments and other problems (respectively) were resolved in ways that were up-setting and unpleasant (reverse coded) and that resolution of problems and disagreements left people feeling good about themselves (Cronbach's α = .80). Positive work team climate was measured by asking respondents to report their agreement (1 = *strongly disagree*, 5 = *strongly agree*) with statements reflecting staff perceptions of psychological climate. Specific items asked whether staff who offered new ideas were likely to get "clobbered," whether staff were afraid to express their real views, whether staff members have respect for each other, the degree to which participation is encouraged, and the degree to which there is constant bickering in the group home (Cronbach's α = .81).

Overall outcomes. Mental health was measured with a multidimensional index of symptoms that included 24 items from the SCL-90-R subscales (Der-ogatis, Rikels, & Rock, 1976) for anxiety, depression, somatization, and anger. The mental health measure was coded so that higher scores indicated fewer symptoms (Cronbach's α = .81). The job satisfaction measure (Cronbach's α = .85) used nine items to tap employees' feelings about various aspects of the

Table 1. CSP Participant Reports of the Training Activities They Conducted in Their Group Homes

Content of training activity	% of Participants who reported conducting training
Clarifying misunderstandings	28.6
Providing effective feedback	45.7
Making requests of others	41.7
Identifying and prioritizing problems	35.1
Group problem-solving techniques	28.4

Note. CSP = Caregiver Support Program.

job such as task variety, skill utilization, opportunities for promotion, and job content (Andrews & Withey, 1976).

Results

Participation in the Caregiver Support Program

Of the 785 employees in the experimental group at Time 2, 617 (79%) worked in homes that had at least one employee who had attended a minimum of one session of the CSP. The rest of the experimental group worked in "no-show" homes (i.e., no one from the group home attended any CSP sessions). Thus, 21% of the experimental group had no exposure to the CSP.

Among the 134 attendees still employed at Time 2, 97 (72%) attended five or six sessions, 23 (17%) attended three or four sessions, and 14 (10%) attended only one or two sessions. Nonattenders—those employees who did not attend the CSP sessions but who worked in a home that had an employee attend— had varying amounts of "indirect" exposure to the program. Indirect exposure was measured by the total number of person-sessions attended by employees from a home. Forty-seven nonattenders had an indirect exposure of 1–4 person-sessions, 106 had 5–8 person-sessions, and 320 nonattenders had 9–16 person-sessions.

Effectiveness of the "Train-the-Trainer" Approach

At the last CSP session, participants reported whether they had conducted training activities that addressed various CSP concepts and skills in their group homes. One third of these participants stated that they had not conducted any training activities up to that point. Only 10% claimed that they had conducted five or more activities. Table 1 shows the percentage of participants who reported having conducted training activities for each of the five skill areas.

The data shown in Table 1 provide only a partial picture of the extent to which participants transferred the CSP concepts to the staff in their group

Table 2. Amount of Discussion About CSP Concepts That Took Place in Group Homes After Training Began

Discussion topic[a]	Overall mean	Control group	No-show homes	Nonattenders			Attenders			Overall F
				1–4	5–8	9–16	1–2	3–4	5–6	
				(person-sessions)			(sessions attended)			
Providing constructive feedback	2.38	2.28	2.10	2.28	2.32	2.51	2.86	2.64	2.97	7.14*
Making requests of others	2.52	2.48	2.29	2.15	2.53	2.58	2.73	2.80	3.01	4.89*
Clarifying misunderstandings	2.73	2.70	2.55	2.46	2.75	2.75	3.20	2.96	3.15	3.55*
Handling disagreements	2.33	2.22	2.11	2.15	2.40	2.43	2.80	2.52	2.89	5.86*
All topics	2.51	2.44	2.28	2.33	2.56	2.57	2.85	2.82	2.99	6.64*

Note. CSP = Caregiver Support Program.
[a]All items were measured on a 5-point scale: none (1), a little (2), some (3), quite a bit (4), and a great deal (5).

homes. Participants could have conducted training activities after the completion of the CSP program. In addition, participants who did not attend the last session did not have a chance to report their training activities (and thus are not included in the table).

All of the caregivers in the study were asked on the second survey (conducted 5 weeks posttraining) to report the amount of discussion about topics covered in the CSP that had taken place in the past 2 months in their group homes. Table 2 shows the overall means on these items and the means for the control group and subgroups of the experimental group. These subgroups are defined by the amount of exposure that employees had to the CSP (as explained earlier). The overall sample means indicate that, in general, respondents reported that between "a little" to "some" discussion on these topics had taken place. The F tests indicated that the groups of employees did report different mean levels of discussion. Pairwise comparisons (not shown in the table) indicated that nonattenders reported having had more discussion about constructive feedback and handling disagreements than did employees in the control group. However, there were no differences between nonattenders and control group employees for the other items. In addition, although the pattern of means showed a trend for nonattenders with more indirect exposure to the CSP to report having had more discussions about these topics than nonattenders with less indirect exposure, the differences between the groups of nonattenders were not statistically significant. This suggests that the attenders, no matter how much exposure they had to the CSP, did not discuss the material with others in the group home to any great extent and that the train-the-trainer approach was therefore not successful.

Interestingly, pairwise comparisons showed that attenders reported significantly greater amounts of discussion of these topics than did all the other groups. (The number of sessions attended did not affect the amount of discussion reported.) The attenders worked in the same group homes as did the nonattenders. Why did they report that more discussion had taken place than their coworkers reported? There are a few possible explanations for this finding. If the discussions took place informally rather than at a meeting, attenders would have been involved in all of the discussions, but only a few of the nonattenders might have been involved. A second possibility is that attenders were better at recalling the discussions because they had initiated them, and the topics were more salient to them having had attended the CSP training. A third possibility is that the attenders thought they were having discussions about these topics but that the discussions were so abstract or obtuse that nonattenders did not even understand what the foci of the discussions were. Finally, demand characteristics may explain why attenders reported having had more discussion in their group homes. Having attended the CSP sessions, they were well aware that the facilitators of the sessions hoped and expected that they would conduct training sessions on these topics back at the group homes. Wanting to appear compliant, attenders might have inflated their reports of the amount of discussion that took place. Unfortunately, from the data available, we cannot choose between these rival explanations.

Table 3. Regression Coefficients for Intervention Effects by Amount to Exposure of CSP Training

Exposure to intervention	Interpersonal skills-related outcomes				Group problem-solving outcomes			Overall outcomes	
	Supervisor support ($n=1{,}267$)	Supportive feedback ($n=1{,}282$)	Self-appraisal of coping ($n=1{,}271$)	Handling disagreements ($n=1{,}270$)	Group problem solving ($n=1{,}248$)	Positive work team functioning ($n=1{,}276$)	Work team climate ($n=1{,}269$)	Mental health ($n=1{,}240$)	Job satisfaction ($n=1{,}237$)
Experimental–control comparisons[a]	—	.15**	.15***	—	.08**	.08**	.09**	.04**	—
Dosage comparisons									
No shows[b]	—	—	—	—	—	—	—	—	-.12**
Nonattenders in show homes	—	—	—	—	—	—	—	—	—
Attenders									
1–2 Sessions	—	—	.59***	.38**	—	—	—	—	—
3–4 Sessions	—	—	.71***	—	.26*	.33**	—	—	—
5–6 Sessions	.40****	.69****	.68****	.26**	.32****	.35****	.33****	.14***	.21***

Note. Regression models include Time 1 dependent variable and seven variables for which there were experimental–control differences at Time 1: role overload, coping with overload, support from provider agency, support from neighbors and the community, support from clients' families, group home coping style of bringing problems out in the open, and group home coping style of smoothing things over.

[a] Dummy variable coded 1 = experimental group, 0 = control group.

[b] Control group is the omitted category.

*$p < .10$.   **$p < .05$.   ***$p < .01$.   ****$p < .001$.

Impact of the Caregiver Support Program

Table 3 shows standard experimental–control comparisons. Regression models for each dependent variable included the Time 1 measure of the dependent variable, seven variables on which the experimental and control groups differed at Time 1, and a dummy variable coded 1 for the experimental group and 0 for the control group. From this table, one can see that the intervention group experienced greater increases than the control group in supportive feedback, self-appraisal of coping, group problem solving, positive work team functioning, work team climate, and overall mental health. There were no differences between the two groups on job satisfaction, supervisor support, and handling disagreements.

Given the rates of participation in the CSP and the lack of success of the train-the-trainer approach, it is not surprising that the experimental–control comparisons indicate weak intervention effects. All of the outcome measures assume transfer to the worksite. In other words, study participants were asked about processes, events, and behaviors that took place at the workplace, not in the training context.

When subgroups of the experimental group were compared with the control group (see Table 3), results indicate that all of the significant intervention effects were for CSP attenders and that employees who attended five or six sessions of the CSP experienced significantly more improvement on all of the program outcomes than did the control group employees. Nonattenders differed from the control group only on one outcome: They experienced a greater increase in supportive feedback. The level of indirect dosage experienced by nonattenders did not make a difference in terms of the outcomes.

The dosage comparisons should be interpreted with caution. The advantages of random assignment are lost when subgroups of the experimental group are examined. Thus, selection effects could have contributed to the between-groups differences. Controlling for the Time 1 level of the dependent variable minimized the effect of selection, but we could not ascertain that selection had no effect on the results. Keeping this caveat in mind, the results do suggest that the CSP increased the coping resources and enhanced the mental health and job satisfaction of those employees who attended all or almost all of its six sessions.

Conclusions

The results of the field experiment reported here show that the worksite coping resources of social support and positive work team functioning can be enhanced through a programmatic change effort. Individual skill training and modifications in team decision-making processes increased the amount of supportive feedback on the job, strengthened participants' perceptions of their abilities to handle disagreements and overload at work, and enhanced the work team climate in the group homes. This suggests that work team processes and skills in mobilizing social support are causal determinants of worksite coping resources. Thus, even though personality characteristics and macrosocial structures may have an impact on levels of social support (House, Umberson, & Landis, 1988) and climate for participation (Karasek & Theorell, 1990), so, too, do proximal work processes and individual skill training.

The CSP also enhanced the mental health and job satisfaction of those who attended at least five of the six training sessions. Job satisfaction has been shown to be strongly negatively correlated with both intent to leave one's job and with turnover in various human-services occupations (Shore & Martin, 1989). In the current study, 22% of the caregivers left their jobs during the 4.5 months of the study. Thus, a program that increased job satisfaction could reduce the high rate of staff turnover in community residential care, thus enhancing the quality and continuity of care received by clients in the group homes.

That benefits from the CSP were experienced only by those who attended the CSP sessions calls into question the usefulness of the train-the-trainer approach. As described previously, the program's learning processes were carefully developed to maximize the transfer of learnings from the training context to the worksite. Even with this careful attention, neither formal training activities nor informal discussions about CSP issues were conducted to any great extent with the rest of the staff. Perhaps the burden of planning, scheduling, and facilitating training activities was too onerous for caregivers who already felt overworked. Although the opportunity to increase the competence of home managers and direct-care staff in training other staff is attractive and theoretically useful in a high-turnover occupation, it may not be workable in a high-stress work environment.

Another possible explanation for the limited effects of the CSP is that efforts to change individuals' work-related attitudes and behaviors may have little success unless the organizational environment reinforces them (House, 1981). House managers, who attended the training sessions, were likely to support and reinforce efforts by their staff to try to improve interpersonal relationships and work team functioning. However, house managers might not have been rewarded for or encouraged in their own efforts by their supervisors. Provider agencies were encouraged by the project team to support the goals of the CSP, but they were given no specific guidelines on how to do so.

The CSP is a first step toward the development of effective approaches for increasing coping resources and reducing stress-related symptoms in human services workers. Future efforts to increase work-related coping resources should build on the learning activities and processes used in the CSP. Modifications might include providing training to all members of the work teams and developing organizational level reward structures for successful implementation of CSP concepts and skills.

References

Abbey, A., Abramis, D. J., & Caplan, R. D. (1985). Effects of different sources of social support and social conflict on emotional well-being. *Basic and Applied Social Psychology, 6*, 111–129.

Andrews, F. M., & Withey, S. B. (1976). *Social indicators of well-being: Americans' perceptions of life quality*. New York: Plenum.

Antonovsky, A. (1979). *Health, stress and coping*. San Francisco: Jossey-Bass.

Baldwin, T. T., & Ford, J. K. (1988). Transfer of training: A review and directions for future research. *Personnel Psychology, 41*, 63–105.

Bandura, A. (1977). *Social learning theory*. Englewood Cliffs, NJ: Prentice Hall.

Cherniss, C. (1980). *Staff burnout: Job stress in the human services*. Beverly Hills, CA: Sage.

Cherniss, C., & Egnatios, E. (1978). Participation in decision-making by staff in community mental health programs. *American Journal of Community Psychology, 5*, 171–190.

Cox, T. (1987). Stress, coping, and problem solving. *Work and Stress, 1*, 5–14.

Derogatis, L. R., Rikels, K., & Rock, A. F. (1976). The SCL-90 and MMPI: A step in the validation of a new self-report scale. *British Journal of Psychiatry, 128*, 280–289.

Eckenrode, J. (1983). The mobilization of social supports: Some individual constraints. *American Journal of Community Psychology, 11*, 509–528.

Edelwich, J., & Brodsky, A. (1980). *Burn-out: Stages of disillusionment in the helping professions*. New York: Human Sciences Press.

Fleishman, J. A. (1984). Personality characteristics and coping patterns. *Journal of Health and Social Behavior, 25*, 229–244.

Ganster, D. (1988). Improving measures of worker control in occupational stress research. In J. Hurrell, L. Murphy, S. Sauter, & C. Cooper (Eds.), *Occupational stress: Issues and developments in research* (pp. 88–99). Washington, DC: Taylor & Francis.

Goldstein, A. P., Lopez, M., & Greenleaf, D. O. (1979). Introduction. In A. P. Goldstein & F. H. Kanfer (Eds.), *Maximizing treatment gains* (pp. 1–15). San Diego, CA: Academic Press.

Gottlieb, B. H. (1988). Marshalling social support: The state of the art in research and practice. In B. H. Gottlieb (Ed.), *Marshalling social support* (pp. 11–51). Beverly Hills, CA: Sage.

Heaney, C. A., & van Ryn, M. (1990). Broadening the scope of worksite stress programs: A guiding framework. *American Journal of Health Promotion, 4*, 413–420.

House, J. S. (1981). *Work stress and social support*. Reading, MA: Addison-Wesley.

House, J. S., Umberson, D., & Landis, K. R. (1988). Structures and processes of social support. *Annual Review of Sociology, 14*, 293–318.

Ivancevich, J. M., Matteson, M. T., Freedman, S. M., & Phillips, J. S. (1990). Worksite stress management interventions. *American Psychologist, 45*, 252–261.

Jackson, S. E. (1983). Participation in decision making as a strategy for reducing job-related strain. *Journal of Applied Psychology, 68*, 3–19.

Janis, I. L. (1983). *Short-term counseling*. New Haven, CT: Yale University Press.

Johnson, D. W., & Johnson, F. P. (1982). *Joining together: Group theory and group skills*. Englewood Cliffs, NJ: Prentice Hall.

Karasek, R. (1979). Job demands, job decision latitude, and mental strain. *Administrative Science Quarterly, 24*, 285–307.

Karasek, R. A., & Theorell, T. (1990). *Healthy work: Stress, productivity and the reconstruction of working life*. New York: Basic Books.

Lazarus, R. S. (1966). *Psychosocial stress and the coping process*. Elmsford, NY: Pergamon Press.

Meichenbaum, D. (1985). *Stress inoculation training*. Elmsford, NY: Pergamon Press.

Menaghan, E. G. (1983). Individual coping efforts: Moderators of the relationship between life stress and mental health outcomes. In H. B. Kaplan (Ed.), *Psychosocial stress: Trends in theory and research* (pp. 157–191). San Diego, CA: Academic Press.

Morris, J. H., Steers, R. M., & Koch, J. L. (1979). Influence of organizational structure on role conflict and ambiguity for three occupational groupings. *Academy of Management Journal, 22*, 58–71.

Murphy, L. R. (1988). Workplace interventions for stress reduction and prevention. In C. L. Cooper & R. Payne (Eds.), *Causes, coping and consequences of stress at work* (pp. 301–339). New York: Wiley.

Pearlin, L. I., & Schooler, C. (1978). The structure of coping. *Journal of Health and Social Behavior, 19*, 2–21.

Shinn, M., Rosario, M., March, H., & Chestnut, D. E. (1984). Coping with job stress and burnout in the human services. *Journal of Personality and Social Psychology, 46*, 864–876.

Shore, L. M., & Martin, H. J. (1989). Job satisfaction and organizational commitment in relation to work performance and turnover intentions. *Human Relations, 42*, 625–638.

Spector, P. (1986). Perceived control by employees: A meta-analysis of studies concerning autonomy and participation at work. *Human Relations, 39*, 1005–1016.

Thoits, P. (1986). Social support as coping assistance. *Journal of Consulting and Clinical Psychology, 54*, 416–423.

U.S. Department of Health and Human Services, Public Health Service. (1993). 1992 National survey of worksite health promotion activities summary. *American Journal of Health Promotion, 7*, 452–464.

U.S. Department of Health and Human Services, Public Health Service, Office of Disease Prevention and Health Promotion. (1987). *National survey of worksite health promotion activities: A summary*. Washington, DC: U.S. Government Printing Office.

Van de Ven, A. H. (1982). Group decision-making and effectiveness. In D. Roben & S. Altman (Eds.), *Organizational development: Progress and perspectives* (pp. 207–221). New York: Macmillan.

8

An Investigation of Job-Related Coping Strategies Across Multiple Stressors and Samples

Carlla S. Smith and Lorne M. Sulsky

A consistent theme permeating the psychological stress literature is that stress has potentially deleterious effects on individual attitudes and behaviors, as well as on physical and mental well-being. Therefore, it is not surprising that researchers have focused their investigative efforts on how people manage or cope with stress in a variety of life domains (e.g., Lazarus & Folkman, 1984; Osipow & Davis, 1988; Roth & Cohen, 1986). Toward that end, theoretical models of stress and coping have been developed to describe how people cope generally with a variety of life stressors (e.g., Lazarus & Folkman, 1984; Roth & Cohen, 1986) and specifically with organizational stressors (e.g., Beehr & Bhagat, 1985).

In the current study we used one theoretical framework of organizational stress, Schuler's (1985) integrative transactional process model of coping in organizations, as a general referent for examining the coping process at work. In focusing on the role of cognitive appraisal, Schuler's conceptualization draws heavily from Lazarus's cognitive–transactional model of stress (see Lazarus & Launier, 1978). Specifically, Schuler's model states that environmental (work) stressors serve as a "coping trigger" to initiate primary appraisal, where the question "What are the relevant stressors?" is posed. Identification of relevant stressors is followed by the coping strategy development and selection phase or secondary appraisal, where the question "What should I do now?" is asked. These coping strategies are implemented and, through a process of feedback and evaluation, affect individual responses (outcomes or strains), stress levels, and perhaps the environmental stressors themselves, all of which may influence future coping efforts. (Although we do not consider their effects here, Schuler's model also addresses other aspects of the appraisal process, such as the impact of the uncertainty and importance of the situation.)

Previous empirical research has largely attempted to link the reported use of coping strategies to personal and organizational outcomes (e.g., Latack, 1986; Osipow & Davis, 1988). The specific form of that link has often assumed that coping moderates the stressor–strain relation (e.g., Osipow & Davis, 1988). Other studies have examined individual differences, such as neuroticism or

Type A behavior, as potential predictors of coping type (e.g., Kirmeyer & Diamond, 1985; Parkes, 1986). However, to our knowledge, no organizational research has systematically investigated primary appraisal (i.e., "What are the relevant job stressors?") or the link between primary appraisal and secondary appraisal (i.e., given certain job stressors, "What should I do now?"). In other words, these critical, initial stages of the coping process at work have mostly been unexplored in empirical research.

Although researchers have not generally attempted to investigate primary appraisal in work settings, some mention is usually made of the stressor referents participants use when describing their coping episodes. Most commonly, the stressor referents are some type of work role stressor (e.g., Latack, 1986) or a generalized or unspecified job stressor (e.g., Dewe & Guest, 1990). There also is little evidence on whether different types of job stressors influence secondary appraisal. The results of studies investigating general life stressors (e.g., Folkman & Lazarus, 1980) and organizational stressors (e.g., Parkes, 1986) have suggested that coping may vary with the type of stressor encountered. For example, Folkman and Lazarus (1980) reported that their respondents coped with work-related events differently from with health- or family related events. Parkes (1986) also found that coping type varied across five different categories of stressful work episodes.

If job-related coping is contextually determined (i.e., yoked to stressors or types of stressors), generalized comparisons of coping across studies may be somewhat akin to comparing apples and oranges. Researchers' preoccupation with work role stressors might have also restricted the range of reported coping responses in prior organizational research.

The purpose of the present study was, within the work context, to examine primary appraisal, the relation between primary appraisal and secondary appraisal, and the relation between secondary appraisal and coping outcomes. Clarification of the role of appraisal in the coping process should facilitate the development of substantive organizational coping theory and the design of more effective stress management programs for industry.

First, for a broad cross section of workers, we wanted to identify the most bothersome job-related stressors from a varied array of stressors. Such information should help researchers identify the content domain of stressors generally experienced in work settings.

Second, we wanted to determine how workers would actually cope with these diverse stressors; specifically, do workers cope similarly with several different stressors or are their coping strategies tailored to specific stressors? For example, stressors such as physically dangerous work environments or time pressure to complete work projects may elicit much different coping behaviors from workers than dealing with an incompetent coworker or interpersonal friction with a supervisor.

Third, we wanted to investigate the link between secondary appraisal and coping outcomes. To achieve that goal, we examined relations between coping behaviors, stress levels, and individual and organizational outcomes. Consistent with prior research, we expected that active coping strategies, or attempts to change the stressful situation, should be positively related to job satisfaction and negatively related to health problems, stress levels, and (organizational) turnover intentions. Palliative coping, or attempts merely to manage the emotional distress triggered by the stressful situation, should be negatively related to job satisfaction and positively related to health problems, stress levels, and turnover intentions (e.g., Folkman & Lazarus, 1980; Latack, 1986; Pearlin & Schooler, 1978).

Because researchers have found support for both additive or main effects (e.g., Folkman & Lazarus, 1980; Latack, 1986) and interactive (Kobasa, Maddi, & Puccetti, 1982; Parkes, 1990) models of coping, we examined both types in our data. In main effects models, the relations between coping and outcomes do not vary with the level of stress. In interactive models, coping functions as a moderator of the stress–outcome relation (i.e., type of coping covaries with the level of reported stress). For example, palliative coping may be used predominately when stress levels are perceived to be high.

Our study also extended prior research in two ways. We used coping scales designed specifically for the work context. Organizational coping research has frequently used coping scales developed for general life stressors (e.g., Parkes, 1990), which may be less appropriate. Also, to enhance generalizability, these issues were examined in three diverse samples of workers.

Method

Participants and Data Collection

Sample 1. The sample consisted of 160 faculty, administrative, and support staff in a community college in southeastern Canada. The sample was 62% female. More than 70% were 31–50 years of age; 17% were older than 50. More than 38% of the sample had completed college, of which 47% had graduate training or graduate degrees. Forty percent of the sample had been with their organizations 3–10 years, whereas more than 30% had more than 10 years of tenure. Examination of organizational records indicated that this sample was demographically representative of employees within the organization.

The college personnel department requested that all faculty and staff participate in answering questionnaires that assessed employee job satisfaction, stress, and health in the college system. Participation was totally voluntary. Employees answered the surveys in two sessions at their workstations.

Of the original 160 surveys distributed, 82 usable surveys were returned from both sessions, a response rate of 54%. The final sample was demographically similar to the original sample.

Sample 2. Fifty-five salaried personnel at a small heavy metal foundry in northwestern Ohio participated in the study. More than 46% of the workers were 30–50 years old; 29% were older than 50. Sixty-three percent were male. Slightly more than 50% had graduated only high school, whereas 50% had either attended or graduated college. Almost 65% of the sample had been with their company more than 10 years. They were drawn from the accounting, engineering, general office, machine shop, and sales departments and were demographically representative of salaried workers in the organization.

Participants voluntarily attended a meeting during normal working hours to answer an organizational survey measuring employee attitudes and health. All 55 questionnaires provided usable data.

Sample 3. The sample consisted of 432 full-time workers of organizations, primarily from Ohio and surrounding states. The occupations of these workers included substantial representation from both white-collar (70%) and blue-collar (30%) jobs, ranging from business executives to foundry workers. The sample was predominantly female (60%), of whom 32% were younger than 25 years of age and 28% were older than 40. Approximately 35% had finished some college work, whereas almost 40% had completed college or some graduate work. More than 50% of the sample had been with their present company 3 years or less.

These data were collected as part of course requirements for a class field project in an advanced undergraduate organizational psychology course. The students were provided with questionnaires assessing demographic characteristics, organizational stress, job attitudes, and self-reported health and were trained to administer them. They were instructed to administer the surveys to 10 adults employed full time in any work setting. Responses were totally anonymous. Of the 432 surveys returned, 415 were usable.

Measures

Job-related stressors. Organizational stressors were measured with the Job Stress Index (JSI; Sandman, 1992; Sandman & Smith, 1988), an 82-item scale with 11 distinct subscales: lack of feedback, lack of participation, lack of achievement, lack of competence of supervision, lack of interpersonal skills of supervisor, lack of competency of others, lack of interpersonal skills of others, red tape, time pressure, job insecurity, and physical demands and dangers. The 11 scales have a 3-point response format that assesses the presence of each stressor (1 = no, 2 = undecided, and 3 = yes).

These scales were developed in a series of studies in five diverse organizations: civil service, a large grocery store chain, university maintenance workers, a mental health facility, and a large astronautics firm (sample sizes ranged from 265 to 4,487). Sandman and Smith (1988) reported that in the most recent large sample (N = 4,487), the coefficient alpha was .79 for an average of the 11 scales (ranging from .70 for job insecurity to .91 for time pressure); comparable internal consistency reliabilities have been found across other samples. The range of the reliability estimates in the present samples was highly similar. The construct validity of the scales has been supported by their relations with variables such as job satisfaction, management attitudes, and intent to quit (the job). Definitions of the dimensions and examples of one item from each scale are provided in the Appendix.

Job satisfaction. Job satisfaction was measured with the Job In General scale (JIG; Ironson, Smith, Brannick, Gibson, & Paul, 1989). The scale has 18 global evaluative items and a scale format similar to the Job Descriptive Index (Smith, Kendall, & Hulin, 1969) and the JSI. Ironson et al. (1989) reported that the scale has a coefficient alpha of .91 and demonstrates adequate convergent and discriminant validity.

Global job stress. Global job stress was measured with the Stress In General scale (SIG; Smith et al., 1992), which was patterned after the JIG scale discussed previously. The scale has 18 global evaluative items that assess general perceptions of stress at work. Smith et al. (1992) reported that results from four separate samples demonstrated stability in psychometric properties and evidence of convergent and discriminant validity.

Self-reported health. Self-reported health was measured with three scales developed by Moos, Cronkite, Billings, and Finney (1986). A 14-item scale assesses medical conditions during the past 12 months (e.g., diabetes, high blood pressure). A 12-item scale assesses physical symptoms that have occurred fairly often within the past 12 months (e.g., headaches, acid stomach). A six-item scale assesses depressed mood during the past 12 months (e.g., felt irritable, felt you were a worrier). Moos et al. (1986) reported coefficient alphas of .80 for physical symptoms and .69 for depressed mood in a large adult sample. (They considered the internal consistency reliability for medical conditions to be inappropriate because the items are essentially independent.) All scales require the respondent to check applicable terms.

Coping behaviors. Coping behaviors were measured with Latack's (1986) Control, Escape, and Symptom Management Coping scales. Control coping strategies are active or problem-focused cognitions and behaviors (e.g., "Think about the challenges I can find in this situation," "Devote more time and energy to doing my job"), and escape coping strategies are palliative or emotion-focused cognitions and behaviors (e.g., "Remind myself that work isn't everything," "Avoid being in this situation if I can"). Symptom management strategies are used merely to alleviate stress-related symptoms (e.g., take tranquilizers, sedatives, or other drugs; do physical exercise) and also are assumed to be a form of palliative coping.

Latack (1986) attempted to establish the validity of these coping dimensions by examining relations among the coping behaviors and various personal and job-related outcomes. As hypothesized, she found that control coping was related to positive outcomes and that escape and symptom management coping were related to negative outcomes. The coping scales are demonstrated acceptable internal consistency reliabilities (Control = .70–.85; Escape = .54–.71; Symptom Management = .70).

In the current study, respondents in Sample 1 were randomly assigned their stressor referent from a pool of work stressors (i.e., items on the JSI) they previously rated as stressful. However, because of organizational constraints, respondents in Samples 2 and 3 were allowed to choose their stressor referent; this stressor could be chosen from the items on the JSI or individually generated. (All respondents selected an item either from the JSI or one similar to an item on the JSI.) They were instructed to select any stressor that was particularly bothersome for them. This simplified procedure allowed the data from Samples 2 and 3 to be collected in single administrations of the survey. All participants were asked to refer to their stressor referent when responding to the items on the coping scales and to check off any strategies they had actually used in managing the stressor. (Because of organizational time constraints, Latack's original 5-point coping scale format was not used.)

Intent to quit. Organizational turnover intentions were assessed with a three-item scale ("Are you presently looking for another job?"; "How likely is it that you will quit your present job?"; "How frequently do you think about leaving your present job for good?"). Responses to the three items are indicated by referring to a 5-point Likert-type response format. This variable was included because organizational turnover is a probable outcome of experiencing job-related stress (Jackson & Schuler, 1985).

Data Analyses

The relation between primary appraisal and secondary appraisal was examined with a Coping Behaviors × Stressor Types repeated measures analysis of variance (ANOVA). Each respondent checked off applicable items for all three coping scales and consequently received a score of zero or higher on each. Therefore, coping was treated as a repeated measures variable. Because each coping scale has a different number of items, these frequency counts were converted to proportions of total possible within-coping category responses for statistical analyses. Each respondent referred to only one stressor, so type of stressor served as the between-subjects variable.

In the repeated measures ANOVA, a main effect of coping would indicate that proportions of reported coping behaviors were not equal across the three coping types. A main effect for stressor type would mean that stressor types were differentially represented (i.e., more coping behaviors were used for one type of stressor than for others). An interaction between coping and stressor types would indicate that the proportion of different types of coping strategies varied across different types of stressors.

For Samples 1 and 2, any stressor category that contained three or fewer responses across respondents was omitted from the ANOVA analysis, which created missing data ($ns = 44$ and 37 for Samples 1 and 2, respectively; ANOVA only). This criterion was arbitrary, although it was based on cell size (statistical power) considerations. This criterion produced a 3 (coping types) × 5 (stressor types) design in Sample 1 and a 3 (coping types) × 6 (stressor types) in Sample 2. Given the much larger size of Sample 3, we adopted a more stringent criterion for inclusion in the ANOVA: Stressor categories were excluded if they contained fewer than 15 responses ($n = 232$ for Sample 3; ANOVA only), which produced a 3 (coping types) × 8 (stressor types) design for Sample 3. To determine whether our arbitrary criteria for inclusion were biasing the results, we performed the ANOVAs using both larger and smaller categories of stressors and found no overall differences in the results for each sample.

Because both proportional (i.e., coping data) and frequency (i.e., health data) data are not normally distributed, both types of data were normalized before submitting them to statistical analyses. However, the results were highly similar in both the unnormalized and normalized solutions. To preserve the original scale metrics, we present unnormalized results here.

To examine the main effects and interactions between coping behaviors and perceived stress on strains, we used hierarchical moderated regression analyses (Cohen & Cohen, 1983). The data were entered into the regression equations in three blocks: The main effects for the perceived stress and coping scales were entered in the first and second blocks, respectively; in the third block, the Coping × Stress interactions for the three coping types were entered.

In Sample 3, all analyses were repeated for one demographic variable, white- and blue-collar subgroups. Classification by "collar color" was achieved by referring to the *Dictionary of Occupational Titles'* occupational categories. If a job could not be classified as either professional, technical, clerical, or sales, it was classified as blue-collar (e.g., processing, benchwork, or machine trades).

Results

To answer one of our research questions—"What are the relevant stressors?" (primary appraisal)—we examined the stressor types most frequently nominated as being stressful in each sample. In Sample 1, time pressure, which was chosen by 26% of the respondents, was the most frequently cited stressor. In Sample 2, lack of competence of others, which was chosen by 22% of the respondents, was the most frequently cited stressor. The most frequently nominated stressor in Sample 3 was time pressure, with 27% of the respondents indicating that it was stressful for them. Collapsing across the three samples, "people-oriented" stressors (i.e., lack of competence of supervisor and coworkers, and lack of interpersonal skills of supervisor and coworkers) accounted for 24% of the total stressor nominations.

To investigate the link between primary and secondary appraisal, we conducted repeated measures ANOVAs of the coping categories and stressor dimensions for the three samples. The repeated measures analyses across the samples indicated a large main effect for coping; Sample 1, $F(2, 78) = 54.13$, $p < .01$; Sample 2, $F(2, 62) = 39.44$, $p < .01$; Sample 3, $F(2, 448) = 73.52$, $p < .01$ (Greenhouse-Geiser correction for nonindependence of the repeated measures variable). Neither the main effect for stressor type nor the interaction between stressor type and coping was significant in any analysis. The cell means (proportions of total possible coping strategies) are provided for each sample in Table 1. In all three samples, respondents reported that they used primarily control-type coping strategies in managing the job-related stressors, followed by escape strategies; symptom management coping was reported the least frequently.

Table 1. Cell Means: Total Within Category Proportions of Coping Behaviors Across Samples

Management	Coping behaviors		
	Control	Escape	Symptom
Sample 1	.79	.66	.41
Sample 2	.43	.27	.11
Sample 3	.40	.28	.21

To show the associations between secondary appraisal and coping outcomes, Tables 2 and 3 show the correlations between coping, perceived stress, and coping outcomes for the three samples. All correlations functioned as predicted except control coping, which was generally positively related to stress and health and unrelated to job satisfaction across samples. The three coping variables were also moderately positively intercorrelated across samples.

More complex relations between coping and strains were examined with hierarchical moderated regression analyses. These regression analyses, which examined the associations between coping outcomes, stress, coping, and the Stress × Coping interactions, revealed no significant interactions when the interaction terms were entered last. These results indicate support for the additive model. That is, the relationships between coping and strains did not vary as a function of the level of perceived stress.

Because entering the interaction terms last provides a conservative test of their effects, we varied the order of entry of the blocks of predictors in a usefulness analysis (Darlington, 1968); specifically, the interaction terms were entered first, followed by the other two blocks. This second set of regression analyses showed more support for interactive coping models in two of the samples. However, given the statistically liberal nature of these tests and the complexity of the effects, we do not present the results here. (The results of the usefulness analyses can be obtained from the first author.)

Splitting Sample 3 into white- and blue-collar subgroups yielded similar patterns of results between the subgroup and total sample analyses. However, when white- and blue-collar responses were compared, some specific differences became apparent. Relative to white-collar workers, blue-collar workers reported lower job satisfaction, $t(402) = 4.20$, $p < .01$; more physical symptoms, $t(415) = 2.98$, $p < .01$; higher depressed mood, $t(415) = 2.32$, $p < .05$; higher intent to quit, $t(413) = 2.54$, $p < .05$; and greater use of escape coping, $t(416) = 1.96$, $p < .01$.

Discussion

When asked to identify their most bothersome job-related stressor, workers in three diverse samples selected several different types of stressors from 11 categories of stressors. In two of the three samples, time pressure was nominated most frequently as stressful; lack of competence of coworkers was most frequently chosen in the other sample. People-oriented stressors, which involve

Table 2. Intercorrelations Between Coping Behaviors, Stress, and Outcome Measures for Samples 1 and 2

Sample and variable	Control	Escape	Symptom measurement	Global job satisfaction	Global job stress	Medical conditions	Physical symptoms	Depressed mood
Sample 1 (n = 82)								
Control	.66							
Escape	.41*	.68						
Symptom management	.41*	.51*	.85					
Global job satisfaction	.02	−.25*	−.27*	.79				
Global job stress	.21	.17	.25*	−.37*	.88			
Medical conditions	.02	.08	.19	−.22*	.20	—		
Physical symptoms	.11	.06	.22*	−.18	.41*	.32*	.74	
Depressed mood	.03	.10	.39*	−.34*	.28*	.25*	.56*	.70
Sample 2 (n = 55)								
Control	.82							
Escape	.56*	.92						
Symptom management	.56*	.66*	.92					
Global job satisfaction	−.08	−.33*	−.17	.88				
Global job stress	.35*	.51*	.45*	−.22	.88			
Medical conditions	.35*	.37*	.19	−.09	.36*	—		
Physical symptoms	.21	.47*	.35*	−.29*	.42*	.61*	.81	
Depressed mood	.15	.38*	.28*	−.16	.35*	.44*	.64*	.78

Note. Coefficient alphas are on the diagonal.
*$p \leq .05$.

Table 3. Intercorrelations Between Coping Behaviors, Stress, and Outcome Measures for Sample 3 ($n = 415$)

Variable	Control	Escape	Symptom management	Global job satisfaction	Global job stress	Medical conditions	Physical symptoms	Depressed mood	Intention to quit
Control	.84								
Escape	.46*	.80							
Symptom management	.49*	.49*	.89						
Global job satisfaction	.04	−.15*	−.14*	.93					
Global job stress	.16*	.14*	.20*	−.43*	.91				
Medical conditions	−.03	.02	.04	−.07	.10*	—			
Physical symptoms	.06	.12*	.22*	−.28*	.33*	.31*	.81		
Depressed mood	.15*	.25*	.22*	−.28*	.28*	.19*	.60*	.77	
Intent to quit	−.07	.00	.10*	−.52*	.16*	−.08	.14*	.20*	.74

Note. Coefficient alphas are on the diagonal.

*$p \leq .05$.

interpersonal or competency issues with coworkers or supervisors, were nominated by almost 25% of the respondents across the three samples. These results clearly indicate the need to investigate stressors other than typical work role stressors (i.e., role conflict and ambiguity) in organizations, a sentiment echoed by other researchers (Jex & Beehr, 1991).

We examined the link between primary appraisal and secondary appraisal. That is, we investigated whether specific types of stressors would be associated with certain types of coping behaviors. Our results are consistent across the three samples and demonstrate that workers used primarily active (control) coping strategies when managing job-related stressors. However, palliative coping (i.e., escape and, to a lesser extent, symptom management) was also reported. Workers did not indicate that they used different types or amounts of coping behaviors in managing varied types of stressors at work.

Similar to prior research (Folkman & Lazarus, 1980; Folkman, Lazarus, Dunkel-Schetter, DeLongis, & Gruen, 1986; Parkes, 1986), we found that workers reported using a variety of different types of coping strategies in managing their job-related stressors, although active coping predominated. This finding simply suggests that workers generally turned to active coping when managing several types of organizational stressors, but it suggests nothing about the effectiveness of their efforts. Contrary to conventional wisdom, which assumes that people should be taught to increase their use of active coping strategies, our data indicate that such stress management interventions may be unnecessary; workers reported that they tried large numbers of active coping strategies. However, they may indeed need to be trained to more effectively use these active strategies or to manage the stress generated from unsuccessful coping attempts.

Our last research goal was to examine the relation between secondary appraisal and coping outcomes. Across two or more samples, we found that increased use of escape and symptom management strategies was associated with higher global job stress, more physical symptoms, increased depressed mood, and lower job satisfaction. In more than one sample, the increased use of control strategies was associated with higher global job stress and more health problems (i.e., medical conditions, physical symptoms, or depressed mood). Surprisingly, across all samples, the use of different types of coping did not vary with the levels of reported stress. In the third sample, although investigations of primary and secondary appraisal yielded a similar pattern of results across blue- and white-collar subgroups, some differences were apparent. These differences (i.e., increased palliative coping and health problems, higher intent to quit, and lower job satisfaction in blue-collar workers) are consistent with previous research on blue-collar workers (e.g., Wallace, Levens, & Singer, 1988).

The relations between escape and symptom management coping, stress, and outcomes were stronger and more consistent across samples than comparable relations between control coping and these variables, a finding that is consistent with the results of prior research (Holahan & Moos, 1985). In addition, the three coping scales were moderately positively intercorrelated (see Tables 2 and 3), which is also consistent with prior research (Holahan &

Moos, 1985; Roth & Cohen, 1986). When experiencing stress at work, most people drew on both active and palliative coping strategies. However, the palliative strategies were typically more strongly associated with the development of strains, especially health problems.

Our results indicate that palliative coping strategies functioned as predicted. However, contrary to predictions and the results of prior research, control coping appeared to function similarly to palliative coping. These results may indicate a general stress mobilization effect such that, when confronted with an organizational stressor of sufficient magnitude, workers responded by drawing on any type of coping activity at their disposal. Because control coping would function similarly to the palliative strategies in this case, the effects should be similar regardless of the type of strategy used. We investigated this possibility by partialing perceived stress from the bivariate correlations between control coping and coping outcomes. The results of these analyses plus the usefulness analyses (see the Results section) showed a reversal in direction for some of the correlations that conformed to our original predictions.

Considering our results across three diverse samples, active or control coping appears to be governed by processes beyond the somewhat simplistic notions advanced in prior research (and in our hypotheses). Complex relations between control coping and stress-related variables may explain some unexpected results between active coping and strains in earlier studies (e.g., Kuhlmann, 1990; Osipow & Davis, 1988). Unraveling this complexity lies beyond the focus of our research; however, current methodological explorations of organizational coping behavior may shed some light on these issues (Sulsky & Smith, 1993).

Some limitations of our study should be addressed. One obvious criticism is that reports of control coping merely represent a social desirability bias of respondents (i.e., to present themselves favorably, people indicate they deal with stressors in a problem-solving manner). However, across all samples, respondents reported that they also used many palliative strategies. Latack (1986) also provided evidence that social desirability was not a strong alternative explanation of responses to the control and escape coping scales.

A more serious criticism is the cross-sectional nature of our (and much prior) coping research. Coping is essentially a longitudinal process, and to capture fully the dynamics of that process, a longitudinal design ideally should be used. One weakness of our design is that it is not sensitive to the dynamic relations among coping strategies. For example, using one strategy may preclude choosing a second strategy, which could have conceivably affected the final proportions of coping strategies reported for each category. Clearly, we need to study organizational coping "as it happens" through the use of a diary approach or another technique that captures the longitudinal nature of the coping process.

In conclusion, the results of our study demonstrate three important points. First, our data indicate that stress researchers should broaden their efforts to include organizational stressors other than only work role stressors. The discipline's almost myopic focus on work role stressors might have seriously limited the theoretical domains previously investigated. Second, because they already report using large numbers of active coping strategies, workers probably do not need to be trained to engage in even more active coping. However, they may benefit from stress management training that focuses on how to use active coping more effectively or to manage the stress generated from unsuccessful coping attempts. Third, the common, simplistic distinction between active and palliative coping may not be warranted in the work context, and active organizational coping may be governed by more complex processes than previously realized. These results have some direct implications for the focus of future organizational stress research and the design of stress management programs in industry.

References

Beehr, T. A., & Bhagat, T. S. (1985). *Human stress and cognition in organizations*. New York: Wiley.

Cohen, J., & Cohen, P. (1983). *Applied multiple regression/correlation analysis for the behavioral sciences*. Hillsdale, NJ: Erlbaum.

Darlington, R. B. (1968). Multiple regression in psychological research and practice. *Psychological Bulletin, 69*, 161–182.

Dewe, P., & Guest, D. (1990). Methods of coping with stress at work: A conceptual analysis and empirical study of measurement issues. *Journal of Organizational Behavior, 11*, 135–150.

Folkman, S., & Lazarus, R. (1980). An analysis of coping in middle-aged community sample. *Journal of Health and Social Behavior, 21*, 219–239.

Folkman, S., Lazarus, R. S., Dunkel-Schetter, C., DeLongis, A., & Gruen, R. (1986). Dynamics of a stressful encounter: Cognitive appraisal, coping, and encounter outcomes. *Journal of Personality and Social Psychology, 50*, 992–1003.

Holahan, C. J., & Moos, R. H. (1985). Life stress and health: Personality, coping, and family support in stress resistance. *Journal of Personality and Social Psychology, 49*, 739–747.

Ironson, G., Smith, P., Brannick, M., Gibson, Q., & Paul, K. (1989). Construction of a Job In General scale: A comparison of global, composite, and specific measures. *Journal of Applied Psychology, 74*, 193–200.

Jackson, S. E., & Schuler, R. S. (1985). A meta-analysis and conceptual critique of research on role ambiguity and role conflict in work settings. *Organizational Behavioral and Human Decision Processes, 36*, 16–28.

Jex, S. M., & Beehr, T. A. (1991). Emerging theoretical and methodological issues in the study of work-related stress. *Research in Personnel and Human Resources Management, 9*, 311–365.

Kirmeyer, S. L., & Diamond, A. (1985). Coping by police officers: A study of role stress and Type A and Type B behavior patterns. *Journal of Occupational Behavior, 6*, 183–195.

Kobasa, S. C., Maddi, S. R., & Puccetti, M. C. (1982). Personality and exercise as buffers in the stress–illness relationship. *Journal of Behavioral Medicine, 5*, 391–404.

Kuhlmann, T. (1990). Coping with occupational stress among urban bus and tram drivers. *Journal of Occupational Psychology, 63*, 89–96.

Latack, J. (1986). Coping with job stress: Measures and future directions for scale development. *Journal of Applied Psychology, 72*, 377–385.

Lazarus, R. S., & Folkman, S. (1984). *Stress, appraisal, and coping*. New York: Springer.

Lazarus, R. S., & Launier, R. (1978). Stress-related transactions between person and environment. In L. Pervin & M. Lewis (Eds.), *Perspectives in interactional psychology* (pp. 287–327). New York: Plenum.

Moos, R., Cronkite, R., Billings, A., & Finney, J. (1986). *Health and daily living from manual*. Palo Alto, CA: Social Ecology Laboratory.

Osipow, S., & Davis, A. (1988). The relationship of coping resources to occupational stress and strain. *Journal of Vocational Behavior, 32*, 1–15.

Parkes, K. R. (1986). Coping in stressful episodes: The role of individual differences, environmental factors, and situational characteristics. *Journal of Personality and Social Psychology, 51,* 1277–1292.

Parkes, K. R. (1990). Coping, negative affectivity, and the work environment: Additive and interactive predictors of mental health. *Journal of Applied Psychology, 75,* 399–409.

Pearlin, L., & Schooler, C. (1978). The structure of coping. *Journal of Health and Social Behavior, 19,* 2–21.

Roth, S., & Cohen, L. J. (1986). Approach, avoidance, and coping with stress. *American Psychologist, 41,* 813–819.

Sandman, B. A. (1992). The measurement of job stress: Development of the Job Stress Index. In C. Cranny, P. Smith, & E. Stone (Eds.), *Job satisfaction: How people feel about their jobs and how it affects their performance.* New York: Lexington Books.

Sandman, B., & Smith, P. (1988). *The Job Stress Index.* Perrysburg, OH: Smith, Sandman & McCreery.

Schuler, R. (1985). Integrative transactional process model of coping with stress in organizations. In T. Beehr & R. Bhagat (Eds.), *Human stress and cognition in organizations* (pp. 347–374). New York: Wiley.

Smith, P. C., Balzer, W. K., Ironson, G. H., Paul, K. B., Hayes, B., Moore-Hirschl, S., & Parra, L. F. (1992, April). *Development and validation of the Stress in General (SIG) scale.* Paper presented at the 7th Annual Meeting of the Society for Industrial and Organizational Society, Montreal.

Smith, P. C., Kendall, L. M., & Hulin, C. L. (1969). *The measurement of job satisfaction in work and retirement.* Chicago: Rand McNally.

Sulsky, L. M., & Smith, C. S. (1993). *Methodological concerns associated with research examining relationships between alternative coping strategies and outcomes.* Unpublished manuscript.

Wallace, W., Levens, M., & Singer, G. (1988). Blue collar stress. In C. Cooper & R. Payne (Eds.), *Causes, coping and consequences of stress at work* (pp. 53–76). New York: Wiley.

Appendix: Examples of Items From the 11 Dimensions of the Job Stress Index

1. *Lack of feedback:* Report of inadequate information from supervisor or the task itself concerning the level and quality of job performance ("Too little feedback about my performance").
2. *Lack of participation:* Feeling that the individual has too little influence on decisions that affect him or her ("My supervisor does not ask my opinion").
3. *Lack of achievement:* Report that job does not use abilities or give knowledge of task completion or feeling of accomplishment ("Job doesn't use my abilities").
4. *Lack of competence of supervision:* Perceived lack of job knowledge and competence of the supervisor ("My supervisor doesn't understand my job").
5. *Lack of interpersonal skills of supervisor:* Frictions and/or conflicts with the supervisor which interfere with a smooth working relationship ("My supervisor is inconsiderate").
6. *Lack of competence of others:* Perceived lack of competence and poor job performance of coworkers ("Other employees lack technical knowledge").
7. *Lack of interpersonal skills of others (coworkers):* Frictions and/or conflicts with coworkers which cause tensions impeding a smooth working relationship ("Other employees don't cooperate").
8. *Red tape:* Too much dealing with fixed procedures, paperwork, and regulations in the course of doing work ("Too many approvals needed to get things done").
9. *Time pressure:* Experience of inadequate time to do work and heavy work load, with resultant reports that the job is "hectic, tense," etc. ("Too many things are due at once").
10. *Job insecurity:* Fear and uncertainty about one's future on the job ("Uncertain about how company changes will affect my job").
11. *Physical demands and danger:* Discomfort and danger of the job ("Uncomfortable working conditions").

9

The Jobs I Preventive Intervention for Unemployed Individuals: Short- and Long-Term Effects on Reemployment and Mental Health

Amiram D. Vinokur, Richard H. Price,
Robert D. Caplan, Michelle van Ryn,
and Joan Curran

Because the fundamental causes of unemployment are rooted in societal economic processes, remedies to the adverse social effects of unemployment must be sought in comprehensive economic and social policies. Although social and economic policies need to address the problems that result from unemployment, various community efforts can be undertaken to reduce the taxing impact of unemployment at the local level. The Jobs Project at the University of Michigan was designed by Caplan, Vinokur, Price, and van Ryn (1989) as a research and evaluation project to test a preventive intervention for unemployed individuals. The intervention goals were to prevent the deterioration in mental health that often results from unemployment and to promote high-quality reemployment. To achieve its goals, the intervention was designed to provide participants with social support and a promotive learning environment to acquire job-search skills and inoculate the participants from common setbacks that are part of the job-seeking process. We tested this intervention in a large-scale randomized experimental field study using a large heterogeneous sample of 1,087 unemployed individuals who were recruited from Michigan unemployment offices in the greater Detroit area.

Caplan et al. (1989) described theories that address the enhancement of self-efficacy (Bandura, 1986), inoculation against setbacks (Kanfer & Goldstein, 1991; Marlatt & Gordon, 1985; Meichenbaum, 1985), and vigilant coping (Janis, 1982) that were used to guide our model of the effects of the Jobs intervention project. Following Lazarus's (1966) theory of stress and adaptation, we view coping with job loss as a process that starts with primary and secondary appraisal that include diagnosis and motivation to respond in spe-

This chapter is based on research conducted under National Institute of Mental Health Grants MH39675 and 2P50MH38330, with the latter representing the Michigan Prevention Research Center.

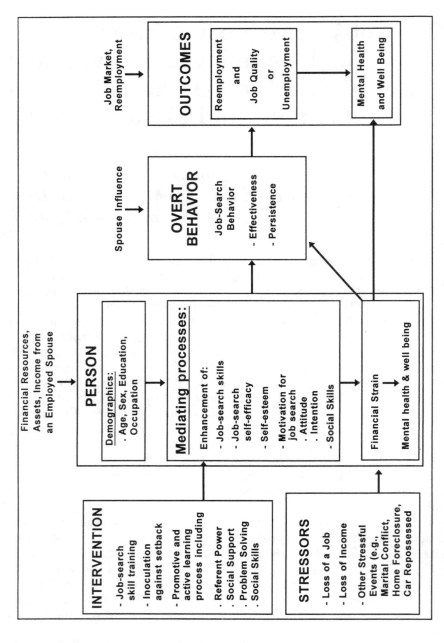

Figure 1. Effects of a self-efficacy-based job-search intervention for unemployed individuals on reemployment and well-being outcomes.

cific ways. Resultant coping may lead to reappraisals that the action is useful or, in the case of setbacks, that it is not. Such setbacks may undermine further use of the specific coping behavior. Consequently, to produce continued adherence to a new course of coping requires an additional intervention, referred to by Meichenbaum as "inoculation against setbacks." Such inoculation involves the acquisition of both cognitive and behavioral repertoires for continuing action despite temporary setbacks.

The quality of coping is assumed to be a multiplicative function of motivation to perform and skill. It follows that an adequate preventive intervention must provide substantive skills as well as the motivational concomitants (social reinforcement, inoculation against setbacks, increased self-esteem, and perceived competence). These motivational assets are associated with perceived control, or self-efficacy (e.g., Abramson, Seligman, & Teasdale, 1978; Bandura, 1977, 1986; Rotter, Chance, & Phares, 1972; Weiner, 1979). Unless job search self-efficacy is enhanced through the intervention, unemployed persons may restrict their information seeking, limit the alternatives they generate, and engage in less advanced contingency planning (Friedrich, 1987).

This rationale was used in our jobs search study to define the necessary elements of the preventive intervention for the recently unemployed (Price & Vinokur, in press) and to generate a set of reliable measures of the processes in that intervention. The model, as presented in Figure 1, also served to guide the analyses of our results.

Method

Research Design

The Jobs preventive intervention project was embedded in a field experiment with random assignment of the recently unemployed to an experimental (i.e., the intervention treatment) and a primary control condition. The participants in the primary control condition were sent self-instructional materials consisting of a brief booklet with extremely general descriptions on job seeking. The intervention was conducted and administered to a series of 15 groups between January and June 1986. The project has completed collection of one pretest and three posttests at 1, 4, and 32 months after the intervention. Figure 2 is a flow chart representing the design of the study and its waves of data collection.

The intervention delivery. To make the intervention truly preventive, only participants who had been unemployed for less than 4 months were selected. In groups of 16–20 individuals, participants took a training program delivered in eight 3-hr sessions covering a 2-week period. Three male–female pairs of trainers followed an extensively pretested 8- to 10-page protocol for each session. Each protocol incorporated the elements of the various theories that guided the construction of the intervention, such as enhancement of self-efficacy and inoculation against setbacks. Other elements intended to ensure

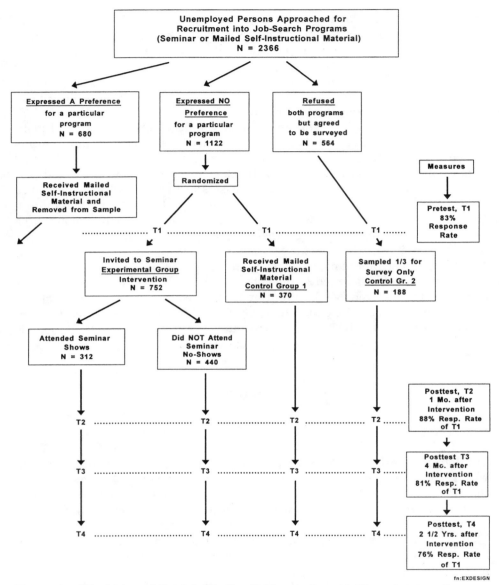

Figure 2. The design of the Jobs Project field experiment with an intervention program for unemployed individuals.

that the trainers established trust (referent power), established a base of expertise as trainers, and established positive expectancies that the intervention would lead the participants to achieve the desired outcomes.[1] The intervention included the following set of topics and activities: dealing with obstacles to reemployment, handling emotions related to unemployment and job seeking,

---

[1]A comprehensive implementation manual that includes information on the selection and training of the trainers and detailed protocols of the intervention sessions is available on request.

thinking like an employer, identifying sources of job leads, finding job leads in social networks, contacting potential employers, completing the job application and preparing a résumé, conducting the information interview, practicing and rehearsing interviews, and evaluating a job offer.

Throughout the program, participants were encouraged to analyze their situation for problems or potential difficulties and to generate their own solutions. We hypothesized that a person who feels he or she owns the solution to a problem will be more committed to implementing the solution. The group setting was considered to be a crucial element in this process because even if the person cannot come up with a solution, he or she is exposed to people who can.

Theory-drawn preventive intervention. The Jobs project emphasizes a theory-driven approach to test some generic principles of intervention and methods of evaluation that could be more widely used in preventive interventions. Two such important principles of intervention are (a) the necessity of highly intensive training of the trainers before program delivery and (b) the importance of close monitoring of the intervention by observers during program delivery. Both of these elements help maintain a high-quality intervention.

Much of the intervention's rationale derives from research on vigilant coping that shows that people under pressure often narrow their search for solutions and tend to become prematurely invested in a certain course of action. Vigilance promotes the search for problem diagnosis and alternative solutions. Participants are therefore trained in diagnosing unemployment problems and generating alternatives for reemployment. Moreover, they receive inoculation against setbacks by anticipating potential setbacks and building up repertoires to cope with counterpressures.

The Jobs intervention project also derives from theory that emphasizes the importance of self-efficacy, the knowledge that one can succeed, as a motivational force for attempting difficult behaviors. The Jobs intervention project was designed to provide these conditions, and the research findings showed that enhancement in job search self-efficacy stimulated participants to engage in intensive job-search activities (van Ryn & Vinokur, 1992).

Finally, research and theory on social resources also drives the intervention. Skills, social support, and knowing how to cope with setbacks are all critical social resources that can have powerful preventive effects for people who would otherwise be vulnerable to the adversity of life transitions such as job loss.

Recruitment of Participants

Participants were recruited from the lines of the Michigan Employment Security Commission. Trained recruiters approached each person, asked a set of screening questions, and arranged for the person to enter the study if eligible. Those who stated that they had "no preference" for either the eight-session (experimental) or self-taught (control) program were then randomly assigned to the control or experimental condition. Individuals with a preference were excluded from the study. Consequently, participants were randomized with regard to initial motivation to enter a particular condition. The control group respondents received in the mail self-instructional materials consisting of a booklet with information on successful job-search strategies. Because the follow-up evaluation period lasted for more than 28 months, it was not possible to invite the respondents in the control group to the intervention at the end of the study.

Outcome Measures and Variables

Pretest data collection included basic information about the past job and its quality, attitudes toward work and toward job seeking, job-seeking intentions, and behavior, job-search self-efficacy, mental health and well-being (the SCL-90), health status, social support and social undermining, and personality dispositions (self-esteem, locus of control, and assertiveness). During the intervention, process measures were administered. Follow-up measures included all of the pretest measures and additional information on reemployment outcomes, such as number of hours working, wage rate, and job quality. Measures are described in detail by Caplan et al. (1989), Vinokur, Price, and Caplan (1991), Vinokur, van Ryn, Gramlich, and Price (1991), and Price, van Ryn, and Vinokur (1992).

Results

Sample Characteristics

The recruitment process produced a sample of unemployed people whose demographic characteristics were highly similar to the U.S. unemployed population older than 16 years of age and to representative community samples of unemployed (Caplan et al., 1989; U.S. Bureau of Labor and Statistics, 1986). Men constituted 46% of the sample; 15% of the sample were Black. The average age was 35.9 years (SD = 10.6 years), and the average education was approximately 12.9 years (SD = 1.9 years). Finally, 53% of our respondents included those who were unmarried at the time (respondents who were divorced, separated, widowed, or never married). Nearly one third of the sample fell into each of the following three broad occupational classifications: professional and managerial (33%), service and clerical (28%), and blue-collar (38%). The participants in this study were, on the average, well into their careers; respondents reported being with their previous employer an average of 6 years (SD = 6.3 years). The average length of unemployment was 13 weeks (SD = 9 weeks).

Dropouts and Participants

Among those assigned to the experimental condition, 59% failed to show up for the intervention. This percentage varied only by about 5% over the course of recruiting 15 experimental groups in a 4-month period, during which successively recruited groups were entered into the experimental and control conditions. "Participants," by contrast, were defined as having completed at least six of the eight sessions.

Response Rate

Of the experimental and control group respondents who received a pretest questionnaire, 83% mailed it back. The response rates for those receiving the Time 2, Time 3, and Time 4 posttest questionnaires were 88%, 80%, and 76%, respectively. Most important, there were no significant interaction effects between respondent status (responders vs. nonresponders) and experimental condition (experimental vs. control) on any demographic, mental health, or job-search variables at pretest. Thus, differences in response rate (or dropout mortality) between the experimental and the control groups cannot provide plausible explanation for the findings on the basis of the follow-up data.

Analyses

Two basic types of analyses were conducted. The first type included analyses that were based on the complete randomized (true) experimental design. The experimental condition in these analyses included those who were originally assigned to the experimental condition, regardless of whether they showed up and participated in the intervention.

The second type of analysis focused on experimental respondents who actually participated in the intervention seminar and excluded those who did not show up. In these analyses, the participants' outcomes were compared with the outcomes of the subset of respondents in the control group who constituted their counterparts (i.e., those who would have participated in the intervention had they been invited). These analyses involved estimation procedures of those in the control group who would and those who would not show up to the intervention on the basis of the no-show group in the experimental group as suggested by Bloom (1984).

A special feature of this study was the process measures. At Sessions 1, 7, and 8, participants filled out detailed measures assessing the elements of the intervention that were based on self-efficacy theory (e.g., the establishment of referent power, inoculation against setbacks, and rehearsal of skills). Using these process measures, internal analyses within the experimental group of participants demonstrated that the various intervention elements were implemented and operated as designed.

Manipulation Checks, Integrity, and Strength of the Intervention

The measures of degree of participant engagement provided a close indication of the integrity and strength of the intervention. These measures were based on multi-item scales that assessed referent power, trainer and group attractiveness, practice of skills, and generation of alternatives for dealing with setbacks. The means of these measures ranged from 3.6 to 4.6 on the 5-point scales, with standard deviations ranging from 0.4 to 1.3. These means suggest that the experimental intervention was perceived by the participants as establishing trust and that the participants actively practiced skills and dealt with potential setbacks. Furthermore, natural variation in the delivery of these parameters was associated with predicted variation in immediate outcomes relating to job-search confidence and motivation as well as emotional well-being. The analyses showed that participants' level of engagement had beneficial effects on job-seeking attitudes, employment-related outcomes (e.g., number of hours of reemployment, pay, rates of reemployment), and emotional well-being 1 and 4 months after the intervention.

Effectiveness of Randomization

There were no significant differences at pretesting between the experimental and control groups on demographic variables, job-seeking motivation, mental health, or other dependent variables.

The intervention effects using the original randomized experimental design are displayed in Table 1. The strongest short-term effects emerged on the reemployment outcomes. The finding demonstrated that the experimental intervention yielded significantly greater percentages of reemployed individuals at both posttests, with the difference at Time 3 being a continuation of the advantage that appeared at Time 2.

Among the reemployed, at the 1-month posttest, there was a statistically nonsignificant trend for the experimental group to score higher than the control group on quality of working life. By the 4-month posttest, this difference had become statistically significant. Furthermore, the percentage of individuals who had found reemployment in what they characterized as their main occupation was higher for the experimental group at both Time 2 (82% vs. 64%) and Time 3 (88% vs. 77%). Among the reemployed, those in the experimental group also reported higher monthly earnings than did those in the control group (a $359 difference) at Time 2. This difference almost disappeared at Time 3 and was no longer significant.

Finally, these findings also show that of those who remained unemployed, the respondents in the experimental condition has significantly higher levels of job-search self-efficacy than did the respondents in the control condition at both Time 2 and Time 3 follow-ups.

Table 1.   Effects of Treatment on Quantity and Quality of Reemployment and Job-Seeking Attitudes at 1 (Time 2) and 4 (Time 3) Months Posttest

Variable	Experimental		Control		$t(df)$	p
	M	SD	M	SD		
All participants						
% Reemployed						
Time 2	33	0.47	26	0.44	1.74(608)[a]	.04
Time 3	59	0.49	51	0.50	2.00(623)[a]	.025
Monthly earnings						
Time 2	$512	769	$322	607	3.12(622)	.001
Time 3	$853	923	$723	977	1.65(664)	.05
Reemployed participants						
Quality of working life						
Time 2	5.02	1.02	4.81	1.07	1.23(175)	ns
Time 3	4.97	1.02	4.76	1.10	1.70(343)	.045
Monthly earnings						
Time 2	$1,456	780	$1,097	774	2.28(148)	.01
Time 3	$1,467	857	$1,407	1128	0.79(307)	ns
% in Main occupation						
Time 2	82	0.38	64	0.48	2.75(177)[b]	.004
Time 3	88	0.34	77	0.43	2.41(343)[b]	.008
Unemployed participants						
Self-efficacy in job-seeking ability						
Time 2	3.92	0.80	3.75	0.87	2.02(411)	.02
Time 3	3.94	0.79	3.72	0.87	2.09(255)	.02
Motivation to job seek						
Time 2	4.93	1.06	4.85	1.07	0.63(468)	ns
Time 3	4.64	1.24	4.38	1.24	0.62(304)	.06

Note.   Adapted from Caplan, Vinokur, Price, and van Ryn (1989, Table 2). Copyright 1989 by the American Psychological Association.

[a] t Tests were computed on means based on assigned scores of 1 or 0 for reemployed and unemployed, respectively.

[b] t Tests were computed on means based on assigned scores of 1 or 0 for employed in main occupation or in other-than-main occupation, respectively.

Intervention Effects on Actual Participants

The effects of participation were estimated by comparing the means of the subgroup of actual participants with the means of the control group would-be participants on the basis of a procedure developed by Bloom (1984). Comparison of the effects of the intervention according to the original randomized assignment with the effects based on participation was discussed by Vinokur, Price, and Caplan (1991) using effect sizes (Cohen, 1977) as well as t tests for the difference between the means.

The results of the analysis that focused on the participating subgroup compared with their counterparts in the control group indicate that participation in the intervention yielded significantly greater percentages of reemployed individuals at both posttests. At the Time 3 4-month follow-up, 53% of the experimental group participants were reemployed compared with 29% of their control group counterparts. This 24% difference appears to be a continuation of the 20% advantage for the experimental group participants over their control counterparts, which appeared at Time 2 4-week follow-up.

The comparison of the effect size and level of significance in the results of the two analyses, one based on the intact randomized design (cf. Table 1) and the other on actual participation, demonstrates clearly that the intervention effects were far more dramatic for the participants than might be inferred from the analyses that were based on the full experimental design. For example, regarding the percentage of reemployed, the effect sizes for the participants at Time 2 and Time 3 were .60 and .48, which is more than three times larger than the .15 and .17 for the full experimental design groups.

Among the reemployed, at the Time 2 1-month posttest, there was a significantly higher level of earnings in the full experimental than the control group. By the 4-month posttest, this difference was no longer significant because the proportion of reemployed in both groups increased sharply. Furthermore, the percentage of those who had found reemployment in what they characterized as their main occupation was significantly higher for the experimental group at both Time 2 (82% vs. 64%) and Time 3 (87% vs. 76%). The same results were found in the comparisons for the participants only with consistently larger effect sizes. Moreover, the comparisons for the participants were statistically significant only at both posttests with respect to two additional outcomes. Compared with their control counterparts, the reemployed participants enjoyed significantly better quality of life at work and were more likely to obtain jobs that were permanent rather than temporary.

Attitudes and behaviors of unemployed participants. Self-reports of posttest job-seeking behaviors were not significantly different between the experimental and control groups. At both posttests, however, the unemployed participants in the experimental group had higher perceived confidence, or self-efficacy, in their job-seeking ability. A similar but nonsignificant pattern also occurred for motivation to engage in job seeking. Once again, these same effects that appeared for the full design were far more pronounced in the comparisons for the participants with statistically significant effects for these variables at Time 3. The intervention had the effect of maintaining confidence and a sense of efficacy even in the face of setbacks.

Effects on mental health. Replicating other studies (e.g., Feather & O'Brien, 1986; Vinokur, Caplan, & Williams, 1987), we found that people who became reemployed scored significantly lower on anxiety, depression, and anger and higher on self-esteem and quality of life than those who remained unemployed. However, the comparisons that were based on the full experimental design did not yield any statistically significant results with respect to all these variables. By contrast, a number of significant differences on these variables, in particular on depression, were revealed in the analyses only for the participants. Depression was, for the unemployed participants, consistently lower at both

Table 2. Benefits and Costs of the Preventive Intervention for Unemployed Individuals Present-Value Terms per Person

Benefits and costs	Individual	Federal	State	Total
Benefits				
Gain in after-tax earning 32				
months after program[a]	5,392	0	0	5,392
Gain in taxes paid	0	1,006	308	1,314
Total benefits	5,392	1,006	308	6,706
Total costs	0	286	0	286
Net total for 32 months	5,392	720	308	6,420
Net total for 5 years				
0% Discount rate	10,784	1,726	616	13,126
2.5% Discount rate	10,575	1,686	604	12,865
5% Discount rate	10,377	1,649	593	12,619
Net total until age 60				
0% Discount rate	58,913	10,705	3,370	72,988
2.5% Discount rate	49,290	8,909	2,819	61,018
5% Discount rate	38,944	6,979	2,228	48,151

Note. Adapted from Vinokur, van Ryn, Gramlich, and Price (1991, Table 3). Copyright 1991 by the American Psychological Association. Data were based on TOBIT estimates of predicted mean differences of $239.50 between full experimental group and control group in earnings per month adjusted for age, sex, education, and family income at Time 1 using the LIMDEP Program.
[a]Gain occurred within last 28 month period as recorded by Time 4 data collection. During the first 4 months, most respondents were still looking for a job.

posttests. Surprisingly, the reemployed participants displayed a significantly higher level of depression and anxiety at Time 2 than did their counterpart controls. However, the direction of this difference was reversed at Time 3, with the reemployed participants showing significantly lower levels of depression.

Long-term effects on reemployment at the 32-month follow-up were found for the entire sample with respect to earnings per month. The experimental intervention group had statistically significant higher earnings than did the control group in each of the follow-ups. The mean difference was $178 at the Time 2 4-week follow-up, $227 at the Time 3 4-month follow-up, and $239 at the Time 4 32-month follow-up.

The intervention was found to have additional effects on the respondents who reported earnings of at least $1 per week. Compared with these respondents in the control group, the intervention group respondents were working a significantly greater percentage of the time and were having more stable work (fewer employers and job changes) during the proceeding 2.5 years. The results of our benefit–cost analyses are shown in Table 2. The intervention resulted in net benefits of $6,420 per respondent at the end of the follow-up period and will result in a conservative projected net benefits of $12,619 at the end of 5 years and $48,151 by the time the respondents retire at an estimated age of 60 years.

Additional preventive effects on depressive episodes were found in more detailed analyses that identified high-risk respondents on the basis of their pretest combined score of depression, financial strain, and low social assertiveness. As shown in Figure 3, during the 2.5-year follow-up period, the in-

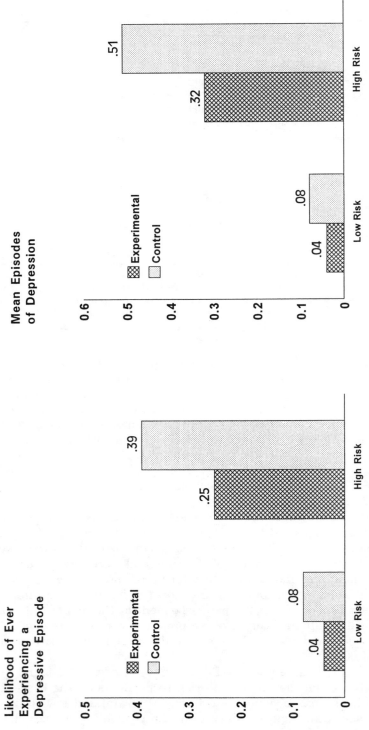

Figure 3. Impact of Jobs intervention project and risk status on likelihood of ever experiencing a depressive episode and number of depressive episodes (32-month follow-up).

tervention had a statistically significant preventive impact on both the incidence and prevalence of more severe depressive symptoms among the high-risk individuals (Price et al., 1992).

Discussion and Conclusions

These analyses provide strong evidence that the intervention accomplished its goals. Analyses of the 1- and 4-month follow-up data showed that the Jobs intervention project produced higher quality reemployment in terms of earnings and job satisfaction and higher motivation among those who remained unemployed. Furthermore, the long-term follow-up, 2.5 years later, demonstrated continued beneficial effects of the intervention on wage rate, monthly earnings, and fewer episodes of job changes. More detailed analyses identified the characteristics that placed unemployed individuals at higher risk for experiencing depressive symptoms and for remaining unemployed. The individuals at the highest risk for depression were found to have baseline depressive symptoms, financial hardship, and low social assertiveness. Our analyses showed that the intervention buffered the effects of these risk factors on depression. In other words, the intervention benefited more those who needed it most.

This randomized field experiment was designed to test hypotheses about the effect of providing social support and improving skills and cognitions relevant to coping with a major life stressor: loss of employment. The long-term effects of the Jobs intervention project embedded in this experiment demonstrated that it can be implemented as a cost-effective community program that provides net benefits to the unemployed participants as well as to society.

At the most general level, this field experiment has demonstrated that interventions that establish trust, engender skills and the motivation to use them, inoculate against setbacks, and provide social support are capable of helping people succeed in a difficult task in spite of setbacks and failures. The experiment was aimed specifically at providing job-search skills to those who had lost their jobs. Nevertheless, we believe that because the theoretical components of the intervention are derived from basic research on motivation and coping, they are potentially applicable to preventive interventions dealing with a wide range of difficult life tasks and decisions. For unemployed people, the foundations of the Jobs search intervention project can be used to design additional intervention components to help them cope with other tasks and stressors in their lives. For example, providing skills and knowledge of financial planning and management, loan restructuring, assistance programs, and so on, an intervention that addresses the financial hardship during the period of unemployment can help unemployed individuals cope with the strain of losing their income as a result of the job loss. Furthermore, with changing technologies and economic conditions, interventions that address the need for and stresses of a career change could help unemployed individuals make the occupational changes that will be required from a significant portion of the displaced workforce.

References

Abramson, L. Y., Seligman, M. E. P., & Teasdale, J. D. (1978). Learned helplessness in humans: Critique and reformulation. *Journal of Abnormal Psychology, 87,* 49–74.

Bandura, A. (1977). Self-efficacy: Toward a unifying theory of behavior change. *Psychological Review, 84,* 191–215.

Bandura, A. (1986). *Social foundations of thought and action.* Englewood Cliffs, NJ: Prentice Hall.

Bloom, H. S. (1984). Accounting for no-shows in experimental evaluation designs. *Evaluation Review, 8,* 225–246.

Caplan, R. D., Vinokur, A. D., Price, R. H., and van Ryn, M. (1989). Job seeking, reemployment, and mental health: A randomized field experiment in coping with job loss. *Journal of Applied Psychology, 74,* 759–769.

Cohen, J. (1977). *Statistical power analysis for the behavioral sciences.* San Diego, CA: Academic Press.

Feather, N. T., & O'Brien, G. E. (1986). A longitudinal study of the effects of employment and unemployment on school-leavers. *Journal of Occupational Psychology, 59,* 121–144.

Friedrich, J. R. (1987). Perceived control and decision making in a job hunting context. *Basic and Applied Social Psychology, 8,* 163–176.

Janis, I. (1982). *Short term counselling: Guidelines based on recent research.* New Haven, CT: Yale University Press.

Kanfer, F. H., & Goldstein, A. P. (Eds.). (1991). *Helping people change* (4th ed.). Elmsford, NY: Pergamon Press.

Lazarus, R. S. (1966). *Psychological stress and the coping process.* New York: McGraw-Hill.

Marlatt, A. G., & Gordon, J. R. (1985). *Relapse prevention.* New York: Guilford Press.

Meichenbaum, D. (1985). *Stress inoculation training: A clinical guidebook.* Elmsford, NY: Pergamon Press.

Price, R. H., van Ryn, M., & Vinokur, A. D. (1992). Impact of a preventive job search intervention on the likelihood of depression among the unemployed. *Journal of Health and Social Behavior, 33,* 158–167.

Price, R. H., & Vinokur, A. D. (in press). The Michigan Jobs Program: Supporting career transitions in a time of organizational downsizing. In M. London (Ed.), *Employee development and job creation: Human resources strategies for organizational growth.* New York: Guilford Press.

Rotter, J. B., Chance, J. E., Phares, E. J. (1972). *Applications of a social learning theory of personality.* New York: Holt, Rinehart & Winston.

U.S. Bureau of Labor Statistics. (1986, July). Current labor statistics: Employment data. *Monthly Labor Review, 109*(2):74.

van Ryn, M., & Vinokur, A. D. (1992). How did it work? An examination of the mechanisms through which a community intervention influenced job-search behavior among an unemployed sample. *American Journal of Community Psychology, 5,* 577–597.

Vinokur, A., Caplan, R. D., & Williams, C. C. (1987). Effects of recent and past stress on mental health: Coping with unemployment among Vietnam veterans and non-veterans. *Journal of Applied Social Psychology, 17,* 708–728.

Vinokur, A. D., Price, R. H., & Caplan, R. D. (1991). From field experiments to program implementation: Assessing the potential outcomes of an experimental intervention program for unemployed persons. *American Journal of Community Psychology, 19,* 543–562.

Vinokur, A. D., van Ryn, M., Gramlich, E. M., & Price, R. H. (1991). Long-term follow-up and benefit-cost analysis of the Jobs Project: A preventive intervention for the unemployed. *Journal of Applied Psychology, 76,* 213–219.

Weiner, B. (1979). A theory of motivation for some classroom experiences. *Journal of Educational Psychology, 71,* 3–25.

10

When Couples Cope With Job Loss: A Strategy for Developing and Testing Preventive Interventions

George W. Howe, Robert D. Caplan, David Foster, Mindy Lockshin, and Claire McGrath

Work is a fundamental determinant of how Americans feel about the quality of their life. In the past 15 years, employment has gained a central role in the lives of women as well as men, with married women and single mothers greatly increasing their participation in the workforce (Nieva, 1988). As economic changes trigger workplace shutdowns and reductions in the workforce, an estimated 10 million employees annually lose their jobs (U.S. Department of Labor, 1986). Findings from the Great Depression to the present, based on cross-sectional, longitudinal, and prospective designs, have documented the psychological and social costs of job loss for the unemployed person, for individual members of the person's family, and for the family as a whole (Dew, Penkower, & Bromet, 1991). Numerous studies have shown that job loss is associated with increased depressive symptoms, increased anxiety, lower self-esteem, and increased risk of suicide attempts by the unemployed person (Cobb & Kasl, 1977). Job loss also appears to affect the family of the job seeker. The husband's loss of a job is related to increased incidence of wife battering (Windschuttle, 1980), wife mortality (Moser, Fox, & Jones, 1984), wife psychiatric disorder (Bebbington, Hurry, Tennant, Sturt, & Wing, 1981), and child abuse (Taitz, King, Nicholson, & Kessel, 1987).

As a whole, the research literature provides consistent evidence that job loss puts the recently unemployed individual and his or her family at significant risk for emotional disorders and for deterioration of the quality of family life. As such, this research suggests that interventions delivered before or shortly after job loss hold great promise for reducing these risks and for preventing the harmful social and emotional sequelae just described. Experimental trials of preventive interventions aimed at helping the individual job seeker cope effectively with job loss have demonstrated significant financial and psychological benefits for the job seeker (Vinokur, van Ryn, Gramlich, & Price, 1991). Research also has shown that families may have an important role to

This work was supported in part by Grant R01 MH47292 from the National Institute of Mental Health. The order of the last three authors is random.

play in coping with the sequelae of job loss and in promoting reemployment (Vinokur & Caplan, 1987). Consequently, preventive interventions aimed at the families of job seekers are logical outgrowths of initial preventive trials that involve only the individual job seeker.

This chapter is concerned with how to design and test family-focused preventive intervention programs aimed at reducing the risk of emotional disorders and family dysfunction in the period after job loss. To our knowledge, there have been no true experiments involving such family-focused interventions. We explore what will be required to develop such preventive interventions. On the basis of a literature review, we propose a programmatic strategy that joins survey and experimental methods such that the results of epidemiological studies are used to inform field experiments. We propose a process-oriented conceptual framework for guiding such research. This framework is intended to address two related questions: Why do families differ in how successfully they cope with job loss? What are the likely points of preventive intervention that are implied by such findings?

In this chapter, we also examine recent research indicating that the marital or partner relationship is particularly important in understanding the link between job loss and depression. We then discuss research on family support interventions in situations other than unemployment. On the basis of this literature, we present a set of guidelines for developing programmatic research that would identify and test fruitful family-focused preventive interventions. Finally, we present a detailed conceptual model of family processes that is serving as a specific guide for our research and for designing family-focused interventions.

What Is the Potential for Family-Focused Preventive Intervention?

To date, all experimental trials to reduce distress and depression during unemployment have targeted and studied only individual job seekers. These interventions have proved highly successful, and results of this work are described elsewhere (Caplan, Vinokur, Price, & van Ryn, 1989; Vinokur, Price, & Caplan, 1991; Vinokur, van Ryn, et al., 1991). Because these trials have not studied the effects of interventions on the family members of the job seeker, there is little information on their effectiveness in preventing negative sequelae in these family members. However, these studies have provided some initial suggestions on the importance of family factors in determining how the individual job seeker copes with job loss.

As part of the program of research on individually focused preventive interventions, Vinokur and Caplan (1987) examined the role of the wife's social support in the coping and well-being of the unemployed husband. This research suggested that partners can play a significant role in the job-seeking process through two forms of social support: motivational support and unconditional regard. With regard to motivational support, partners could either support or undermine the job seeker's cognitions about whether it was worthwhile to look for a job. Such cognitions were predictive of the husband's amount of job-seeking behavior 6 months later.

Unconditional regard had a much different function. When job seeking, an individual often experiences repeated setbacks. Previous research has shown that when a job seeker experiences such setbacks, the risk of depression increases, particularly for job seekers who are highly motivated to succeed (Feather & Davenport, 1981). Vinokur and Caplan's (1987) findings suggest that support in the form of unconditional regard (e.g., messages such as, "Regardless of whether you succeeded or not, we still love you") can counteract such depression-inducing effects, particularly among those who are highly motivated to look for reemployment, a group that is at higher risk for depression.

Although many family factors are likely to be important in determining successful coping with job loss, these and other findings point to the relationship with a spouse or committed partner as having a major influence on outcome. There is substantial evidence that this relationship is closely linked to the mental health of each partner. The presence of a supportive confidant, usually a spouse or partner, is one of the few factors likely to reduce the risk of psychological and emotional problems in individuals experiencing severe life stress (Barnett & Gotlib, 1988). On the negative side, Beach, Sandeen, and O'Leary (1990, p. 17) cited epidemiological data indicating that 50% of women experiencing a major depressive episode are in distressed marriages. Conversely, roughly half of all women who report marital discord are also experiencing major depression. There is also evidence for causal direction in this link. In their recent review of research on risk factors for major depression, Barnett and Gotlib (1988) concluded that marital conflict is one of the few factors that predicts the onset of depression prospectively.

These general findings are consistent with the thesis that, when job loss disrupts the marital or partner relationship, this disruption contributes to increased depression in both job seekers and their partners. These findings suggest that the relationship with a partner can have powerful effects, both negative and positive, on the capacity of both the job seeker and the job seeker's partner to weather the stresses of a period of unemployment and point to this relationship as a possible target for preventive intervention. Although we found no reports of experimental trials with such a focus, studies of couple-focused interventions in other contexts provide some insight into the feasibility and direction of such efforts.

Job seeking can introduce a particular class of problems for couples. Unlike situations in which couples must make joint decisions, such as the division of household roles, job seeking involves an asymmetry of roles in which only one person is the job seeker. Although both partners are likely to be greatly affected by the outcome of the search, the final responsibility for carrying the search to a successful conclusion falls most heavily on the partner seeking employment.

There have been a number of experimental interventions targeting such asymmetric situations in contexts other than job loss. Some investigators have developed spouse-assisted therapies for psychiatric conditions such as depression (Rush, Shaw, & Khatami, 1980), obsessive–compulsive disorder (Emmelkamp & de Lange, 1983), and agoraphobia (Hafner, 1977), in which only one of the partners is experiencing the problem. Spouse-assisted therapy, in which the spouse is engaged as an aid in carrying out therapeutic tasks to ameliorate the symptoms of the partner, is distinguished from marital therapy, in which conflict and other issues between the partners are the targets of intervention.

Dewey and Hunsley (1990) reviewed the findings of outcome studies for spouse-assisted treatment of agoraphobia. Although this approach did not appear to differ from individual therapeutic approaches in its capacity to reduce the symptoms of agoraphobia, attrition rates during therapy were substantially lower than those reported for individual exposure-based therapy or pharmacological treatment. Furthermore, more general indicators of the quality of the marriage as measured before treatment began were significantly related to reduction in symptoms up to 1 year after treatment.

Other reports of experimental interventions into such asymmetrical relationships, particularly with regard to health behavior modification, suggest that interventions involving the assistance of a spouse often have no effect on promoting the intended behavior and may make things worse (Cohen et al., 1987). The studies that have shown beneficial effects also include those in which the spouse was generally encouraged to show no interest in the other spouse's behavior (Hoebel, 1976).

These findings suggest that simply using the spouse as an "assistant" can have unpredictable and even negative effects. There also is evidence from the agoraphobia studies that using the spouse as an assistant may be less important than attending to the quality of the marital relationship itself. Therefore, it seems wise to proceed cautiously in developing preventive interventions that include partners or spouses, attending to two general issues. First, asking partners to assist in interventions to help the job seeker may ignore the unique context of the couple's relationship. As a result, reinforcing general categories of "supportive behavior" by the partner, such as offers of aid in job-search activities, may lead to unexpected outcomes. Research on stranger interaction, for example, has indicated that providing aid can be experienced as supportive or can be perceived as a threat to self-esteem and autonomy, depending on the context and the relationship of the provider to the recipient (Fisher, Nadler, & Witcher-Alagna, 1982). Although none of these studies have included couples, it is likely that similar issues will arise in this context and will depend on how the couple has incorporated such aid provision into its regular interactions. Such offers may actually undermine the job seeker's self-esteem if the offers are perceived as implicit criticisms.

Second, these findings suggest that it may be more important to strengthen the partner relationship itself than to use the partner as an assistant in the intervention. Findings from the studies of both weight loss and agoraphobia point in this direction, as do the findings reviewed earlier concerning the strong correlation between increased depression and general marital conflict.

Pursuing a Research Agenda in Studying Couple Factors and Job Loss

Given the mixed findings concerning couple-focused interventions in other areas, it seems important to ask two interrelated questions: (a) What patterns of transaction among couples determine how effectively partners cope with a major negative life event such as loss of a job? (b) Once helpful and harmful patterns of such transactions are identified, what are their antecedents? These questions remain unanswered. By identifying such transaction patterns and their antecedents and by determining which are open to social influence, it should be possible to lay a conceptual and empirical foundation for the design of effective preventive interventions.

As such, we suggest that the best strategy to pursue is to develop a more elaborate picture of how couples function under stress and to test this model using survey research designs before developing couple-focused interventions. Here, we lay out this general strategy in more detail; in the following section, we describe a conceptual model of couples coping that we are currently testing as part of the second stage of this strategy.

Theory-driven programmatic research of the sort articulated by a number of prevention researchers (Caplan et al., 1989) should involve four stages when applied to family-focused interventions: (a) identification of an array of potential family factors that mediate or moderate the impact of job loss on individual adjustment; (b) integration of these factors into a process model and testing of that model through survey research designs; (c) development of preventive interventions that are based on findings from these studies, with rigorous testing of their effectiveness; and (d) engineering of successful interventions so they can be applied within real-world settings. Each of these stages is discussed relative to couple-based interventions for those experiencing job loss.

Stage 1. Identifying mediating and moderating factors. Mediating factors reflect aspects of family life that are altered or disrupted by job loss and that subsequently have an impact on individual functioning. For example, Elder, Conger, Foster, and Ardelt (1992) documented how economic strain is associated with increased irritability in men and showed that such irritability can lead to increased conflict of fathers with children, which in turn is related to the emergence of childhood disorders such as aggressive behavior and depression. Here, the influence of economic deprivation on child adjustment is mediated through changes in family interaction patterns. Strong mediating factors provide a natural target for intervention, because changes in such factors will break the link between job loss and individual maladjustment. The model we develop includes a number of mediating factors, including couple transaction styles, appraisals about the job loss and the job search, and appraisals each partner has about the couple's relationship and about the other partner.

Although there may be a large number of mediating factors, several criteria can be used to select among this set. First, mediating factors need to reflect processes that most likely can be altered by an intervention. The ultimate practical goal of this research is the development of family-based interventions that are effective, efficient, and applicable in real-world settings. Therefore, any mediation model should be limited to processes that could be targeted for change through relatively brief interventions. For example, stable, ingrained attitudes and values about family life are probably not amenable to such intervention, whereas specific approaches to family problem solving are more likely to be malleable.

Second, highest priority should be given to family processes that are functionally related to a limited and well-specified set of individual outcomes. In the case of job loss, prior research points to two outcome domains: (a) the prevention of depression in the job seeker and other family members and (b) the promotion of cognitive and behavioral aspects of job-search activities most likely to lead to successful and stable reemployment.

Finally, there is substantial recent research literature on family process indicating the need to focus on both family-level processes and individual-level variables. Research on social support provides an obvious starting point in considering how families might influence the job seeker and the job search. By the late 1980s, a substantial amount of research had been conducted on the general relationship between social support and mental health, and several summary reviews had appeared (Barnett & Gotlib, 1988). The most robust finding for support effects appeared to be in the area of marital relationships.

Coyne and DeLongis (1986), among others, have used this finding to argue for a radical shift in social support research. They suggested that social support research should be wedded to interpersonal process research methods to tease apart the complexities of the support process and that only by doing so would researchers be able to advance the understanding of social support to the point where it becomes useful for designing concrete interventions. Following this line of thinking, we propose that the interpersonal processes occurring between partners in a long-term, committed relationship are likely to provide an excellent focus for family-based interventions. This position requires some revision of thinking, because the models that emerge focus on interaction patterns in this dyad as the unit of analysis rather than on individual behaviors.

Moderating factors reflect characteristics of families that alter the causal linkage between job loss variables and individual outcome. The length of unemployment following job loss is generally related to level of depression in male job seekers. However, Vinokur and Caplan (1987) provided evidence that depression is less likely for job seekers who report having spouses or partners who provide unconditional positive support. The presence of such a partner moderates the relationship (and perhaps the causal effect) between duration of unemployment and the job seeker's mental health. Some moderators may be subject to direct intervention. Other moderators, such as ethnicity, gender, or employment history, may help to identify subgroups that are most likely to benefit from particular types of interventions. These latter types of moderating variables can point to ways of tailoring preventive interventions for particular subgroups of families, for whom influence processes may differ. The model that we develop includes the gender of job seeker, the traditionality of the couple, and the extent of financial hardship as potential moderators of this type.

Stage 2. Integrating couple factors into a process model to drive survey designs. The second stage of a general research program involves the specification and testing of process models involving family factors as both mediators and moderators of effect. Such specific process models are important because they provide guidance in programmatic research to develop highly specific interventions. Such models would need to (a) specify the aspects of job loss that are most likely to influence outcome, such as duration of unemployment, perceived and objective economic hardship, and disruption of daily life; (b) make predictions as to how these job loss factors would influence important family mediating factors; (c) specify how these family mediators influence individual functioning of family members, including general indicators of mental health, job-search activity, and reemployment; and (d) identify family variables that moderate these relationships. In the early stages of a research program, when less is known about the validity of the models, longitudinal panel designs can provide a relatively economical way of collecting data to test them.

Stage 3. Theory-driven interventions. Findings from such surveys can suggest the most likely targets of intervention. In the third stage, on the basis of this information, methods of intervention can then be selected from other intervention research that has demonstrated effectiveness in influencing targets of this type. The studies of Meichenbaum (1985) and others provide numerous tests of interventions aimed at elements such as those presented in our process model. Unfortunately, it is rare to find true experiments targeted at unemployed individuals, and those targeted at the job-seeking family seem to be even more rare.

Such interventions would be tailored specifically to influence those couples' mediating processes that have shown the most powerful relationships to job loss and to outcome during the second stage of research. Rigorous evaluation designs during this stage should serve two purposes: They should provide careful assessment of the effectiveness of preventive interventions and a more stringent experimental test of the theoretical models developed in earlier stages.

The results of experiments in intervention can then be applied in several directions. They can lead to respecification of theoretical models for further evaluation of longitudinal panel designs as well as to a recasting of intervention techniques to increase the effectiveness and efficiency of their social technologies.

Stage 4. Enhancing and disseminating preventive technologies. The fourth stage of this research program involves the engineering of preventive intervention techniques that can be applied in real-world settings. For example, family-based interventions provide different challenges from those focused on individuals. Recruitment strategies may require different approaches, because factors that lead individuals to participate may be different from those that cause families to use preventive services. In addition, family-based interventions may fit naturally into one community setting, such as the schools, but they may be much more challenging to deliver within settings that are traditionally concerned primarily with the job seeker, such as state unemployment offices.

A Model of Transactional Patterns Within Couples Coping With Job Loss

Following the strategy just outlined, we have developed and articulated a working model for understanding how couples cope with job loss. The model we present here reflects the set of hypotheses we elaborated as part of the first two stages of this general strategy.

Figure 1 shows the various components of our model and how we hypothesize they are linked to individual depression and motivation for job-search activities. The core of this model involves the day-to-day transaction patterns engaged in by a couple. By the use of the term *transactions*, we refer to behavioral interactions between the partners as well as the thoughts and feelings that occur during these interactions. These daily transactions have shape and regularity. They span time simply spent in one another's company, as well as periods of intense discussion and planning. They involve the mundane and the intimate. Such transaction patterns are themselves possible targets for preventive intervention, as Markman, Duncan, Storaasli, and Howes (1987) demonstrated.

In addition, the model also attends to the cognitive stances of both partners that help to shape these interactions. For example, beliefs held by the partner of the job seeker may influence how that partner acts to support the self-esteem of the other. Some partners believe the job seeker is working as hard as possible to find a new job; others believe the job seeker is unwilling to put in enough effort and willing to risk keeping the family in financial hardship. The former belief is likely to support esteem-building interactions. The latter belief is likely to support guilt induction and criticism, and critical, angry exchanges by the couple are likely to influence the job seeker's mood and motivation, which may lead to avoidance of job-search activities and provide further evidence for the partner's belief.

Forms of Couple Transactions

Four aspects of transaction seem to be particularly relevant for the motivation of job seekers and for the emotional health of each member of the couple. These include valuing and esteem maintenance, a climate of openness, problem-solving capacity, and maintaining a climate of hope.

Valuing and esteem maintenance. Communication between partners often involves the expression of likes and dislikes. Expressions of how positively or negatively people evaluate their partners and their partner's actions are important determinants of partner mood. Evaluative statements are also likely

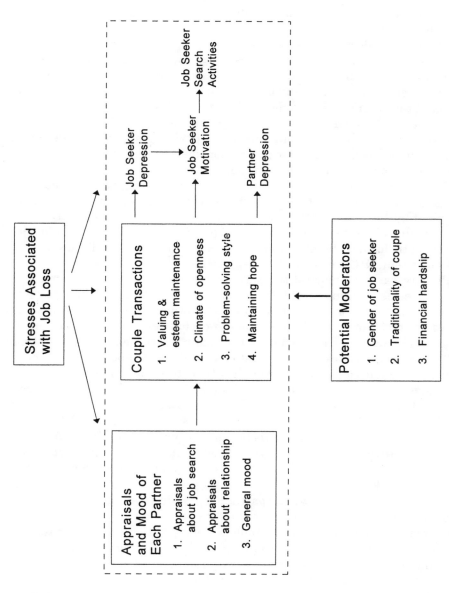

Figure 1.   Model of couple coping with job loss, including mediating and moderating factors.

to influence self-evaluation or, more generally, self-esteem. Certain general categories of partner behavior are likely to communicate positive evaluation. These include direct statements of confidence in the other's capabilities and skills or direct statements that the partner does positively value aspects of the other. Nonverbal aspects of communication also appear to communicate that one partner values the other positively; these include attentiveness and responsiveness during transaction.

Other general categories of behavior, however, communicate negative evaluation. Devaluing communications carry the message that the other is experienced as worthless, incompetent, or unable or unwilling to do things correctly. Verbal expressions involve sarcasm about the other, criticism of the other or of the other's actions, and "guilt induction" statements that imply the other has caused the partner or other people harm or pain. Nonverbal aspects of behavior that appear to communicate a devaluing stance include unwillingness to pay attention and lack of responsiveness, particularly when they follow expressions of feeling by the other.

Expressions of positive or negative evaluation can have profound implications for the sense of self-esteem experienced by each family member. For example, high levels of critical statements (and accompanying critical attitudes) in family members are predictive of more severe clinical manifestations of psychopathology, including childhood depression (Asarnow, Tompson, Hamilton, Goldstein, & Guthrie, 1994).

Prior research on marital transaction in severely distressed couples suggests that esteem maintenance or undermining of esteem is likely to be the outcome of patterns of transaction to which both members contribute. Such couples are much more likely to engage in exchanges of negative statements that are self-generating and that crowd our more positive exchanges (Gottman, 1979). Such reciprocal exchanges must be considered a function of the couple, not just of one individual member or the other. In some instances, the couple operates as an "esteem maintenance" system. Members of such couples come to know what kinds of comments are likely to undermine the partner's positive feelings about self and what kinds of comments will enhance that feeling.

Indirect evidence for these effects comes from the observational studies by Gottman (1979). Sequence analysis of couple transaction indicated that, in the early stages of problem-solving discussions, couples who had reported significant marital discord were likely to engage in "cross-complaining" sequences, where a statement by one partner expressing feelings about a problem is most likely to be followed by a similar statement by the other partner. In couples reporting no distress, such problem feeling statements were most likely to be followed by a statement of agreement by the other rather than by a complaint. This pattern was termed a *validation sequence* because the second partner appeared to be attending to and validating the feelings and concerns of the other rather than responding to a complaint with another complaint.

A climate of openness. Couples responding to a crisis such as job loss can have many decisions to make in a short time. These may involve small adjustments, such as eliminating minor luxuries, or major adjustments, such as whether to move to a new state where employment opportunities may be better. As couples face these dilemmas, their styles of engaging such issues can have an important bearing on how decisions are finally made and enacted. Engagement of issues during couple transaction may be straightforward, with both members of a couple able to discuss their thoughts and feelings openly. These couples are able to maintain an atmosphere in which the concerns of each person can be brought up, even when they involve disagreement or conflict. There is a capacity to engage issues to allow problem solving to occur.

However, some couples may not have such a straightforward style. These couples may raise concerns indirectly and break off discussion of a difficult issue at the first sign of disagreement or conflict. Indirectness, conflict avoidance, and failure to engage openly with one another about areas of concern in family life can have a number of negative consequences. Decisions can be made unilaterally that do not take into account the goals or needs of the other partner, leading to resentment and anger. Unresolved disagreements can color all couple transactions, making them more aversive and leading to escalation of avoidance, with its concomitant disruption of esteem maintenance activities. Finally, issue avoidance can become chronic, contributing to the sense of hopelessness found in couples reporting marital distress.

Problem-solving style. Couples may also differ in their capacity to explore an issue and work out acceptable solutions, even if they are able to get the issue out on the table successfully. Problem-solving styles may also depend on the nature of problems to be worked out. Couples are faced with two different types of problems following job loss. Many problems are sequelae of the job loss and involve adjustments to financial hardships or to changes in family routines. For example, parents may need to renegotiate child-care roles and household chores, particularly if the primary caretaker of the children gets a job to help supplement family income. There is substantial research literature on how couples go about solving problems of this type. Research by Gottman (1979), for example, suggests that distressed couples are more likely to engage in cross-complaining cycles during problem solving, are less likely to validate one another's feeling statements, and are less likely to move toward negotiated agreements in the latter part of problem-solving discussions.

As we discussed earlier, the issue of finding employment for the newly unemployed adult is a different type of problem, involving a fundamental asymmetry of roles. Although job search has traditionally been defined as something done by an individual, our observations suggest that job-search activities also can involve both partners. There is little research on the various ways that couples approach such a problem. Some couples may come to employ the partner as an assistant to the job seeker, helping with concrete activities such as typing résumés and making telephone calls. This fits with Thoits's (1986) notion of support as "coping aid." In other couples, the partner may be called on as a consultant by the job seeker and asked to provide advice or to evaluate new strategies. In still other couples, offers of such aid may never be attempted by partners, because to do so could elicit defensiveness or anger on the part of the job seekers, who perceive such offers as expressions of a lack of faith in their abilities and experience offers of assistance as threats to self-esteem and independence. Although there is substantial research on how offers of help can be perceived as threats to esteem (Fisher et al., 1982), none of this work has involved helping in intimate relationships.

Maintaining a climate of hope. A large body of research on individuals supports the idea that expectancies for success are essential factors in maintaining motivation. This thesis is at the core of the social learning theory (Rotter, Chance, & Phares, 1972) and learned helplessness (Seligman, 1975) models of behavior. There is, however, much less research on the interpersonal context of expectancies for success and concomitant motivation. We contend that the couple relationship may have a substantial impact on such expectancies, particularly concerning job-search activities. A job seeker may express confidence about his or her ability to find a job, and the partner may in turn echo and reinforce that expectation. Alternately, a partner may speak discouragingly about the job seeker's chances, and the job seeker may agree with this interpretation. This may lead to a general stance of hopelessness that is reinforced by both members of the couple.

Couples' discussions may also shape expectancies more indirectly. Couples may discuss the causes of job loss and the causes of failure to find a job. Causal attributions have been linked to expectations for success and to motivation in achievement situations (Weiner, 1980) and more globally (Seligman, Abramson, Semmel, & von Baeyer, 1979). The attributional "frame" for failure or setback can emerge from couples' discussions and can be shaped by both members during the transaction. If the consensus is that failures are attributable to stable characteristics of the job seeker, such as personality or basic lack of competence, expectancies for success are likely to be undermined. Attributions that the job seeker is to blame are also likely to be perceived as devaluing by the job seeker and can contribute to reductions in self-esteem.

Summary. These four domains of couple transaction—valuing and esteem maintenance, a climate of openness, problem-solving capacity, and maintaining a climate of hope—are clearly not independent of one another. For example, engaging in problem solving may involve openness and may, by its very presence, communicate an atmosphere of hope. Nevertheless, these dimensions do provide an initial framework for observing couple transactions. They are dimensions of transaction that are most likely to be influenced by the stresses surrounding job loss and in turn are likely to influence depression and motivation. These aspects of couple transactions are thus primary candidates for mediating variables in a process model of coping with job loss. As such, they involve concrete aspects of couple transaction that can become targets for preventive intervention.

Potential Antecedents of Couple Transactions

As illustrated in Figure 1, a number of cognitive and affective variables are likely to shape transactions among couples. These potential antecedents fall into three domains: appraisals about the job loss and the job search, appraisals about the couple relationship, and general mood. Each of these has the capacity to be altered by stresses of job loss, and each is likely to have some influence on couple transactions.

Appraisals about job loss and job search. As we hypothesized earlier, couple transactions may help to shape the appraisals held by the job seeker about the effectiveness of job-search activities. It is likely that these transactions are themselves shaped by more general appraisals held by both the job seeker and partner. Two types of general appraisals may be particularly relevant for the motivation and mental health of the job seeker: those related to *hopelessness* and those related to *blame*. Appraisals related to hopelessness include general expectations that job-search activities are not likely to bear much fruit. Such expectations of failure also can be linked to attributions that job loss occurred because of some stable and unchangeable aspect of the job seeker. Appraisals related to blame involve beliefs that the job seeker was responsible for the job loss and has not been willing to carry out the activities necessary to find a new job. These appraisals may include self-blame, with the job seeker attributing failure to stable, negative aspects of self, such as laziness, incompetence, or lack of effort.

Appraisals about the relationship. Appraisals of hopelessness and blame about the couple's relationship are also likely to shape the couple's transactions. A number of studies have demonstrated links between blame attributions and marital discord, with maritally dissatisfied individuals being more likely to attribute negative behaviors by their partner to causes within the partner, including intent to harm or hurt (Bradbury & Fincham, 1990). There also is evidence that partners in distressed couples are more likely to attribute conflict to global and stable causes (Bradbury & Fincham, 1990) and that such attributions are related to low expectations for success in resolving conflicts (Howe, 1987). Finally, there is evidence that, in couple transactions, members of a distressed couple are less likely to use language that is oriented toward joint responsibility for problems and more likely to use language that placed the responsibility for the problem on the other partner (Leftwich, 1989).

General mood. There is substantial evidence that job loss is associated with irritability and dysphoria in all family members. General mood states also are likely to influence couple transactions. There is evidence that depressive mood may inhibit acceptance of aid (Coyne et al., 1987). It is also possible that dysphoria in the partner can lead to increases in offers of aid at low-to-moderate levels of discomfort as an attempt to change the partner's own mood but that it may lead to reductions in offers of aid when the partner's mood is more severely depressed.

Coyne et al. (1987) observed increased hostility in couples in whom at least one member was experiencing severe depressive symptoms. In addition, Elder et al. (1992) documented increased negative interaction in families that were experiencing recent economic hardships, including unemployment. This negative family interaction appears to be linked to increased general anger and irritability in the unemployed individual. Overall, these findings suggest that changes in general mood, particularly in depressive symptoms and irritability, are common in couples experiencing job loss and are likely to influence couple transaction patterns during this period of stress.

Moderators of the Effects of Couple Transactions

Some variables, although not providing direct targets for preventive intervention, may act to moderate the impact of couple transaction patterns on individual adjustment and motivation for the job search. Three likely candidates for moderator variables include the gender of the job seeker, the traditionality of the couple, and the extent of financial hardship brought about by the job loss.

Gender. There have been few studies of the effects of women's lob loss on individual or family outcomes. As may be evident in the studies already reviewed, almost all of the literature relating to the absence or presence of work in people's lives had the following focus: If women were the object of study, the research was concerned with whether *employment* might undermine or improve the woman's quality of life. If men were the object of study, the research dealt with whether the *loss of employment* might undermine the man's and his family's well-being. There appeared to be little research dealing with the psychological impact of job loss on female job seekers. Indeed, a literature review on the topic described it as "relatively small, and at times obscure" (Dew, Bromet, & Penkower, 1992, p. 752).

This lack of research is particularly significant in that women, as noted by Dew et al. (1992), are more likely than men to lose their jobs during layoffs and plant closings, to be single heads of households, to fail to find reemployment, to experience a drop in income if reemployed, and to find job loss as psychologically distressing as it is for men. In one of the first longitudinal studies of blue-collar women coping with job loss, Dew et al. found that symptoms of distress did not disappear with reemployment. They suggested that the loss of employment generated feelings of insecurity and ambiguity about the future for these women that were not assuaged by reemployment. This finding has been reported elsewhere in cross-sectional research (Rosen, 1987). Further evidence that women's experience of job loss is at least as negative as that experienced by men comes from a field experiment involving a broad range of age and occupational groups (Caplan et al., 1989). Caplan et al. found that men and women in the control group were just as likely to report demoralization and depression in the face of setbacks.

It is also likely that the pattern of relationship between the job seeker and partner will be much different depending on whether the job seeker is male or female. Little research has addressed this question for couples facing unemployment. Other research, however, supports the importance of taking gender into account. In general, research suggests that women have greater empathic concern for others and more ties to extended family and external social networks (Kessler & McLeod, 1985). Women are also more likely to experience negative network events (Wethington, McLeod, & Kessler, 1987) and more overload due to demands from social networks (Williams, 1985). These differences may explain the higher levels of emotional strain and psychopathology reported among women.

These findings suggest that couples involving women who lose their jobs will deal with the crisis in different ways than couples involving women who are partners of recently unemployed men. It is possible, for example, that the needs of the unemployed individual for social support from the partner may be more strain producing for female than male partners. The research by Dew et al. (1991) on postlayoff sequelae of husband job loss indicated that two factors—poor perceived social support from their husbands and the experience of financial difficulties—were most predictive of subsequent emotional distress for wives. These predictions are further supported by findings suggesting that women are more sensitive than men to issues of intimacy and caring (Rubin, Peplau, & Hill, 1981) and that women's attributions regarding negative relationships with their spouses are more likely to influence their feelings of marital distress (Fincham & Bradbury, 1987). Such feelings are likely to be exacerbated by the stresses of job loss on the relationship.

Whereas the larger social networks of female partners may constitute a source of overload with regard to providing social support, such networks may also provide more resources for female job seekers. Accordingly, one might expect that women who lose their jobs would be less likely then men to turn solely to their partners for support. On the other hand, men, who are more likely to have a social network that is tied largely to associates at work, may be more likely to turn to their spouse for support. Such a finding was reported by Pearlin (1975) in one of the few studies that compared male and female patterns of coping with job loss. That study also indicated that job loss was more likely to lead to depression for men than for women. This means that, in addition to issues that job-seeking couples face, such as managing finances and planning strategies for job seeking, female partners in Pearlin's study were more likely than male partners to have the additional stressor of dealing with a depressed partner (Coyne et al., 1987).

Nearly 20 years have passed since the publication of Pearlin's (1975) findings, and such findings on sex differences in depression may not be as relevant in today's workforce, given the increased participation of women who view the role of employee as a significant part of their self-identity. Regardless, the generic importance of the finding is that understanding the burden placed on the couple may depend (a) on the additional demands for support caused by job loss, (b) the meaning of work for the job seeker, and (c) the skills of each partner in meeting needs for support of the other partner, and (d) the emotional reactions of each partner. Whether these parameters differ because of the gender of the job seeker may depend on the social period in which the study is being conducted as well as the traditionality of the couple's relationship in terms of the definition of male and female roles in the marriage. Research on job loss that integrates these parameters would fill an important gap in the literature and would provide a conceptual and empirical framework for designing interventions that respected differences among couples in their particular social, behavioral, and emotional needs as job seeker and partner.

Traditionality. Couples vary substantially on how much they embrace traditional or more modern role divisions in family life. Traditional couples are more likely to value gender-based allocation of homemaker and provider roles. In addition, traditional couples are more likely to value problem-solving styles that do not involve as much discussion or direct confrontation with one another (Fitzpatrick, 1988). Less traditional, more egalitarian attitudes in couples are likely to be associated with more equal valuing of employment for both members and a more collaborative and confrontive style of approaching problems or conflicts. These findings suggest that traditional couples and egalitarian couples are challenged in different ways by job loss and that the two types of couples may bring different transactional strengths and weaknesses to the situation. As a result, couple transaction patterns that help to reduce the negative effects of job loss for traditional couples may be much different from those transaction patterns that are most productive for egalitarian couples.

Financial hardship. Several studies have suggested that the financial strain generated by job loss may be responsible for the incidence of poor mental health. Although both employed and unemployed individuals may have to cope with negative life events, research suggests that the confluence of job loss with other negative events with a loss of financial flexibility accounts for more variance in symptoms of emotional strain than does either the job loss or other life events alone (e.g., Kessler, House, & Turner, 1988; Vinokur & Caplan, 1987). These findings suggest that differences in a couple's abilities to negotiate how to manage finances could be a powerful determinant of their mental health.

It seems reasonable that higher levels of financial hardship and associated stressors would have different effects on couple transactions than would lower levels. However, it is unclear whether the effects of financial hardship operate through the objective burdens that result from reduced finances or whether financial hardship is most influential through the perceived threat implied by reduced income. For example, Elder et al. (1992), in their study of rural families experiencing economic stress, found that perceived hardship was related to increased hostility toward each other in both the wife and the husband but that objective hardship was actually related to *decreased* hostility of the wife toward the husband. In addition, only perceived hardship predicted the husband's depression, and neither variable predicted depression experienced by the wife.

Summary. Gender, traditionality, and financial hardship are potential moderators of how couple transactions may influence the mental health of the partners and the economic outcomes of their coping. Knowledge of such moderators may allow social scientists and practitioners to identify particular groups of couples for whom the mediating model is particularly likely to hold.

For example, if men rather than women depend more on the spouse for social support, it is possible that couple transactions will be much more predictive of job-search motivation for male job seekers than for female job seekers. Second, moderators may help researchers to identify different subsets of mediating factors for different subgroups. For example, engagement and open problem solving may prove to be more important for egalitarian couples, whereas esteem maintenance functions may prove to be more important for traditional couples. Such findings would suggest specific directions for tailoring interventions so they might have the maximal impact for each couple.

Next Steps

In this chapter we have attempted to make the case that, although family-focused interventions may hold great promise for reducing the emotional and economic costs of job loss, they need to be guided by a clear understanding of how families and couples cope as a group with the demands of this crisis. Furthermore, we have argued that theory-driven survey research may need to precede experimental intervention projects to identify those couples and family factors that are the best targets for such intervention. We have also presented a specific set of hypotheses concerning the factors that may lead to successful problematic coping by couples experiencing job loss. The emphasis on couple transactions points to an important gap in the understanding of coping processes: that is, how to think about coping and social support as functions of the dyad rather than of individuals.

On the basis of these premises, we believe that family-focused interventions, or any preventive intervention that attempts to target the social milieu of people at risk for emotional distress, will be more successful if they are based on close observation of "situated coping," or coping as it emerges from and helps to shape the day-to-day transactions within this milieu. To address these issues in the domain of unemployment, we are conducting what appears to be one of the first studies to address these issues. This study has involved going into the homes of job seekers, identified through state unemployment centers, and directly observing couples discussing a variety of coping issues. It also involved returning to these homes twice over the course of a year to understand how such coping changes in the face of new crises and how various couple coping styles influence emotional distress and job-search activities over time. Measures are based on the process model outlined earlier, with an emphasis on observing those processes that are most likely to be amenable to intervention. Although such survey studies can be time-consuming and expensive, particularly those involving longitudinal designs and direct observation of family transactions, they hold major promise for advancing the understanding of coping processes and for guiding the development of preventive interventions that are effective in reducing the suffering associated with transitional crises such as job loss.

References

Asarnow, J. R., Tompson, M., Hamilton, E. B., Goldstein, M. J., & Guthrie, D. (1994). Family-expressed emotion, childhood-onset depression, and childhood-onset schizophrenia spectrum disorders: Is expressed emotion a nonspecific correlate of child psychopathology or a specific risk factor for depression? *Journal of Abnormal Child Psychology, 22,* 129–146.

Barnett, P. A., & Gotlib, I. H. (1988). Psychosocial functioning and depression: Distinguishing among antecedents, concomitants, and consequences. *Psychological Bulletin, 104,* 97–126.

Beach, S. R. H., Sandeen, E. E., & O'Leary, K. D. (1990). *Depression in marriage.* New York: Guilford Press.

Bebbington, P., Hurry, J., Tennant, C., Sturt, E. Y., & Wing, J. K. (1981). Epidemiology of mental disorders in Camberwell. *Psychological Medicine, 11,* 561–579.

Bradbury, T. N., & Fincham, F. D. (1990). Attributions in marriage: Review and critique. *Psychological Bulletin, 107,* 3–33.

Caplan, R. D., Vinokur, A. D., Price, R. H., & van Ryn, M. (1989). Job-seeking, reemployment, and mental health: A randomized field experiment in coping with job loss. *Journal of Applied Psychology, 74,* 759–769.

Cobb, S., & Kasl, S. V. (1977). *Termination: The consequences of job loss* (DHEW [NIOSH] Publication No. 77-224). Washington, DC: U.S. Government Printing Office.

Cohen, S., Lichtenstein, E., Mermelstein, R., Kingsolver, K., Baer, J. S., & Kamarck, T. W. (1987). Social support interventions for smoking cessation. In B. H. Gottlieb (Ed.), *Creative support groups: Formats, processes, and effects* (pp. 211–240). Newbury Park, CA: Sage.

Coyne, J. C., & DeLongis, A. (1986). Going beyond social support: The role of social relationships in adaptation. *Journal of Consulting and Clinical Psychology, 54,* 454–460.

Coyne, J. C., Kessler, R. C., Tal, M., Turnbull, J., Wortman, C. B., & Greden, J. F. (1987). Living with a depressed person. *Journal of Consulting and Clinical Psychology, 55,* 347–352.

Dew, M. A., Bromet, E. J., & Penkower, L. (1992). Mental health effects of job loss in women. *Psychological Medicine, 22,* 751–764.

Dew, M. A., Penkower, L., & Bromet, E. J. (1991). Effects of unemployment on mental health in the contemporary family. *Behavior Modification, 15,* 501–544.

Dewey, D., & Hunsley, J. (1990). The effects of marital adjustment and spouse involvement on the behavioral treatment of agoraphobia: A meta-analytic review. *Anxiety Research, 2,* 69–83.

Elder, G. H., Jr., Conger, R. D., Foster, E. M., & Ardelt, M. (1992). Families under economic pressure. *Journal of Family Issues, 13,* 5–37.

Emmelkamp, P. M. G., & de Lange, J. (1983). Spouse involvement in the treatment of obsessive-compulsive patients. *Behavioral Research Therapy, 21,* 341–346.

Feather, N. T., & Davenport, P. R. (1981). Unemployment and depressive affect: A motivational and attributional analysis. *Journal of Personality and Social Psychology, 41,* 422–436.

Fincham, F. D., & Bradbury, T. N. (1987). The impact of attributions in marriage: A longitudinal analysis. *Journal of Personality and Social Psychology, 53,* 510–517.

Fisher, J. D., Nadler, A., & Witcher-Alagna, S. (1982). Recipient reactions to aid. *Psychological Bulletin, 91,* 27–54.

Fitzpatrick, M. A. (1988). *Between husbands and wives. Communication in marriage.* Newbury Park, CA: Sage.

Gottman, J. M. (1979). *Marital interaction: Experimental investigations.* San Diego, CA: Academic Press.

Hafner, J. (1977). The husbands of agoraphobic women and their influence on treatment outcome. *British Journal of Psychiatry, 131,* 289–294.

Hoebel, F. C. (1976). Brief family-interactional therapy in the management of cardiac-related high-risk behaviors. *Journal of Family Practice, 3,* 613–618.

Howe, G. W. (1987). Attributions of complex cause and the perception of marital conflict. *Journal of Personality and Social Psychology, 53,* 1119–1128.

Kessler, R. C., House, J., & Turner, B. (1988). The effects of unemployment on health in a community survey: Main, modifying, and mediating effects. *Journal of Social Issues, 44,* 443–452.

Kessler, R. C., & McLeod, J. D. (1985). Sex differences in vulnerability to undesirable life events. *American Sociological Review*, *49*, 443–452.

Leftwich, L. (1989). *Attributional locus in marital problem solving and its relationship to marital satisfaction*. Unpublished doctoral dissertation, Vanderbilt University, Nashville, TN.

Markman, H. J., Duncan, S. W., Storaasli, R. D., & Howes, P. W. (1987). The prediction and prevention of marital distress: A longitudinal investigation. In K. Hahlweg & M. J. Goldstein (Eds.), *Understanding major mental disorder: The contribution of family interaction research* (pp. 266–289). New York: Family Process Press.

Meichenbaum, D. (1985). *Stress inoculation training: A clinical guidebook*. Elmsford, NY: Pergamon Press.

Moser, K. A., Fox, A. J., & Jones, D. R. (1984). Unemployment and mortality in the OPCS longitudinal study. *Lancet*, *ii*, 1324–1328.

Nieva, V. (1988). Work and family linkages. In B. Gutek, A. Stromber, & L. Larwood (Eds.), *Women and work* (Vol. 3, pp. 162–191). Newbury Park, CA: Sage.

Pearlin, L. I. (1975). Sex roles and depression. In N. Datan & L. H. Ginsberg (Eds.), *Life-span developmental psychology: Normative life crises* (pp. 191–207). San Diego, CA: Academic Press.

Rosen, E. I. (1987). *Bitter choices: Blue-collar women in and out of work*. Chicago: University of Chicago Press.

Rotter, J. B., Chance, J. E., & Phares, E. J. (1972). *Applications of a social learning theory of personality*. New York: Holt, Rinehart & Winston.

Rubin, Z., Peplau, L. A., & Hill, C. T. (1981). Loving and leaving: Sex differences in romantic attachments. *Sex Roles*, *7*, 821–835.

Rush, A. J., Shaw, B., & Khatami, M. (1980). Cognitive therapy of depression: Utilizing the couples system. *Cognitive Therapy and Research*, *4*, 103–113.

Seligman, M. E. P. (1975). *Helplessness: On depression, development and death*. San Francisco: W. H. Freeman.

Seligman, M. E. P., Abramson, L. Y., Semmel, A., & von Baeyer, C. (1979). Depressive attributional style. *Journal of Abnormal Psychology*, *88*, 242–247.

Taitz, L. S., King, J. M., Nicholson, J., & Kessel, M. (1987). Unemployment and child abuse. *British Medical Journal*, *294*, 1074–1076.

Thoits, P. A. (1986). Social support as coping assistance. *Journal of Consulting and Clinical Psychology*, *54*, 416–423.

U. S. Department of Labor. (1986, December). *Economic adjustment and worker dislocation in a competitive society: Report of the Secretary of Labor's Task Force on Economic Adjustment and Worker Dislocation*. Washington, DC: Author.

Vinokur, A., & Caplan, R. D. (1987). Attitudes and social support: Determinants of job-seeking behavior and well-being among the unemployed. *Journal of Applied Social Psychology*, *17*, 1007–1024.

Vinokur, A. D., Price, R. H., & Caplan, R. D. (1991). From field experiments to program implementation: Assessing the potential outcomes of an experimental intervention program for unemployed persons. *American Journal of Community Psychology*, *19*, 543–562.

Vinokur, A. D., van Ryn, M., Gramlich, E. M., & Price, R. H. (1991). Long-term follow-up and benefit-cost analysis of the Jobs Program: A preventive intervention for the unemployed. *Journal of Applied Psychology*, *76*, 213–219.

Weiner, B. (1980). A cognitive (attribution) emotion-action model of motivated behavior: An analysis of judgments of helpgiving. *Journal of Personality and Social Psychology*, *39*, 186–200.

Wethington, E., McLeod, J. D., & Kessler, R. C. (1987). The importance of life events for explaining sex differences in psychological distress. In R. C. Barnette, L. Bierner, & G. Baruch (Eds.), *Gender and stress* (pp. 144–156). New York: Free Press.

Williams, D. G. (1985). Gender differences in interpersonal relationship and well-being. In A. Kerckhoff (Ed.), *Research in sociology of education and socialization* (Vol. 5, pp. 239–267). Greenwich, CT: JAI Press.

Windschuttle, K. (1980). *Unemployment: A social and political analysis of the economic crisis in Australia*. New York: Penguin Books.

11

Coping With Job Loss and Career Stress: Effectiveness of Stress Management Training With Outplaced Employees

Miya Maysent and Stefanie Spera

Corporate closings have been occurring at an unprecedented rate since the mid-1980s. According to Offerman and Gowing (1990), more than 57,000 corporations experienced a reduction in force or complete shutdown in 1986 alone. More recent statistics estimated that 9 million workers were permanently and involuntarily separated from their jobs between January 1991 and December 1993 (Walsh & Dillon, 1994). This report also indicated that the greatest number of job displacements occurred among managers and professionals (1.2 million) and among technical, sales, and administrative support personnel (1.3 million).

The challenge to unemployed workers and perhaps even more so to the professional and management-level worker is to develop job-search strategies that are effective and to maintain a high level of motivation throughout their job search. Studies have consistently shown that job loss ranks between seventh and ninth in the severity of stress it creates when compared with more than 60 other life events (Holmes & Rahe, 1967). Research indicates that job loss increases an individual's risk for emotional and physical illness (DeFrank & Ivancevich, 1986; Iverson & Sabroe, 1988).

Studies investigating the relation between health and job loss have shown that general health reports became progressively more negative and numerous as the length of unemployment increased (Cook, Cummins, Bartley, & Shoper, 1982; Warr & Jackson, 1984). Warr and Jackson found that psychological distress increased as individuals went from employed to unemployed status and that the reverse pattern occurred when workers became reemployed. O'Brien and Kabanoff (1979) surveyed employed and unemployed individuals and found that the jobless sample had elevated levels of stress symptoms, increased heart trouble, shortness of breath, and vision problems. Researchers also found more heavy drinking and alcohol abuse among unemployed individuals (Cook et al., 1982).

Unemployment affects individuals on emotional and psychological levels. Bebbington, Harry, Tennant, Sturt, and Wing (1981) found that unemployed people had more "psychiatric problems" than comparable employed groups. Finlay-Jones and Eckhardt (1981) suggested that these effects were found across age lines. They studied young job seekers and found that a significant number of their participants experienced emotional distress and that 70% of those individuals began experiencing the emotional problems after they had begun their job searches. Feather (1982) found that respondents with the highest motivation to find a job, and with the highest rating of attractiveness of work, were also those with the highest scores on various depression indexes.

Considering the research that supports the belief that unemployment can play a role in increasing an individual's vulnerability to illness combined with the belief that job is generally experienced as a highly stressful change event, a program that prepares newly displaced workers for the difficulties that are likely to occur during their job search may ameliorate some of the physical and emotional trauma frequently experienced by job seekers.

In this chapter, we describe a stress management program developed for the outplacement clients of Drake Beam Morin, Inc., (DBM) one of the nation's largest outplacement firms (Kirkpatrick, 1991). The purpose of the intervention was to aid displaced employees in managing their stress levels during their job searches. The intervention involved training, counseling, and coaching in various stress management strategies and techniques. The study was based on the belief that by increasing an individual's ability to cope with job-search stress, he or she would be better able to conduct a thorough job-search campaign. First, we outline the major components of the program; we then evaluate the effectiveness of this stress intervention for an unemployed population.

Method

Managing Career and Lifestyle Stress Program

The intervention developed for the unemployed participants had five primary focuses: understanding the nature of stress, recognizing individual stress responses, techniques to minimize the negative effects of stress, an opportunity to use these techniques, and developing strategies to deal with future stressors. The program, titled *Managing Career and Lifestyle Stress* (Drake Beam Morin, Inc., 1994), was divided into the following sections: (a) understanding and assessing stress, (b) managing stress by managing your thinking, (c) managing stress by strengthening yourself; (d) managing stress by taking control, and (e) planning to improve stress management. The intervention was presented as a two-part workshop facilitated by trained counselors. A more thorough examination of each of the components of the workshop follows.

Understanding and assessing stress. This section focused on participant introductions, rapport building, and education of the clients. The participants were asked to fill out the Social Readjustment Rating Scale (Holmes & Rahe, 1967), which appropriates values to 43 life change events. These 43 events are representative of health, work, family, personal, social, and financial areas of life adjustment. The goal of having participants complete this stress inventory was not for the counselor to measure each individual's stress level but to illustrate to the participants that stress could be induced by both positive and negative events. The primary stress agent was that of change. All the events on the inventory caused the individual to move from a steady state of psychological adjustment into a state of disequilibrium. This view of stress is supported by several researchers who have found that the greater the individual's degree of disequilibrium, the greater the risk for psychological distress (Rahe, 1979). The counselor used this measure to provide participants with tangible evidence of the stress they were experiencing.

During this period, the counselor assessed the participants' functional level by discussing their personal experiences with and perception of stress. The facilitator guided the discussion in a didactic fashion, explaining various models of stress. The didactic and cognitive approach was supported by Lazarus and Folkman (1984), who suggested that stress interventions should provide individuals with information concerning the processes they experience while stressed.

The first model is based on Roskies' (1987) theory that Type A behavior and stress do not automatically lead to dysfunction or physical impairment. She posited that in the standard stress situation, individuals are faced with a change event. The individual mobilizes all of their resources, thoughts, feelings and actions to deal with the threat. After they have adjusted to or eliminated the distressing event, they regroup to replenish their resources to meet the next challenge. Roskies suggested that it is the Type A individual's nature to maintain a level of hypervigilance for stressful stimuli as well as a higher-than-normal level of physical activity. People with Type A personalities are more highly aroused by all environmental stimuli (Glass, 1977), and, as a result, even if they cope with the initial distressing event effectively, they are unlikely to allow themselves time to regroup following the event. Therefore, when the next stressor occurs, Type A individuals must meet the challenge with fewer resources than those who have had sufficient time to replenish their energy resources.

The second model focused on the physical outcomes of stress. Because many high-functioning individuals have difficulty recognizing when they are experiencing stress, the participants are presented with a list of stress symptoms. Researchers have attributed a plethora of symptomatology to stress (Catalano & Dooley, 1977; Kelvin & Jarrett, 1985). This exercise was intended to aid participants in recognizing their own unique stress triggers (Roskies, 1987) and the individual manifestations of responses to an identical stressor.

The third model presented to participants was Bridges' (1980) transitional model. He suggested that individuals are continually moving through and dealing with change and that people are not normally aware of the changes going on around them. Individuals classify events in their life as expected, predictable developments. It is only when those events are not expected or their impact is detrimental to one's well-being that it is classified as a stressor.

Bridges adopted a long-term perspective of the individual's life in which he or she is continually moving from one change event to the next.

Bridges (1980) suggested that there are some consistent phases and experiences that a person goes through during any change, either positive or negative. He labeled these phases as "the ending," "the neutral zone," and "the new beginning." The ending is a period of letting go, loss, and sadness. The unemployed individual can easily relate to this phase, especially because most of the outplacement clients are actively in this phase. The neutral zone, by Bridges' own admission, is a misnomer. He described this as a period of confusion, hope, despair, anxiety, and excitement. During this period, the individual is well on his or her way to saying goodbye and letting go of the emotional burdens attached to the ending; however, they also have a futuristic perspective in anticipating their next step. This is the phase in which outplacement clients spend the majority of their time. Excitement about their possible future is sometimes diminished by anxiety or anger about their present or past. As a result, individuals during this period may feel emotionally out of control. The last stage in Bridges' model is the new beginning. This period is marked by a sense of renewal and revitalization. The individual is now committed to the next step and the actions necessary to being successful within it. Bridges noted that these stages are not discreet; rather, each stage flows into and overlaps one another at different periods. He suggested that if one can put all life's transitions, both good and bad, into this perspective, the way in which one chooses to deal with them can be less damaging and painful.

The fourth model is the cognitive–behavioral model proposed by Burns (1980). He suggested that the way people think about a situation or about themselves will directly affect their affective and behavioral responses. According to Burns, people have great difficulty modifying their emotional responses to a situation. Thoughts are more easily reshaped than are emotions. Therefore, rather than allowing patterns of emotions to lead to thoughts and on to behaviors, one should alter the cycle so that thoughts lead to behaviors that lead to a change in emotional responses. In essence, he recommended removing emotions from the early stages of the process, allowing them to exist, but focusing on shaping one's thoughts so that they are more motivating rather than deflating.

Burns (1980) and Bridges (1980) proposed that the stressor or environmental stimuli is not inherently good or bad. Rather, it is the individual's historical perspective, current situation, and cognitive appraisal that deems an event as positive or negative. These proactive approaches parallel the cognitive perspectives of individuals high in hardiness and effective coping skills (Kobasa & Puccetti, 1983; Lazarus & Folkman, 1984).

Managing stress by managing your thinking. This section of the intervention focused on identifying, challenging, and replacing cognitive distortions with more effective and realistic self-talk. The first step in removing irrational thoughts was to begin recognizing these thoughts as irrational. The aim of this module was to make participants aware of how their own expectations and judgments contributed to the intensity and duration of stress experienced and to demonstrate that modification of these habitual thought patterns could lead to a reduction of stress.

Ellis (1970) and others (e.g., Meichenbaum, 1985) have focused extensively on the nature and treatment of irrational beliefs. Some typical distorted beliefs are "I can't change myself," "I must be perfect and absolutely competent," and "I have no control over my unhappiness." Therefore, treatment began with increasing participants' awareness of when, how, and why irrational thoughts occurred to build up their commitment to the purpose of this intervention. Participants were provided with a list of 10 typical cognitive distortions (McKay, Davis, & Fanning, 1981). These were slight derivations from Ellis's (1970) distortions in that they were related specifically to job-search issues. Participants were asked to look through the list and their descriptions and to select those patterns or beliefs that most closely resembled themselves. This activity provided examples of beliefs that lead to increased tension and discomfort, such as unrealistic expectations of themselves or others, catastrophizing, and constantly focusing on the uncontrollable rather than the controllable elements of their life (Roskies, 1987).

After participants were introduced to the idea of irrational or distorted beliefs, they completed an exercise on recognizing and challenging distortions. A scenario was set up in which a character faced a stressful situation. The character's internal dialogue was written out. The participants were asked to label the emotions the character might be experiencing, the distortions being used, and healthier, more productive thoughts that could replace them. After going through two examples, participants were asked to apply the same technique to a personal situation that they perceived to be stressful.

The scenarios addressed two categories of stressful situations: predictable and unpredictable (Roskies, 1987). The two situations required different types of preparation and adaptive skills. In the predictable situation, one was able to prepare for the typical reactions to the stimulus. By evaluating the situation from a distance, one could select the tactic that would be most useful when the situation eventually occurred. Mental rehearsal increases an individual's perception of having control over the situation.

The second scenario reflected the unpredictable type of stress encountered on a daily basis, such as long lines at a grocery store, traffic jams, and canceled appointments. Because it is impossible to eliminate these types of daily hassles (Lazarus & Cohen, 1977) from life, the ability to affect one's reactions to these situations can significantly decrease their negative impact. The first step in dealing with unpredictable stressors is recognizing the signs of increasing tension. Once the tension is recognized, the individual can interrupt the process by "braking" (Meichenbaum, 1985; Roskies, 1987). This braking process is not intended to deny the existence of the stressor but to allow the individual to regain control so that he or she is better able to deal with the situation.

One of the greatest challenges the facilitators faced was to overcome participants' perceptions that modifying and replacing negative self-talk was merely a game of semantics, which was an artificial externally imposed pattern of thoughts and actions. It was the facilitator's obligation to point out that all patterns of thought are learned and as such can be unlearned or relearned.

Managing stress by strengthening yourself. This module focused on be-havioral changes that reduced the experience of stress. Participants were trained in relaxation exercises that were individualized and focused on the particular stress triggers they experienced. Relaxation and visualization have proved to be effective in combating stress (Lehrer, Woolfolk, Rooney, McCann, & Car-rington, 1983). Goldfried (1977) pointed out that although individuals find different forms of relaxation more effective than others, not all are practical for situations that arise during the day. The methods discussed during the workshop focused on the individual's stress-inducing internal dialogue and the behavioral consequences of this type of thought pattern. The individual re-placed the negative internal dialogue with more effective statements and vis-ualized the behavioral outcome of that dialogue. By visualizing the desired behavior and desired outcome, the individual increased his or her sense of control and lowered his or her autonomic responses to the stressor.

The second component of the relaxation module trained participants in deep muscle relaxation techniques. Researchers have found that using a slow, well-modulated tone that guides the listeners through the various muscle groups, instructing them on how to relax their muscles, is highly effective in reducing physical tension and anxiety (Heide & Barkovec, 1984). After being guided through the exercise, participants were asked to evaluate their tension levels before and after the exercise.

The participants were taught that relaxation in its various forms (visu-alization, deep breathing, and muscle relaxation) could be used in a number of ways. Roskies (1987) offered three main ways in which relaxation can be used as a coping skill: to modulate physical tension throughout the day; to prepare for potentially stressful situations; and as the first step in regaining control when in a high state of tension. Participants were encouraged to share their stress triggers and to apply these techniques to diminish their negative effects.

Managing stress by taking control. This module explored three approaches for evaluating and coping with stressors. The concept of evaluating, increasing, and accepting control over situations has been researched by several profes-sionals (Dooley & Catalano, 1988; Folkman, 1984). Their findings indicated that control expectancies or beliefs about control greatly affected one's ap-praisals and responses to situations. In general, the more controllable a sit-uation seemed, the less stressful it was for an individual. This module focused on helping participants realistically evaluate situations by looking at the amount of control they had over it, the importance of the situation to them, and de-veloping action plans for taking and relinquishing control when appropriate.

The first exercise in this module involved assessing control. This exercise guided participants through the process of assigning degrees of control to an upsetting event. Glass (1977) found that individuals with Type A personalities typically struggle to achieve an unlimited number of poorly defined goals while maintaining control over uncontrollable factors. Because many of the partic-ipants fit the Type A profile, helping them clarify their primary objectives and determine how attainable they were increased their effectiveness in coping. The second exercise, decision clarification, helped participants prioritize and make their goals tangible. The decision clarification process required participants to write out all areas of current concern, selecting the three most important areas, and making a list of pros and cons for dealing with the situation in the current fashion or developing novel alternatives. This is a practical technique used in decision-making processes (McKay et al., 1981), but it is frequently forgotten when an individual is in distress.

The final exercise in this module focused participants' attention on areas that were controllable within their lives. During the job-search process, there are many areas that, for all practical purposes, are outside of his or her control, such as waiting for a returned phone call, the speed of negotiating a job offer, or the economic slump of certain industries. When an individual is faced with significant uncontrollable areas in his or her life, it has been found that successfully attending to areas that are more controllable can help the individual generalize these control expectancies to other areas of his or her life (Folkman, 1984). Participants selected an area of their life that they had not attended to that was important to them (commitment) and that was under their control. They developed an action plan for taking steps affecting that area and markers to measure their success. The goal of the exercise was two-fold: to encourage a positive change within the individual's life and to expand the perceptions and expectations for control in other areas of his or her life.

Planning to improve stress management. This module summarized the previous modules. The goal of the module was to reinforce the principles and skills offered in the earlier modules. The discussion focused on stress management as a lifelong process rather than a gimmick used within circumscribed parameters. Participants were encouraged to develop an individualized stress management plan that outlined their particular stress triggers, techniques that worked most effectively for them, and strategies for dealing with an isolated stressor. In concluding the workshop, participants were provided with a list of reading materials and audiotapes used to facilitate relaxation. They were encouraged to use these materials as they deemed necessary. They had access to trained staff to discuss concerns or pitfalls they experienced following treatment.

Having developed and implemented this approach to educate our clients on stress and the management of it, we then needed to evaluate the effectiveness of the program. This study was conducted over a 2-year period using evaluations and test materials provided by participants and nonparticipants in the stress management training.

Participants

The treatment group consisted of 101 (89 men and 12 women) unemployed DBM clients. Their ages ranged from 27 to 67 ($M = 47$ years). Seventy-six of the 101 participants completed all phases of the stress management program and the follow-up questionnaires. Of the 76 participants, there were 70 men,

6 women, 1 Asian American, 2 Mexican Americans, and 3 African Americans. These individuals had left careers in insurance, finance, real estate, and engineering, to name a few. All participants were white-collar workers and generally held mid- and upper-level management positions prior to being unemployed.

The control group was randomly selected from the existing DBM client population who had not opted to participate in the stress management training. Fifty people were asked to participate in the control group, with 37 completing all the necessary questionnaires to be a member of the group. Of the 37 control group members, there were 33 men, 4 women, 2 Mexican Americans, and 1 African American. Their ages ranged from 32 to 59 years (M = 46 years).

Measures

The Occupational Stress Inventory (OSI; Osipow & Spokane, 1984) was given to participants to test for treatment effects. This instrument was developed by Osipow (Osipow & Davis, 1988; Osipow & Spokane, 1984), whose research linked an individual's perception of stress and strain with his or her ability to use appropriate coping resources, such as those taught in the stress management training program. Osipow and colleagues reported that as an individual's coping resources increased, his or her experience of stress and strain diminished. The OSI consists of three major scales that assess stress related to the work environment, the individual's perception of stress and strain, and the coping skills used by the individual. Because this study was directed at unemployed individuals, the first scale used to assess the work environment was deemed inappropriate and was not filled out by the participants.

Two OSI scales were deemed appropriate: the Personal Strain Questionnaire (PSQ) and the Personal Resources Questionnaire (PRQ). The PSQ has four subscales: Vocational Strain, Physical Strain, Interpersonal Strain, and Psychological Strain. The PRQ also has four subscales: Use of Recreation, Health Maintenance, Social Support, and Rational/Cognitive Coping Skills.

Procedure

The treatment consisted of attending and participating as a group in the Managing Career and Lifestyle Stress workshops conducted by mental health professionals working for DBM. All workshops were conducted at the offices of DBM in Dallas, Texas. The group sizes ranged from 3 to 12 people per workshop. The workshops were offered as needed by DBM clients. The treatment results were gathered over a 2-year period to have a sufficient number of participants for this study. The workshops were conducted as two 3-hr classes spread out over a 1-week period. During the first 3-hr session, the facilitator covered the first three sections. Between the two sessions, participants were asked to practice some of the techniques taught. The second session began with participants sharing related experiences from that week while applying some of the stress management techniques. The remainder of the second session

Table 1. Observed and Adjusted Means of the Personal Strain Questionnaire (Pre- and Posttreatment)

Strain variables	Treatment group			Control group		
	Observed M	Adjusted M	SD	Observed M	Adjusted M	SD
Vocational pre	19.513	19.550	4.203	17.135	17.098	4.423
Vocational post	19.645	20.326	5.401	21.081	20.399	4.633
Psychological pre	25.316	25.402	6.761	21.676	21.589	7.401
Psychological post	24.000	24.371	6.790	23.784	23.411	6.929
Interpersonal pre	21.408	21.761	4.828	19.135	18.781	5.855
Interpersonal post	21.329	21.476	5.563	22.405	22.258	5.439
Physical pre	19.921	20.123	5.430	17.837	17.635	5.263
Physical post	19.395	19.458	6.212	20.243	20.179	5.320

was devoted to last two sections and wrapping up. At the conclusion of the workshop, participants filled out program evaluations and the PSQ and the PRQ.

All DBM clients are given a vocational assessment when they begin their tenure, and included in this assessment is the OSI. The results from this initial assessment were used as the baseline measure for the treatment and control groups. Individuals in the control group were given the PSQ and the PRQ to complete between September 1 and 15, 1992.

Results

Statistical Analysis

To analyze the results, we conducted a one-way repeated measures multivariate analysis of variance. The variance of each of the eight subscales of the PSQ and the PRQ was analyzed (see Tables 1 and 2). The time that elapsed

Table 2. Observed and Adjusted Means for the Personal Resources Questionnaire (Pre- and Posttreatment)

Resource variable	Treatment group			Control group		
	Observed M	Adjusted M	SD	Observed M	Adjusted M	SD
Recreation pre	26.592	26.356	6.169	28.919	29.154	5.428
Recreation post	26.684	26.683	6.473	27.810	27.811	6.724
Self-care pre	27.947	27.493	6.136	29.351	29.805	6.901
Self-care post	28.868	28.606	6.791	27.946	28.207	7.627
Social support pre	40.250	40.099	7.412	42.216	42.366	7.087
Social support post	40.934	40.767	8.057	40.108	40.274	7.430
Rational pre	36.395	35.927	5.104	38.973	39.440	6.216
Rational post	36.947	36.721	5.151	36.892	37.118	6.458

between pretesting, done at the start of DBM's services, and posttesting, done following treatment, varied from individual to individual. To reduce the risk that this variance might confound the data, we entered the elapsed time between pre- and posttesting as a covariate in the analysis, resulting in both observed and adjusted means and standard deviations.

The repeated measures comparison between treatment and control groups yielded several significant results. Of the eight scales that were evaluated, seven resulted in significant findings. The four scales that measured the level to which individuals perceived themselves to be experiencing stress or strain indicated that although both the treatment and control groups were experiencing relatively similar levels of strain initially, as time passed the treatment groups were able to maintain that level of strain, whereas the control group significantly increased their perception of strain. This occurred on the Vocational Strain, Psychological Strain, Interpersonal Strain, and Physical Strain subscales.

The perceived resources of these individuals were then evaluated, and an inverse relationship was found. On three of the four resource scales, the treatment group was able to maintain its ability to use effective coping resources to challenge their perceptions of stress and strain. By comparison, the control group decreased its use of effective resources over time. The scales that differed significantly between the two groups included Self Care, Social Support, and Rational/Cognitive coping resources.

Discussion

A multiple analysis of covariance yielded results that support the hypothesis that stress management interventions can be beneficial to an outplaced population. These results suggest that some form of education or training for individuals going through a job loss and job-search situation might be helpful in containing some of the negative emotional effects that often are associated with these events. This program was specifically developed for individuals conducting a job search, so the generalizability of these effects may be limited to programs geared to the populations they are meant to serve.

The greatest benefit of the program appeared to be in its ability to assist individuals in maintaining their effective coping resources and minimizing elevations of their perceived stress and strain. After the treatment, the participants did not show significant decreases in their pretreatment levels of functioning. This effect is not interesting until compared with the outcomes for the control group members, who, on seven of eight scales, either increased their experience of strain or decreased their use of coping skills.

In evaluating the effects of the stress management program, it appears to have supported the appropriate and helpful activities that participants were already doing to deal with their stressful situations. Perhaps through discussions focused on their stressful experiences and recommendations of appropriate coping activities, participants were simply reminded of strategies that had worked for them in the past and reinforced their continued use.

Through the informal information-gathering technique of program eval-uations, it became apparent that one of the informal benefits of this program was providing the participants with a forum in which they shared their own personal frustrations and concerns as they went through the job-search process. Many individuals who conduct job-search campaigns are doubly burdened with the belief that they must go it alone. By providing a safe and accepting en-vironment in which to vent and seek feedback, some of this sense of isolation might have been diminished.

Of greatest concern are those individuals who are unemployed but who lack the guidance or support from either professional consultants or colleagues to seek out stress management techniques. Several state employment commis-sions have begun to offer outplacement seminars for individuals whose em-ployers do not provide this type of support as part of their severance program. This is a positive first step in assisting those individuals; however, long-term assistance and monitoring needs to accompany this first step to ensure that unemployed individuals are given the tools and knowledge to successfully seek out their next job.

References

Bebbington, P., Harry, J., Tennant, C., Sturt, E., & Wing, J. K. (1981). Epidemiology of mental disorders in Camberwell. *Psychological Medicine, 11*, 561–579.

Bridges, W. (1980). *Transitions: Making sense of life's changes.* Reading, MA: Addison-Wesley.

Burns, D. (1980). *Feeling good.* New York: William Morrow.

Catalano, R., & Dooley, C. D. (1977). Economic predictors of depressed mood and stressful life events in a metropolitan community. *Journal of Health and Social Behavior, 18*, 292–307.

Cook, D. G., Cummins, R. O., Bartley, M. J., & Shoper, A. G. (1982). Health of unemployed middle-aged men in Great Britain. *Lancet, 5*, 1290–1294.

DeFrank, R. S., & Ivancevich, J. M. (1986). Job loss: An individual level review and model. *Journal of Vocational Behavior, 28*, 1–20.

Dooley, D., & Catalano, R. (1988). Recent research on the psychological effects of unemployment. *Journal of Social Issues, 44*(4), 1–12.

Ellis, A. (1970). *The essence of rational psychotherapy: A comprehensive approach to treatment.* New York: Institute for Advanced Study in Rational Psychotherapy.

Feather, N. T. (1982). Unemployment and its psychological correlates: A study of depressive symptoms, self-esteem, Protestant ethic values, attributional style, and apathy. *Australian Journal of Psychology, 34*, 309–323.

Finlay-Jones, R. A., & Eckhardt, B. (1981). Psychiatric disorder among the young unemployed. *Australian and New Zealand Journal of Psychiatry, 15*, 265–270.

Folkman, S. (1984). Personal control and stress and coping processes: A theoretical analysis. *Journal of Personality and Social Psychology, 46*, 839–852.

Glass, D. C. (1977). *Behavior patterns, stress, and coronary disease.* New York: Wiley.

Goldfried, M. R. (1977). The use of relaxation and cognitive relabeling as coping skills. In R. Stuart (Ed.), *Behavioral self-management: Strategies, techniques and outcomes* (pp. 82–116). New York: Brunner/Mazel.

Heide, F. J., & Barkovec, R. D. (1984). Relaxation-induced anxiety: Mechanisms and theoretical implications. *Behaviour Research and Therapy, 22*, 1–12.

Holmes, T. H., & Rahe, R. H. (1967). The Social Readjustment Rating Scale. *Journal of Psychosomatic Research, 11*, 213–218.

Iversen, L., & Sabroe, S. (1988). Psychological well-being among unemployed and employed people after a company closedown: A longitudinal study. *Journal of Social Issues, 44*(4), 141–152.

Kelvin, P., & Jarrett, J. E. (1985). *Unemployment: Its social psychological effects.* Cambridge, England: Cambridge University Press.

Kirkpatrick, D. (1991, April 8). The new executive unemployed. *Fortune,* pp. 44–51.

Kobasa, S. C., & Puccetti, M. C. (1983). Personality and social resources in stress-resistance. *Journal of Personality and Social Psychology, 43,* 13–23.

Lazarus, R. S., & Cohen, J. B. (1977). Environmental stress. In I. Altman & J. F. Wohlwill (Eds.), *Human behavior and environment: Advances in theory and practice* (Vol. 2, pp. 89–127). New York: Plenum.

Lazarus, R. S., & Folkman, S. (1984). *Stress, appraisal, and coping.* New York: Springer.

Lehrer, P. M., Woolfolk, R. L., Rooney, A. J., McCann, B., & Carrington, P. (1983). Progressive relaxation and meditation. *Behaviour Research and Therapy, 21,* 651–662.

McKay, M., Davis, M., & Fanning, P. (1981). *Thoughts and feelings: The art of cognitive stress intervention.* Oakland, CA: New Harbinger Press.

Meichenbaum, D. (1985). *Stress innoculation training.* Elmsford, NY: Pergamon Press.

O'Brien, G. E., & Kabanoff, B. (1979). Comparison of unemployed and employed workers on work values, locus of control, and health variables. *Australian Psychologist, 14,* 143–154.

Offerman, L. R., & Gowing, M. K. (1990). Organizations of the future: Changes and challenges. *American Psychologist, 45,* 95–108.

Osipow, S. H., & Davis, A. S. (1988). The relationship of coping resources to occupational stress and strain. *Journal of Vocational Behavior, 32,* 1–15.

Osipow, S. H., & Spokane, A. R. (1984). Measuring occupational stress, strain, and coping. *Applied Social Psychology Annual, 5,* 67–86.

Rahe, R. H. (1979). Life change events and mental illness: An overview. *Journal of Human Stress, 5,* 2–10.

Roskies, E. (1987). *Stress management for the healthy type A: Theory and practice.* New York: Guilford Press.

Walsh, D. P., & Dillon, H. (1994). Where the workers are: A state by state guide to occupations. *Occupational Outlook Quarterly, Fall 1994* (pp. 10–23). Washington, DC: U.S. Government Printing Office.

Warr, P., & Jackson, P. (1984). Men without jobs: Some correlates of age and length of unemployment. *Journal of Occupational Psychology, 57,* 77–85.

Part III

Understanding and Treating Posttraumatic Stress

12

Prevention of Work-Related Posttraumatic Stress: The Critical Incident Stress Debriefing Process

George S. Everly, Jr., and Jeffrey T. Mitchell

According to the National Council on Compensation Insurance, excessive stress accounts for about 14% of all "occupational disease" workers' compensation claims (McCarthy, 1988). The council noted that medical and other benefit payments averaged $15,000 for stress-related claims. This amount is twice the average amount paid per claim for workers with physical injuries.

Although even more difficult to document, the total financial costs of excessive stress to business and industry, beyond just workers' compensation claims, appear formidable. Estimates place the overall cost of stress on the economy as high as $150 billion per year (Miller, 1988).

By many estimations, posttraumatic stress disorder (PTSD) represents the most severe and disabling type of occupational stress (Everly, 1989). An epidemiological investigation conducted by Helzer, Robins, and McEvoy (1987) revealed that PTSD has a prevalence of about 1–2% of the general population of the United States, a prevalence comparable to that of schizophrenia. Davidson (1991) noted that its prevalence may reach close to 10% of the young adult population in the United States. The statistical risk of PTSD may be misleading, however. Lifton (1988) argued that vulnerability to psychological trauma is merely a matter of degree: All human beings are vulnerable. For those employed in high-risk professions (e.g., public safety, emergency services, military, etc.), occupational demands dramatically increase the risk of psychological traumatization. Yet, there is no generally agreed on "treatment of choice" for PTSD. The severity, prevalence, and lack of generally agreed on therapeutic interventions argue strongly for the development of a program to prevent PTSD, especially in high-risk populations. *Critical incident stress debriefing* (CISD; Mitchell, 1983) is a form of psychological debriefing developed to mitigate the harmful effects of work-related trauma and ultimately prevent PTSD.

CISD appears to be the most widely used group intervention technique in the world for the prevention of work-related PTSD among high-risk emergency response personnel. There are more than 360 quick-response CISD teams around the world.

In this chapter we describe the development of CISD, its basic components, and its 12-year operational history as a preventive intervention for PTSD among high-risk occupational groups.

Background

As a direct result of his field experience working with firefighting and emergency medical services workers, Mitchell (1983) developed CISD and its shorter variant, "defusing." These group processes were explored in the mid-1970s and published in 1983. The CISD and defusings were developed with two main goals: (a) to mitigate the harmful effects of traumatic stress on emergency personnel and (b) to accelerate normal recovery processes in normal people who were experiencing normal reactions to abnormal events. In short, it was believed that the CISD, as a structured small-group process, would be a positive factor in the prevention of posttraumatic stress and PTSD among high-risk occupational groups, specifically firefighters, law enforcement officers, emergency medical workers, disaster response personnel, emergency dispatchers, and public safety personnel (Mitchell, 1983, 1988a, 1988b, 1991). These processes have subsequently been adopted by numerous organizations, including the military, the clergy, and school systems, especially pupil personnel services. CISDs and defusings are frequently used in high-risk business and industrial settings, such as the banking industry, mining, oil discovery and refining operations, life guard services, and other recreational programs. Employee assistance programs are now using debriefings and defusings in their work with traumatized employees in a wide range of workplace settings.

Currently, the formal trauma response teams throughout the world use the CISD and defusing models in the prevention of posttraumatic stress. CISD and defusing protocols have been estimated to have been used in more than 20,000 group sessions during the past 12 years in a variety of settings that range from small-scale traumatic incidents to large-scale disasters. CISD protocols have been used in numerous major disaster situations, including the Barneveld, Wisconsin, tornado in 1984; the massive Mexico City earthquake in 1985; the Cerritos, California, air disaster in 1986; the devastating earthquake in El Salvador in 1986; the Palm Bay, Florida, mass shooting of 1987; the Bridgeport, Connecticut, building collapse in 1987; the San Francisco, California, earthquake of 1989; the New York City fire bombing in 1990; the aftermath of Hurricane Hugo in South Carolina in 1990; the Los Angeles, California, civil riots of 1992; the aftermath of Hurricane Andrew in South Florida in 1992; Hurricane Iniki in Hawaii in 1992; the combat in Kuwait in 1992; and the civil unrest in Somalia in 1993 and 1994. Canadian peacekeepers in Bosnia and body recovery personnel in the Pittsburgh air disaster and in the Indian air crash received CISD support.

In the past, the primary emphasis for CISD and defusings was on emergency service personnel, especially law enforcement, rescue workers, firefighters and emergency medical service personnel. Today, any organization that experiences work-related trauma uses CISD.

The seeds of critical incident stress teams were actually planted during combat situations in World War I and World War II. Brown and Williams (1918), Salmon (1919), and Appel, Beebe, and Hilger (1946) found that soldiers in those wars were more prone to return to combat when given immediate psychological support after combat than when managed later in hospitals, where they were far behind the combat lines. The debriefings in those times were unstructured, small-group meetings held during lulls in the battles. There was not much provided in the way of teaching. The debriefings mostly provided a brief opportunity for soldiers to talk about the turmoil of combat.

After the 1967 war, the Israeli Defense Forces began to use group and individual psychological support services after combat situations in the Middle East. The research on these posttrauma activities indicated that the incidence of psychiatric disturbance, including posttraumatic stress disorder, was trimmed by as much as 60% since the inception of their support services (Breznitz, 1980). In 1983, the first formal emergency services CISD team was established in Arlington, Virginia, and Alexandria, Virginia. The growth of CISD teams since then has been extensive.

Creating the CISD Team

Critical incident stress teams are in actuality a partnership between mental health professionals and peer support personnel from emergency or other high-risk professions. Both groups are interested in preventing and mitigating the negative impact of acute stress on themselves and on other workers. Teams provide stress education programs and defusings or debriefings as required to emergency personnel. They also are interested in accelerating the recovery process once an emergency person or a group has been seriously stressed or traumatized. As a team organizes, it obtains approval from the administrations of the various groups that will use the team's services. Once a group of emergency workers or others decide that they need a traumatic events team, they begin to look for a mental health professional to assist them in the team's work. Choosing the appropriate mental health professional is one of the most challenging factors in CISD team development. Mental health professionals need to have a sincere interest in the special groups they wish to assist. Mental health professionals who serve on the teams have at least a master's degree in psychology, social work, psychiatric nursing, or mental health counseling. In addition to their regular training in counseling and other mental health services, they usually need special training in crisis intervention, stress, PTSD, and the CISD process.

A critical incident stress team typically has 3–5 mental health professionals and 20–30 peer support personnel who are drawn from the ranks of emergency service organizations: police, fire, emergency medical services, dispatch, disaster response agencies, and nursing programs (especially those in emergency or critical care centers). Both the mental health professionals and peer support personnel form a pool of critical incident team members from which a response team is developed when needed. An incident that is predominantly police oriented is worked by police peers with the support of mental health professionals who are familiar with police activities and procedures. Likewise, an incident that is predominantly fire related will have fire peers who provide the support services, and so on. If an incident involves various response agencies, a mixed cadre of peers is developed to provide support services. Critical incident stress teams meet regularly to review their cases and to continue their service education.

CISD Defined

The CISD and defusing processes may be defined as group meetings or discussions about a traumatic event or series of traumatic events. Although they are not considered psychotherapy, the CISD and defusing processes are designed to mitigate the psychological impact of a traumatic event, prevent the subsequent development of PTSD, and serve as an early identification mechanism for individuals who will require professional mental health followup after a traumatic event. They also are intended to accelerate the recovery of traumatized people.

The formal CISD process is a seven-stage intervention. These stages are delineated in Table 1 (Mitchell & Everly, 1993).

The debriefing process has both psychological and educational elements, but it should not be considered psychotherapy or a substitute for psychotherapy. Instead, it is a structured group meeting or discussion in which personnel are given the opportunity to discuss their thoughts and emotions about a distressing event in a controlled, structured, and rational manner. Participants also get the opportunity to see that they are not alone in their reactions but that many others are experiencing the same reactions.

The CISD process allows for catharsis and for the exchange of information between participants and between team members and the participants. It is a good opportunity to evaluate the need for referral for some group members. The seven phases of the debriefing process are carefully structured to move in a nonthreatening manner, from the usual cognitively oriented processing of human experience, which is common to high-risk professional personnel, through a somewhat more emotionally oriented processing of these same experiences. The debriefing ends by returning the personnel to the cognitive processing of their experiences where they started.

The first segment of the seven-phase process is the *introduction*. The trained critical incident stress team lays out the ground rules of the debriefing process, describes an overview of how a debriefing works, and encourages active involvement on the participants' part. Confidentiality is emphasized throughout the process. Space constraints do not permit a full discussion of the introductory remarks that are made to the participants. Additional details of the process can be found in Mitchell and Everly (1993).

The second phase of the debriefing is the *fact* phase. Participants are asked to discuss the general facts of the incident (not aspects that would jeopardize an investigation or cause them difficulties with their supervisors). The usual questions that begin this discussion are "Who are you?"; "What was your job

Table 1. Stages of the Critical Incident Stress Debriefing

Stage	Phase	Domain	Objective
1	Introduction	Cognitive	To introduce intervention team members, explain process, set expectations.
2	Fact	Cognitive	To have each participant describe a traumatic event from his or her personal perspective.
3	Thought	Cognitive to affective	To have each participant describe his or her cognitive reactions to the event and to begin the transition to emotional reactions.
4	Reaction	Affective	To have each participant identify the most traumatic aspect of the event to facilitate affective catharsis.
5	Symptom	Affective to cognitive	To allow the identification of personal symptoms of distress and transition back to the cognitive level.
6	Teaching	Cognitive	To educate about normal reactions and adaptive coping mechanisms (i.e., stress management). Provide a cognitive anchor.
7	Reentry	Cognitive	To clarify ambiguities and prepare for termination.

Note. Adapted from Mitchell and Everly (1993) with permission of Chevron Publishing Corporation.

during the incident?"; and "What happened?" If the group is small enough (less than 20), the team leader has everyone in the room answer the same question one after the other, going around the room. If the group is larger than 20, a different technique may be used. The leader may then ask "Who arrived first, then what happened?" and then "Who arrived next and what happened?" until enough people (usually 6–8) have spoken to re-create the incident for the purpose of the debriefing.

The third phase is the *thought* phase. Participants are asked what their first thoughts were about the incident once they got off the "autopilot" mode. This phase personalizes the experience for the participants. It makes it part of them rather it being than a collection of facts outside of them.

The fourth phase, *reaction*, is the phase in which the debriefing participants discuss emotions by answering the question, "What was the worst part of the event for you personally?" This segment may last between 30–45 min depending on the intensity of the event.

The fifth phase is the *symptom* phase, in which the participants describe the signs and symptoms of distress. Usually three occurrences of signs and symptoms are discussed: those symptoms that appear immediately during the event, those that arose during the next few days, and those that are left over and still being experienced at the time of the debriefing.

The sixth phase is the *teaching* phase. In it, the critical incident stress team teaches practical, useful information that can be used to reduce the person's stress at work, at home, or both.

The seventh and final phase of the debriefing process is the *reentry* phase. In it, participants can ask whatever questions they want. They may also repeat certain portions of the incident and review aspects that still bother them. They

Table 2. Stages of Posttrauma Defusings

Stage	Phase	Domain	Objective
1	Introduction	Cognitive	To introduce intervention team members, explain the process, set expectations.
2	Exploration	Cognitive to affective to cognitive	To discuss the traumatic experience. This is achieved by having each participant relate to the facts of the event. Inquiry is also made into any cognitive or affective reactions to the event. Finally, participants are encouraged to discuss any symptoms or "unusual" reactions they had in response to the traumatic event.
3	Information	Cognitive	To ensure that participants have returned to the cognitive domain in their processing of the event. This is achieved by teaching trauma concepts and stress management techniques while attempting to "normalize" symptoms.

Note. Adapted from Mitchell and Everly (1993) with permission of Chevron Publishing Corporation.

may also bring up new pieces of information that were brought out earlier in the debriefing. Advice, encouragement, and support are offered by the critical incident stress team members. Participants are given referrals should they need additional assistance. Handouts including resource phone numbers are also distributed.

Posttrauma Defusing Defined

The defusing process is typically a three-stage intervention. It may be considered a shortened version of the CISD. Defusings are designed to be (a) implemented immediately or shortly after a traumatic event; (b) shorter in length than a formal CISD (about 1 hr compared with a 2- to 3-hr CISD); (c) more flexible than a CISD (greater latitude for questions in the three-stage format); and (d) used to either eliminate the need for a formal CISD or to enhance a subsequent CISD. The stages of a defusing are shown in Table 2 (Mitchell & Everly, 1993).

Defusings are given more frequently by a CISD team than are debriefings. They are easier to organize and have substantial advantages over formal CISDs. They clearly demand fewer team members (2 instead of 3 or 4). They are applied rapidly (within 8 hr of the completion of an event). Because they do not go into as much depth on the distressing material, a mental health professional is not always present. The team members are supervised later by a mental health professional who is on the CISD team.

Defusings are used for the same types of traumatic events that would trigger a formal CISD. The only factor that causes a team to choose a defusing over a debriefing is the time elapsed since the incident. Defusings are always given immediately after an incident, and debriefings are provided an average of 3–5 days afterward.

Putative Mechanisms of Action

CISD and defusing interventions appear to derive their effectiveness from several aspects of their phenomenology.[1]

Early Intervention

More than 50 years of research on crisis intervention support the concept of early intervention and suggest that the speed at which help is applied is related to the speed of recovery. CISD and defusings are simply methods of applying basic crisis intervention principles to a specific population of traumatized people. Therefore, they are crisis intervention practices. They have positive effects for the same reasons that crisis intervention has positive effects. They intervene quickly in a period of maximum chaos and quickly restore a sense of order. CISD and defusing are most typically used as early intervention strategies, often within hours or days of the traumatic event. Friedman, Framer, and Shearer (1988) found that early detection of and early intervention with posttrauma reactions led to lower costs and more favorable prognoses associated with individuals who have experienced trauma. Indeed, it is universally recognized that the prevention and early intervention efforts are preferable to having to use traditional treatment of full-blown posttraumatic sequelae (Butcher, 1980; Duffy, 1978; Kentsmith, 1980; Yandrick, 1990).

Opportunity for Catharsis

The term *catharsis* refers to venting emotions. CISD provides a safe, supportive, structured environment in which individuals can do this. Kahn (1966) concluded that catharsis initiates autonomic nervous system recovery after arousal. In a review of studies specifically investigating the relation between the disclosure of traumatic events and stress arousal, Pennebaker and Susman (1988) concluded that disclosure of traumatic events leads to reduced stress arousal and improved immune functioning. Heider (1974) commented on the universal applicability of catharsis to any condition of emotional discord.

Opportunity to Verbalize Trauma

CISD not only allows individuals to release emotions, but they can also verbally reconstruct and express specific traumas, fears, and regrets. van der Hart, Brown, and van der Kolk (1989) recounted the views of master traumatologist Pierre Janet, who noted at the turn of the 20th century that the successful treatment of posttraumatic reactions was based largely on the patients' ability to not just express feelings (catharsis) but to reconstruct and integrate the

---

[1]See Mitchell and Everly (1993) for a more detailed discussion of the critical incident stress debriefing and its elements for mitigating arousal. The section Putative Mechanisms of Action is adapted from Mitchell and Everly (1993) with permission of Chevron Publishing Corporation.

trauma using the verbally expressive medium. The work of Pennebaker (Pennebaker, 1985; Pennebaker & Beall, 1986) appears to confirm the critical role that verbal reconstruction and expression of the traumatic event plays in the successful resolution of posttrauma syndromes for many individuals. Bettelheim (1984) commented that "what cannot be talked about can also not be put to rest" (p. 166).

The collective value of catharsis and the verbalizing of the trauma appears to be that they lead to (a) reduced stress; (b) reduced strain on the homeostatic mechanisms of the body; (c) a reduced tendency to ruminate and obsess; and (d) an increased likelihood of making sense of the trauma (i.e., reintegration of the person's worldview, or *weltanschauung*).

Structure

With its seven specific phases, CISD provides a finite structure (i.e., a group debriefing represents a finite beginning and a finite end) superimposed on a traumatic event representing chaos, suffering, and a myriad of unanswered questions. CISD is the antithesis of the cacophony of the traumatic milieu. Borkovec, Wilkenson, Folensbee, and Lerman (1983) found that providing a structured environment where the participant could worry actually reduced the overall tendency for worry to contaminate, or interfere with, other activities.

CISD follows a psychological structure that starts in the cognitive domain and gradually moves into the affective domain. The cognitive domain helps group members to effectively use their defenses before proceeding to emotional catharsis.

Group Support

CISD, in its classic application, uses a group education model. The value of using a group format to address distressing issues is well documented: Yalom (1985) noted that the group format provides numerous healing factors intrinsic to the group format itself. Among them are the exchange of useful constructive information, catharsis, the dissolution of the myth of a unique weakness among individuals, the modeling of constructive coping behavior, the opportunity to derive a sense of group caring and support, the opportunity to help oneself by helping others, and, perhaps most important, the generation of feelings of hope. Jones (1985) commented on the value of using group discussion formats following trauma: "There is real value, especially for young men, in understanding that others feel the same strong emotions under such circumstances, that each is not alone in the strength of his shock, grief, and anger" (p. 307). To put it another way, it is impossible for one individual to believe that he or she is unique and isolated when every member of the group describes the same cognitive, physical, emotional, and behavior symptom pattern.

Peer Support

Although mental health professionals oversee the CISD process, it is a peer-driven process. Carkhuff and Truax (1965) long ago demonstrated the value of lay support models. Indeed, peer support interventions offer unique advantages over traditional mental health services, especially when the peer-group views itself as being highly unique, selective, or otherwise "different" compared with the general population.

Follow-Up

The CISD allows people with trauma to engage in group discussion, information exchange, and support. It also represents a mechanism wherein individuals who do require formal psychological care can be identified and helped to reach a quick and total recovery.

Possible explanations about how CISD works can be derived from other lines of research. True experimental designs are just beginning to be used to assess the CISD process. Such designs are obviously difficult to use in the field, but they are still needed nonetheless.

The efficacy of the CISD may be deduced naturalistically on the basis of thousands of applications over a 10-year history. One possible empirical comparison does emerge from the records of two air disasters: the San Diego air crash of 1978 and the Cerritos air crash of 1986. In San Diego, there were 125 deaths compared with 82 in Cerritos. There were no survivors in either crash. In each disaster, 16 homes were destroyed and 15 civilians were killed on the ground by airplane wreckage. More than 300 emergency response personnel were engaged in each of the two crashes. More than 10,000 body parts were recovered from each disaster scene during 8 days of recovery efforts. Thus, one can see the somewhat comparable psychotraumatogenetic circumstances facing rescue and recovery personnel.

In San Diego, crisis intervention teams provided individual on-scene support as the primary mental health response. In Cerritos, 12 formal CISD interventions were used, along with on-scene crisis intervention and a telephone hotline.

Although clearly not a controlled assessment of the CISD interventions alone, CISD represented the main traumatic stress mitigation response in Cerritos. The outcome is noteworthy. Although there was a loss from service of 5 law enforcement and 7 fire personnel within 1 year in San Diego, Cerritos lost none. San Diego lost 15 paramedics in one year, and Cerritos lost 1. Finally, there was a 31% increase in mental health utilization in San Diego; in Cerritos there was only a 1% increase according to available records.

Clearly, controlled research studies need to be conducted to demonstrate the efficacy of the CISD and to analyze, componentially, its most effective mechanisms. Until then, it may be useful to recall the comment of Kurt Lewin (1945), who said, Nothing is as practical as a good theory" (p. 129).

Enhancing the CISD: Pretrauma Education

In their review of the field of psychotraumatology, Everly and Lating (1995) noted the importance of the cognitive domain in the etiology of and recovery from posttraumatic stress. Consistent with Everly's (1993) two-factor formulation of posttraumatic stress, the cognitive appraisal and expectation of the traumatic venue may enhance or mitigate the posttraumatic stress sequelae. Thus, it would seem useful to provide workers in high-risk occupational settings with pretrauma education regarding the nature of traumatic events on the job. Similarly, learning about the early signs and symptoms of posttraumatic stress seems warranted. Such preparation is likely to functionally enhance the outcome of the CISD by assisting the stabilization and normalization processes inherent in the CISD. Everly and Mitchell (1993) reviewed pretrauma "immunization" in some detail.

Summary

CISD and its parallel intervention, posttraumatic stress defusing, are interventions designed by Mitchell (1983, 1988a, 1988b, 1991) specifically to prevent posttraumatic stress and PTSD among high-risk occupational groups such as firefighters, emergency medical personnel, law enforcement personnel, public safety workers, dispatch personnel, and disaster workers. The recently modified CISD appears especially suited for mass disasters and community response applications (Mitchell & Everly, 1993). CISDs and defusings also have been widely used to assist traumatized workers in a wide range of settings and with children in school systems.

Although pretrauma education is a prevention tactic that is used before the traumatic event, the defusing and the CISD are posttrauma prevention techniques. It is likely that the generic principles of defusing and CISD will continue to be used and will spawn variations specifically for use in school settings, nursing homes, general community settings, and so on.

Without doubt, the CISD process will be scrutinized by researchers and clinicians alike. It needs such scrutiny to determine the reasons for its perceived success and its wide acceptance in managing work-related trauma.

References

Appel, J. W., Beebe, G. W., & Hilger, D. W. (1946). Comparative incidence of neuropsychiatric casualities in World War I and World War II. *American Journal of Psychiatry, 103*, 196–199.

Bettelheim, B. (1984). Afterword to C. Vegh. *I didn't say goodbye.* New York: Dutton.

Borkovec, T. D., Wilkenson, L., Folensbee, R., & Lerman, C. (1983). Stimulus control applications to the treatment of worry. *Behavioral Research and Therapy, 21*, 247–251.

Breznitz, S. (1980). Stress in Israel. In H. Selye (Ed.), *Selye's guide to stress research* (pp. 71–89). New York: Van Nostrand Reinhold.

Brown, M. W., & Williams, J. (1918). *Neuropsychiatry and the war: A bibliography with abstracts.* New York: National Committee for Mental Hygiene.

Butcher, J. (1980). The role of crisis intervention in an airport disaster plan. *Aviation, Space and Environmental Medicine, 51*, 1260–1262.

Carkhuff, R., & Truax, C. (1965). Lay mental health counseling. *Journal of Consulting Psychology, 29*, 426–431.

Davidson, J. (1991, September). Clinical efficacy shown in pharmacologic treatment of post-traumatic stress disorder. *Psychiatric Times*, 62–63.

Duffy, J. (1978). Emergency mental health services during and after a major aircraft accident. *Aviation, Space and Environmental Medicine, 49*, 1004–1008.

Everly, G. (1989). *A clinical guide to the treatment of the human stress response*. New York: Plenum.

Everly, G. S. (1993). Psychotraumatology: A two-factor theory of posttraumatic stress. *Integrative Physiological and Behavioral Science, 28*, 270–278.

Everly, G. S., & Lating, J. M. (1995). *Psychotraumatology: Key papers and core concepts in post-traumatic stress*. New York: Plenum.

Friedman, R., Framer, M., & Shearer, D. (1988, September–October). Early response to post-traumatic stress. *EAP Digest*, pp. 45–49.

Heider, J. (1974). Catharsis in human potential outcome. *Journal of Humanistic Psychology, 14*, 27–47.

Helzer, J., Robins, L., & McEvoy, L. (1987). Post-traumatic stress disorder in the general population. *New England Journal of Medicine, 317*, 1630–1634.

Jones, D. R. (1985). Secondary disaster victims. *American Journal of Psychiatry, 142*, 303–307.

Kahn, M. (1966). The physiology of catharsis. *Journal of Personality and Social Psychology, 3*, 278–286.

Kentsmith, D. (1980). Minimizing the psychological effects of a wartime disaster on an individual. *Aviation, Space, and Environmental Medicine, 49*, 1004–1008.

Lewin, K. (1945). The Research Center for Group Dynamics at Massachusetts Institute of Technology. *Sociometry, 2*, 126–136.

Lifton, R. J. (1988). Understanding the traumatized self. In J. Wilson, Z. Harel, & B. Kahanan (Eds.), *Human adaptation to extreme stress* (pp. 7–31). New York: Plenum.

McCarthy, M. (1988, April 7). Stressed employees look for relief in workers' compensation claims. *Wall Street Journal*, p. 34.

Miller, A. (1988, April 25). Stress on the job. *Newsweek*, pp. 40–41.

Mitchell, J. T. (1983). When disaster strikes: The critical incident stress debriefing process. *Journal of Emergency Medical Services, 8*, 36–39.

Mitchell, J. T. (1988a). History, status, and future of CISD. *Journal of Emergency Medical Services, 13*, 49–52.

Mitchell, J. T. (1988b). Development and functions of a critical incident stress debriefing team. *Journal of Emergency Medical Services, 13*, 43–46.

Mitchell, J. T. (1991). Law enforcement applications of critical incident stress debriefing teams. In J. T. Reese (Ed.), *Critical incidents in policing* (pp. 289–302). Washington, DC: U.S. Department of Justice.

Mitchell, J. T., & Everly, G. S. (1993). *Critical incident stress debriefing: An operations manual for the prevention of trauma among emergency service and disaster workers*. Baltimore: Chevron Publishing Corporation.

Pennebaker, J. W. (1985). Traumatic experience and psychosomatic disease. *Canadian Psychologist, 26*, 82–95.

Pennebaker, J. W., & Beall, S. (1986). Confronting a traumatic event. *Journal of Abnormal Psychology, 95*, 274–281.

Pennebaker, J., & Susman, J. (1988). Disclosure of traumas and psychosomatic processes. *Social Science and Medicine, 26*, 327–332.

Salmon, T. W. (1919). War neuroses and their lesson. *New York Medical Journal, 109*, 993–994.

van der Hart, O., Brown, P., & van der Kolk, B. (1989). Pierre Janet's treatment of post-traumatic stress. *Journal of Traumatic Stress, 2*, 379–396.

Yalom, I. (1985). *Theory and practice of group psychotherapy* (3rd ed.). New York: Basic Books.

Yandrick, R. (1990, January). Critical incidents. *EAPA Exchange*, pp. 18–23.

13

Traumatic Stress and Organizational Strain in the Fire Service

Wayne Corneil

Stress in the Fire Service

Firefighting ranks as the fifth most dangerous occupation in North America, with an overall job-related mortality rate of 48.8 deaths per 100,000 workers (Leigh, 1988). However, despite the popular images and the beliefs of the firefighters themselves, only slightly more than one third of these deaths are fire related (i.e., caused by burns or building collapse). The National Fire Protection Association's (1988) annual report on firefighter deaths reported that for 1987, stress-related diseases accounted for 58.8% of job-related deaths.

Both acute stressors resulting from disasters and chronic stressors such as difficult working conditions have been linked to various kinds of illnesses among emergency service providers. Research on firefighters has tended to focus on biochemical or physiological indicators of stress: electrocardiographic findings, pulse rate, blood pressure, and working energy metabolism (Blimkie, Rechnitzer, & Cunningham, 1977; Dutton, Smolensky, Leach, Lorimor, & Bartholomew, 1978; Kuorinka & Korkonen, 1981). This has been the result of concerns over the high rates of cardiovascular disease (CVD) and coronary heart disease (CHD) found among firefighters.

Firefighters are a highly select population, both physically and psychologically. Applicants must pass rigorous medical examinations, meet stringent fitness standards, and, in a growing number of departments, undergo psychological screening. Anyone with a risk factor for disease particularly CVD, is rejected (Dutton et al., 1979). Accordingly, on the average, firefighters across all age groups are in better physical condition than the rest of the population. Despite such fitness levels, the incidence of CVD and CHD is two to three times that which one would expect (National Fire Protection Agency, 1988).

Physiological strain has been studied by several researchers (Blimkie et al., 1977; Dutton et al., 1979; Kalimo, Leheonen, Daleva, & Kuorinka, 1980; Kuorinka & Korkonen, 1981; Lim, Ong, & Phoon, 1987; Wong, 1990). The results of these studies have shown that firefighting is strenuous work; however, the data do not conclusively link physical effort to disease outcomes.

Given firefighters' high level of physical fitness compared with those in the general population, extraordinary stressors have to account for their increased levels of mortality (Kalimo et al., 1980).

Person–Environment Fit Model

The predominant model used by researchers to explain these results has been the person–environment fit. Typically, this is defined as follows: Certain events (stressors) occur in the environment that produce a reaction in the individual (stress), leading to wear and tear on the physical and emotional capacities (strain; Myers, 1985).

As a result, investigators have focused their efforts on identifying individual factors or environmental stimuli that cause these health effects. Considerable attention has been devoted to fitness levels (Cady, Thomas, & Karwasky, 1985), nutritional and dietary habits (Friel, Gabriel, & Stones, 1988), and smoking behavior (Sardinas, Miller, & Hansen, 1986) as explanatory variables. Most stress management programs designed for fire service personnel have concentrated on the findings of this line of inquiry.

Another line of investigation has been directed at the environmental events confronted by firefighters. Exposure to toxic chemicals, noxious fumes, and other products of combustion, extreme heat, explosions, building collapse, and other severe environmental stressors has been studied widely. Two studies have reported on high distress levels resulting from exposure to hazardous materials. Markowitz (1989) found that stress symptoms persisted 22 months after exposure to a serious chemical fire. The National Institute for Occupational Safety and Health (1981) found higher stress scores for those who had greater exposure to smoke and hazardous fumes at the MGM Grand Hotel fire.

Considerable attention has been paid to firefighters' responses to the fire alarm bell (Kalimo et al., 1980; Kuorinka & Korkonen, 1981). These researchers have found that the alarm triggers the onset of physical reactions such as increased heart rate and catecholamine excretion. Yu-Chun (1986) found higher stress levels in firefighters from busy stations responding to more alarms. However, these have all been short-term studies that did not provide a link to the long-term consequences of such repeated arousal reactions.

Kalimo et al. (1980) found that sleep disturbances, the continuous levels of high alertness required, and the mental demands of the job were reported as the most stressful factors by firefighters. The overall stress scores for the firefighters in his study were lower than the average in the Finnish population.

A number of factors have been examined for their contribution to firefighter stress: organizational, demographic, individual, interpersonal, and environmental. There is evidence that administrative and organizational stress, conflict with management, and promotional policies and procedures are important determinants of stress levels among firefighters.

Innes and Clarke (1985) reported that stress responses at a fire were predicted more by concerns about maintaining one's self-image in the eyes of superior officers and the public than by the perceived threat of the fire. They also noted that on-scene reactions varied according to the role of the individual in organizing firefighting activity, other organizational factors, and social support from coworkers.

Yu-Chun (1986) reported that poor relationships between firefighters and their superior officers resulted in significantly higher stress scores. Low social support at work among colleagues also was associated with higher stress levels. No relation was found between stress and rank.

McLeod and Cooper's (1992) literature review on firefighter stress suggested that firefighters in busier stations appeared to have more stress. They also noted that the relationship of stress to age and rank was not clear because contradictory results were found in several different studies. They concluded that some firefighters are affected by traumatic stress, whereas the majority are affected by organizational stressors.

Job Demand–Control Model

Most of the work on traumatic stress has focused on individual perceptions and susceptibility, and most interventions have been directed at individual coping strategies. This is different from other areas of occupational health, in which environmental exposures and organizational factors are assessed for their contribution to risk. From an occupational health perspective, one wants to identify factors from the workplace that contribute to the disorder as well as those from within the individual. Because stress reactions have a multifactorial etiology, investigations should reflect the workplace and personal factors in the construction of models that have a strong theoretical basis.

Baker's (1985) review of work-related stress noted that there are several work-related factors that have been identified as contributing to health outcomes: work environment (physical hazards and dangers); job content (workload and decision making); work organization (structure and level of participation); and extraorganizational (family and community stressors). He noted that occupational stress has consistently been demonstrated to be strongly associated with mental health outcomes.

The job demand–control model has come to be regarded as a more potent explanatory model for health outcomes than the person–environment fit model (Baker, 1985; Syme, 1988) when examining the influence of work. The two component factors of the job demand–control model are (a) job demands, which are primarily task related and include workload, time deadlines, shiftwork, and other structural factors; and (b) control, or job-decision latitude, the amount of constraint placed on the individual that allows for participation in routine decision making over skill usage or organizational activities.

This model holds that a primary source of stress originates in the structure and nature of the organization of work, not the individual. It assumes that the psychological and physical capacities of most individuals are sufficient to meet the demands of most occupations. It is the way in which the job allows the individual to exercise these capacities that leads to strain.

The principal finding reported in the literature and research on occupational stress has been that work that is characterized by high demands in conjunction with low decision-making latitude create high levels of strain that in turn result in deleterious health outcomes. Karasek and Theorell (1990) found that among those occupations with higher risk for CHD, firefighters were in the high-strain group. Their findings indicated that high strain had as great an association with CHD as did other, more traditional risk factors such as cholesterol level.

The person–environment fit model has led to a focus on individual coping responses to stress. This approach has been less predictive of health outcomes, either physiologic or psychologic, than the job demand–control model (Baker, 1985; Syme, 1988).

Studies of air traffic controllers (Burke, 1990) have made a distinction between unavoidable demands directly related to the actual nature of the work and those that are artificially imposed by the organizational environment. Similar responses have been found for workers in palliative care (Burke, 1990). Actual exposure to death and dying was less stressful than job organization and administration.

In virtually every study (Brown & Campbell, 1991) that has surveyed firefighters directly to obtain their subjective identification of stressors, the most frequently mentioned causes of distress are related to organizational and working conditions, not traumatic events. Given that highly stressful events do not occur on a frequent basis except for certain areas in large cities, the daily existence of the firefighter is more likely to be subject to routine stressors such as the quality of the physical environment, workloads, role conflicts or ambiguity, work relationships, and organizational culture. These day-to-day events form the backdrop against which traumatic incidents unfold.

It has been argued by Brown and Campbell (1991) that these routine stressors outweigh the effects of traumatic stressors, both in terms of the impact on the individual and on the organization. However, a review of the literature did not reveal any studies that used more rigorous methodology or standardized measures to assess the degree or impact of the demand–control relationship on firefighters or its interaction with traumatic stress.

Only one study was found (Beaton & Murphy, 1993) in which the researchers attempted to examine sources of work stress and stress outcomes using the Sources of Occupational Stress, a self-administered job stress questionnaire. Their multiple regression results suggested that leadership and organizational sources of stress were more predictive of self-assessed job satisfaction and morale. They also reported that previous critical incidents were also predictive of current job satisfaction. Beaton and Murphy concluded that firefighter stress is more complex than the simple demand–control paradigm proposes.

There has been ample evidence that a simple stressor is not the determining factor in health outcome. Social support from both the workplace (supervisor and peers) and the home buffers the effects of job-related stress. The lack of social support both in the workplace and from family has been shown to be an important predictor of emotional well-being (Cooper & Davidson, 1989). Workers who appear to be most at risk are those who have high levels of strain and lower levels of social support (Johnson, 1989).

Traumatic Stress

There seem to be a variety of events that initiate reactions characterized by intrusion and avoidance. These have led to the description *traumatic stress reactions* as a specific range of responses with expected patterns of reactions and symptoms.

Traumatic stress can be distinguished from job stress by the actual encounter with a horrible or threatening situation. Training and experience can develop mechanisms that allow firefighters to handle most situations with the necessary professional detachment. Such a calm, cool, and collected demeanor can be breached by a life-threatening situation or by a particularly terrifying incident. The reaction may not end with the shift but may emerge much later.

The literature on disaster stress has identified a wide range of stressors that appear to have both short- and long-term consequences for rescue workers. Research in this area has tended to be event specific and has not provided conclusive evidence of cumulative effects.

Posttraumatic Stress Disorder

Although part of the legacy of the Vietnam War, posttraumatic stress disorder (PTSD) is not viewed as being unique to war; it is recognized as a long-standing and pervasive disorder caused by exposure to human tragedy. The essential feature of PTSD in the development of characteristic symptoms following the experience of a traumatic event that is "outside of the range of normal human experience." According to the revised third edition of the *Diagnostic and Statistical Manual of Mental Disorders* (*DSM-III-R*; American Psychiatric Association, 1987), many situations confronting firefighters may be considered among the abnormally stressful events that may precipitate symptoms of PTSD. The characteristic symptom clusters involve (a) reexperiencing the traumatic event; (b) numbing of responsiveness to the external world; and (c) other autonomic, dysphoric, or cognitive reactions such as hypervigilance, sleep disturbances, survivor guilt, memory impairment, avoidance of reminders, and intensification of symptoms when exposed to reminders of the event. These must be persistent and last longer than 1 month to be classified as PTSD.

Method

In the current study, I used a cross-sectional, retrospective design to identify prevalence and exposure rates. The cross-sectional aspect consisted of the administration of a questionnaire consisting of standardized measures to the entire firefighter population ($N = 625$) of a major metropolitan fire department. This yielded data on diagnostic symptoms, social support, organizational factors, and other demographic information.

The retrospective aspect entailed the collection of information on exposure from fire department records. The list of events that have been hypothesized to cause trauma was used to obtain a computer printout of all such incidents in the preceding 12-month period. Fire department data are routinely collected in a way that identifies all the fire companies that responded to a particular event. The station log book for each company provided the names of the firefighters who were exposed to the event.

The names of the firefighters exposed were matched to the data from the questionnaires to provide exposure rates. The data on exposures gathered in this fashion is an objective measure of exposure that avoids recall error if self-reported exposure were used. Such a research plan is administratively difficult to coordinate in most settings. Fire departments are usually meticulous in maintaining records of incidents for legal, workers' compensation, and disability claim reasons.

PTSD Scale

Burge (1988) matched the individual test items from the Brief Symptom Index (BSI) and the Impact of Events Scale (IES) to the *DSM-III-R* criteria for PTSD. This allowed the use of two scales to reinforce the findings of traumatic stress and to differentiate the levels of chronic stress in arriving at a diagnosis for PTSD.

To develop a framework to evaluate the severity of PTSD symptoms and to arrive at a diagnosis for each participant, I used Burge's (1988) approach to constructing a PTSD symptom profile. This profile is constructed using participants' responses to selected BSI and IES subscale items to correspond to the *DSM-III-R* diagnostic criteria of PTSD. The items selected from the BSI scales also correspond to Saunders, Arata, and Kilpatrick (1990), who derived a 28-item PTSD scale from the SCL-90, the parent of the BSI. Their items, when compared with the Diagnostic Interview Schedule for PTSD as a criterion, showed a sensitivity of .75 and a specificity of .90 in screening PTSD cases.

Mediating Variables

Two measures of social support were used to tap the differences between workplace and family social resources. Billings and Moos (1987) developed the Work Relationship Index (WRI) and the Family Relationship Index (FRI) to evaluate the quality of social relationships in these contexts. The WRI has three components: involvement (i.e., the extent one is involved and committed to the job); peer cohesion (i.e., how friendly and supportive coworkers are); and supervisor support (i.e., encouragement and support from management). This scale has substantial internal consistency ($\alpha = .88$) and moderate test–retest reliability (.59 over 12 months; Heitzmann & Kaplan, 1988). The FRI also has three dimensions: cohesion (i.e., degree of family support and helpfulness); expressiveness (i.e., extent one can freely and openly express feelings); and conflict (i.e., extent of anger and conflict within the family). The internal consistency alpha is .89 and test–retest reliability over 12–15 months is .62 (Heitzmann & Kaplan, 1988).

Work Organization

Organizational climate variables, demand, control, and strain were measured by the Work Environment Scales (WES; Billings & Moos, 1987) for task orientation, manager control, and worker autonomy. The WES has been widely used to assess the relationship between work organizational stress and health outcomes (Caldwell, 1991).

Two variables were created from the WES subscales to reflect the influence of work organization: demand and work pressure. Demand is a measure of how much routine pressure is imposed by the organizational procedures and administration. It was created by adding the scores from the Work Pressure (i.e., the degree to which the press of work and time urgency dominate the work milieu) and Control (i.e., the extent to which management uses rules and pressures to keep firefighters under control) subscales. The mean for demand was 6.93 (SD = 2.46, range = 0–15). The correlation between work and control was .25, p = .0001. The correlations between demand and work and between control and demand were .82 and .76, respectively.

FF control is a measure of how much influence the individual firefighter feels he or she has over the routine demands of administration and work pressures. This variable was created by summing the scores for the WES Autonomy (i.e., the extent to which firefighters are encouraged to be self-sufficient and to make their own decisions), Clarity (i.e., the extent to which firefighters know what to expect in their daily routine and how explicitly rules and policies are communicated), and Involvement (i.e., the extent to which firefighters are concerned about and committed to their jobs) subscales. The mean for FF control was 18.75 (SD = 5.19, range = 0–27).

The literature (Karasek & Theorell, 1990) on the work demand–control model has emphasized that it is the interaction between demand and control that is of most interest in predicting health outcomes. Those individuals who have high demands but low control experience the most strain in their work and have the worst health outcomes. An interaction variable for strain specific to high levels of demands and low levels of control was created (Demand × Control; high demand = 1, low demand = 0, low control = 1, high control = 0). This variable considers strain to be present only when high levels of demand are combined with low levels of control. It does not, as conventional wisdom might indicate, assess situations in which steadily increasing demands even in the presence of control would create higher levels of strain.

Results

The firefighter population in this sample was male; their mean age was 38.9 years (SD = 10.2 years). The mean number of years of service on the fire department was 13.4 years (SD = 10.9 years), and 70.6% were firefighters with 29.4% classed as officers. Eighty-one percent were currently in a coupled relationship. Almost half (49.3%) had completed some form of postsecondary education.

The relationships among each of the new variables were explored using a correlation matrix. The strongest associations were found between work social support and the sense of control in the workplace. This appears to support other findings (Johnson & Hall, 1988) that social support plays an important role in the modification of the demand–control paradigm.

The associations between the two social support variables and demand, although in the predicted direction, were weak and not significant. Similarly, the relationship between control and demand was not significant. This may indicate that the average firefighter does not feel that he or she has much influence over the paramilitary nature of the work organization and the daily routine in the fire station. Officers reported both higher levels of work $t(393.9) = -3.61, p = .0003$, and of control $t(349.9) = -4.89, p = .0001$. This is likely due to heavier burdens with regard to routine administration and paperwork, coupled with greater control over day-to-day operations in the station.

Much of the literature on the job demand–control model has focused on comparisons between occupational groups. In this study, the comparison was between ranks within a homogeneous occupational group. An examination of the relationship between demand and control indicated that there was almost no one in the high demand–low control category that was identified in the literature as the high-risk group. This is consistent with other findings that this population does not constitute a large proportion of the workplace (Johnson, 1989).

What one does find is that high demand appears to be associated with high control. There appear to be differences in one's level in the organization such that with additional responsibilities come increased authorities. What may be important is the sense of active as opposed to passive involvement with the organization.

A dichotomous variable for strain was created using the demand and firefighter control variables split on the mean. Twelve percent ($n = 75$) had high strain and 88% had low strain. A chi-square analysis on the relationship between rank and strain showed that firefighters had the highest levels of strain and officers the lower levels, $X^2(1, N = 625) = 27.32, p = .000$.

As noted earlier, when looking at work demands and control, one needs to look at the interaction between these two factors, which results in the amount of strain experienced by the individual. A person experiences strain when there are high demands but low control over those demands. The variable created for strain reflected this situation and categorized strain into low and high levels for the bivariate analysis. The first odds ratio tested the influence of strain by itself. The crude odds ratio for strain was 2.68 (95% confidence interval [CI] = 1.49–4.77).

When strain was examined in the presence of exposure, the crude odds ratios were as follows: low strain = 2.27 (CI = 1.15–4.58) and high strain = 4.91 (CI = 1.42–17.99). These findings were based on crude risk ratios and were not adjusted for the influence of the other variables.

In the multivariate analysis, logistic regression models were used to take into account the variables that the gross analyses showed to be linked in the frequency of PTSD.

The model was estimated in stages. The first stage estimated the impact of exposure on its own when regressed on PTSD. In the second stage, the effects of the various variables on exposure when regressed on the diagnosis. In the third stage, each of the variables that was found to be significant in the preliminary analysis (serious injury, prior counseling) was entered individually to determine its effect on exposure, with PTSD as the dependent variable. When this was done, a forward stepwise analysis was done with the addition of the modifier variables to determine which variables would be retained given the criterion of $p < .05$ for inclusion. On the basis of the stepwise regression and the previous three stages' models, I constructed a final model. Variables that were found to be significant in the stepwise and preceding analysis were retained for the final model.

The models were estimated by entering all variables together into the equation to test for main effects. If variables were observed to be significant, they were retained for further models. Nonsignificant variables were removed from the model using a significance level of .05 as the criterion for inclusion.

As recommended by Checkoway, Pearce, and Crawford-Brown (1989), all variables in the logistic regression were dichotomized. This allowed the modeling of the prevalence odds across all of the possible confounding and moderating variables to estimate their effects on the dependent variable as an odds ratio. Odds ratios were calculated by taking the antilog of the logistic coefficient. Ninety-five percent CIs were calculated using the standard error of the regression coefficient.

The odds ratio estimated the change in risk for PTSD from any exposure, adjusted for the other covariates in the model. This allowed the prediction of relative odds of PTSD for a given individual who was exposed relative to the unexposed individual. Logistic regression allowed for the examination of any change in risk for PTSD from any covariate adjusted for other covariates in the model. This helped to model the need for interventions on the basis of relative risk and to identify the factors that appeared to increase the relative risk of PTSD so that these could be addressed in intervention efforts.

Tables 1 and 2 show the results of the logistic regression equations. The odds ratios for each of the various variables are presented as the relative odds for being diagnosed as having PTSD if one has that variable present.

Model 1 indicates that exposure alone had an increased odds for PTSD of 2.18. Thus, any exposure in the preceding 12-month period increased the individual's risk of PTSD twofold.

Model 2 shows the odds ratios for work and family social support, along with organizational strain when combined with exposure. Once again, exposure retained its independent effect. However, both work and family social support when examined independently served a protective function, reducing the risk for PTSD in the presence of exposure. Most striking was the elevated risk (odds ratio = 3.29) for job strain. Those who were under pressure from work stressors (i.e., high demands and low control) had three times the risk of PTSD than did those with lower levels of job strain.

A forward stepwise procedure was used to choose the variables that improved the maximum likelihood. All of the vulnerability, modifier, and ex-

Table 1. Odds Ratios of Posttraumatic Stress Disorder for Exposure

Variable	Logit coefficient	Odds ratio	95% Confidence interval	p
Model 1				
Exposure	0.78	2.18	1.26–3.77	.006
Model 2				
Exposure	0.82	2.27	1.28–3.99	.003
Work social support	−0.77	2.15	1.54–3.32	.0005
Model 3				
Exposure	0.78	2.18	1.23–3.86	.006
Family social support	−0.92	2.51	1.63–3.85	.0001
Exposure	0.84	2.32	1.31–4.08	.003
Work strain	1.19	3.29	1.80–6.02	.0001

posure variables were included in the procedure. None of the vulnerability variables were retained in the model. Prior help seeking, job strain, and exposure were the major predictors of risk for PTSD. Family social support had a protective influence, and previous serious on-the-job injury was still important.

Given the emphasis in the critical incident stress debriefing interventions as well as the literature on social support as a modifier of job stress, I constructed a final model to determine the influence of work social support.

Table 2 shows that exposure in the presence of all other variables remained consistently at a two-fold or better predictor of risk for PTSD. Thus, exposure alone is sufficient to produce this traumatic stress response in firefighters.

Exposure predicted PTSD even after adjustments for vulnerability, social support, and work strain. Those who were exposed to an event in the previous 12-month-period were at significantly greater risk for PTSD than were the others. Throughout all of the models, the strength of the association between exposure and PTSD was not diminished by any interaction between or among the other variables. Being exposed continued to be associated with significantly higher risk when other variables were controlled.

Additionally, prior seeking of help for a personal problem increased risk,

Table 2. General Logistic Model for Odds Ratios of Posttraumatic Stress Disorder Among Firefighters

Variable	Logit coefficient	Odds ratio	95% Confidence interval	p
Exposure	0.94	2.56	1.42–4.59	.002
Serious injury	0.55	1.73	1.06–2.82	.03
Help	1.23	3.42	1.97–5.91	.0001
Work social support	−0.44	1.55	0.95–2.53	.07
Family social support	−0.62	1.86	1.15–2.94	.01
Work strain	0.83	2.29	1.19–4.45	.01

as did organizational strain. A serious on-the-job injury that led to more than a week off from work also contributed significantly to increased risk.

Family social support helped to diminish the effects of stress, indicating that firefighters appear to turn to family members to assist them in resolving their distress. Work social support also helped to reduce the risk for PTSD among firefighters.

Discussion

The results of the univariate analyses showed significant relationships among PTSD and exposures, vulnerability, social support, and organizational strain. Multivariate analyses that were based on logistic regression models that took into account the interactions among these variables revealed significant links among exposure, prior counseling experience, organization strain, and the protective effects of social support. These results suggest that occupational and organizational risk factors may be as important as exposure to traumatic events in determining the risk for PTSD among firefighters.

These findings reinforce the notion that traumatic events overwhelm the individual's normal protective environment and personal capacities. Exposure to these powerful events is sufficient in itself to create the psychological re-actions. This is strong evidence that such exposures overwhelm the normal individual with a reaction that is beyond his or her ability to simply "will it away."

These analyses indicate that in addition to the high risk from exposure to traumatic events, the risk for PTSD among firefighters was significantly increased by job strain and previous experience in counseling. They also dem-onstrate that work and family social support help to decrease the risk for PTSD.

The results of this investigation demonstrate that work characteristics are associated with PTSD. Unfortunately, the specific factors that contribute to strain have yet to be determined. To further develop intervention strategies, more powerful study designs that will allow for the elaboration of specific stressors are required.

My findings also underscore the importance of both individual and or-ganizational factors in the prevalence of PTSD. The respective roles played by these factors in causing PTSD are not yet entirely clear.

Traditional Counseling

Although one might assume that the data from this study, which indicate that those who have previously sought counseling or assistance for a personal prob-lem are at greater risk and that this is due to their inability to cope or some inherent deficiency, there is an alternate explanation.

Interventions aimed at reducing personal risk factors may contribute to the severity of the reaction. The person–environment fit model leads to a type of "blame the victim" response that focuses on the inherent weaknesses of the individual. Recent efforts to increase psychological prescreening for firefighter candidates exacerbates this attitude, which mitigates against the individual seeking assistance.

Traditional clinical approaches have focused on individual interventions intended to provide symptomatic relief from stress and its attendant physiologic and psychologic manifestations. Individually oriented measures are unlikely to have any lasting effect on jobs such as firefighting, with its physical demands and safety hazards. In fact, the emphasis on individual responsibility and coping through lifestyle change (i.e., physical fitness) may increase vulnerability by creating unrealistic expectations.

Those who believe that they are responsible for controlling and coping with organizational stressors may be disillusioned when these prove to be ineffective. They may come to question their self-efficacy and resort to more maladaptive behaviors or withdrawal. If these individuals do not normally feel in control of their routine work environment, they are unlikely to generalize their sense of adequacy to traumatic events. When a traumatic event occurs, they may be less prepared and able to respond.

Secondary victimization occurs when others blame the individual for the occurrence of the event or when the person is provided with the wrong advice for how to deal with it. Pearlin and Schooler (1978) noted that in the workplace, individual coping efforts were largely ineffective in reducing the stressor or the strain. They suggested that collective efforts are more realistic given the limited power of the individual in changing organizational structures or the informal social work culture.

Methods that emphasize individual stress reduction methods are at best a "bandaid" solution because exposure and work structures are beyond the influence of the individual. The findings of this study indicate that interventions need to take into account social support and collective interventions designed not only to deal with the immediate impacts of exposure but the organizational contexts that increase strain and deplete the individual's sense of control.

This investigation indicates that management and organizational aspects of firefighting contribute significantly to PTSD outcomes. What it does not show are which factors, workloads, role conflicts, or organizational culture contribute to increased risk.

References

American Psychiatric Association. (1987). *Diagnostic and statistical manual of mental disorders* (3rd ed., rev.). Washington, DC: Author.

Baker, D. B. (1985). The study of stress at work. *Annual Review of Public Health, 6*, 367–381.

Beaton, R. J., & Murphy, S. A. (1993). Sources of occupational stress among firefighters/EMTs and firefighter/paramedics and correlations with job-related outcomes. *Prehospital and Disaster Medicine, 8*, 140–150.

Billings, A. G., & Moos, R. H. (1987). *The Social Climate Scales: A users guide.* Palo Alto, CA: Consulting Psychologists Press.

Blimkie, C. J. R., Rechnitzer, P. A., & Cunningham, D. A. (1977). Heart rate and catecholamine responses of fire fighters to an alarm. *Canadian Journal of Applied Sports Science, 2*, 153–156.

Brown, J. M., & Campbell, E. A. (1991). Stress among emergency services personnel: Progress and problems. *Journal of the Society for Occupational Medicine, 41,* 149–150.

Burge, S. K. (1988). Post-traumatic stress disorder in victims of rape. *Journal of Traumatic Stress, 1,* 193–210.

Burke, R. J. (1990, November). *Issues and implications for health care delivery systems: A Canadian perspective.* Paper presented at the APA/NIOSH Conference, Washington, DC.

Cady, L. D., Thomas, P. C., & Karwasky, R. J. (1985). Programs for increasing health and physical fitness of firefighters. *Journal of Occupational Medicine, 27,* 110–114.

Caldwell, B. S. (1991). A new view of quantifying organizational climate through the Work Environment scale. In *Proceedings of the Human Factors Society 35th Annual Meeting* (Vol. 2, pp. 930–933). San Francisco: Human Factors Society.

Checkoway, H., Pearce, N. E., & Crawford-Brown, D. J. (1989). *Research methods in occupational epidemiology.* New York: Oxford University Press.

Cooper, G. L., & Davidson, M. (1989). Sources of stress at work and their relation to stressors in non-working environments. In R. Kalimo, M. A. El-Batawi, & G. L. Cooper (Eds.), *Psychosocial factors at work and their relation to health* (pp. 99–111). Geneva: World Health Organization.

Dutton, L. M., Smolensky, M. H., Leach, C. S., Lorimor, R., & Bartholomew, P. H. (1979). Stress levels of ambulance paramedics and firefighters. *Journal of Occupational Medicine, 20,* 111–115.

Friel, J. K., Gabriel, A., & Stones, M. (1988). Nutritional status of firefighters. *Canadian Journal of Public Health, 79,* 275–276.

Heitzmann, C. A., & Kaplan, R. M. (1988). Assessment of methods for measuring social support. *Health Psychology, 7,* 75–109.

Innes, J. M., & Clarke, A. (1985). The responses of professional fire fighters to disaster. *Disasters, 9,* 149–154.

Johnson, J. V. (1989). Collective control: Strategies for survival in the workplace. *International Journal of Health Services, 19,* 469–480.

Johnson, J. V., & Hall, E. M. (1988). Job strain, work place social support and cardiovascular disease: A cross sectional study of a random sample of the Swedish working population. *American Journal of Public Health, 78,* 1336–1342.

Kalimo, R., Leheonen, A., Daleva, M., & Kuorinka, I. (1980). Psychological and biochemical strain in fireman's work. *Scandinavian Journal of Work and Environmental Health, 6,* 179–187.

Karasek, R., & Theorell, T. (1990). *Healthy work.* New York: Basic Books.

Kuorinka, I., & Korkonen, O. (1981). Firefighters' reaction to alarm: An ECG and heart rate study. *Journal of Occupational Medicine, 23,* 762–766.

Leigh, J. P. (1988). *Job related deaths in 347 occupations.* San Jose, CA: San Jose University Press.

Lim, C. S., Ong, C. N., & Phoon, W. O. (1987). Work stress of firemen as measured by heart rate and catecholamine. *Journal of Human Ergology, 16,* 209–218.

Markowitz, J. S. (1989). Long-term psychological distress among chemically exposed firefighters. *Behavioral Medicine, 15,* 75–83.

McLeod, J., & Cooper, D. (1992). *A study of stress and support in the Staffordshire fire and rescue service.* Staffordshire, England: Keele University Centre for Counselling Studies.

Myers, D. G. (1985). Helping the helper: A training manual. In D. Hartsough & D. G. Myers (Eds.), *Disaster work and mental health* (pp. 45–136). Washington, DC: U.S. Government Printing Office.

National Fire Protection Agency. (1988). *Annual report of firefighter deaths and injuries.* Quincy, MA: Author.

National Institute for Occupational Safety and Health. (1981). *Health hazard evaluation report: Federated Fire Fighters of Nevada* (Rep. No. 81-137-990). Washington, DC: U.S. Government Printing Office.

Pearlin, L. I., & Schooler, C. (1978). The structure of coping. *Journal of Health and Social Behavior, 19,* 2–21.

Sardinas, A., Miller, J. W., & Hansen, H. (1986). Ischemic heart disease mortality of firemen and policemen. *American Journal of Public Health, 76,* 1140–1141.

Saunders, B. E., Arata, C. M., & Kilpatrick, D. G. (1990). Development of a crime-related post-traumatic stress disorder scale for women with the Symptom Checklist-90-Revised. *Journal of Traumatic Stress, 3*, 439–448.

Syme, S. L. (1988). Social epidemiology and the work environment. *International Journal of Health Services, 18*, 635–645.

Wong, A. W. C. (1990, June). Physical and psychological effects of B.A. wearers. *Fire Engineers Journal*, pp. 29–31.

Yu-Chun, K. (1986, December). A study of work and illness in Hong Kong firefighters. *Fire Engineers Journal*, pp. 15–17.

14

The Assaulted Staff Action Program: An Approach to Coping With the Aftermath of Violence in the Workplace

Raymond B. Flannery, Jr., M. Annette Hanson, Walter E. Penk, Georgina J. Flannery, and Charles Gallagher

Violence in the United States is disquietingly commonplace and increasing with time. As violence has increased in society, there has been a similar increase in violence in the workplace. Offices, courts, schools, health care settings, and the like are no longer safe havens from crime. The four major societal crimes of homicide, assault, rape, and robbery have now become frequent occurrences in the workplace (Flannery, 1995).

A newly emerging body of evidence repeatedly documents acts of aggression toward college students (Utterbach & Caldwell, 1989), corporate employees (Brom & Kleber, 1989), emergency services personnel (Mitchell & Bray, 1990), grade school students (Nader, Pynoos, Fairbanks, & Frederick, 1990), mental health care providers (Carmel & Hunter, 1989; Thackrey & Bobbitt, 1990), police officers (Anderson & Bauer, 1987), shelter staff (McKenna, 1986), and teachers (Lowenstein, 1991).

Some of these episodes of violence are minor events, such as a mild threat, and usually do not unduly distress the employee who remains at work. Other events are more destructive and may result in bodily injury and psychological fright. Again, some employees with good coping skills take such events in stride and continue at the worksite, but not all. Some become victims of psychological trauma and eventually victims of posttraumatic stress disorder (PTSD) when the aftermath of such violence is left untreated (Caldwell, 1992). Such violence is costly in terms of human suffering (Caldwell, 1992), medical expense, and lost productivity (Hunter & Carmel, 1992).

Although many researchers have documented the presence of aggressive behavior (Brom & Kleber, 1989; Carmel & Hunter, 1989; Lowenstein, 1991; McKenna, 1986), less attention has been directed at treating the impact of these events on employee-victims.

In this chapter we address this need by presenting both a short review of the latest findings on psychological trauma and PTSD and a systems treatment intervention for such employee-victims. This treatment approach is called the assaulted staff action program (ASAP; Flannery, Fulton, Tausch, & DeLoffi, 1991) and is the first empirically data-based systems intervention for mental health care providers assaulted by patients in a state mental hospital. Although the ASAP focus here is on nursing personnel, this model could be readily adapted for any of the at-risk employee groups noted earlier.

Psychological Trauma

The term *psychological trauma* is defined as a person's response to a sudden, unexpected, potentially life-threatening event over which he or she has no control, regardless of how hard the person tries.

These victims are at first stunned and then extremely frightened. This is usually followed by anger, as the mind and body mobilize to restore some sense of personal control. The reasonable mastery, caring attachments to others, and a meaningful purpose in life that have been identified as the three domains associated with improved physical and mental health (Flannery, 1992) may all be disrupted by psychological trauma.

Victims lose reasonable mastery of their everyday living. There is nothing they can do to control the violence. In addition, extreme fright or physical injury can disrupt normal routines at home and at work. One's safety in a particular locale must be fully reexamined and revised. Similarly, caring attachments are disrupted. Friends may be injured or killed by the same event; colleagues and neighbors may blame the victim; and many victims of interpersonal violence understandably choose to withdraw from others to prevent being revictimized. Finally, the victim's meaningful purpose in life may be shattered (Janoff-Bulman, 1985). Most humans believe that the world is orderly, that they are reasonably safe, and that the world is worthy of the investment of one's energy. Psychological trauma proves these beliefs to be illusory, and the victim's motivation to go on is often impaired.

Along with the disruption of these three basic domains of functioning, victims may develop the symptoms of the acute distress associated with psychological trauma and PTSD. These include physical symptoms, such as hypervigilance, an exaggerated startle response, and sleeping difficulties; intrusive symptoms of memories, nightmares, and flashbacks of the violence; and avoidant symptoms of withdrawing from people and activities associated with the violence. Untreated trauma is also associated with the presence of many forms of addictive behavior, and these behaviors may reflect attempts to self-medicate the unpleasant symptoms noted here (Flannery, 1992).

If left untreated (and much trauma *is* left untreated), these initial attempts to restore some sense of control may evolve into PTSD. PTSD is characterized by two distinct phases. The first 6-month period is marked by anger and protest as the victim continues to attempt to restore some sense of mastery, attachment, and meaning. If these tasks are not resolved, the victim enters a chronic, or numbing, phase. This period is marked by less cognitive integration, less behavioral interaction with the environment, and a restricted affective life that is characterized primarily by continuous depressive affect and the numbing of other feelings. If the aftermath of the numbing phase is left unresolved, the effects may last for the victim's lifetime.

It was in this context of untreated violence that the ASAP (Flannery et al., 1991) was developed to address psychological sequelae in the aftermath of duty-related patient–staff violence.

The Assaulted Staff Action Program

The ASAP is a voluntary, peer help, crisis intervention, systems approach for dealing with psychological sequelae of assaults by patients in a state mental hospital. Within 20 min of an assault, an ASAP team member debriefs the victim at the site and provides any further ASAP services needed. The system is voluntary to avoid passive resistance by staff victims and is a peer help model so that services are provided by colleagues who themselves understand the risks. It is a systems approach to ensure supportive outreach to self-blaming victims who might not come forward on their own, and it is a crisis intervention model to ensure swift intervention.

ASAP Philosophy

The ASAP program assumes that (a) staff members may experience a crisis as a result of being assaulted by a patient; (b) these staff are deserving of compassion and clinical care; (c) violence is not the deliberate fault of the employee; and (d) victims of psychological trauma who are given the opportunity to discuss the event immediately after it occurs will cope more effectively and avoid long-lasting disruptions (Caldwell, 1992; Carmel & Hunter, 1989; Thackrey & Bobbitt, 1990).

ASAP Rationale

For 12 years, Flannery (1990) studied 1,200 men and women to see who coped well with life stress and to determine the skills used by adaptive problem solvers to ensure good physical and mental health. He referred to these individuals as *stress-resistant persons.*

Six characteristics of stress-resistant persons have been identified. These include reasonable mastery or personal control over the events in one's life; a personal commitment to some important life task; a lifestyle guided by reduced dietary stimulants, relaxation periods, and aerobic exercise; meaningful relationships with others; a sense of humor; and concern for the welfare of others.

Recent research has suggested that the six skills of stress-resistant individuals lead not only to better outcomes in coping with daily stressful situations but may be helpful in buffering the impact of traumatic events and enhancing recovery from such violent episodes (Flannery, 1992; Flannery,

Perry, & Harvey, 1993). The skills of stress-resistant people make up the domains of mastery, attachment, and meaning that are disrupted by traumatic events, and the ASAP rationale has been derived from these findings.

Deliberate attempts are made during the crisis period to reduce symptomatology associated with the acute disasters of psychological trauma and PTSD, to restore reasonable mastery, to reestablish caring attachments to others, and to foster an initial sense of renewed meaningful purpose in life to preclude the long-term consequences of untreated PTSD.

1. *Reasonable mastery.* Although personal control is associated with better health and productivity (Rotter, 1966), staff victims of patient violence frequently conclude that they have lost control of their work environment. The ASAP program reinforces the appreciation that one's actions shape one's work environment and that staff must develop, maintain, and restore personal skills necessary for effectively exercising control over one's environment.

2. *Caring attachments to others.* Social support from caring others has been shown to be related to enhancing effective problem solving with the information and emotional support gained from others (Kobasa, 1979). When staff are victims of interpersonal violence, there is an understandable initial response of withdrawing from others. In addition, victim blaming often further isolates the assaulted employee. Because these types of negative outcomes are not beneficial to recovery, ASAP counseling fosters restoration of support networks as one of its first goals. The ASAP peer help model is itself a basic component in establishing a supportive environment.

3. *Meaningful purpose in life.* Antonovsky (1987) wrote about the "sense of coherence," a global predisposition that leads to more meaningful coping. It is composed of three factors: (a) comprehensibility—the belief that the world is predictable; (b) manageability—the belief that one can shape the environment for one's needs; and (c) meaningfulness—the belief that the world is worthy of personal investment. As noted earlier, Janoff-Bulman (1985) showed how all of these assumptions are shattered when violence occurs. The work world no longer appears to be a safe place for innocent people, and many staff find their assumptions about their devotion and dedication to caregiving equally in need of being reexamined. ASAP interventions address the need for a restored purposeful meaning in life by examining with the staff victim what in the patient's behavior or in the ward community environment might have led to aggressive outbursts. Frequently, assaultive patients apologize to staff victims. The combination of these two events is often helpful in finding a renewed purpose to remain as a health care provider.

ASAP Structure

The ASAP team is made up of 15 volunteer clinicians from nursing, psychology, psychiatry, and social work. (Mental health workers were not included initially because union contracts required employees to be paid overtime for extra duty. Because the ASAP was a volunteer program, extra monetary compensation beyond base salary was not possible. The union requirements have since been changed to include mental health workers as ASAP participants.)

Eleven of the volunteers are line staff or first responders. Each responder is assigned to be on-call for a 24-hr period and carries a page beeper when on-call. Team members respond to any patient–staff assault that occurs on their shift, attend a weekly team meeting to review cases, and attend a monthly in-service training program for continuing preincident training or lectures on various aspects of PTSD and relevant intervention approaches. Each first responder spends an average of 3 hr per week on ASAP-related duties. These hours, along with monthly in-service training, total 72 hr a month for line staff.

Three ASAP supervisors, who are nurses from the staff development office, are also on-call by page to serve as support and consultant for line staff and as backup in case of multiple assaults or particularly difficult situations. The nurse ASAP supervisors rotate their coverage weekly. All three supervisors attend weekly ASAP team meetings to track the subsequent needs of staff victims individually and to assess the need for further staff training in various patient care sites. Nurse supervisors were chosen from the staff development office because, in this role, they are in a unique position to provide an array of supports to staff victims without calling attention to the fact as such. Supervisors, along with the ASAP director, provide critical incident stress debriefing (CISD; Mitchell & Bray, 1990) to wards where an assault on a staff member has been particularly distressing to the ward community. An ASAP supervisor spends 10 hr a week on ASAP-related tasks for a total of about 40 hr a month for the supervisors.

The ASAP director is responsible for administering the program. This includes monitoring the continued quality of ASAP care, providing CISD (Mitchell & Bray, 1990) to wards where indicated, and conducting a weekly short-term support group for staff victims. The director also oversees management of team resources, provides supervision, conducts in-service trainings, acts as a backup to the entire program, and continuously evaluates team members for vicarious traumatization and burnout (Flannery, 1992). The team leader also is responsible for supporting and debriefing ASAP members if they become victims of patient assault or other acts of random violence. During the first 2 years of the ASAP program, one ASAP team member was assaulted by a patient, one was confronted with the sudden death of her young child, and one experienced the murder of her two best friends by a drug-addicted thief who broke into the friends' home and killed them. The ASAP director spends about 15 hr a week on the program.

The hospital's six operators, although not formal members of the ASAP team, were an integral part of the service delivery system. They were included in all ASAP in-service trainings, were debriefed by the ASAP director regularly, and were included in all ASAP social gatherings.

ASAP Functions

Crisis intervention. When an assault occurs, the ward charge nurse is required to report the assault to the hospital switchboard operator. The operator logs the call and summons the on-call ASAP team member by beeper. (To minimize errors in summoning the correct on-call person, only two beepers were used. The line staff had one beeper that was passed on daily, and the nurse supervisors had one beeper that was passed on weekly.) The first responder goes immediately to the patient care site where the assault has occurred and is expected to arrive within 20 min of the assault. Any necessary medical care is provided off-site under agreement with a local general hospital, and any immediate medical first aid at the site is provided first before debriefing begins.

During the clinical debriefing interview, the ASAP team member notes any symptoms of psychological trauma and assesses the extent of loss of reasonable mastery and the extent to which such mastery may be restored quickly. The victim, in conjunction with the team member, determines whether the victim can continue at the worksite, can manage the unpleasant effects associated with the aggression, and so forth. The ASAP team leader also pays direct attention to needs for caring attachments by assessing potential support from ward staff, family, and friends. Team staff are especially alert to signs of victim blaming and explain to victims why this happens. Finally, the debriefing team member attempts to help the victim make some initial sense of the violence. For example, the team member may help the victim recognize that the patient was acutely psychotic, the patient was upset because the patient's mother died last week, and so forth.

The staff victim is advised that the same team member will call in 3 days and again in 10 days to evaluate how the victim is doing. If it appears warranted to the ASAP team member, a referral may be made at any time to the weekly support group for assaulted staff.

Although all episodes of severe physical or sexual assaults or threats had to be reported, assaulted employees had the right to refuse on-site ASAP interventions. If an assault occurs when the ASAP team member on-call is off-site, the need for a face-to-face interview is assessed by phone with the victim and the charge nurse. Any team member responding during off-duty hours is given compensatory time off. Finally, when ASAP responders are debriefing a victim, the ASAP member's colleagues on the ASAP member's assigned patient care site cover for the team member during the hour that he or she is off the ward.

Staff victim's support group. This group meets weekly to provide additional short-term support for staff who have experienced assaults. The nature of each assault, possible symptomatology, and the issues of mastery, support, and meaning are addressed at each meeting. Staff victims for whom the assault has led to intrusive memories of previous assaults or other types of traumatic events may be referred for private treatment. To attend the staff victims' group, victims are given release time and are paid their hourly wage for attendance at group sessions. The group is held in midafternoon to make it readily available to employees on two of the hospital's three shifts.

CISD. Particularly violent events on the ward may result in sharp increases in fear, anger, and behavioral disorganization in the ward. These events may affect patients and staff. In such cases, the ASAP offers CISD (Mitchell & Bray, 1990). This process involves a review of the actual facts of the event, an update of the health of any victims, and a focus on the thoughts, feelings, and symptoms that victims or observers might be experiencing. Instruction about psychological trauma and its impact are discussed. The debriefing closes with suggestions for coping more adaptively in coming days with the aftermath of the violent act.

Specialized services. The ASAP offers three additional specialized services: (a) When indicated, the program arranges for family meetings to help families of staff victims adjust to the impact of traumatic assaults. (b) The ASAP team also has representatives on a community crisis response team of a local general hospital psychological trauma team. ASAP team members rotate yearly, and their skills are enhanced for having participated in this community project. (c) The ASAP director conducts a hospitalwide seminar on managing stress for ward staff with the goal of reducing the general level of stress on the ward and thus indirectly reducing the assault rate.

Except for private counseling for staff victims so referred, all ASAP services are free employee benefits conducted on hospital time. All ASAP interventions are completely confidential unless the employee reports a crime. ASAP interventions are not part of the employee's personnel record, medical record, or performance evaluation record.

ASAP setting. The ASAP program was conducted in a 400-bed state mental hospital in an urban metropolitan area. More than 415 nursing personnel on 13 patient care sites provided clinical care to the patients.

When the program was instituted in April 1990, the patient population of 397 was approximately 89% White, 50% Black, 2% Hispanic, and 4% "other." The patients ranged in age from 22 to 77 years; most were 30–40 years old. Most of these patients were diagnosed as having affective and thought disorders, and less than 10% of the patients were voluntarily admitted.

The hospital course for most patients included a short stay on one of three admission units and then discharge to the community or transfer to one of three treatment units. Patients on the treatment units were discharged into the community or transferred to one of the hospital's four transition units to await community residential placement. The average length of stay was 28 days on the admissions service and 180 days on the treatment or transitional housing units. Few patients had any insurance.

The Assaults

The ASAP team responded to assaults that included threats and sexual and physical aggression. Assaults included punching, slapping, kicking, spitting, throwing objects, making threats, making sexual statements or advances, and severe verbal abuse, including racial slurs. The inclusion of threats appears to result in a more accurate representation of institutional abuse because many victims are traumatized by verbal or nonverbal intimidation (Morrison, 1992).

Assaults were either unprovoked as staff performed their duties or were sustained while restraining a patient. The severity of injuries varied greatly.

ASAP teams responded primarily to episodes of patient–staff assault. Infrequent exceptions were made for major events that affected the hospital community, such as the sudden death in the day room of a much loved patient and the murder of an equally esteemed nurse who was killed in the community on his way to work.

For purposes of prevention and management of aggressive patients, all hospital staff were initially trained in effective communication with patients and in both applied nonviolent methods for containing patients' aggressive behavior and basic restraint and seclusion procedures. This training was supplemented at regular intervals with in-service reviews and patient-at-risk consultations.

Because of severe fiscal crisis, the state hospital in which the ASAP program was based was phased down and ultimately closed at the end of the second year of programming. The ASAP data are presented within the context of this facility closure.

Program Evaluation: Preliminary Findings

Clinical Care

Victims who participated. From April 2, 1990, to January 24, 1992, the ASAP program responded to 327 episodes of assault on staff. The ASAP team completed 278 calls for assistance and was declined in 49 incidents.

Staff victims who accepted assistance (165 men and 114 women) were usually victims of an unprovoked assault (62%) by a male patient (56%) during mealtime periods. Assaults were more likely to involve a registered nurse (16%) or a less senior mental health worker (63%), and bruises with swelling were the most likely injuries (34%). Female staff victims were more likely to be victims of unprovoked assaults (75%); male staff victims were more likely to be assaulted during restraint and seclusion procedures (47%).

Several staff victims reported symptoms of psychological trauma. Feelings of fright, anger, and apprehension, as well as hypervigilance, sleep disturbance, and intrusive memories were common in the early hours after the assault. For most staff victims, these psychological sequelae passed, and most victims, as determined by ASAP clinician interviews, had regained a sense of reasonable mastery (81%), had a stable social support network (91%), and were able to make some initial meaning of the assaultive episode (75%) within 3–10 days of the violence.

CISD (Mitchell & Bray, 1990) for ward communities as a whole were requested in more than half the cases in the first 5 months of the ASAP program. As ASAP individual interviews proceeded and staff felt supported, requests for ward interviews decreased to less than 5% within 5 months. Fourteen staff victims came to the staff victims' support group for an average of two sessions. These victims had been involved in particularly severe assaults or were recalling past painful episodes of violence (e.g., rape, incest, domestic battering, car accidents, previous duty-related violence) that were triggered by current patients' assaults. Three staff victims were referred for additional private counseling. In only one case did the family of a staff victim request short-term counseling for the family members. The stress management groups (Flannery, 1990) for staff that were implemented on some patient care sites as a way of reducing the general level of stress appeared to fulfill their purpose by reducing ward staff self-reports of life stress. However, these groups were discontinued early on in the hospital's downsizing, and additional data gathering was precluded. After the ASAP start-up, only one employee left the workforce as a result of patient violence compared with an average of 15 terminations per year prior to ASAP.

Victims who declined. In 49 incidents, staff victims (40 men and 9 women) declined ASAP. Less senior (79%), male (85%) mental health workers on the 3:00 p.m. to 11:00 p.m. shift (53%) were more likely to refuse. In these cases, the assaultive patient was likely to be male (53%) and the act of violence was unprovoked (63%). The most frequently stated reason for refusing ASAP interventions was that assaults "come with the job."

Gender differences. A second analysis of this data by gender differences (Flannery, Hanson, Penk, Flannery, & Gallagher, 1994) revealed that same-gender assaults (male patient against male staff, female patient against female staff) were significantly higher than different-gender assaults, $\chi^2(1, N = 223) = 44.33, p < .001$.

Of the 165 male staff who accepted ASAP (59%), these employees were assaulted by male patients in 117 episodes (71%) and by female patients in 48 cases (29%). Male staff were assaulted in 87 random acts of violence (53%) and in 78 acts during restraint procedures (47%). Of the 114 female staff who accepted ASAP (41%), these employees were assaulted by 39 male patients (35%) and 74 female patients (65%). Female staff were victims in 78 random acts of violence (69%) and 35 acts during restraint procedures (31%).

Reductions in assaults. Although the ASAP program was designed as a treatment intervention for staff victims, there was an unanticipated reduction in the assault rate within the first 5 months of starting the ASAP. This decline in assaults on staff continued and was statistically significant in its reduction from a base rate of 30 to a base rate of 11, when ASAP ended, $t(8) = 16.47$, $p < .005$.

Hospital Costs

The direct and indirect costs associated with the hospital's industrial accident claims were estimated to exceed $2 million a year, and the ASAP team costs were estimated at $40,000 per year in staff salaried hours. This ASAP cost was actually less because ASAP clinicians continued to do all of their regular assigned tasks as well as the ASAP interventions, and no ASAP team member

ever used the compensatory time that he or she accumulated for ASAP interventions provided during off-shift periods.

Incomplete data collection procedures precluded a direct comparison of the
ASAP program and costs incurred during the same period for the preceding 2
years. Notwithstanding, the decline in assaults on staff appeared to have resulted in less injuries, less use of sick leave, and less industrial accident claims.
Hiring and training costs were substantially reduced in that only one employee
left the worksite as a result of patient assault compared with the average of
15 in the years preceding ASAP.

Discussion

Results of this 2-year study reveal three major findings. First, assaultive behavior by patients toward staff may result in psychological trauma and PTSD
(Caldwell, 1992), and a voluntary systems intervention for duty-related assaults may be a helpful intervention for addressing the psychological sequelae
of these acts (Flannery et al., 1991). Second, even with underreporting (Lion,
Snyder, & Merrill, 1981), the findings of assaultive behavior in this study are
remarkably consistent with previously reported studies (Carmel & Hunter,
1989; Thackrey & Bobbitt, 1990), and suggest some variables that may be
associated with patient assaults. Third, in this study, there was a sharp decline
in the level of violence in the hospital social system. This appears to be a
unique finding, and various ways to understand this phenomenon are outlined.

Psychological Trauma

These data reveal a consistent pattern of the presence of traumatic symptoms
in many staff victims (Caldwell, 1992; Flannery et al., 1991). Anger, apprehension, vigilance, and sleep disturbance were common in the aftermath of an
assault. Many victims experienced disruptions in mastery, attachment, and
meaning. Some victims experienced intrusive memories from past episodes of
abuse from previous patient assaults or from episodes of violence in their
personal lives.

The ASAP crisis intervention procedures (Flannery et al., 1991) appear
to have been helpful with these issues. With the exception of severely injured
victims, most victims remained at the worksite after ASAP interventions or
were able to return within 24–48 hr. Few needed the staff victims' group; if
they did, it was only for a few visits. Most victims regained a sense of mastery,
attachment, and meaning, but 9% did not. This finding is highly similar to
that of Caldwell (1992) and suggests that some staff victims remain at high
risk to develop PTSD.

The ASAP program was helpful in other ways. Staff fear about the ASAP
program as a management policing strategy stopped, and overt victim blaming
was virtually eliminated. Morale increased considerably as staff victims realized that they had personal support at a particularly vulnerable point in
their work-related tasks. Staff victims who were later transferred to other

facilities as the hospital was closing requested ASAP teams at their new work-sites. During this time period, 11 ASAP team members left the hospital. New team members were trained and assumed active duty with no disruption of service to staff victims.

This program was implemented with minimal resistance in a large health care system. The implementation was successful because the need was real—assaultive behavior was not an infrequent event. The ASAP also had the full and continued support of the hospital's chief operating officer, the medical–clinical director, and the director of nursing. The chief operating officer chose to be a member of the ASAP team, and her presence reinforced the message of administrative support for employee-victims. It was helpful to have the hospital's clinicians as ASAP team members because ASAP interventions were provided quickly by colleagues known to the staff victim and nursing personnel felt supported by the clinicians who volunteered to be on-call 24 hr a day.

Employee resistance was dealt with directly by offering the employee the option of refusing an intervention and by regularly providing employees with information about psychological trauma and the program. Employee concerns (e.g., whether information supplied to ASAP team members was truly confidential or whether ASAP was a management policing force) were dealt with clearly, directly, and in writing in monthly memorandums to all employees.

Patient Assaults

Male patients committed more assaults than did female patients. These assaults occurred most often during the three mealtime periods (Carmel & Hunter, 1989). During these periods, the ward environment was more active with the administration of medications, meals, going to or returning from day programs, changes in staffing, and family visits. Consistent with the findings of Thackrey and Bobbitt (1990), assaults on male staff were more likely to occur during restraint and seclusion procedures. Assaults against female staff were more likely to have been random events, and less senior nursing employees were at increased risk for such assaults (Carmel & Hunter, 1989). These findings are consistent with several reported studies (Davis, 1991).

Less is known of the staff victims who declined the service. Most were men and less senior mental health workers, but this in itself does not differentiate them from their counterparts in other parts of the hospital. Perhaps this group of victims who declined help from peers was more committed to one particular form of male stereotyping, which holds that "real men" go it alone and are less likely to ask for help. It is also possible that this untreated group who declined remains at increased risk for PTSD at a later time.

Although the risk for assault on male employees is similar to previous findings (Carmel & Hunter, 1989), the present findings for female staff are not consistent with previous research (Flannery et al., 1994). Female staff were at high risk for unprovoked assaults that were often inflicted by female patients. The reason for this finding is not clear. Female staff in this study had more direct patient contact, generally used verbal deescalation strategies rather than active restraint, and were less inclined to take risks than male staff. These factors might have increased the risk. It also is possible that female patients have become acculturated to violence and that female staff became the focus for some of this displaced aggression.

Decline in Violence

The substantial decline in violence in this study appears to be unique to this hospital, and it remains unclear why this decline occurred. Some explanations, however, may be tentatively ruled out. For example, there were no changes in levels of clinical skills among nursing staff, nor were there any changes in basic approaches for staff development before or after the ASAP started. Moreover, "crowding" would not appear to be an adequate explanation. Calhoun (1970) proposed a theory of crowding and violence that states that there is a limit to the amount of social interactions that can be reasonably tolerated within any physical space. As noted earlier, the hospital with the ASAP team was closed due to a severe fiscal crisis. Although Calhoun's theory might explain some occasions of reductions in violence, in the present study the reduction in violence occurred during the first 10 months of the ASAP program, before there were any significant discharges or transfers of patients and before any staff were laid off or transferred.

The decline in violence might have been due to the closing of the hospital, which resulted in the staff and patient community becoming depressed and the patients less likely to be assaultive. Second, hospital strategies for assessing and managing violence (e.g., tracking of incidents, consultations on the wards, patient-at-risk conferences, etc.) were improved to some degree, and this might have reduced the level of violence. Third, it also is possible that the ASAP program as a peer help model might have somehow empowered the staff. This sense of improvement might have resulted in better problem solving of work-related tasks, a subsequent reduction in worksite stress, and an increase in worksite safety. Reasons for such effects cannot be determined from the current study, but the finding of reduced violence does underscore the vital importance for further research and points out ways to identify dimensions that could be studied when researching effects of peer help programs for improving occupational safety.

Methodological Issues

Several methodological issues need to be addressed. Future studies will need to replicate the ASAP approach (Flannery et al., 1991) and will need to have better operational definitions and measurement of mastery, attachment, and meaning in staff victims. If future studies of the ASAP model note the same reduction in violence, research designs will need to be incorporated that provide ways to test competing hypotheses that might explain this phenomenon. Attention also needs to be given to the similarities and differences of patient–staff assaults with other types of traumatic events, such as combat, physical abuse, and sexual abuse (Flannery, 1992) and to the cost-effectiveness of this approach (Hunter & Carmel, 1992). Empirical studies are needed in which data are gathered before and after intervention (ABA designs) in multiple baseline designs across sites or in control group designs.

The definition of assault needs further clarification. Several previous studies have used the Occupational Safety and Health Administration's definition of physically assaultive behavior that results in lost work days (Hunter & Carmel, 1992). In the current study, the addition of threats (Morrison, 1992) and the tracking of assaults that do not necessarily result in lost work time appeared helpful in assessing more accurately the frequency and impact of violence. In this study, there were frequent occurrences of both male and female staff experiencing intense fright in the absence of serious injury and several cases in which verbal abuse and noninjurious assault resulted in intrusive memories and flashbacks of past non-work-related histories of abuse.

The ASAP program appears to offer a flexible model of an occupational trauma program that would appear to be suitable for many kinds of settings, including police and corrections facilities, homeless shelters, emergency services, schools, nursing homes, and domestic violence programs. Violence is a complex environmental–interpersonal event. To the extent that the salient factors can be assessed and contained, the quality of care for employee-victims should be enhanced.

References

Anderson, W., & Bauer, B. (1987). Law enforcement officers: The consequence of exposure to violence. *Journal of Counseling and Development, 65*, 381–384.

Antonovsky, A. (1987). *Unraveling the mystery of health: How people manage stress and stay well.* San Francisco: Jossey-Bass.

Brom, D., & Kleber, R. (1989). Prevention of post-traumatic stress disorders. *Journal of Traumatic Stress, 2*, 335–351.

Caldwell, M. F. (1992). The incidence of PTSD among staff victims of patient violence. *Hospital and Community Psychiatry, 43*, 838–839.

Calhoun, J. B. (1970). Space and the strategy of life. *Ekistics, 29*, 425–437.

Carmel, H., & Hunter, M. (1989). Staff injuries from inpatient violence. *Hospital and Community Psychiatry, 40*, 41–46.

Davis, S. (1991). Violence in psychiatric inpatients: A review. *Hospital and Community Psychiatry, 42*, 585–590.

Flannery, R. B., Jr. (1990). *Becoming stress-resistant through the Project SMART program.* New York: Continuum Press.

Flannery, R. B., Jr. (1992). *Post-traumatic stress disorder: The victim's guide to healing and recovery.* New York: Crossroad Press.

Flannery, R. B., Jr. (1995). *Violence in the workplace.* New York: Crossroad Press.

Flannery, R. B., Jr., Fulton, P., Tausch, J., & DeLoffi, A. Y. (1991). A program to help staff cope with the psychological sequelae of assaults by patients. *Hospital and Community Psychiatry, 42*, 935–938.

Flannery, R. B., Jr., Hanson, M. A., Penk, W. E., Flannery, G. J., & Gallagher, C. F. (1994). Violence against women: Psychiatric patient assaults on female staff. *Professional Psychology: Research and Practice, 25*, 182–184.

Flannery, R. B., Jr., Perry, J. D., & Harvey, M. R. (1993). A structured reduction approach modified for victims of post-traumatic stress disorder. *Psychotherapy, 30*, 646–650.

Hunter, M., & Carmel, H. (1992). The cost of staff injuries from inpatient violence. *Hospital and Community Psychiatry, 43*, 586–588.

Janoff-Bulman, R. (1985). The aftermath of victimization: Rebuilding shattered assumptions. In C. R. Figley (Ed.), *Trauma and its works: The study and treatment of post-traumatic stress disorders* (pp. 15–35). New York: Brunner/Mazel.

Kobasa, S. C. (1979). Personality and resistance to illness. *American Journal of Community Psychology, 7,* 413–423.

Lion, R. J., Snyder, W., & Merrill, G. L. (1981). Underreporting of assaults on staff in a state hospital. *Hospital and Community Psychiatry, 32,* 497–498.

Lowenstein, L. (1991). Teacher stress leading to burnout: Its prevention and cure. *Education Today, 41,* 12–16.

McKenna, L. S. (1986). Job stress in shelters. *Response to the Victimization of Women and Children, 9,* 21–23.

Mitchell, J. T., & Bray, G. R. (1990). *Emergency services stress: Guidelines for preserving the health and careers of emergency services personnel.* Englewood Cliffs, NJ: Prentice Hall.

Morrison, E. F. (1992). A hierarchy of aggressive and violent behaviors among psychiatric inpatients. *Hospital and Community Psychiatry, 43,* 505–506.

Nader, K., Pynoos, R., Fairbanks, L., & Frederick, C. (1990). Children's PTSD reactions one year after a sniper attack at their school. *American Journal of Psychiatry, 147,* 1526–1530.

Rotter, J. B. (1966). Generalized expectancies for internal versus external control of reinforcement. *Psychological Monographs, 80,* 1(Whole No. 6091).

Thackrey, M., & Bobbitt, R. G. (1990). Patient aggression against clinical and nonclinical staff in a VA medical center. *Hospital and Community Psychiatry, 41,* 195–197.

Utterbach, J., & Caldwell, J. (1989). Proactive and reactive approaches to PTSD in the aftermath of campus violence: Forming a traumatic stress react team. *Journal of Traumatic Stress, 2,* 171–183.

THE WORK SETTING

Introduction

In contrast to the chapters in the first section of this book, the chapters in this section are concerned with interventions at the job and organizational level, such as job redesign and organizational change efforts focusing on reducing or eliminating the source of stress in the work environment. In the leading chapter, Cartwright, Cooper, and Murphy provide a discussion of how to identify job and organizational stressors, and they offer guiding principles for designing stress reduction strategies. Next in chapter 16, Schurman and Israel describe their experience with a participatory action research approach for designing, implementing and evaluating a system-level stress intervention. Terra, in the following chapter, presents a case study of a participatory approach to job redesign and stress reduction in the Dutch metal can industry. In chapter 18, Lindström describes six different stress intervention approaches, involving job redesign and organizational development, used by work psychologists at the Finnish Institute for Occupational Health. In chapter 19, Scharlach emphasizes the importance of family-oriented personnel policies in stress reduction programs. Joplin and Quick, in the next chapter, describe and evaluate an intervention aimed at developing and promoting interdependence among workers. In chapter 21, Ganster performs a critical review of the stress intervention literature and highlights the many challenges that exist for future research. The chapter by Houtman and Kompier finishes this section of the book by assessing the quality of stress management training courses offered in the Netherlands and emphasizes the need for such training to address characteristics of the work situation in addition to the worker's capacity to cope with stress.

15

Diagnosing a Healthy Organization: A Proactive Approach to Stress in the Workplace

Sue Cartwright, Cary L. Cooper, and Lawrence R. Murphy

Organizational health can be measured in a variety of ways other than by an analysis of the profit and loss account. Profitability is a clear indicator of the success and financial health of an organization at a given point of time. However, it is not necessarily a good predictor of future performance, unless account is taken of the ability of the organization and its workforce to continue to sustain and possibly increase that level of performance over time. An automobile may be running perfectly well one day, despite a neglectful owner, but it is invariably only a matter of time before a costly breakdown occurs. Similarly, the performance and financial health of an organization is dependent upon the physical and psychological health of its members.

There are a range of indices that are indicative of organizational ill health, other than the more obvious data such as sickness absenteeism, high labor turnover, and low productivity. These indices include high insurance and health care costs, poor accident and safety records, low levels of organizational commitment and job satisfaction, and generally deteriorating industrial relations.

As the human and financial costs of occupational stress to business and industry have become increasingly well documented (Elkin & Rosch, 1990), a growing number of organizations have introduced initiatives designed to reduce stress and improve employee health in the workplace. DeFrank and Cooper (1987) suggest that stress intervention in the workplace can focus on the individual, the organization, or the individual–organizational interface. Interventions that focus on the individual are concerned with extending the physical and psychological resources of employees to enable them to deal more effectively with stress. Health and stress education and skills training in the area of time management or assertive behavior are examples of such interventions. In contrast, organizationally focused interventions are concerned with reducing workplace stress by addressing factors that operate at the macro level. Such interventions might include changing aspects of the organizational structure, reviewing selection and training procedures, or developing more flexible and "employee-friendly" systems and personnel policies that more closely meets the needs and demands of the workforce.

Exhibit 1. Stress Management Interventions and Outcomes

Interventions	Outcomes
Focus on individual	Focus on individual
Relaxation techniques	Mood states (e.g., depression, anxiety)
Cognitive coping strategies	Psychosomatic complaints
Biofeedback	Subjectively experienced stress
Meditation	Physiological parameters (e.g., blood pressure, catecholamines, muscle tension)
Exercise	
Employee Assistance Programs (EAP)	Sleep disturbances
	Life satisfaction
Time management	Focus on individual–organizational interface
Focus on individual–organizational interface	Job stress
Relationships at work	Job satisfaction
Person–environment fit	Burnout
Role issues	Productivity and performance
Participation and autonomy	Absenteeism
Focus on organization	Turnover
Organizational structure	Health care utilization and claims
Selection and placement	Focus on organization
Training	Productivity
Physical and environmental characteristics of job	Turnover
	Absenteeism
Health concerns and resources	Health care claims
Job rotation	Recruitment/retention success

From DeFrank and Cooper (1987). Reprinted with permission.

Finally, there are interventions that operate at a more local, work group level, focusing on the individual–organizational interface. These are likely to address issues relating to work relationships and roles, person–environment fit, participation, and autonomy (see Exhibit 1). Ivancevich and Matteson (1988) proposed three points of possible organizational intervention: (a) changing the stress potential of a situation by reducing the intensity and number of stressors; (b) helping individuals modify their appraisal of a stressful situation and the threat it presents; and (c) helping individuals cope more effectively with the stress response. Murphy (1988) also emphasized three levels of intervention: (a) primary (e.g., stressor reduction), (b) secondary (e.g., stress management), and (c) tertiary (e.g., employee assistance programs [EAPs]).

Primary level interventions (stressor reduction) can be considered as being essentially concerned with modifying environmental stressors by direct action to eliminate or reduce their negative impact on the individual. In contrast, secondary and tertiary level interventions focus on managing distress and dealing with the outcomes or consequences of the stress process, and to a lesser extent, helping the individual modify the meaning of the stressor(s).

This chapter will start to highlight the current initiatives in the workplace, then explore the effectiveness of stress management and EAPs, and finally develop the case for a "front-end" approach by encouraging diagnosis and organizational interventions of structural problems.

Current Initiatives in the Workplace

Most workplace initiatives operate at the secondary or tertiary levels. Typically, they involve the provision of on-site fitness facilities, smoking cessation programs, dietary control, relaxation and exercise classes, health screening, alcohol and stress education, or psychological counseling, or some combination of these, packaged as a multimodular program available to employees and possibly, their partners. In a recent survey of some 3,000 worksites, the U.S. Department of Health and Human Services found that more than 60% of worksites with 750 or more employees now offer some form of stress management or health promotion activity. It is estimated (Feldman, 1991) that more than 75% of all Fortune 500 companies and about 12,000 smaller companies currently operate EAPs.

Initiatives, such as EAPs, by definition have tended to be "employee"-rather than "organization"-directed strategies, whereby the focus is directed at changing the behaviors of individuals and improving their lifestyles or stress management skills. Earlier definitions within the literature conceptualized stress as being an external stimulus, a physiological response, or an environmental condition. Later definitions (Cooper, Cooper, & Eaker, 1988; Edwards & Cooper, 1990) have emphasized the active role played by the individual in the stress process and suggested that stress is best understood as resulting from the interaction or "lack of fit" between the individual and his or her environment. However, the primary aim of most workplace intervention strategies is to improve the adaptability of the individual to the existing work environment by increasing physical and psychological resilience to stress. Inherent in such an approach is a recognition that the working environment is stressful but that the onus is on the individual to adapt and extend his or her coping skills to meet the given demands of that environment. Consequently, this strategy is often described as the "band-aid," or inoculation approach.

In contrast, there appears to be markedly less organizational concern with adapting the environment to "fit" the individual. One suggested reason (Ivancevich, Matteson, Freedman, & Phillips, 1990) is that the "interventionists"—the counselors, physicians and clinicians—are more comfortable with changing individuals than changing organizations. Furthermore, secondary and tertiary level interventions present a high profile means by which organizations can "be seen to be doing something about stress and taking reasonable precautions to safeguard employee health without unduly disrupting business activities."

The Effectiveness of Stress Management and Employee Assistance Programs

There have been some dramatic reports attesting to the cost benefits of EAPs and health promotion activities. Figures typically show savings-to-investment ratios of anywhere from 3:1 to 15:1. Such reports have not been without criticism. Many studies are considered to be methodologically weak in that they lack control groups, fail to use objective multiple measures, and are of cross-sectional rather than longitudinal design. Many programs are multimodal in their approach; therefore, it is often difficult to isolate the effectiveness of individual component modules. Furthermore, increasingly, schemes are evaluated by the managed care companies responsible for their implementation, who may even be under contract to deliver a preset dollar saving (Smith & Mahoney, 1989).

However, it has been well documented that the New York Telephone Company's wellness program designed to improve cardiovascular fitness saved the organization $2.7 million in absenteeism and treatment costs in one year alone. General Motors Corporation report a 40% decrease in lost time and a 60% decrease in accident and sickness benefits as a result of their program. Evidence from Control Data Corporation's Staywell Program shows an increase in productivity and an impressive reduction in health care costs and absenteeism among employees who quit smoking, underwent exercise training, and enrolled in the cardiovascular fitness programs (Cooper, Cooper, & Eaker, 1988).

Counseling programs, such as those introduced by Kennecott in the United States (Cooper, Cooper, & Eaker, 1988) and the U.K. Post Office (Cooper & Sadri, 1991) both resulted in a reduction in absenteeism of approximately 60% in one year. The Post Office study involved pre- and postcounseling measures of employee mental health, job satisfaction, self-esteem, organizational commitment, and health behaviors, and it included control groups. Counseling was found to result in a significant improvement in the mental health and self-esteem of the participating employees. Neither job satisfaction nor organizational commitment, however, showed significant changes as a result of counseling.

Evidence as to the success of secondary interventions or stress management training is generally confusing and imprecise (Elkin & Rosch, 1990), which possibly reflects the idiosyncratic nature of the form and content of this kind of training. Programs differ in content and are often embedded in broader health promotion programs. Recent studies that have evaluated the outcomes of stress management training have found a modest improvement in self-reported symptoms and psychophysiological indices of strain (e.g., Reynolds, Taylor, & Shapiro, 1993), but little or no change in job satisfaction, work stress, or blood pressure. Newman and Beehr (1979) reviewed 24 employee-directed stress management programs that involved teaching relaxation or other coping skills, of which only 3 produced credible positive findings. Similarly, Murphy (1984) assessed 13 empirically based studies that included muscle relaxation, cognitive restructuring, meditation, and diaphragmatic breathing and concluded that although such techniques can be effective, "too few studies have been conducted to determine the relative merits of select techniques and compute cost–benefit ratios." Overall, it would seem that stress management programs may have a positive effect (Ivancevich et al., 1990), but if employees return to an unchanged work environment and its intrinsic stressors, those beneficial effects are likely to be eroded. Assessing the cost and long-term benefits of stress management programs remains problematic, particularly when, as has been suggested (Sutherland & Cooper, 1990), account is taken of the characteristics and health status of those who voluntarily attend such programs.

Research findings which have examined the impact of lifestyle and health promotion programs also suggest that any benefits may not necessarily be sustained. Lifestyle and health habits appear to have a strong direct effect on strain outcomes in reducing anxiety, depression, and psychosomatic distress but do not necessarily moderate the stressor–strain linkage. Ivancevich and Matteson (1988) suggest that after a short time, 70% of individuals fail to maintain a long-term commitment to exercise habits and are likely to revert to their previous lifestyle. They also highlight the possibility of a placebo effect, which may be inherent in such programs.

The Front-End Approach: Dealing With the Sources of Stress

It has been argued that the simplistic philosophy of "one size fits all" (Elkin & Rosch, 1990) implicit in current secondary and tertiary interventions may be appropriate for smoking cessation programs, but it is less appropriate for stress reduction. Stress may have common manifestations and symptomatology (i.e., raised blood pressure, irritability, insomnia, depressed mood, etc.), but the potential sources of workplace stress are many and various and are not necessarily easy for the individual to identify and deal with effectively. Cardiovascular fitness programs may be successful in reducing the harmful effects of stress on the high-pressured executive, but such programs will not eliminate the stressor itself, which may be overpromotion or a poor relationship with the executive's boss. Identifying and recognizing the problem and taking steps to tackle it, perhaps by negotiation (i.e., a front-end approach) might arguably arrest the whole stress process.

Self-awareness is recognized as a key component in stress management. The completion of some form of stress diary or self-report diagnostic measure is often helpful to the individual (Cooper, Cooper, & Eaker, 1988) in increasing awareness and identifying individual stressor patterns.

Treatment may, therefore, often be easier than a cure, but it may be only an effective short-term strategy, as perhaps will be demonstrated by longer term cost–benefit analysis of secondary and tertiary interventions. In focusing on the outcome or "back end" of the stress process (i.e., poor mental and physical health, maladaptive coping strategies, etc.) and taking remedial action to redress that situation, the approach is essentially reactive and recuperative rather than proactive and preventative.

Awareness activities and skills training programs designed to improve relaxation techniques, cognitive coping skills, and work/lifestyle modification skills (e.g., time management courses or assertiveness training) have an important part to play in extending the individual's physical and psychological resources. Their role, however, is essentially one of "damage limitation," often addressing the *consequences* rather than the *sources* of stress that may be inherent in the organization's structure or culture. Indeed, individuals are likely to perceive themselves as lacking the "resource or positional power" to change most of these stressors; they are perceived as simply beyond their control.

A number of general recommendations for reducing job stress have been put forth by the National Institute for Occupational Safety and Health (NIOSH) in their *National Strategy for the Prevention of Work-Related Psychological Disorders* (Sauter, Murphy, & Hurrell, 1990). A few of these recommendations are listed here:

> *Workload and work pace.* Demands (both physical and mental) should be commensurate with the capabilities and resources of workers, avoiding underload as well as overload. Provisions should be made to allow recovery from demanding tasks or for increased control by workers over characteristics such as work pace of demanding tasks.
>
> *Work schedule.* Work schedules should be compatible with demands and responsibilities outside the job. Recent trends toward flextime, a compressed work week, and job sharing are examples of positive steps in this direction. When schedules involve rotating shifts, the rate of rotation should be stable and predictable.
>
> *Job future.* Ambiguity should be avoided in opportunities for promotion and career or skill development and in matters pertaining to job security. Employees should be clearly informed of imminent organizational developments that may affect their employment.
>
> *Social environment.* Jobs should provide opportunities for personal interaction, both for purposes of emotional support and for actual help as needed in accomplishing assigned tasks.
>
> *Job content.* Job tasks should be designed to have meaning and provide stimulation and an opportunity to use skills. Job rotation or increasing the scope (enlargement/enrichment) of work activities are ways to improve narrow, fragmented work activities that fail to meet these criteria.

Elkin and Rosch (1990) also summarize a useful range of possible organization-directed strategies to reduce stress:

- Redesign the task.
- Redesign the work environment.
- Establish flexible work schedules.
- Encourage participative management.
- Include the employee in career development.
- Analyze work roles and establish goals.
- Provide social support and feedback.
- Build cohesive teams.
- Establish fair employment policies.
- Share the rewards.

Many of these strategies are directed at increasing employee participation. Indirectly, they are often a vehicle for culture change moving the organization toward a more open and "employee-empowered" culture. Previous reviews of the behavioral science literature have demonstrated that employee participation has a positive impact upon productivity and quality control (Guzzo, Jette, & Katzell, 1985). Quality Circle (QC) programs, which, it has been suggested, represent the ultimate form of employee involvement, have been shown to favorably impact upon productivity (Barrick & Alexander, 1987) and employee attitudes (Rafael, 1985).

In a study comparing the attitudes of QC members (n = 455) and non-QC members (n = 305), it was found that QC membership increased employee perceptions of the influence they had over their jobs, and overall job satisfaction (Rafael, 1985). The link between locus of control (Rotter, 1966) and vulnerability to stress is well recognized as a mediator of the stress response. Stress is commonly experienced by individuals as a feeling of powerlessness and of being out of control. Research studies have suggested that perceived control over a situation is an advantage in managing environmental stress agents (Sauter, Hurrell, & Cooper, 1989). However, the effects of strategies such as QC in improving psychological well-being and reducing employee anxiety and stress have been little investigated.

Similarly, different types of organizational culture nurture particular values, attitudes, and styles of work organization to create psychologically different work environments and forms of psychological contract between employer and employee. Although culture change is a potentially stressful event, certain types of culture are generally experienced by employees as more satisfying than others (Cartwright & Cooper, 1989, 1992). In a recent study of more than 600 Norwegian managers and employees in the aluminum industry, it was found that individual perception of the culture type of the organization was a strong predictor of organizational commitment and job satisfaction. Those employees who perceived the culture to be of a Task Achievement type (Harrison, 1972) reported significantly higher levels of organizational commitment and job satisfaction than those employees who perceived the culture as being fragmented or ambiguous or of a different type (Rasmussen, 1992).

Although the relationship between commitment and job performance is generally weak (Matthieu & Zajac, 1990), attitudinal commitment has been found to be predictive of employee turnover (Angle & Perry, 1981). Similarly, evidence reported by Chadwick-Jones, Nicholson, and Brown (1982; as cited in Zaccaro, Craig, & Quinn, 1991) concerning the direct relationship between job satisfaction and performance, absenteeism, and turnover is mixed because decisions to leave organizations are often determined more by labor market conditions than dissatisfaction alone. However, stress studies that have included job satisfaction as an outcome measure (Cooper & Roden, 1985) have found that employees with low job satisfaction also record poorer levels of mental health. However, the stressors predicting these outcomes are often different.

One might argue that the truly "healthy" organization, which has been successful in creating and maintaining a healthy and relatively stress-free environment, will be an organization in which secondary (stress management) and tertiary (EAP) interventions are unnecessary. Such an organization will have effectively targeted its resources at reducing or eliminating stressors before their longer term consequences on employee and organizational health impact the balance sheet.

However, once again, one size does *not* fit all. Not all of the stress that impacts the workplace is necessarily or exclusively caused by the work environment. As evidenced by the U.K. Post Office study, which evaluated the impact of stress counseling at work (Cooper & Sadri, 1991), the largest cluster of problems presented by employees fell into the broad category of mental and stress issues and formed 46% of the caseload; the second most significant cluster concerned "relationship" problems. Relationship problems accounted for 24% of the caseload, the majority of which focused on marital difficulties. A number of other non-work-related problems were presented, including bereavement, assault, and physical illness or disability.

This suggests that primary interventions cannot totally displace the need for secondary and tertiary interventions such as counseling, which address the problems associated with stressful life events, but rather should be complementary. However, primary or organizational level (stressor reduction) strategies appear to be preferred less than other levels of intervention. Although organizations have recognized the benefits of providing health screening to employees, they have been less concerned about or slower to recognize the potential diagnostic benefits of conducting regular "stress audits" to ascertain the current state of health in their organization as a whole (and its constituent parts) through occupational or organizational stress screening.

The Stress Audit: A Diagnostic Approach

As has been suggested (Elkin & Rosch, 1990), there are a variety of organization-directed strategies to prevent or limit stress, which generally fall in the area of organizational development (OD). Implementation is often expensive and potentially disruptive, and it may result in major restructuring. Few organizations would be prepared to commit themselves to extensive OD programs without justification for their necessity or else a baseline measure by which to evaluate their effectiveness, or both. In the same way that different stressors are responsible for different outcomes (Cooper, Rout, & Faragher, 1989), the potential sources of stress have been shown to vary among different occupational groups. For example, money handling and the risk of personal assault was found to be a major occupational stressor among bus drivers in the U.K. transport industry (Duffy & McGoldrick, 1990), whereas the major source of stress for U.K. income tax officers was autocratic management style and lack of consultation (Cooper & Roden, 1985). Furthermore, differences have been found between institutions and organizations in the same industry or business sector (Cooper & Mitchell, 1990) and between different subcultures and status groups within the same organization (Cooper & Bramwell, 1992). Consequently, the type of action required by an organization to reduce or eliminate workplace stressors will vary according to the kinds of stressors operating, the level of coping skills of those involved, and the culture of the

SOURCES OF
STRESS   SYMPTOMS OF STRESS   DISEASE

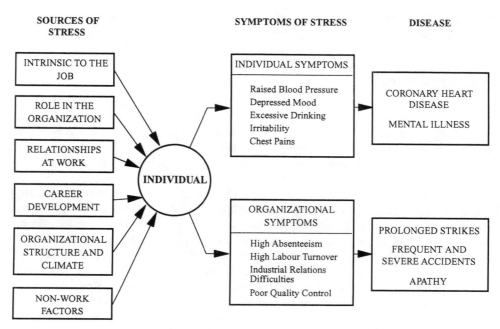

Figure 1.   Stress: a research model. From Cooper and Marshall (1978). Reprinted with permission.

organization. In the examples just given, stress reduction might suggest a possible ergonomic solution in the case of bus drivers, whereas a change in management style that leads to increased employee participation is more likely to reduce the stress experienced by income tax officers.

Tailoring action to suit the assessed needs of the organization is likely to be more effective than any "broad brush" approach. As Levering (1988) points out, "A great workplace cannot be equated with the presence or absence of a particular set of policies and practices." In order to direct its resources effectively in reducing stress in the workplace, an organization first needs answers to the following questions:

1. What is the existing level of stress within the organization? Are job satisfaction and physical and psychological health better in some areas than others? How does the organization compare with other occupational groups or populations? In other words, "Is there a problem?"
2. If so, can the problem and what is causing it be determined? What are the stressors? Are they department- or site-specific or organization-wide?

There are a number of occupational stress models within the literature (Cooper & Payne, 1988); later models (Bruckman & Peters, 1987) have tended to focus on merger stress but have general applications. The Cooper-Marshall (1978) model (see Figure 1) conceptualizes the sources of occupational stress as falling within six broad categories: (a) factors intrinsic to the job; (b) role in the organization; (c) relationships with others; (d) career development; (e) organizational structure, climate, and culture; and (f) home–work interface.

Factors Intrinsic to the Job

There are a variety of factors intrinsic to the job that are potentially stressful and have been linked to poor mental health (Cooper & Smith, 1985; Kelly & Cooper, 1981). These include poor physical working conditions, shift work, long hours, travel, risk and danger, new technology, and work overload or underload (of both a qualitative and quantitative nature).

The quality of the physical working environment is recognized as an important factor in employee health. In 1983, the World Health Organization defined the concept of the "sick building syndrome." Sick building syndrome is characterized by a range of physiological symptoms, including sensory irritation, headache, nausea, and dizziness and fatigue, which grow worse over the course of a day and disappear after the workers leave the building. Research has found the concentration of macromolecular organic dust, floor covering, number of workplaces in an office, age of the building, type of ventilation, and other indoor climatic factors to be associated with the occurrence of the syndrome (Skov, Valbjórn, & Pedersen, 1990). However, work-related mucosal irritation has been found to be associated with psychosocial and job-related factors such as work overload and dissatisfaction with one's superior (Skov, Valbjórn, & Pedersen, 1989). The same study also found that office workers who considered the pace of work at their workplace too fast and believed that they had little influence on their work activities were significantly more likely to report general symptoms.

Eliminating or reducing stressors relating to factors intrinsic to the job may involve ergonomic solutions and have implications for task or workplace redesign. Problems of work overload or underload may indicate a need to recruit, skills deficiencies, underutilization, inappropriate selection decisions, or delegation problems.

Role in the Organization

Karasek (1979) postulated that the amount of work does not seem to be as critical to worker health as the interaction of workload with the amount of control or discretion the worker has over the work and related work processes. Karasek and colleagues (Karasek et al., 1988) combined a database containing information on worker self-reports of job conditions with national health databases to examine the relationship between workload, work pace, and degree of worker control (referred to as "decision latitude"). Their findings indicated that workers in jobs with higher psychological workload, coupled with lower decision latitude, had increased risk of coronary heart disease, had higher blood pressure, and smoked more than workers in jobs without these characteristics. Indeed, the concept that worker control or discretion (a role-related

factor) over working conditions is integral to health has become almost ubiquitous in the occupational stress area.

Three other critical factors—role ambiguity, role conflict, and the degree
of responsibility for others—are also major potential sources of stress. In a
study of U.S. dentists (Cooper, Mallinger, & Kahn, 1978), for example, a high
level of role conflict was found to be a major predictor of abnormally high blood
pressure. Essentially, this conflict stemmed from the discrepancy between the
idealized "caring/healing" role and the actuality of being "an inflictor of pain."
Eliminating or reducing role-related stress requires clear role definition and
role negotiation.

Relationships at Work

Relationships with others at work (i.e., superiors, colleagues, and subordinates)
are potentially stressful. Most studies have concluded that mistrust of coworkers is associated with high role ambiguity, poor communication, low job
satisfaction, and diminished psychological well-being (Cooper & Payne, 1988).

Improving personal relationships in the workplace is a complex process
and may have implications for a range of interpersonal skills training. Oldham
(1988) investigated the impact of physical layout on communication and employee satisfaction among clerical staff. It was found that employees were more
satisfied when working in traditional partitioned offices than open plan. Partitioned offices were recognized as providing greater possibilities for focusing
on the task and for communicating in private.

Career Development

Job insecurity and career development have increasingly become a source of
stress during the merger and acquisition boom of the 1980s, and they seem
likely to continue as such throughout the recessionary 1990s (Cartwright &
Cooper, 1992). Ivancevich and Matteson (1980) have demonstrated that "career
stress" is associated with multiple negative outcomes (e.g., job dissatisfaction,
poor work performance).

The introduction of regular appraisals, the provision of retraining opportunities, career sabbaticals, and counseling are ways in which career stress
may be reduced. Because redundancy or job loss appears likely to remain a
feature of organizational life in the near future, the provision of outplacement
facilities becomes increasingly important.

Organizational Structure and Climate

Sources of stress that may be described as relating to the organizational structure and climate are frequently the outcome of organizational culture and
management style. They include factors such as lack of participation and
effective consultation, poor communication, and office politics. As organizations have increasingly found themselves involved in mergers, acquisitions,

and joint ventures or have felt the pressure to conduct downsizing (what is now popularly called "rightsizing") activities, a result has been major restructuring. This frequently results in turn in culture change or "collisions" that create ambiguous working environments and individual cultural incongruence, which are likely to be experienced as stressful.

In a recent study comparing employee stress in four autonomous divisions of the same parent company, it was found that employee differences in physical and mental health were linked to the culture and practices of the operating division (Cartwright, Cooper, & Barron, 1993). Furthermore, such factors were associated also with motor fleet accident rates.

Nonwork Factors

As shown in Figure 1, individual factors can alter or modify the way workers exposed to the stressors perceive or react to the work environment. These "moderator" variables have received increased research attention in recent years, and following are descriptions of the most common of these (Hurrell & Murphy, 1992).

The most prominent individual factor related to stress has been the coronary-prone *Type A behavior* pattern, characterized by intense striving for achievement, competitiveness, urgency, excessive drive, and overcommitment to one's vocation or profession. Many investigators have reported the Type A pattern to be independently associated with coronary artery disease (Cooper & Payne, 1991).

Social support that an individual receives from work and nonwork sources has powerful influences on the stressor–health relationship. One of the earliest studies in this area reported that social support served to buffer or protect the worker from the ill effects of stress (LaRocco, House, & French, 1980), although later studies have provided mixed support for the "buffering" hypothesis. In a similar way, certain *coping styles* have been found to be related to better health, especially those referred to as problem-focused coping, compared with emotion-focused coping (Folkman & Lazarus, 1980).

Finally, it is clear that workers do not leave their family and personal problems behind when they go to work, nor do they forget job problems upon returning home. Nearly all models of job stress acknowledge the importance of *nonwork factors*, and their interaction with work factors, in affecting health outcomes.

Managing the interface between work and home is particularly problematic, especially for dual career couples (Cooper & Lewis, 1993) and those who may be experiencing financial difficulties or life crisis. Although the organization arguably can do little to alleviate the stress caused by domestic circumstances such as a bereavement in the family other than by providing counseling services, it can help reduce the pressure on, for example, dual-career couples and single parents by introducing more flexible working arrangements and adopting family-friendly employment policies.

Stress Audit Instruments

Instruments such as the Occupational Stress Indicator (OSI) devised by Cooper, Sloan, and Williams (1988), have been increasingly used as a diagnostic instrument in occupational stress research in Europe. The OSI is based upon the Cooper-Marshall (1978) model and consists of six scales (each of which provides a number of subscale scores). In addition to identifying sources of pressure at work, it incorporates personality measures of Type A behavior, perceived locus of control, and employee coping strategies. The OSI also measures job satisfaction and self-reported mental and physical health. The instrument has established reliability and both predictive and criterion-oriented validity (Cooper & Bramwell, 1992; Cooper, Sloan, & Williams, 1988; Rees & Cooper, 1991; Robertson & Cooper, 1990).

The OSI and other similar instruments provide an effective means whereby organizations can regularly audit and monitor organizational health and be proactive in stress reduction. Such audits can be used to provide a baseline measure whereby stress reduction techniques can be evaluated. The use of audits could be extended to ascertain employee attitudes and perceived needs for secondary (stress management) and tertiary (EAPs) interventions and to provide valuable information regarding the likely rates of use of such programs before any expenditure is incurred.

Many other questionnaires have been developed to assess job stress–health relationships, far too many to be reviewed in this short chapter. However, a few other assessment instruments will be briefly described. For example, the Occupational Stress Inventory (Osipow & Spokane, 1983) measures a wide range of job stressors, employee resources for coping with stress, and mental and physical strains. The various subscales have demonstrated good test–retest reliability, and occupational norms are available. Plotting standardized scores on each subscale produces a "stress profile" for workers.

The Generic Job Stress Questionnaire (Hurrell & McLaney, 1988) was developed by NIOSH. This instrument assesses many different job stressors as well as stress reactions or strains. Most of the scales were adapted from prior scales with known reliability and validity. This instrument was designed to be modular; organizations can select individual scales, or the entire instrument can be used. Normative data on this questionnaire are currently being gathered.

Another commonly used instrument, the Work Environment Scale (WES; Moos, 1981) was not developed to assess job stress; rather, it was designed to assess the general work climate. It contains 90 items that comprise 10 subscales, and it uses a True–False response format. The subscales have demonstrated good reliability and validity and have been used often by researchers over the past 15 years. Also, occupation norms are available for this instrument.

Organizational Interventions

Following stress assessment and problem identification, interventions need to be designed, installed, and evaluated. The intervention itself needs to be comprehensive and contain an element of stressor reduction through organizational change, in addition to any individual-oriented elements. Stressor reduction interventions require a knowledge of the dynamics of change processes in organizations, so that potentially undesirable outcomes can be minimized. Stressor-targeted interventions must initially deal with the problem that organizations, like individuals, tend to resist change, and this inertia is reinforced by the belief among many managers that the work environment does not contribute to employee distress. Despite these difficulties, stressor reduction interventions remain the preferred approaches to employee stress problems because of the focus on the source of the problem(s), not the symptoms.

Regardless of the specific intervention strategy selected, the involvement and participation of workers in the process is critical to its success. An example from the research literature illustrates this point. Lawler and Hackman (1969) introduced identical incentive pay plans in groups of workers and discovered that the effects of the pay plans on employee attendance varied as a function of *how* the plans were introduced to workers. The three work groups that participated in the development of the pay plans showed increased attendance in the 16 weeks after the plans were introduced, relative to the 12 weeks before the plans went into effect. A year later, two of the three pay plans were discontinued. Interviews with the managers who discontinued the plans revealed that they felt little commitment to the plans and had not themselves participated in their development (Scheflen, Lawler, & Hackman, 1971). Lasting, effective change in organizations requires involvement of individuals at all levels in the organization.

Conclusion

Occupational stress appears to be a growing problem as many organizations increasingly find themselves functioning in rapidly changing internal and external environments. However, it is not just change and its attendant uncertainty that are the significant precursors of stress in the 1990s. As organizations have become leaner and more aggressively competitive, the effect has been to increase individual workloads as well as to fuel endemic fears concerning future job security. The changing structure of the family unit has placed increased and new demands on the home–work environment. The extent to which organizations and their individual members learn to cope effectively with the stresses and strains of work has important implications for their continued survival and for society generally.

Organizational preoccupation with the outcome of the stress process has tended to detract from the more proactive approach of addressing the source or causal factors in the stress process. Clearly, it is important for organizations to recognize that primary, secondary, and tertiary levels of intervention are complementary and that the diagnostic stress audit has a useful and potentially cost-effective role to play in identifying appropriate primary level interventions to reduce workplace stressors. The substantial yet piecemeal growth in the number of organizations providing some form of stress management activity or EAPs in the United States and United Kingdom has rapidly overtaken the pace of academic research in systematically evaluating the effectiveness of such interventions. Strategies that in effect shift the responsibility for dealing with workplace stress onto the individual, in isolation are unlikely to prove effective.

References

Angle, H. L., & Perry, J. L. (1981). An empirical assessment of organizational commitment and organizational effectiveness. *Administrative Science Quarterly, 26*, 1–14.

Barrick, M. R., & Alexander, R. A. (1987). The efficacy of quality circles. *Personnel Psychology*, 579–590.

Bruckman, J. C., & Peters, S. C. (1987). Mergers and acquisitions: The human equation. *Employment Relations Today, 14*, 55–63.

Cartwright, S., & Cooper, C. L. (1989). Predicting success in joint venture organizations in information technology: A cultural perspective. *Journal of General Management, 15*, 39–52.

Cartwright, S., & Cooper, C. L. (1992). *Mergers and acquisitions: The human factor.* Oxford, England: Butterworth Heinemann.

Cartwright, S., Cooper, C. L., & Barron, A. (1993). An investigation of the relationship between occupational stress and accidents amongst company car drivers. *Journal of General Management, 19*(2), 78–85.

Cooper, C. L., & Bramwell, R. (1992). Predictive validity of the strain components of the occupational stress indicator. *Stress Medicine, 8*, 57–60.

Cooper, C. L., Cooper, R. D., & Eaker, L. (1988). *Living with stress.* Harmondsworth, England: Penguin Health.

Cooper, C. L., & Lewis, S. (1993). *Managing the new workforce.* San Diego, CA: Pfeiffer.

Cooper, C. L., Mallinger, M., & Kahn, R. (1978). Identifying sources of occupational stress amongst dentists. *Journal of Occupational Psychology, 51*, 227–234.

Cooper, C. L., & Marshall, J. (1978). *Understanding executive stress.* London: Macmillan.

Cooper, C. L., & Mitchell, S. (1990). Nursing the critically ill and dying. *Human Relations, 43*(4), 297–311.

Cooper, C. L., & Payne, R. (1988). *Causes, coping and consequences of stress at work.* New York: Wiley.

Cooper, C. L., & Payne, R. (1991). *Personality and stress.* New York: Wiley.

Cooper, C. L., & Roden, J. (1985). Mental health and satisfaction amongst tax officers. *Social Science Medicine, 21*(7), 474–751.

Cooper, C. L., Rout, U., & Faragher, E. B. (1989). Mental health, job satisfaction and job stress among GPs. *British Medical Journal, 298*, 366–370.

Cooper, C. L., & Sadri, G. (1991). The impact of stress counselling at work. In P. L. Perrewe (Ed.), Handbook of job stress [Special issue]. *Journal of Social Behavior & Personality, 6*(7), 411–423.

Cooper, C. L., Sloan, S. J., & Williams, S. (1988). *Occupational Stress Indicator management guide.* Windsor, England: NFER-Nelson.

Cooper, C. L., & Smith, M. J. (1985). *Job stress and blue collar work.* New York: Wiley.

DeFrank, R. S., & Cooper, C. L. (1987). Worksite stress management interventions: Their effectiveness and conceptualization. *Journal of Managerial Psychology, 2*, 4–10.

Duffy, C. A., & McGoldrick, A. (1990). Stress and the bus driver in the UK transport industry. *Work and Stress, 4*(1), 17–27.

Edwards, J. R., & Cooper, C. L. (1990). The person–environment fit approach to stress: Recurring problems and some suggested solutions. *Journal of Organizational Behavior, 11*, 293–307.

Elkin, A. J., & Rosch, P. J. (1990). Promoting mental health at the workplace: The prevention side of stress management. *Occupational Medicine: State of the Art Review, 5*(4), 739–754.

Feldman, S. (1991). Today's EAP's make the grade. *Personnel, 68*, 3–40.

Folkman, S., & Lazarus, R. S. (1980). An analysis of coping in a middle-aged community sample. *Journal of Health and Social Behavior, 120*, 219–239.

Guzzo, R. A., Jette, R. D., & Katzell, R. A. (1985). The effects of psychologically based intervention programs on worker productivity: A meta-analysis. *Personnel Psychology, 38*, 275–292.

Harrison, R. (1972, May–June). Understanding your organization's character. *Harvard Business Review*, 119–128.

Hurrell, J. J., Jr., & McLaney, A. M. (1988). Exposure to job stress: A new psychometric instrument. *Scandinavian Journal of Work Environment and Health, 14*(Suppl. 1), 27–28.

Hurrell, J. J., Jr., & Murphy, L. R. (1992). An overview of occupational stress and health. In W. M. Rom (Ed.), *Environmental and occupational medicine* (2nd ed.). Boston: Little, Brown.

Ivancevich, J. M., & Matteson, M. T. (1980). *Stress and work*. Scott Foresman City, IL: Scott Foresman.

Ivancevich, J. M., & Matteson, M. T. (1988). Promoting the individual's health and well-being. In C. L. Cooper & R. Payne (Eds.). *Causes, coping and consequences of stress at work*. New York: Wiley.

Ivancevich, J. M., Matteson, M. T., Freedman, S. M., & Phillips, J. S. (1990). Worksite stress management interventions. *American Psychologist, 45*, 252–261.

Karasek, R. A. (1979). Job demands, decision latitude and mental strain: Implications for job redesign. *Administrative Science Quarterly, 24*, 285–307.

Karasek, R. A., Theorell, T., Schwartz, J. E., Schnall, P. L., Pieper, C. F., & Michela, J. L. (1988). Job characteristics in relation to the prevalence of myocardial infarction in the U.S. Health Examination Survey (HES) and the Health and Nutrition Examination Survey (HANES). *American Journal of Public Health, 78*, 682–684.

Kelly, M., & Cooper, C. L. (1981). Stress among blue collar workers. *Employee Relations, 3*, 6–9.

LaRocco, J. M., House, J. S., & French, J. R. P., Jr. (1980). Social support, occupational stress and health. *Journal of Health and Social Behavior, 21*, 202–218.

Lawler, E. E., & Hackman, J. R. (1969). Impact of employee participation in the development of pay incentive plans: A field experiment. *Journal of Applied Psychology, 53*, 467–471.

Levering, R. (1988). *A great place to work*. New York: Random House.

Matthieu, J. E., & Zajac, D. M. (1990). A review and meta-analysis of the antecedents, correlates and consequences of organizational commitment. *Psychological Bulletin, 108*(2), 171–194.

Moos, R. H. (1981). *Work Environment Scale manual*. Palo Alto, CA: Consulting Psychologists Press.

Murphy, L. R. (1984). Occupational stress management: A review and appraisal. *Journal of Occupational Psychology, 57*, 1–15.

Murphy, L. R. (1988). Workplace interventions for stress reduction and prevention. In C. L. Cooper & R. Payne (Eds.), *Causes, coping and consequences of stress at work*. New York: Wiley.

Newman, J. D., & Beehr, T. (1979). Personal and organizational strategies for handling job stress: A review of research and opinion. *Personnel Psychology, 32*, 1–43.

Oldham, G. R. (1988). Effects of changes in work space partitions and spatial density on employee reactions: A quasi-experiment. *Journal of Applied Psychology, 73*, 253–258.

Osipow, S. H., & Spokane, A. R. (1983). *A manual for measures of occupational stress, strain and coping*. Odessa, FL: Par, Inc.

Rafael, A. (1985). Quality circles and employee attitudes. *Personnel Psychology, 38*, 603–615.

Rasmussen, L. (1992). *Cultural change and its effect on job satisfaction, organizational commitment and motivation with Hydro Aluminium*. Unpublished master's thesis, University of Manchester Institute of Science & Technology, Manchester, England.

Rees, D., & Cooper, C. L. (1991). A criterion-oriented validation of the OSI outcome measures on a sample of Health Services employees. *Stress Medicine, 7*, 125–127.

Reynolds, S., Taylor, E., & Shapiro, D. A. (1993). Session impact in stress management training. *Journal of Occupational and Organizational Psychology, 66*, 99–113.

Robertson, I. T., & Cooper, C. L. (1990). The validity of the Occupational Stress Indicator. *Work and Stress, 4*, 29–39.

Rotter, J. B. (1966). Generalized expectancies for internal v. external control of reinforcement. *Psychological Monographs, 80*, 609–619.

Sauter, S., Hurrell, J. J., & Cooper, C. L. (1989). *Job control and worker health*. New York: Wiley.

Sauter, S. L., Murphy, L. R., & Hurrell, J. J., Jr. (1990). A national strategy for the prevention of work-related psychological disorders. *American Psychologist, 45*, 1146–1158.

Scheflen, K. C., Lawler, E. E., & Hackman, J. R. (1971). Long-term impact of employee participation in the development of pay incentive plans: A field experiment revisited. *Journal of Applied Psychology, 55*, 182–186.

Skov, P., Valbjórn, O., & Pedersen, B. V. (1989). Influence of personal characteristics, job-related factors and psychosocial factors on the sick building syndrome. *Journal of Work Environment, 15*, 286–295.

Skov, P., Valbjórn, O., & Pedersen, B. V. (1990). Influence of indoor climate on the sick building syndrome in an office environment. *Scandinavian Journal of Work, Environment and Health, 16*(5), 363–371.

Smith, D., & Mahoney, J. (1989, August). McDonnell Douglas Corporation's EAP products hard data. *The Almacan*, 18–26.

Sutherland, V. J., & Cooper, C. L. (1990). *Understanding stress*. London: Chapman & Hall.

Zaccaro, S. J., Craig, B., & Quinn, J. (1991). Prior absenteeism, supervisory style, job satisfaction, and personal characteristics: An investigation of some mediated and moderated linkages to work absenteeism. *Organizational Behavior and Human Decision Processes, 50*(1), 24–44.

16

Redesigning Work Systems to Reduce Stress: A Participatory Action Research Approach to Creating Change

Susan J. Schurman and Barbara A. Israel

Although definitions of stress continue to be the subject of debate, there is broad agreement that the experience of stress emerges as an outcome of interactions among the characteristics of individuals and of their social and physical environments. In particular, evidence suggests that people are at increased risk for occupational stress-related illness or behavioral problems when the externally (environmentally) determined performance demands of their work do not match their capacities or latitude for effective responses (Dimartino, 1992; Karasek & Theorell, 1990).

In theory, occupational stress interventions could seek to improve the match between demands and response capacities or latitudes by attempting to change one or all of the following: (a) work demands, (b) response latitudes, and (c) response capacities. Alternatives (a) and (b) require changes in the underlying social, technical, and organizational characteristics of the work system, whereas alternative (c) targets changes in the behavior of individual employees. In practice, this latter option has been the most common stress-related intervention. In particular, the bulk of intervention practice appears aimed at increasing employees' capacities to cope with stressful working conditions by teaching them how to better "manage" their psychological, physiological, or behavioral responses (Israel, Schurman, & House, 1989; Karasek, 1992). Although helping individuals learn to protect themselves from the effects of job stress will remain an important intervention component, the prevention and reduction of stress requires a more comprehensive intervention strategy that includes fundamental changes in the work system.

Many contributing factors account for the relatively slow adoption of stress

The authors deeply thank the members of the United Auto Workers (UAW)/General Motors (GM)/University of Michigan Stress and Wellness Project for their contribution to the efforts described in this chapter. We also thank Charles Heckscher for helpful comments on a previous draft. The participatory action research project described in this chapter was initially supported by grant #501 AA065353 from the National Institute on Alcohol Abuse and Alcoholism and later by a grant from the UAW/GM National Joint Committee on Health and Safety.

interventions aimed at system-level changes, but one factor has received considerable attention recently: the relatively poor track record of interventions aimed at creating organizational change at levels beyond the individual or immediate working group (Golembiewski, 1990). This failure has been attributed to the lack of useful theories of how complex human systems develop and change, which could serve as guides for practitioners engaged in the design and implementation of organizational-level interventions (Burdine & McLeroy, 1992; Golembiewski, 1990; Heckscher, Eisenstat, & Rice, 1994; Porras & Robertson, 1987; Sarason, 1971, 1990). Sarason's (1971) comment on the difficulties posed by "reforming" educational institutions applies equally well two decades later to efforts to redesign other organizations and institutions:

> We do not have adequate descriptions of the change process so as to allow us to begin to understand the high frequency of failures or the occasional successes . . . . *The relationship between knowledge of the setting and the conception of how to introduce change into it is by no means self-evident.* (p. 60, emphasis added)

Our purpose in this chapter is to describe one particular approach to system-level intervention: participatory action research (PAR). PAR, in our experience, has proven itself as an effective means of linking knowledge of the setting with a conception of how to introduce change. It therefore deserves serious attention as a strategy for redesigning work systems to prevent the onset of stress-related health problems.

We assume, based on our experience and our reading of the health and safety literature, that many occupational health and safety interventions are designed by professionals whose expertise lies primarily in the substance of particular health issues (e.g., ergonomics, hazardous materials, stress) rather than in change processes at either the individual or organizational level. Therefore, our emphasis in this chapter is less on the concept of stress and more on the change process, although, as will be discussed further, the two are highly intertwined in our model of preventing work-related stress. We begin by explaining the conceptual framework used to guide our approach to intervention, followed by an outline of the core characteristics of the PAR methodology. After this conceptual overview, we illustrate the notorious difficulty in translating theory into practice by describing our use of the PAR methodology in an intervention aimed at reducing sources of stress in an automobile factory. We conclude with an assessment of the key lessons from this case. Drawing on reports from several other recent PAR interventions, we present some recommendations for strengthening PAR interventions.

Analyzing the Stress Process: A Framework for Developing Interventions

Building on considerable research evidence, Figure 1 schematically depicts the systemic nature of the stress process (French & Kahn, 1962; House, 1981; Israel, Schurman, & House, 1989). Reading the figure from right to left, health

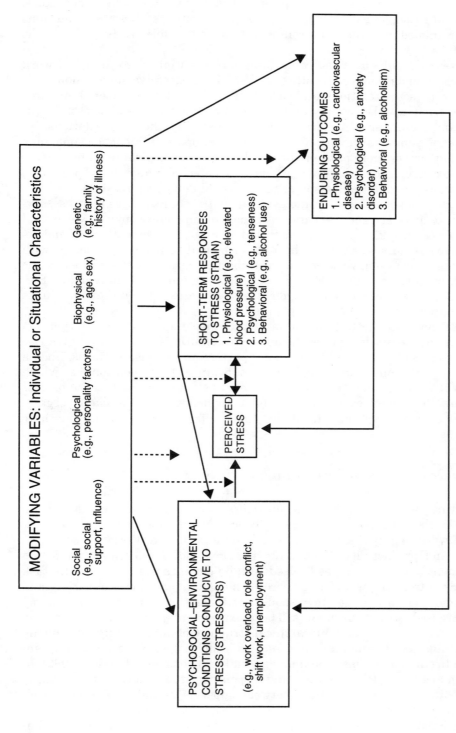

Figure 1. Conceptual framework of the stress process. Solid arrows between boxes indicate presumed causal relationships (direct effects) among variables. Broken arrows intersecting solid arrows indicate an interaction between the modifying variables and the variables in the box at the source of the solid arrow in predicting variables in the box at the head of the solid arrow.

and behavioral problems are conceptualized as the long-term effects of people's short-term response patterns to "stressors"—specific psychosocial conditions in their immediate work environment that they subjectively interpret as "stressful."

Research results have indicated numerous potential stressors such as work overload or underload, role conflict, task variety, excessive supervision, negative interpersonal relations, and lack of influence on decisions (see Dimartino, 1992 for a review). Depending on their personal perceptions of stressful situations and a number of moderating factors that may affect the relationships among stress and health variables (e.g., social support, influence), people may respond on one or more of the following levels: psychological (e.g., feelings of anxiety or anger), physiological (e.g., elevated catecholamines, blood pressure), or behavioral (e.g., absenteeism, drug or alcohol abuse, aggression).

Because of the generality and systemic nature of responses to stress, several causes may trigger the same response, or one cause may have several responses (Karasek, 1992). As illustrated in Figure 1, perceptions of and responses to stressors—as well as the long-term health outcomes associated with the stress process—have been shown to be influenced by differences in the genetic, biophysical, psychological, and social resources of individuals. Significantly, some stressors may trigger stress responses without the individual's being consciously aware of feeling stressed.

This model suggests that the most preventive approach to intervention would be to attempt to change the objective conditions of work that give rise to perceptions of stress and that trigger particular response patterns. Such a view poses questions concerning both the substance of intervention (i.e., which aspects of working conditions are amenable to change) as well as the process (i.e., how to attempt such interventions). Evidence from the early "organizational change" experiments of the 1970s offers some guidance on these questions.

Substance of Stress Reduction Interventions

Though not specifically aimed at job stress, early organizational change interventions sought to change working conditions to improve both the experience of work (e.g., job satisfaction) and the outcomes of work activity (e.g., quality and productivity). Under the headings "job enlargement" and "job enrichment," typical changes focused both on changes in the immediate task demands of frontline workers to decrease monotony and increase variety and challenge, and on changes in response latitudes through greater autonomy and increased skill requirements. These experiments also typically included modest amendments to the hierarchical structure of authority by introducing work group decision-making processes in which supervisors permitted employees to participate in selected managerial decisions (e.g., Landen, 1982). In addition to altering task demands and response latitudes, these latter changes also modified the social relations between supervisors and employees as well as among coworkers.

On balance, these experiments were generally quite successful at improving job satisfaction as well as quality and productivity at the job and work group level (see, e.g., Goodman, 1980; Trist, 1981; Walton, 1975 for reviews). In addition, some of these experiments also provided early field evidence suggesting two characteristics of work systems that could be modified to reduce the risks of stress-related illness: the amount of influence employees have on work-related decisions and the quality of social interaction (e.g., Gardell, 1975; Jackson, 1983).

Intervention Process

Organizational change interventions in the 1970s typically sought first to introduce innovative work practices at the microlevel of work groups or departments and then to "diffuse" the innovation throughout the system. Although these microlevel interventions were a clear conceptual and practical improvement on intervention approaches targeting solely the individual level, they generally failed to be adopted beyond the immediate implementation context (see Golembiewski, 1990; Goodman, 1980; Karasek, 1992; Walton, 1975 for thorough discussions of these experiments). In fact, as Katz and Kahn pointed out (1978), these were not really *organizational* change interventions but rather *job design* interventions. As such, they failed to address the core techno-structural features of the system and consequently failed either to diffuse or to persist.

Broadening the Framework

With the benefit of hindsight, the typical design of early organizational change interventions can now be seen as suffering from the "error of local determinism" (Katz & Kahn, 1978), that is, the assumption that one part of a system can be changed without affecting the rest of the structure. In practice, the larger system usually reacted in ways that nullified local changes. The nature of complex bureaucratic organizations is such that the major "objective" features of the immediate work environment are "overdetermined," that is, the system has multiple mechanisms for reproducing desired behavior and resisting change. For example, selection, training, and reward practices are all geared to producing and maintaining stability (i.e., preventing change) in the prescribed role behavior of individuals. Moreover, changes in these policies are almost always made at levels of the system outside the direct influence of all but the highest ranks of managers (Berg, Freedman, & Freeman, 1979; Kochan, Katz, & McKersie, 1986; Lazarus, 1985). Consequently, in order to effect system-level change, interventions need to incorporate the strategic decision-making level of the organization as well as, in some cases, factors in the external environment and not just the microlevels of workplaces, work groups, and individual jobs.

As a practical matter, however, as Karasek (1992) has pointed out, interventions targeting the individual worker or work microsystem level are much easier to implement. Interventions that seek to modify features at other system levels—although theoretically more preventive—are also more difficult to implement because they involve an increasingly complex set of social factors and interest groups. At the same time, interventions implemented at the individual or microsystem level will quickly reveal that many of the desired changes have implications for the entire system and require the consent of decision makers far outside the direct influence of those immediately affected. The problem for intervention designers is to conceptualize a structure and process of intervention that incorporates multiple levels of the system in the change process.

Integrating the Role of Individual and Collective Learning

In most theories of organizational change, actual behavior change at either the individual or organizational level is presumed to occur through the direct learning experiences of individuals and groups at different levels of the system (see Porras & Robertson, 1987 for a review of this literature). However, until recently, the actual processes through which such learning is presumed to occur have generally been taken for granted (Porras & Robertson, 1987; Schurman, 1992). Yet the problem of how organization members develop their "causal maps" of the organization's operating system that guide their own role performances and, more important, how they unlearn old maps and learn new ones is central to the design of organizational change strategies (see, e.g., Weick & Bougon, 1986). Frei, Hugentobler, Schurman, and Alioth (1993) proposed that such learning *requires* the direct participation of system members in both designing and implementing the change process. Direct participation in the reconstruction of their own work activities allows employees at different levels of the system to gain greater insight into the patterns of interaction among the technical, social, and organizational features of their work environment. Through opportunities to formulate their own goals and interests, together with their coworkers, employees learn about the "invisible" interdependencies in the work system and the needs and interests of others in different positions or areas. They also develop greater understanding of their own work and greater influence over the demands posed by the newly redesigned activities. At the same time, employees can contribute their own expert knowledge to improving the work process (Frei et al., 1993).

The experience of participating in the change of one's immediate work can lead to a qualitative change in employee knowledge as well as a reinforcement of the expectation that one's actions can result in desired changes and that one can learn new things. Karasek and his colleagues (Karasek, 1992; Karasek & Theorell, 1990) argued that such "active learning" through direct participation can in itself enhance health and reduce the risk of stress-related illness. This process of active learning through participating in change processes has also been termed "empowerment learning" (Kornbluh, Pipan, & Schurman, 1987). Similarly, direct participation in the change process allows managers and professionals at higher levels of the system to learn about the effects of their decisions and policy formulations on the performance and health outcomes of people in other parts of the system.

These conceptual perspectives on the occupational stress process and the learning process have several implications for intervention design. First, the contextual nature of the stress process, combined with recognition of individual differences, suggests that approaches to intervention need to be context-specific rather than rely on packaged, context-independent "off-the-shelf" programs that are marketed to be implemented in any setting. Second, the framework suggests that the intervention process needs to engage people in direct learning activities that allow them first to develop a systemic understanding of the nature of the occupational stress process in their organization and then to influence the kinds of changes that will be adopted. Third, it suggests that such learning processes need to be initiated in, and eventually link, multiple levels of the system—that is, that the intervention strategy needs to be interactive (Heckscher, 1994), combining top-down and bottom-up approaches (Frei et al., 1993). With these guidelines in mind, the authors selected PAR as an appropriate methodology for an intervention aimed at changing the objective psychosocial environmental conditions conducive to stress.

What Is Participatory Action Research?

PAR is an emerging approach within the applied social and behavioral sciences. Although its complete genealogy is open to dispute and would require a separate chapter, its primary roots can be linked to three sources: (a) the "classical action research" method usually attributed to the work of Kurt Lewin and his followers (e.g., Lewin, 1946, 1951; see Elden & Chisholm, 1993 for a review); (b) the "operations (or operational) research" method developed by members of the Tavistock Institute in London and in the United States by Russell Ackoff and C. West Churchman (see Choukroun & Snow, 1993; Trist, 1981 for conceptual and historical reviews of these approaches); and (c) the "participatory research" method derived from the work of Paulo Freire (see Freire, 1971, 1973, 1985) and used especially by practitioners concerned with combating powerlessness and oppression (see Brown, 1983, 1985, 1993; Brown & Tandon, 1983; FalsBorda, 1985; and Gaventa, 1988 for conceptualization and case examples). The first two traditions have been accused of paying insufficient attention to the problem of power inequalities in human systems; the latter specifically addresses issues of power and oppression (Brown, 1993). PAR researchers have been drawing from these traditions to fashion a distinctive approach to intervention in human systems (Brown & Tandon, 1983; Whyte, 1991).

The PAR Process

Although definitions of PAR abound (see Elden & Chisholm, 1993 for a review), a general definition and description of key characteristics is provided here. PAR is a methodology in which researchers and members of a social system collaborate in a process of data-guided problem solving for the dual purposes of (a) improving the system's ability to provide members with desired outcomes and (b) contributing to general scientific knowledge. This is accomplished through

1. enhancing the system's ability to take action to meet identified needs,
2. improving its ability to use data as feedback to guide actions and to contribute to a body of knowledge,
3. increasing its capacity to learn from experience, and
4. decreasing the power inequities among system members.

The core PAR methodology involves identifying and assembling the major stakeholders—or, in the case of large systems, a representative group—and helping them design a knowledge acquisition and change strategy. The strategy involves a cyclical process of reflection and action in which the stakeholders (a) identify aspects of the system that they wish to change, (b) analyze "causes" of system dysfunction, (c) develop and implement action plans, (d) create a plan to evaluate the effects of their actions, (e) specify key lessons learned from their experiences of making changes, and (f) consolidate their learning into revised action plans that directly benefit the system members and into general knowledge that benefits others.

Because of its focus on concrete human systems problems, PAR is, by definition, "contextually bounded" (Susman & Evered, 1978). Consequently, each PAR inquiry can be expected to assume a different structure and employ different methods of inquiry, based on the needs and interests of the stakeholders involved. Indeed, designing the structure and process of the inquiry is the most significant conceptual challenge of PAR interventions. Despite the flexibility of its procedures, however, the methodology is distinguished by a common set of characteristics or principles that its practitioners seek to employ (Israel, Schurman, Hugentobler, & House, 1992):

1. PAR focuses on **system development** rather than individual behavior change. The intent of a PAR intervention is to help the system institutionalize the cyclical process of (a) diagnosing and analyzing problems and (b) planning, implementing, and evaluating actions as an ongoing approach to "managing" the system.
2. PAR is a **co-learning process** in which outside researchers can contribute their theoretical knowledge, preference for data-based judgments, and methodological expertise, and insiders can contribute their "local theories" and practical knowledge of the setting. Hence, change strategies are both contextually relevant and also grounded in accumulated general knowledge.
3. PAR is **participatory and cooperative**. The purpose of the approach is to involve researchers and system members in all aspects of both the research and action components of the inquiry from framing the problem(s), to collecting and analyzing data, to formulating action plans, conducting evaluation, and forming generalizations and conclusions.

4. PAR is an **empowering process** in which, through direct participation in inquiry and in action, system members gain increased influence and control over their lives.

5. PAR seeks a **balance between research and practical action** outcomes. In contrast to traditional research that is primarily focused on contributing advances to knowledge and theory, the research conducted by PAR investigators aims to solve practical problems. At the same time, in contrast to most organizational interventions, which focus primarily on solving practical problems, PAR researchers strive to contribute to theoretical advances, especially concerning organizational functioning and change.

PAR Outcomes

Successful PAR interventions should result in a number of changes in the structure and functioning of a system. First, the intervention should lead to increased use of data to guide planning and decision making. Second, it should lead to the development of new structures and decision-making processes that alter the distribution of power and authority in the system and provide more system members greater opportunities to participate in problem solving and influence decision making. These new structures and processes will be likely to involve more group-based problem solving and decision making, which will in turn lead to increased opportunities for positive social interaction and feelings of social support. Third, a successful PAR intervention should result in the institutionalization of these new structures and processes as the "normal" behavior patterns of the system. In addition to these direct benefits to the system, the intervention should result in increased scientific knowledge about organizational behavior and change, as well as about the particular topic on which the intervention is focused, such as—in this case—the occupational stress process.

PAR as a Methodology for Preventing or Reducing Sources of Work-Related Stress: Putting the Theory Into Practice in an Auto Plant

In this section, we describe our experience using the PAR methodology to design, implement, and evaluate a systemic intervention aimed at reducing sources of stress in an automobile factory. Given the iterative nature of the PAR process, this 6-year study evolved through a series of different developmental phases of reflection and action. In analyzing the data from the extensive field notes in which we documented the qualitative aspects of the change process, it became clear that movement from one phase to the next occurred as the result of the consolidation of learning by the participants in the project. Overall, this learning process involved a developmental change in problem-solving styles and strategies as participants in the intervention—including us as investigators—learned from the experience of planning and implementing action strategies. These changes in problem solving can be characterized as a shift in the way problems and solutions were framed away from a tendency to focus on generating isolated solutions to isolated problems toward a more complex, systemic, and multivariate understanding of both the problems and potential solutions (Israel, Schurman, Hugentobler, & House, 1992). After first presenting a brief overview of events leading to the intervention and a description of the organizational context, we will describe the intervention as it moved through these developmental shifts.

Background and Context

Our first encounter with the systemic nature of organizational change came at the earliest stage of the study. In 1985, we were contacted by the medical director in a parts manufacturing plant of a major American automobile manufacturer, who wanted to institute a stress reduction program. Working with the medical director and a joint union–management committee, we began the first phase of the PAR approach: working with the committee to delineate the problem and develop an intervention strategy. We then obtained a grant to fund the project for 3 years from the National Institute on Alcohol Abuse and Alcoholism's research initiative aimed at evaluating the effects of preventing or reducing occupational stress on alcohol abuse and disorders. In keeping with the PAR methodology, we assembled a multidisciplinary and multimethodological team that included colleagues with different disciplinary orientations, quantitative and qualitative research competencies, and skills in intervention as well as in research. Based on a conceptual model similar to that depicted in Figure 1 and on an extensive review of the stress literature (see Israel et al., 1989; Israel & Schurman, 1990), the project was aimed at reducing the risk of long-term stress-related illness through: (a) changing the objective work conditions conducive to stress, (b) altering patterns of participation in decision making in order to give workers more influence, and (c) creating more supportive social relations. We also argued that the use of a PAR strategy was, in itself, health-enhancing because of the active involvement and influence of participants in the change process (for a more detailed description of the research design and methodology, see Hugentobler, Israel, & Schurman, 1992; Israel et al., 1989).

Shortly after we received the grant, our initial research site informed us that the parent corporation was unwilling to agree to the 3-year longitudinal design and would proceed only on a year-by-year basis. We then confronted two unattractive choices: either risk cancellation of the study prior to completion or find another site that had not been involved in the initial stage of conceptualizing the project. We elected the latter and approached contacts in a large division of a different automobile manufacturer and a different department of the same international union. These initial contacts directed us to a component parts manufacturing plant in south-central Michigan. After several meetings, the local plant management and union leadership decided to participate in the project. Management and the union each appointed a representative to work with us to implement the project.

The plant is one of the oldest automobile plants in continuous operation in the corporation and in the United States. In 1985, as the project commenced, the plant was experiencing a major organizational change in response to a recent reorganization at the corporate level. Faced with the loss of the single product line that had sustained the factory for 75 years, plant managers and union leaders had joined forces to acquire new products. At the time that the stress and wellness project began, the factory was in the early stage of learning to make several new product lines for several different corporate divisions. The manufacturing processes and technology in the plant were in transition, and the conversion process had introduced considerable uncertainty and confusion in the factory. On our first plant tour, we observed traditional mass production methods and old equipment existing side by side with newer production technology and methods. For example, one new product involved the manufacture of precision engine parts using newly developed lightweight metal alloys, computerized technology, and a job redesign intervention to increase "employee involvement."

In 1988—3 years into the study—as part of a broader reorganization effort, the corporation decided to subdivide the plant into two separate plants so that each product area would be directly managed by the corporate division having primary manufacturing responsibility for the product line. A painted line was drawn (literally) on the plant floor, and new signs appeared that denoted the new separate plant identities. Skilled-trades and other nonoperations workers assigned to the central maintenance, materials handling, or housekeeping departments were allowed to bid on which of the plants they wished to be assigned to. As we soon learned, the two divisions had very different labor relations approaches and management styles, one using the more traditional adversarial style associated with mass production and the other, the more cooperative style associated with flexible production (for more detail on these differences and their effects on the intervention process, see Heaney et al., 1993).

At the beginning of the project, the plant employed approximately 1,050 people. By 1987, the recession in the automobile industry had reduced that number to about 800. Following the subdivision of the factory in 1988, new jobs were created, and, at the end of the project, the workforce numbered about 1,100. The following demographic characteristics remained about the same throughout these fluctuations: Approximately 90% of the employees were hourly workers (e.g., in the production and skilled trades), 95% were male, 80% were White, and the average age was in the mid-40s. Because these were primarily machining and not assembly facilities, jobs were desirable because workers were not tied to the assembly line. As a result, the workforce was older than in a typical assembly plant, and the average seniority was more than 20 years. The original plant had a history of relatively good labor–management relations, and the union and management had previous experience with jointly administered employee participation programs.

Phase 1: Entry, Forming the Stress and Wellness Committee, and Creating the Conditions for Joint Inquiry

Following the union and management agreement to participate, the research team, together with the management and union representatives, began the process of jointly developing a PAR committee to conduct the inquiry. This initial group developed a set of criteria that would be used to select committee members, including: (a) representativeness (e.g., coming from different production areas, shifts, and occupational and demographic groups), (b) being knowledgeable about the plant, (c) being trusted and respected by peers, and (d) having the ability to communicate well with others. Using these criteria, specific individuals were nominated and their names submitted to the joint union–management leadership group for approval. This selection process resulted in an initial 26-member committee—much larger than the approximately 12- to 15-member committee the university team had hoped for, based on research concerning effective group functioning. The union and management representatives argued vehemently, however, that previous joint committees had been top-heavy with union and management leaders who were too busy to attend meetings and that, consequently, nothing got accomplished. They felt strongly that this committee should include a substantial number of "shop floor" employees—both supervisory and nonsupervisory—who were usually left out of these efforts and whose participation they believed to be crucial. The so-called Stress and Wellness Committee (SWC) included key union and management leaders but was primarily made up of shop floor employees from both the salaried and hourly ranks and was highly representative of the workforce. This process of forming the committee was the first step in establishing mutual ownership and control of the project and was especially critical because study site members had not been involved in the original conceptualization and design that had led to the grant funding.

In the early meetings of the SWC, the university team focused on helping the committee design a process of dialogue and data-guided inquiry. This involved first generating process rules or "norms" for effective meetings (e.g., have open, honest communication; everyone is equal; everyone's opinion is important; agree to disagree; have consensus decision making; and preserve the confidentiality of discussions), followed by developing shared goals for the project and generating a shared "local theory" of the stress process and how it operated in the factory. The development of shared goals, problems, and procedures was aimed at creating the knowledge, skill, and shared influence that would allow all committee members (including the university team) to participate effectively in the PAR process.

One consequence of the nature of the entry process in this plant and the fact that plant members had not participated in the initial project design was that, during the first phase, the university team had primary responsibility for agenda preparation, meeting facilitation, and overall project coordination. Over time, many of these functions were transferred to other committee members, although never to the degree we would have preferred. We continued to play a major role in project administration and coordination throughout the

6-year intervention. Several times, we suggested that the committee select internal leaders, one from the union and one from management, but they refused, saying that the creation of formal leaders had caused problems in other efforts and they wanted everyone to have equal roles in this project. Eventually, toward the end of the project, after we began to focus on "institutionalizing the process," the SWC selected a team of internal facilitators to take over our role. However, none of the internal members ever really received the release time from their regular functions to perform SWC business, and consequently the research team continued to "staff" the committee.

Phase 2: Isolating "the Problem"

After the SWC had developed a model of the stress process, the next step was to collect data that could be used both as a diagnosis or needs assessment to help guide the development of action plans as well as serve as a baseline against which to evaluate the effects of interventions. The overall data collection strategy incorporated both quantitative and qualitative methods: (a) three administrations of a plantwide survey containing measures of all major variables in the stress model; (b) in-depth, semistructured interviews with all members of the SWC, along with plant union and management leaders at the beginning and end of the project; (c) verbatim field notes from all committee meetings and other important meetings at the site; (d) a series of focus group interviews; and (e) five administrations of a questionnaire to the SWC in which they evaluated their committee process, our role, and their reactions to the project. We also tried unsuccessfully to collect data on plant productivity, quality, and absenteeism and grievance rates. (For more details on the data collection and analysis strategies, see Baker, 1993; Hugentobler et al., 1992; Israel, House, Schurman, Heaney, & Mero, 1989; Israel, Schurman, & House, 1989).

Based on the results of the initial interviews and first wave of survey data, the university team prepared a written report for the committee and, in a series of meetings, helped committee members learn to interpret basic statistical relationships, including correlations. This report became the principal tool through which the SWC members developed an understanding and interpretation of the meaning and implications of the data. In a 2-day meeting held off-site, committee members discussed the findings and prioritized problems. To assist them in using the data to guide their selection of priority problems to work on, the university team developed a set of criteria that included: (a) the prevalance of the problem across different departments and occupational groups; (b) the magnitude of the effects of the problem on job and health outcomes (as indicated by correlational data; and (c) the practical feasibility of influencing the problem, based on their understanding of the plant. By applying these criteria to the data contained in the report, the committee selected four issues as the initial targets for intervention: (a) lack of information, communication, and feedback; (b) poor relations with supervisors; (c) lack of participation in and influence over decision making; and (d) perceived conflicts between demands to produce quality versus quantity of product (for a more thorough discussion of the data on which these selections were based, see Hugentobler et al., 1992).

To develop action plans, the SWC formed four subcommittees to work on the four problem areas. A university team member was assigned to work with each subcommittee. Each subcommittee's charge was to further define the problem and develop recommendations for action to be first considered and approved by the full committee and then presented to the plant leadership for approval and implementation. This process reflected the SWC's "mission" as it had been defined by the union and management as part of their agreement to participate in the project. The committee's role was to diagnose problems and recommend actions; the power and authority to implement changes belonged to the union and management leadership group, eventually termed the "business unit leadership." Initially, this arrangement made sense because key union and management leaders were on the committee and could serve as a link between the SWC and the leadership. Eventually, however, this definition of the scope of the SWC's authority had major consequences; as the project unfolded and factory leaders changed, the committee found itself, in many instances, without the power to get its recommendations implemented.

The initial approach of the four subcommittees reflected what might be termed an "engineering" pattern of problem solving deeply embedded in the culture of this organization and, perhaps, most mass production systems (Ackoff, 1979; Schon, 1983; Schurman, 1992). This pattern, which Reither and Staudel (1985) termed the "isolated variation method" (p. 113) involves dividing a complex problem into its components and developing specific solutions for the parts. In a previous paper, we described this pattern as "discrete solutions for discrete problems" (Israel, Schurman, Hugentobler, & House, 1992). This pattern was captured in a metaphor proposed by one of the SWC members to describe the standard approach to solving problems in the corporation: "If you hear a suspicious noise under the hood of the car, kick the rear end." The following examples from several subcommittees will illustrate.

The first wave of data analysis revealed that employees' relations with their supervisors were an important "variable" in the stress process. Positive relations with supervisors were significantly associated both with higher job satisfaction and with reported better health outcomes (see Israel, House, et al., 1989). Using these data, the Supervisory Relations Subcommittee at first assumed that the "cause" of the "problem" would be found in the behavior of frontline supervisors who directly supervised shop floor production and skilled-trades employees. Their intervention strategy focused on providing training to help these supervisors be more effective in their roles in such areas as interpersonal relations. Similarly, in response to data suggesting that perceived lack of information and poor communication were a significant source of stress, the Information/Communication Subcommittee proposed publishing a daily newsletter that would contain important and up-to-date information about production schedules, meetings, and other items of interest to employees. The Participation and Influence Subcommittee delved more deeply into the reasons that the existing employee participation team (EPT) program appeared not to be working, and discovered that neither hourly team leaders nor supervisors were provided any time off their regular jobs to follow up on the problems discussed during team meetings. Consequently, few items got resolved, and employees became disenchanted with participating. The subcommittee recommended that team leaders and supervisors be allowed time during regular working hours for EPT business.

All SWC recommendations were approved for implementation by the joint business unit leadership. In addition to these proposed interventions aimed at organizational variables, the SWC decided to develop a "health screening and awareness" intervention aimed at increasing employees' awareness of their personal health risks and encouraging them to adopt healthier lifestyles. This intervention, "Healthwatch," was approved and implemented by the committee. It included (a) blood pressure and cholesterol screening and follow-up, (b) health information materials distributed in the plant and sent to employees' homes, (c) administration of health-risk appraisal forms, and (d) changes in the food and hours of operation of the plant cafeteria. Healthwatch was regarded by many as the most successful element of the project (see Baker, Israel, & Schurman, 1994 for a detailed description and evaluation of this intervention).

Phase 3: Systemic Problem Identification—Solutions at the Microsystem Level

In the course of evaluating the first cycle of problem identification and solutions, the SWC recognized that many of their initial recommendations either were not being implemented or were not producing the intended results. This led to a period of further in-depth problem analysis. In the case of the Supervisory Relations Subcommittee, for example, the university facilitator helped the group first to develop a profile of an effective supervisor and then to analyze the organizational factors—in addition to training—that might either encourage or prevent a supervisor from behaving in congruence with this profile. This activity led the subcommittee to request additional data from the survey to see whether there were any differences in how different groups of employees evaluated their relations with their supervisor. The results surprised the group; the data indicated that, rather than being the "cause" of the problem, first-level supervisors reported the highest levels of stress and the lowest amount of supportive relations with their supervisors. In comparison, the hourly unionized employees were relatively satisfied with their relations with the first-level supervisors. As a result of this information, the subcommittee redefined both the problem and its solution; instead of training first-level supervisors, they decided to focus on finding ways to improve relations between upper level supervisors within management and those they supervised.

After receiving approval from union and management to address this problem, the subcommittee decided to obtain the direct input of supervisors through a series of feedback meetings in which the subcommittee members presented the survey findings and solicited suggestions for solutions. In these meetings, supervisors indicated that a great deal of their stress and frustration resulted from the performance evaluation procedures, which primarily measured their ability to "get the numbers" (produce the required quantity of parts) while they were being told, at the same time, to improve product quality and to improve their "people skills," especially by getting employees to participate in solving problems.

These feedback meetings, together with the experience of the other subcommittees, increased the SWC's understanding of the interrelatedness of the problems of quality versus quantity, lack of participation and influence, poor supervisory relations, and lack of information and communication. The committee decided to combine these issues and to integrate the recommendations of different subcommittees into a proposed "pilot project" that was being developed by the Quality/Quantity Subcommittee. The intervention would seek to improve quality by increasing participation and influence, improving communication and information sharing, and developing better supervisory relations. In late 1987, a pilot intervention was proposed and approved by the factory leadership that aimed to develop problem-solving teams in one department. The SWC hoped to learn from this pilot which aspects of the intervention could be developed into recommendations for broader diffusion throughout the plant. At the same time, a new performance appraisal would be piloted involving a group of managers and supervisors willing to experiment with a peer-based performance evaluation system. A steering committee was formed to govern the implementation of the pilot team project that included the product area manager and union representatives, the maintenance supervisor, first-level supervisors, and several SWC members.

From the beginning, it was difficult to get employees to volunteer to serve on a problem-solving team. Many were disillusioned with previous experiences with employee participation teams and adopted a "wait-and-see" attitude. Eventually, nine people from the second shift in one department volunteered to participate. They were joined by the supervisor, a manufacturing engineer, and two skilled-trades workers assigned to the area. The team received training in process analysis using statistical methods, team building, and group problem solving. After 6 months, an evaluation of their experience conducted by the SWC indicated that the experiment was progressing well: The participants reported that they had indeed acquired the skills to work together, had selected important problems to work on, and had the competence to solve production problems. However, evaluation data collected after the first year indicated that the team, although feeling very positive about working together, had encountered a series of barriers to their performance. In particular, they felt that once they identified important problems to work on, one of two things happened: Either they failed to receive the information, follow-up, and assistance needed from the steering committee to complete their work on the problem, or managers and engineers felt threatened by their success and "took the problem away from them" in order to solve it themselves and get the credit. Consequently, the team did not feel sufficiently able to use the skills it had acquired (see Gerschick, 1994 for an in-depth analysis of the pilot project).

Using the evaluation data from the pilot project, the SWC consolidated their learning into a set of recommendations for the establishment of similar teams in other departments throughout the plant. The timing of these recommendations corresponded to a separate initiative sponsored by the corporation to implement "quality teams" (QTs). The SWC suggested to the plant leadership that the experience gained in the pilot team project could be used as the basis for implementing the QTs. Although these recommendations were verbally approved, they were not actually adopted at this point, in part because the plant manager who had supported both the pilot project and the new performance appraisal was transferred to another plant. A key lesson for the SWC from this phase was the manner in which policies and practices in the larger plant and corporate system (e.g., performance appraisal and transfer policies) influenced their efforts with the pilot team and the diffusion of recommendations.

Phase 4: Systemic Approaches to System-Level Problems

Through the ongoing process of diagnosing, planning, action taking, and evaluating outcomes, SWC members began to develop a broader and more complex understanding of the interrelationships of the major sources of stress that their action plans were designed to address, along with the organizational factors that encouraged or inhibited successful intervention. For example, the Communication/Information Subcommittee had initially developed a daily newspaper and, in response to feedback that it was not really meeting the employees' needs, had concentrated on trying to improve it by collecting data on what kind of information people wanted. As they probed further into the problem, the subcommittee realized that the problem was not solely *lack* of information but rather that people did not trust the information they received. What employees really wanted was an opportunity to get honest information about how well the plant was operating in a format that provided an opportunity to ask questions directly of people with information. With this revised understanding, the subcommittee proposed to cancel the daily newsletter and replace it with a four-pronged plantwide "communication strategy": (a) open-door sessions with union and management officials, held twice a month, where employees could drop in to ask questions; (b) quarterly "state-of-the-business" meetings in which managers and union leaders presented performance information to all employees and reserved time for questions and answers; (c) regular meetings between supervisors and hourly team leaders; and (d) special information bulletins to all employees as needed. This comprehensive strategy, the subcommittee felt, would begin to alter the traditional communication system in the plant and create a more supportive atmosphere in which to introduce other changes.

Once again, the union and management leadership agreed with the SWC's recommendations but took little action except to change the newsletter from a daily to a weekly. Several open-door meetings were held, but scheduling was inconsistent.

At this point, many SWC members were becoming very frustrated and confused by the failure of their leadership to follow through on their recommendations. The university team encouraged them to reflect critically on their progress to date and to develop a theory of why "success wasn't taking" (Walton, 1975). Through analysis of their experience, the SWC concluded that achieving their goals required changes in the "way business is done" in the two plants and could not be achieved without the direct and active participation of the top plant leadership, especially management. Union leaders had been consistently supportive of the committee's effort, although they had stopped attending meetings regularly early in the project. The key question became how to regain this participation, which, the committee believed, had been lost primarily as a result of management turnover (five different plant managers in 5 years) and the subdivision of the plant (the management from the new division had not been involved in the original agreement and never developed any investment in the project).

Because the official end of the project was fast approaching, the SWC also had to grapple with their desired future for the stress project. Two major alternatives were considered: (a) Institutionalize the SWC as a "standing committee" of the factories, with support from the leadership and the authority to carry out their recommendations; or (b) institutionalize the goals and methods of the SWC as part of the ongoing approach to managing the factory by the joint union and management business unit leadership. As part of reaching consensus on which of the visions to pursue, the SWC decided to approach the factory leaders and ask their opinion on which alternative was most appropriate. By the end of the project, they never received an official answer from the management in the newer plant, and thus, the remainder of this analysis will focus on events in the original plant.

In early 1990, a new manager was assigned to the plant and immediately expressed an interest in the SWC project. Her involvement was quickly curtailed, however, by a host of serious production problems, and no real progress was made during this period toward getting the plant leadership involved. Many SWC members were ready to simply give up. The university team concentrated on getting them to develop a strategy for getting the leadership's attention. They decided to propose an all-day planning meeting with several key managers and union leaders for the purpose of deciding the future of the stress and wellness project.

During this planning meeting, which took place in April 1991, SWC members briefed the group on the project's goals, methods, and accomplishments, as well as the barriers they had encountered. They explained the goals as (a) identifying sources of stress, (b) designing interventions, (c) evaluating results, and (d) designing additional interventions when appropriate. After their presentation, one manager told them that they had left out one important goal: creating a real understanding among the factory leadership of what they were trying to do and why. Instead, the manager argued, they had made the leaders feel defensive, and this was the reason that they had encountered difficulties in getting their recommendations implemented.

This meeting resulted in a shift in the SWC's thinking about its own role and strategy. Members began to realize that it was the *process of learning* they had gone through that had led them to an understanding of the systemic nature of problems and their solutions. They began to theorize that unless the key union and management decision makers also experienced the same kind of learning process, they would continue to find it difficult to understand the committee's recommendations. This realization led them to start concentrating on replicating learning processes rather than communicating recommendations. The plant manager noted that the committee's group process, norms, and methods of problem analysis were highly consistent with Deming's (1986) ideas about using statistical methods to improve quality and "driving fear out of the workplace," which she was trying to introduce to the factory management group. She proposed an all-day meeting in which the committee would share the results of the third plantwide survey with an expanded group of union and management leaders and engage them in open discussion of whether and how to incorporate the SWC's goals into the ongoing efforts of the leadership to change their approach to managing the business.

During this meeting (in July 1991), the managers and union leaders observed that the problems identified by the committee as stress and health problems were the same problems that they had identified as causing quality and production problems. They noted, too, that the committee's proposed solutions were consistent with solutions that they had been discussing. After this meeting, management and the union agreed to assume the leadership role in improving information and communication, improving relations with supervisors, increasing opportunities to participate in decision making, and removing obstacles to producing sufficient numbers of high-quality parts. The SWC itself would no longer continue to function after feedback from the third survey was provided to the employees, but individual members would be called upon to serve on task forces or projects aimed at incorporating the SWC's goals.

By January 1992, management and the union had jointly conducted meetings in all departments. In these meetings, they shared information concerning the state of the business as well as the results from the third stress and wellness survey. At the time of the official end of the stress project, when the university team left the site, the plant leadership was in the process of planning how to expand and restructure existing employee participation efforts. Part of their plan involved developing improved participation among managers and supervisors in preparation for the more active involvement and influence of the hourly workforce. At a follow-up meeting of the SWC and the university team in May 1993, the plant was in the midst of implementing a corporate-wide quality program that included many of the same elements that the SWC had recommended, based on the pilot project. "We were just ahead of our time," said one management member of the SWC. Another member echoed, "If they'd only listened to us, they'd have done this a long time ago."

Results, Lessons, and Recommendations for Future PAR Interventions

Given the emphasis in this chapter on describing and analyzing the use of a PAR approach for achieving organizational change, the following discussion will focus on the process of conducting PAR. This case study has also contributed knowledge about the relationships among occupational stress and modifying variables (e.g., social support, participation, influence, and control) and measures of health and well-being (see, e.g., Baker, 1993; Baker et al., 1994; Heaney et al., 1993; Heaney, Israel, & House, 1994; Hugentobler et al., 1992; Israel, House et al., 1989; Klitzman, House, Israel, & Mero, 1990). In addition, there are challenges and limitations to using the PAR approach, both in general and in this particular case, that we have discussed elsewhere (Hugentobler et al., 1992; Israel, Schurman, & Hugentobler, 1992; Israel, Schurman, Hugentobler, & House, 1992).

1. *The labor–management relations context is an important determinant of intervention outcomes.* Longitudinal analyses of the first and third waves of survey data (Heaney et al., 1993) suggest that differences in management style and the overall labor–management relations context in the two plants influenced the impact of the intervention. Specifically, involvement in the PAR process enhanced employees' self-reported *actual* participation in decision making in both plants after controlling for baseline levels. However, this increased level of participation enhanced employees' *perceptions* of working in a more participatory environment only in the plant in which management was actively attempting to implement a more participatory style. Conversely, and unexpectedly, involvement in the PAR process enhanced perceptions of supportive relations with coworkers and decreased depressive symptoms only in the plant where management chose not to become involved in the project and where the labor relations climate was perceived as more adversarial. Although we do not know the reason for this effect, we hypothesize—based on our qualitative data—that it may be because there were fewer opportunities to engage in supportive interactions and exercise influence in the more adversarial plant, and therefore, involvement in the PAR process was more salient to employees in this context. These findings underscore the importance of the context in which the intervention is carried out and the need for creating an "intervention-friendly" climate. This result is consistent with Eaton's (1994) finding that union leaders' perceptions of the success of employee involvement programs are influenced more by their perceptions of the overall quality of the labor–management relationship than by the details of the program.

2. *Systemic change requires the direct involvement of strategic decision makers in the PAR inquiry.* The results just cited underscore our earlier discussion of the crucial role played by those who control access to strategic resources and who have the power to shape policy and take action in creating systemic change. This is not a new insight, and it has been consistently highlighted in the literature on organizational change (e.g., Goodman, 1980; Walton, 1975). Yet the problem of *how* to obtain and retain the attention and demonstrable support of those in positions of power and authority, as well as the question of at what level of the system they should be located, continues to pose a major design challenge. For example, although the SWC initially obtained support and participation from top plant and division management, the turnover of key managers at both levels presented the nearly constant challenge of how to educate new managers about the committee's purpose in order to obtain the necessary level of understanding and support. Similarly, upper level managers in the more adversarial plant were not part of the original formation of this project and never became engaged in or supportive of

the process. Furthermore, as we recognized from the beginning, a major obstacle to achieving full leadership support was the fact that the project was not designed jointly with the organization.

Our experience also clearly illustrates the need for involvement of leaders beyond the unit or plant level. The university team had hoped that division management and national union representatives would play a direct role, but this did not occur. The project did receive substantial indirect support from both the corporation and the union. The second 3-year period of the study was funded by the national joint health and safety fund, and the Healthwatch intervention was supported by a grant from the local joint health and safety fund. However, in this industry, as in most U.S. manufacturing contexts, the health and safety function has relatively little power in comparison with the manufacturing function and often has difficulty obtaining manufacturing support for its interventions (see, e.g., Hugentobler, Robins, & Schurman, 1990; Schurman, Silverstein, & Richards, 1994 for further discussion of this issue). Had the project been successful at obtaining the active involvement of division-level management and their union counterparts, we might then have gotten the cooperation of the other plant managers.

This corporation, like most, had a formal executive development policy of moving promising managers around to give them broad understanding of the company. Although this policy makes sense in times of stability, in times of rapid change, it undermines virtually all efforts to create change. To paraphrase one member of the SWC, "These people never stay around long enough to find out if their ideas work, and the people below them know it, so they just pretend to go along, knowing there will be a new boss and a new program soon."

3. *Systemic change requires creating new structures for the involvement and interaction of people at different levels.* The problem of leadership turnover requires the creation of new structures that can sustain change processes when key managers or union leaders leave. Cahill's (1992) PAR approach to reducing stress through technology change in a state welfare agency is a good example. In that case, the union used the results of a survey of burnout conducted by Cahill as part of their testimony in a legislative hearing concerning the agency's performance and staff morale. One result of this action was the formation of a labor–management stress committee to work on problems in the agency. Cahill worked with the committee—which included top agency executives as well as top union officials—to design an intervention that addressed both personal and systemic sources of stress. The result was the introduction and agency-wide diffusion of a new microcomputer technology that employees participated in designing.

In a more far-reaching effort, AT&T and its unions (the Communications Workers of America and the International Brotherhood of Electrical Workers) recently created a system-wide structure to design, implement, and govern their Workplace of the Future (WPOF) contract language (see Eaton, in press for a description). The WPOF contract established structures at multiple levels of the company and the unions—from the boardroom to the worksite level—to engage in the redesign process. The union and management bargainers stated that they learned of the importance of this structure from failures associated with implementing a quality of worklife (QWL) program in the 1980s that did not directly involve strategic decision makers (Heckscher, 1993). Similarly, the United Auto Workers and Ford learned—from their experience in redesigning their health and safety practices in response to federal right-to-know legislation—of the need to establish clear policy mandates and governance mechanisms at the top in order to gain the support and compliance of plant-level union and management officials (Hugentobler et al., 1990).

4. *The learning process is the most important outcome of the intervention.* Despite their frustrations with the slow pace of the change process, the members of the SWC expressed high levels of satisfaction with their participation on the committee. From the first annual committee evaluation survey in 1986 to the last in 1991, members reported increases in trust and openness among committee members and an increased willingness to share their own point of view honestly. All reported satisfaction with the group's internal process (Israel, Schurman, & Hugentobler, 1992). Analysis of the exit interview data, conducted at the end of the project, indicated that most SWC members attributed the longevity and eventual successes of the project to three factors.

One factor was the original committee composition, which included many hourly and salaried shop floor people not usually included in other plant programs. Although the SWC members were keenly aware of the problems posed by failing to keep top management involved, their assessment was that the presence of shop floor employees had helped to retain the union's interest and support from frontline supervisors. A second factor was the process norms that were generated by the committee members and initially adhered to only at meetings but eventually in all their interactions with each other. The committee members especially valued the "equality" norm, which stated that all members' participation is equally valuable, and the "confidentiality" rule, which stated that nothing said during SWC meetings would be shared outside the committee without the explicit permission of the group. This rule was never violated in the 6 years of the project. Members believed that these two norms encouraged and permitted honest, open dialogue about issues and enhanced the development of trust, particularly across labor and management lines. Related to this was a third factor—the university team's presence as "neutral outsiders" (their language, not ours) contributing our general knowledge about stress and organizational change as well as helping to facilitate the change process. Many members stated that our role in helping to create and institutionalize the norms was key to the committee's functioning. In the end, it was the committee's process of inquiry, not its specific recommendations, that attracted management's interest and attention. Our data suggest that it was this internal process that created the conditions for individual and collective learning and change to occur.

5. *The union can play a key role in sustaining the process, even under less-than-ideal circumstances.* What is perhaps most striking in this case is how long it took to establish the conditions for systemic and multivariate thinking within the SWC. In retrospect, no doubt there are things that the university team could have done to speed up the learning process (it took us several

months to analyze the first survey data and prepare a feedback report), but, in large measure, it seems clear that unlearning old patterns of thinking and acting requires feedback and time. Sustaining the intervention through the major obstacles it encountered in order to allow this learning process to progress posed the major challenge. In this project, the plant-level union representatives provided the stability, support, and continuity that allowed the project to survive high levels of managerial turnover. Although they did not play as active a role on the committee nor exert as much leadership in the business unit to encourage management to implement action plans as the SWC would have liked, they did make it clear to managers that they supported the project. This support in itself was probably enough to discourage any attempt by management to scuttle the effort. In part, the union officials did not play a more active role because they experienced competing demands on their time. In addition, several of the SWC members were union activists—informal leaders trusted by union officials to represent the union's interests on the project— and there was close communication between them and the union leadership.

It is interesting again to compare our experience with Cahill's (1992), where the union initiated the intervention and their involvement provided the impetus to obtain management's commitment. In that case as well, once the initial intervention seemed to be gaining support, the union decreased its involvement, claiming the need to devote its attention and limited resources to other problem areas. Heckscher and Hall (1994) argue that the structure of most American unions does not provide the necessary staffing and resources to sustain long-term participation in systemic change processes. If, as former U.S. Labor Secretary Ray Marshall (Marshall, 1991) argues (and we concur), employees need an independent source of power, such as unions, in order to ensure that their interests are represented in work redesign efforts, then the issue of unions' capacities and means to participate as stakeholders is an important one in the intervention design. As two other cases demonstrate (Landsbergis, Silverman, Barrett, & Schnall, 1992; May, 1992), unions are large social systems in their own right and can develop stress reduction interventions independently of employers through their own member services activities and through collective bargaining.

6. *Resources to guarantee the presence of multiple perspectives and methods are mandatory.* Central to the learning process was the inclusion of the perspectives of a representative group of employees. The importance of multiple perspectives to understanding the system and planning change became increasingly evident to everyone involved in the project. It was especially clear to the university investigators because we had been struck, during the initial in-depth interviews conducted as part of the entry/needs assessment phase, by how little people knew about the plant outside their immediate work area. Even many higher level managers seemed to have little understanding of the work processes in the factory beyond their sphere of immediate responsibility. An important outcome of the early committee discussions about the stress process was to help members begin to construct an image of the plant as a whole.

As time went on, the group learned to depend on each member's unique perspective in the decision-making process. The absence of a committee member from meetings always engendered comments such as, "I wish [member's name] were here. I'd like to hear what he/she thinks about this one." Unfortunately, beginning in the second year of the project, layoffs stemming from the major downturn in the U.S. automobile industry made retaining the involvement of shop floor employees as difficult as keeping key managers involved. As part of the corporation's struggle to become more efficient, the plant was forced to reduce its workforce. As a result, the SWC lost some members who transferred to other plants as part of contractual seniority "bumping" provisions. In addition, these reductions in force made it more difficult for shop floor employees, both supervisory and nonsupervisory, to obtain relief coverage in order to participate in SWC meetings and other activities. The most consistent participation came from managers and unionized employees in staff-type jobs who had more control of their own schedule and did not require relief coverage. Several unionized shop floor members of the SWC resigned from the committee because they were not being provided relief coverage, which they argued was unfair to their coworkers and gave both them and the project a bad image on the floor—especially since they could not point to many tangible results from their participation. Thus, employees' participation in the PAR process requires the commitment of resources to support their efforts. As Cahill (1992) notes, one of management's crucial roles was the provision of resources needed to support the intervention, and the union's rule was to insist that management provide the resources.

Obtaining multiple perspectives from system members is only one aspect of this issue. Including multiple research perspectives and methods also requires a major resource commitment, both financial and professional. If PAR interventions are to contribute to the general knowledge about human system functioning and change, then they must include rigorous research components aimed at understanding and explaining the key factors in the change process as well as assessing outcomes. This is particularly true in "single-case" interventions like the one presented here, where a comparison group is neither politically nor methodologically feasible. We sought to overcome this difficulty by designing a research strategy based on the concept of "triangulation" (Denzin, 1978; Fielding & Fielding, 1986), in which multiple research methods are used to increase confidence in the validity of the findings. We made extensive use of both qualitative and quantitative methods both to generate data to guide the intervention as well as to document the process and evaluate effects (see Hugentobler et al., 1992 for a detailed discussion of the multiple methods strategy).

Using a multidisciplinary approach is costly and time-consuming. It requires a substantial investment in research team meetings and "cross-training" so that members who are typically trained in only one research paradigm can develop an understanding and appreciation for each other's contribution. This adds substantially to the cost of a project but, if successfully implemented, significantly increases the likelihood that the PAR inquiry will produce advances in scientific knowledge about organizational change as well as about the topic under investigation (e.g., occupational stress). The classical action research paradigm has been criticized recently as having become primarily an intervention methodology and failing in its second purpose of contributing to scientific advances (e.g., Alderfer, 1982; Porras & Robertson, 1987). Walton and Gafney (1991) argue that finding new ways of conducting PAR inquiries that reduce the costs is crucial to the continued development of the method. There are also personal costs to the researchers involved in a PAR process because this method is not as highly valued within the academy and the results from research often take much longer to reach the publication stage, which can create problems for those in tenure-track academic positions (for a fuller discussion of the costs of PAR to both researchers and organization members, see Israel, Schurman, Hugentobler, & House, 1992).

7. *There is a need for "multiple-case" PAR studies.* In order to advance basic knowledge concerning how to use a PAR approach to systemic change, there is a need for intervention studies that involve a diverse set of organizational contexts and make use of the "case comparison" method. Referring back to Sarason's (1971) comment quoted earlier, there is still a lack of good description in the organizational change literature that allows for meaningful comparison of change processes in different contexts. A recent useful contribution can be found in Dimartino's (1992) edited volume, which contains 19 case studies of stress interventions and which attempted to get the authors to adopt a standard case description protocol. However, the intervention contexts and strategies were so diverse that it is difficult to infer meaningful generalizations (although Karasek [1992] argues that one generalization is that interventions that included employee participation were more successful). A good example of the type of multiple-case study design being recommended here can be found in the University of Michigan's intervention studies of the 1970s (reported in Cammann, Lawler, Ledford, & Seashore, 1984). In these experiments, funded by the U.S. Department of Labor, the classical action research method was used in a variety of organization contexts. The experiments resulted in major contributions both to organizational theory and to the intervention literature.

8. *Diffusing comprehensive stress reduction interventions will require change at the macrosystem level.* Supporting these kinds of intervention studies may require industry-level studies and some public investment, because few employers or even industries are likely to fund this type of research. Two recent PAR interventions suggest the value of such investment. The first is Ledford and Mohrman's (1993) report on their 5-year PAR study in which they helped institutionalize the PAR process of self-design in the manufacturing division of a major food products firm. As Walton and Gafney (1991) point out, however, such corporate-level change may be adequate in industries where each company, together with its unions, is free to develop a unique solution to shared problems. In many industries, however, individual companies or organizations exist in "domains" (Trist, 1981): tightly coupled relationships with other firms, governmental regulatory bodies, central education and training institutions, central labor organizations, and so forth. Systemic changes in these contexts is nearly impossible to achieve at the level of a single company, not to mention

at the level of a single plant or worksite. Instead, the change strategy in these contexts must eventually include these stakeholders in the process.

To illustrate, Walton and Gafney (1991) summarize the development of a PAR intervention aimed at improving both efficiency and safety in the international merchant shipping industry. The intervention began in the Norwegian shipping industry, supported by government funds, and spread to fleets throughout the world, stimulated in part by the interdependencies of the industry. This case also highlights the effects of national industrial and employment laws and regulations on work systems redesign efforts. Levi's (1992) description of the Swedish national investment in redesigning the work environment to benefit all major stakeholders is another example of the role of public policy in creating system change.

Concluding Remarks

PAR is one approach that can contribute both to an enhanced understanding of occupational health and safety issues and to the design, implementation, and evaluation of system-level change strategies aimed at reducing health and safety problems within workplaces. As suggested here, the conduct of successful PAR efforts necessitates attention to (a) both the external and internal environments of the organization, (b) the direct participation of strategic decision makers from both management and labor, (c) the development of a structure for the process of inquiry, (d) the provision of adequate resources to enable the presence of diverse perspectives and the use of multiple methods, and (e) the need for supportive policies and resources at the macrosystem level. Although such a comprehensive and long-term approach may not seem feasible to persons who are primarily engaged in relieving the immediate effects of stress through stress management programs and individual behavior change, we argue, in accordance with the conceptual model of the stress process that guided this intervention, that the complexity of the stress process requires such a multifaceted systemic approach to system-level problems. Our experience indicates that much can be accomplished even in the face of very difficult obstacles because employees really want to participate in redesigning their work system to reduce the health risks and improve the quality of their products. We recognize that there are limits in the time, resources, and skills that any researcher, practitioner, and project can accomplish. Hence, we encourage the formation of multidisciplinary teams and the increased opportunities for dialogue and exchange in order to expand the understanding of occupational health and safety problems and their solution.

References

Ackoff, R. L. (1979). The future of operational research is past. *Journal of Operational Research Society, 30*(2), 90–100.

Alderfer, C. P. (1982). Review of T. G. Cummings (Ed.), *Systems theory for organization development. Contemporary Psychology, 27*(1), 37–38.

Baker, E. A. (1993). *The role of control in occupational stress.* Unpublished doctoral dissertation, University of Michigan, Ann Arbor.

Baker, E. A., Israel, B. A., & Schurman, S. J. (1994). A participatory approach to worksite health promotion. *Journal of Ambulatory Care, 17,* 68–81.

Berg, I., Freedman, M., & Freeman, M. (1979). *Managers and work reform: A limited engagement.* New York: Free Press.

Brown, L. D. (1983). Organizing participatory research: Interfaces for joint inquiry and organizational change. *Journal of Occupational Behavior, 4*(9), 9–19.

Brown, L. D. (1985, February). People-centered development and participatory research. *Harvard Education Review, 55*(1), 69–75.

Brown, L. D. (1993). Social change through collective reflection. *Human Relations, 46*(2), 249–274.

Brown, L. D., & Tandon, R. (1983). Ideology and political economy in inquiry: Action research and participatory research. *Journal of Applied Behavioral Science, 19*(3), 277–294.

Burdine, J., & McLeroy, K. (1992). Practitioners' use of theory: Examples from a workgroup. *Health Education Quarterly, 19*(3), 331–340.

Cahill, J. (1992). Computers and stress reduction in social service workers in New Jersey. In V. DiMartino (Ed.), *Preventing stress at work: Conditions of work digest* (Vol. II). Geneva, Switzerland: International Labour Office.

Cammann, C., Lawler, E., Ledford, G., & Seashore, S. (1984). *Management–labor cooperation in quality of worklife experiments: Comparative analysis of eight cases* (Tech. Rep. to the U.S. Department of Labor). Ann Arbor: University of Michigan.

Choukroun, J. M., & Snow, R. (Eds). (1993). *Planning for human systems.* Philadelphia: University of Pennsylvania.

Deming, W. E. (1986). *Out of the crisis.* Cambridge, MA: MIT Press.

Denzin, N. (1978). *The research act: A theoretical introduction to sociological methods.* New York: McGraw-Hill.

Dimartino, V. (Ed.). (1992). *Preventing stress at work: Conditions of work digest* (Vol. II). Geneva, Switzerland: International Labour Office.

Eaton, A. E. (1994). Factors contributing to the survival of participative programs in unionized settings. *Industrial and Labor Relations Review, 47*(3), 371–389.

Eaton, A. E. (in press). Education for AT&T, CWA and IBEW's workplace of the future. *Proceedings of the 50th annual meeting.* Washington, DC: Industrial Relations Research Association.

Elden, M., & Chisholm, R. (1993). Emerging varieties of action research: Introduction to the special issue. *Human Relations, 46*(2), 121–142.

FalsBorda, D. (1985). *The challenges of social change.* Thousand Oaks, CA: Sage.

Fielding, N., & Fielding, J. (1986). *Linking data.* Thousand Oaks, CA: Sage.

Frei, F., Hugentobler, M., Schurman, S., & Alioth, A. (1993). *Work design for the competent organization.* New York: Quorum Books.

Freire, P. (1971). *Pedagogy of the oppressed.* New York: Herder & Herder.

Freire, P. (1973). *Education for critical consciousness.* New York: Seabury Press.

Freire, P. (1985). *The politics of education: Culture, power and liberation.* South Hadley, MA: Bergin & Garvey.

French, J. R. P., Jr., & Kahn, R. L. (1962). A programmatic approach to studying the industrial environment and mental health. *Journal of Social Issues, 18*(3), 1–47.

Gardell, B. (1975). *Technology, alienation, and mental health* (Report No. 45). Stockholm: Karolinska Institute.

Gaventa, J. (1988). Participatory research in North America. *Convergence, 21*(2/3), 41–46.

Gerschick, T. J. (1994). *The micro-politics of worker participation: Interests, understandings, and consequences of employee involvement.* Unpublished doctoral dissertation, University of Michigan, Ann Arbor.

Golembiewski, R. (1990). *Ironies in organization development.* New Brunswick, NJ: Transaction.

Goodman, P. (1980). Realities of improving the quality of work life: Quality-of-work life projects in the 1980s. *Proceedings of the 1980 Spring Meeting* (pp. 487–494). Washington, DC: Industrial Relations Research Association.

Heaney, C., Israel, B., Schurman, S., House, J., Baker, B., & Hugentobler, M. (1993). Industrial relations, worksite stress reduction and employee well-being: A participatory action research investigation. *Journal of Organizational Behavior, 14,* 495–510.

Heaney, C. A., Israel, B. A., & House, J. S. (1994). Chronic job insecurity among automobile manufacturing workers: Effects on employee satisfaction and health. *Social Science and Medicine, 38*(10), 1431–1437.

Heckscher, C. (1993). *The evolving social contract at work.* Unpublished manuscript, Rutgers University Labor Education Department, New Brunswick, NJ.

Heckscher, C. (1994). Defining the post-bureaucratic type. In C. Heckscher & A. Donnellon (Eds.), *The Post-bureaucratic organization* (pp. 14–62). Thousand Oaks, CA: Sage.

Heckscher, C., Eisenstat, R., & Rice, T. (1994). Transformational processes. In C. Heckscher & A. Donnellon (Eds.), *The post-bureaucratic organization* (pp. 129–177). Thousand Oaks, CA: Sage.

Heckscher, C., & Hall, L. (1994, July). Mutual gains and beyond: Two levels of intervention. *Negotiation Journal,* 235–248.

House, J. (1981). *Work, stress and social support.* Reading, MA: Addison-Wesley.

Hugentobler, M., Robins, T., & Schurman, S. (1990). How unions can improve the outcomes of joint health and safety programs. *Labor Studies Journal, 15*(4), 16–38.

Hugentobler, M. K., Israel, B. A., & Schurman, S. J. (1992). An action research approach to workplace health: Integrating methods. *Health Education Quarterly, 19*(1), 55–76.

Israel, B. A., House, J. S., Schurman, S. J., Heaney, C. A., & Mero, R. P. (1989). The relation of personal resources, participation, influence, interpersonal relationships and coping strategies to occupational stress, job strains and health: A multivariate analysis. *Work and Stress, 3*(2), 163–194.

Israel, B. A., & Schurman, S. J. (1990). Social support, control and the stress process. In K. Glanz, F. Lewis, & B. Rimer (Eds.), *Health behavior and health education: Theory, research and practice* (pp. 187–215). San Francisco: Jossey-Bass.

Israel, B. A., Schurman, S. J., & House, J. S. (1989). Action research on occupational stress: Involving workers as researchers. *International Journal of Health Services, 19*(1), 135–155.

Israel, B. A., Schurman, S. J., & Hugentobler, M. K. (1992). The relationship between employees and researchers in conducting action research: Values, skills, control, politics and rewards. *Journal of Applied Behavioral Science, 28*(1), 74–101.

Israel, B. A., Schurman, S. J., Hugentobler, M. K., & House, J. S. (1992). A participatory action research approach to reducing occupational stress: Phases of implementation and evaluation. In V. DiMartino (Ed.), *Preventing stress at work: Conditions of work digest* (Vol. II, pp. 74–101). Geneva, Switzerland: International Labour Office.

Jackson, S. J. (1983). Participation in decision-making as a strategy for reducing job related strain. *Journal of Applied Psychology, 68*(1), 3–19.

Karasek, R. (1992). Stress prevention through work reorganization: A summary of 19 international case studies. In V. DiMartino (Ed.), *Preventing stress at work: Conditions of work digest* (Vol. II, pp. 23–40). Geneva, Switzerland: International Labour Office.

Karasek, R., & Theorell, T. (1990). *Healthy work: Stress, productivity and the reconstruction of working life.* New York: Basic Books.

Katz, D., & Kahn, R. (1978). *The social psychology of organizations* (2nd ed.). New York: Wiley.

Klitzman, S., House, J. S., Israel, B. A., & Mero, R. P. (1990). Work stress, nonwork stress and health. *Journal of Behavioral Medicine, 13,* 221–243.

Kochan, T., Katz, H., & McKersie, R. (1986). *The transformation of American industrial relations.* New York: Basic Books.

Kornbluh, H., Pipan, R., & Schurman, S. (1987). Empowerment, learning, and control in workplaces: A curricular view. *Journal of Socialization Research and Educational Sociology, 4,* 253–268.

Landen, D. L. (1982). Stress in the workplace—An emerging industrial relations issue. *Proceedings of the 33rd annual meeting* (pp. 276–277). Washington, DC: Industrial Relations Research Association.

Landsbergis, P., Silverman, B., Barrett, B., & Schnall, P. (1992). Union stress committees and stress reduction in blue and white collar workers. In V. DiMartino (Ed.), *Preventing stress at work: Conditions of work digest* (Vol. II, pp. 144–151). Geneva: International Labour Office.

Lazarus, R. S. (1985). Toward an understanding of efficiency and inefficiency in human affairs: Discussion of Schonpflug's Theory. In M. Frese & J. Sabini (Eds.), *Goal directed behavior: The concept of action in psychology* (pp. 189–198). Hillsdale, NJ: Erlbaum.

Ledford, G., & Mohrman, S. (1993). Self-design for high involvement: A large-scale organizational change. *Human Relations, 46*(2), 143–174.

Levi, L. (1992). Managing stress in work settings at the national level in Sweden. In V. Dimartino (Ed.), *Preventing stress at work: Conditions of work digest* (Vol. II, pp. 139–143). Geneva, Switzerland: International Labour Ofice.

Lewin, K. (1946). Action research and minority problems. *Journal of Social Issues, 2,* 34–36.

Lewin, K. (1951). *Field theory in social science.* New York: Harper & Row.

Marshall, R. (1991). *The characteristics of high performance work and learning systems.* Washington, DC: Human Resources Development Institute.

May, L. (1992). A union programme to reduce work and family stress factors in unskilled and semi-skilled workers on the East Coast of the U.S. In V. DiMartino (Ed.), *Preventing stress at work: Conditions of work digest* (Vol. II, pp. 164–171). Geneva, Switzerland: International Labour Office.

Porras, J. I., & Robertson, P. J. (1987). Organization development theories: A typology and evaluation. In R. W. Woodman & W. A. Pasmore (Eds.), *Research in organization change and development* (Vol. 1, pp. 1–57), Greenwich, CT: JAI Press.

Reither, F., & Staudel, T. (1985). Thinking and action. In M. Frese & J. Sabini (Eds.), *Goal directed behavior: The concept of action in psychology* (pp. 110–122). Hillsdale, NJ: Erlbaum.

Sarason, S. B. (1971). *The culture of the school and the problem of change.* Boston: Allyn & Bacon.

Sarason, S. B. (1990). *The predictable failure of education reform.* San Francisco: Jossey-Bass.

Schon, D. (1983). *The reflective practitioner.* New York: Basic Books.

Schurman, S. J. (1992). *Reconstructing work for competence development.* Unpublished doctoral dissertation, University of Michigan, Ann Arbor.

Schurman, S. J., Silverstein, B. A., & Richards, S. E. (1994). Designing a curriculum for healthy work: Reflections on the UAW-GM Ergonomics Pilot Project. In M. Colligan (Ed.), *Occupational medicine: State of the art reviews.* Philadelphia: Hanley & Belfus.

Susman, G., & Evered, R. (1978). An assessment of the scientific merit of action research. *Administrative Science Quarterly, 23,* 582–603.

Trist, E. L. (1981). *The evolution of socio-technical systems: A conceptual framework and an action research program.* Toronto: Ontario Quality of Working Life Centre.

Walton, R. E. (1975). Diffusion of new work structures: Explaining why success didn't take. *Organizational Dynamics, 3*(3), 3–22.

Walton, R. E., & Gafney, M. (1991). Research, action and participation: The merchant shipping case. In W. Whyte (Ed.), *Participatory action research* (pp. 99–126). Thousand Oaks, CA: Sage.

Weick, K., & Bougon, M. (1986). Organizations as cognitive maps. In H. Sims & D. Gioia (Eds.), *The thinking organization* (pp. 102–135). San Francisco: Jossey-Bass.

Whyte, W. (Ed.). (1991). *Participatory action research.* Thousand Oaks, CA: Sage.

17

The Prevention of Job Stress by Redesigning Jobs and Implementing Self-Regulating Teams

Nico Terra

Nowadays, it is common sense to state that the quality of jobs influences the health of workers. However, many jobs are still designed in such a way that their task structure constrains effective performance and is a demotivating factor in further learning and development. Most jobs in production sites are simple and monotonous and offer little scope for choices and competence. Until now there has been little or no association between these types of jobs and stress. Recent figures have shown, however, that psychological disorders are the most significant diagnosis leading to work disablement among younger workers in the Netherlands. Several experiments, like the one presented in this chapter, have shown that redesigning such jobs has a significant and persistent influence on health indicators such as absenteeism from sickness and stress complaints.

The approach to stress reduction presented in this chapter represents a combination of Karasek's Job Decision Latitude theory (Karasek, 1979, 1989, 1990) and basic sociotechnical principles (Emery & Trist, 1965; de Sitter 1981, 1988, 1989). In this approach, the redesigning of work is aimed at the restoration of the balance between job demands and control capacity and at the creation of a complete and complex group task. Balancing demands and control prevents stress complaints, and creating complex tasks stimulates learning behavior. Within this approach, two basic and complementary design strategies are possible (de Sitter, 1989). The first involves decreasing the requisite variety of the system, and the second involves redesigning the system to increase control capacity.

Decreasing the requisite variety of the system is aimed at decreasing avoidable disturbances in the labor process and thereby diminishing the workload. This involves improving the quality of the following five potential sources of disturbance: (a) information (e.g., information that comes too late or is of poor quality), (b) material (e.g., material that is of poor quality or does not meet specifications), (c) equipment (e.g., equipment that is too old or poorly designed), (d) employees (e.g., poorly trained workers), and (e) environment (e.g., noisy or ergonomically inadequate environments). In this scenario, the task structure (the system of division of labor) is left intact. It should be thought of as a supportive scenario for redesigning with certain restricted job-improving characteristics of its own.

To increase control capacity in the system, the social and technical aspects of an organization system are jointly optimized by means of a sociotechnical design: a product- or service-oriented parallelization of the production, called *flows*, and a segmentation of the flows, in which self-regulating teams can operate.

Redesign processes that integrate improvements in the quality of the organization with improvements in the quality of the jobs are rare. The participation of employees in these change processes is even rarer, despite the fact that effects on their jobs and health can be radical.

Design Methodology

In order to make employee participation in these processes effective, a practical, design-oriented methodology is needed. The basic function of such a methodology is twofold. On the one hand, it must create as broad a field of common interest as possible by linking the quality of jobs to the effectiveness of the organization. On the other hand, it must create a clear arena for negotiations on conflicting issues. Employees must become full partners in the discussion. This can be achieved only if the methodology is structure- and design-oriented and if it generates factual information about health risks instead of subjective information, or *satisfaction*. It should therefore fit into the following profile:

1. It creates a common framework for the design of work for all parties involved. The elements of the framework are the inventory of all relevant concepts to be considered concerning the quality of jobs, and standards to assess this quality.
2. It objectively describes and assesses the health risks of the existing work process and jobs, that is, independently of the appraisal of the quality of a job by the individual employee concerned. A subjective appraisal is always biased by processes of adaption (Hackman & Oldham, 1976, 1980) and tends to underestimate the mental health risks of a job because of the relatively high rates of satisfaction caused by this adaption.
3. It generates a number of scenarios for redesign.

Stimulated by a grant from the Dutch Ministry of Social Affairs and Employment, a practical methodology called ASA (Work Setting Analysis) was developed by the Dutch Institute for the Working Environment (NIA) in the period 1985–1988 (Christis, 1989; Terra, 1988a). The case presented here actually played an important role in the development of this methodology. The ASA methodology contains an introduction to the design of healthy jobs and a checklist with instructions. It covers the aspects of safety, health, and well-being in the working environment and permits the integral description, analysis, and assessment of the quality of jobs. As the case will demonstrate, the methodology can be used to create the common framework, survey job-related health risks, establish priorities for the types of measures needed, direct the design process, and evaluate experiments.

Experiments with this methodology have been carried out in several different settings. Research has been done in the metal industry (Terra, 1988b), agricultural industry, administrative organizations, the transport sector, and educational settings. Projects in slaughterhouses, the meat processing industry (Terra, 1993), and the paper industry are at present being carried out using this methodology. Until now, the topic and methodology have drawn the attention principally of larger companies. A recent development is the implementation of projects aimed at the improvement of work content in smaller and medium-sized companies (e.g., greenhouses, the car body repair sector; Terra, 1991), where the problems in the field of quality of working life and productivity are comparably extensive. An important contribution to the possible success of these kinds of projects in small companies can be made by the employers' branch organizations and employees' organizations, such as unions.

A Case From the Metal Can Industry

A metal can industry plant in the north of the Netherlands has successfully changed its organization and way of working as a reaction to both external and internal developments. It has done so by redesigning and reorganizing the traditional functional organization and assembly line structure, with its fragmented and restricted jobs, into a product-oriented production organization operated by self-managing production teams with qualitatively good jobs. In this process, blue-collar workers have played an active role in diagnosing and redesigning jobs. Both management and groups of workers have applied a methodology to assess and redesign jobs from the perspective of integrating the well-being of the workers with organizational effectiveness. The ASA methodology described earlier has effectively functioned in this process as a common framework for improving jobs and working conditions and for negotiating among contrasting points of view.

The Beginning: A Tayloristic Organization

At the start of the project in 1987, the plant was the production site of a Dutch corporation specializing in metal can production. The plant had a workforce of 430 laborers. It operated in a three-shift system and was highly unionized. The production volume was approximately 110 million cans per year. The production organization could be characterized as functional and Tayloristic: many specialized staff and production departments, many hierarchical levels, and an assembly line type of work. The division of labor was excessive, and the conditions and content of most production jobs were of poor quality. Production was carried out on production lines with a straight-line layout. Worksites were situated at different stations in the line, mainly at the beginning,

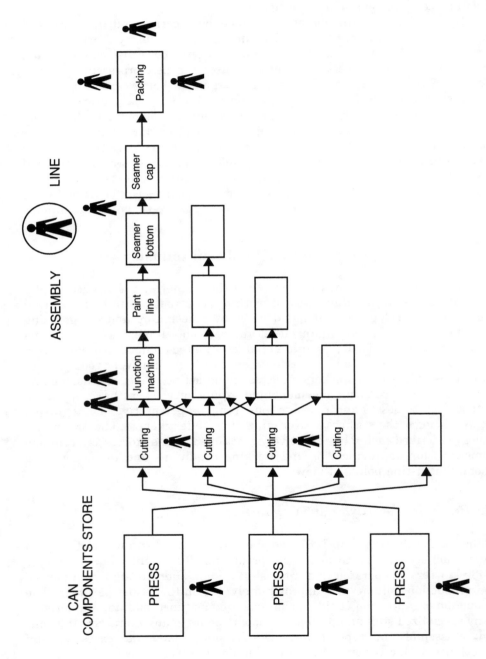

Figure 1. Production layout: former situation.

where the slitting, welding, and seaming operations took place, and at the end of the line, where packing was done. A line had a length of about 20 meters. At every line, about six workers worked at fixed sites, and one supervisor was present (see Figure 1). Tasks like planning, tuning of the installations, the changeover for a new run, repair and maintenance of machines, transport of materials, greasing, and quality control were organized as specialized jobs. This constituted quite a complex organization, consisting mainly of simple jobs. The quality of the work was poor. The workers were subjected to the physical strain of handling heavy pallets with metal and working in nonergonomical postures and to the noise from welding machines. Most jobs were simple and monotonous, with a short working cycle and limited contact possibilities because of distance and noise. The rate of sickness absenteeism was high, although not abnormal for this kind of work compared to other companies. About 15% to 20% of the workforce was absent on any given day. There was high turnover, especially among the better (mostly internally) trained and schooled workers. The plant had increasing difficulties in contracting skilled workers.

Impetus for Change

There were several factors operating that suggested that change was necessary. The corporation had to reorganize as an answer to market problems during the mid-1980s. Collective layoffs took place in almost all production sites. The management wanted to transform the production plants into business units with specific product–market combinations and more opportunities for a local policy. A new general manager was appointed at the site studied. The poor quality of most of the production jobs and the high rate of sickness absenteeism was a serious hindrance to the development and implementation of the new strategy and to the development and implementation of quality management and of technological and organizational innovation. These impulses prompted the new general manager of the plant to start a project aimed at integrated improvement of the quality of the production process, of the working places, and thereby of the product.

Participatory Change

The management team and worker representatives discussed separately and jointly the existing problems and possible strategies for improvements. Several external experts and consultants were invited to make offers to support the change process. Because of the key role that improvement of the quality of the work organization was to play in solving the problems defined and because of the expertise the NIA had in this field, the NIA was selected to carry out the research and consultancy. Another bureau was invited to help with the implementation of quality management. Central elements in the NIA philosophy are the integral improvement of the quality of the working life and the quality of the organization in terms of effectiveness, the combination of a top-down and bottom-up design strategy, and the participation of employees involved. After several meetings of the management team and the workers' council, an agreement on the goals of the change process was reached. This agreement could not be achieved without forcing personnel changes in the management team. Right from the start, it was clear that the project could not be implemented successfully without the unanimous support of the whole team and without the active participation of the middle management and the workers themselves.

The three main goals of the desired change process were explicitly defined by the new management team as:

1. *Improvement of the quality of the organization, of the work organization and the jobs, and of the product.* The quality of the organization has to be created by the implementation of (a) a product-oriented production organization with priority given to the production departments and (b) a service-oriented role for the staff departments. The quality of the work organization has to be created by the design of individual or, preferably, group tasks, meeting the following quality standards:
   - completeness
   - requisite autonomy to influence pace, working method, and sequence of tasks
   - opportunities for contact and cooperation with colleagues inside the group
   - organizational tasks
   - alternation in complexity
2. *The delegation competence and responsibility to lower levels within the organization.*
3. *A maximum of three hierarchical levels in the production organization: team, shift leader, and production manager, instead of four or, in some places, five levels.* The following were regarded as prerequisites for a successful project:
   - reevaluation of wages in the new situation
   - an educational program
   - no forced layoffs, although the plant should lose approximately 60 jobs, owing to the ongoing reorganization at company level
   - participation of workers in the change process

There had been extensive communication about this philosophy with the unions, the workers' council, and all employees. The latter were involved in this phase along two lines: The general manager directly informed the shifts during plenary sessions in the canteen, and members of the management team and the middle management, or shift leaders, discussed the plans during regular work meetings.

The Design Process

Top-down: a new production organization. A more product-oriented organization seemed the most suitable structure in the case of the transformation of a production plant into a market-oriented business unit with external customers and budget responsibilities. An analysis of the markets, customers, and existing product mix and technology showed that a parallelization into three products for two different markets was desirable. In the market for chemical products, the plant was market leader. In the market for aerosols, it wanted to take a "niche" position. A three-flow structure was first created: (a) cans of more than 1 liter content for the paint industry, (b) cans of less than 1 liter content for the same market, and (c) aerosols for the aerosol industry.

Two segments could be distinguished in each flow: the production of the components and the actual assembly of the cans. For the aerosol flow, the two segments were actually integrated, so a group was able to adopt both the installations for the production of the components and the production lines for the assembly of the can. This was a new process, and it involved the replacement of installations and the design of a new layout for this part of the production. For the chemical cans, this integration, although designed, was not finally implemented for physical, logistical, and financial reasons. This new production concept meant the formation of one production group for the production of aerosol cans and three groups—one for components and two for the assembly of the two types of cans—for the chemical cans (see Figure 2) within two flows. Again, communication took place with both the workers' council and the employees about the new structure by means of bulletins and plenary meetings in the canteen.

Bottom-up: a new work organization. At an earlier stage, an inventory was made of the physical working conditions that could be improved. Several surveys were carried out by the Committee for Safety, Health, and Well-Being; the company doctor; and the NIA. As a result, the most urgent ergonomical, climatological, and toxicological problems were solved; the noise produced by the welding machine was diminished; and to improve contact and cooperation, the layout of the lines was changed from a straight line to a U-shaped line (see Figure 3). The new U-shaped layout for production lines created a central working area and, consequently, better opportunities for communication, multifunctionality, and job rotation.

Design teams. Partly parallel to the design of the new production organization, a beginning was made with the improvement of job content. The main instruments for effective participation were the formation of several design teams representing the different jobs in a department and the use of the checklist described earlier for the description and analysis by the members of these teams of the health risks in the work organization. For every production department in the old situation (i.e., components, aerosols assembly, and chemical cans assembly), a design team was installed by the management. The composition of each team with experienced employees was to cover the whole range of jobs in a department. The representatives were selected by the employees. Each team consisted of six or seven members. The assignment given to the teams was to describe the actual work organization and all the different jobs in their department, to analyze the different working environments from

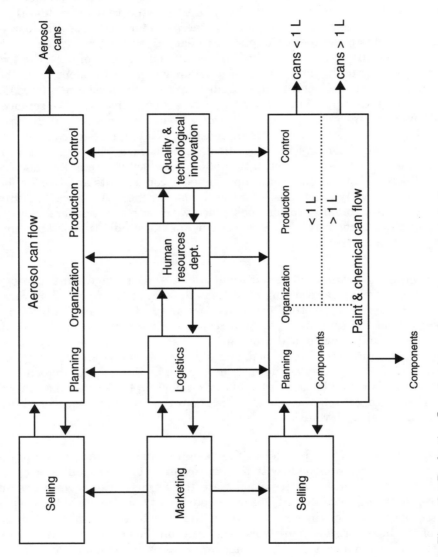

Figure 2.   Production flow structure.

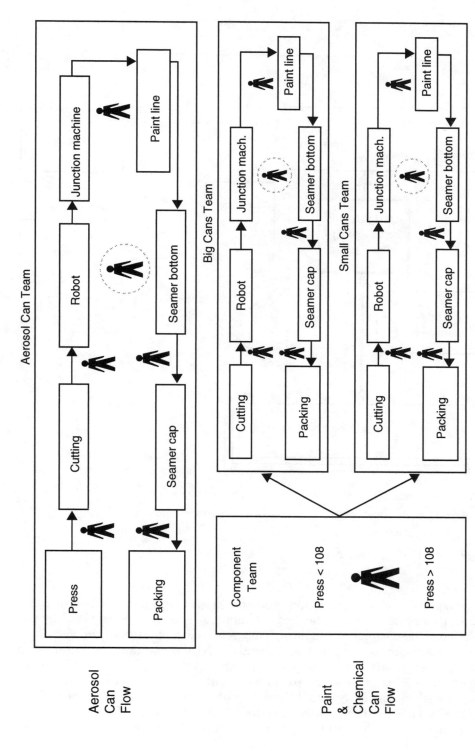

Figure 3. Production layout: new situation.

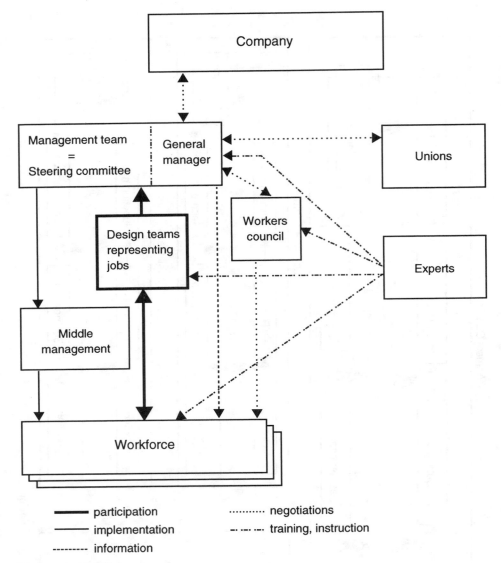

Figure 4. Participation structure.

the perspective of the production problems arising and possible health risks, and to formulate scenarios for improvement. All teams were trained by the NIA to use the design methodology. They received support from the Personnel and Organization department and from the NIA consultant. In Figure 4, a pictorial presentation of the participation network is given. The groups met during working hours, approximately eight times during a 6-month period. They described and analyzed all the different jobs in their department and put together profiles of the health risks found. All groups produced a report of their activities, each containing the profiles of 15 different production jobs, with proposals for improvements. These reports were discussed in the departments and presented to the management team.

The proposals for improvement by the teams in all departments tended toward an integration of the different fragmented jobs into a few all-around jobs; an integration of planning and supportive tasks, such as maintenance and quality control, in these new jobs; and the formation of self-regulating teams running production lines. Another important element in all the reports was the implementation of an extensive cross-functional training program to accompany these changes, partly by intensifying the existing program and partly by setting up new programs for the new work organization (e.g., training in working together in self-regulating teams).

Although the proposals showed a high level of convergence, there was one issue in which the aerosol and chemical can departments differed: the position of the first worker on a line. The discussion was about whether he or she should keep a hierarchical position or be allocated a supportive job inside the group; the latter would make coordination a task for all group members instead of a separate position. According to the philosophy adhered to of fewer hierarchical levels, the latter point of view should prevail.

All reports were discussed within the management team. The concept of self-regulating teams with as few separate positions as possible, with all-around jobs, was accepted. The management team considered the self-regulating team as a basic unit in the organization, which should have a production domain as broad and complete as possible, along with the appropriate competencies and responsibilities.

Tasks to be integrated into the self-regulating production teams were:

- detail planning
- regulation of work activities
- production control
- mechanical maintenance
- quality control
- training of new employees
- internal transport
- regulation of holidays and days off

For each of the product groups, a self-regulating team was to be designed. There were three production lines available for every product group, which meant that a self-regulating team consisted of about 20 employees. This concept was discussed with the workers' council and accepted. The proposals for investments (up to 2 million Dutch guilders) in new machinery and the implementation of the new layout were accepted by the company.

The Implementation of Teams

The functional organization had by now been transformed into a product-oriented organization with three parallel product flows. Each production flow consisted of three production lines.

As a direct result of the activities of the work groups, the production lines in each flow were rearranged into a new layout; if possible and necessary, new production machines were installed, and the physical working conditions were improved (see Figure 3).

Every flow was operated by a self-regulating production team of about 20 all-around workers, of which one was appointed team mentor. The teams were responsible for the production of a complete product, detail planning, quality, transport, maintenance, and training. The number of different jobs was drastically diminished, from 15 mostly specialized and restricted jobs to between 5 and 7 all-around jobs in every new production department. The organization changed from a complicated structure with simple jobs into a simple structure with complex jobs (see Figure 5 for an illustration of this development). This new structure and work organization was implemented during the period 1988–1991 and was accompanied by an extensive training program.

Results

The results were positive and have remained over the years for both the management and the workers. The quality of most jobs in the production has improved and meets the preset high standards concerning health, well-being at work, and productivity. This assessment has been confirmed by various independent measurements. This site in the north of the Netherlands is the only company site that has gone through the reorganization without forced layoffs, partly because of the training program, which functioned as a kind of buffer for employees. This demonstrated that improvement of the quality of jobs can under certain conditions be integrated into economically oriented reorganizations.

Average wages have risen. The number of employees in the lowest wage bracket diminished from 40% in the beginning of 1987 to 6% by mid-1989. The number of employees in the second and third brackets in the same period increased from 13% to 20% and from 7% to 12%, respectively. Sickness absenteeism has structurally decreased by 50%, saving 1 million guilders per year at direct controlling costs, not to mention the savings on the costs of production losses and quality problems due to the high number of temporary and underqualified employees replacing absent workers. Flexibility has improved, creating better opportunities to execute the smaller, specialized orders resulting from the policy of obtaining a "niche position" in the aerosols market. Productivity has increased significantly. For example, overall productivity has risen from 0.26 to 0.43 million cans per worker per year, an increase of 66%. Workers are better qualified, informed, and motivated, and according to the local management, the innovative capacity of the organization has increased. The plant recently received ISO-9000 accreditation for quality assurance, which was facilitated by this project.

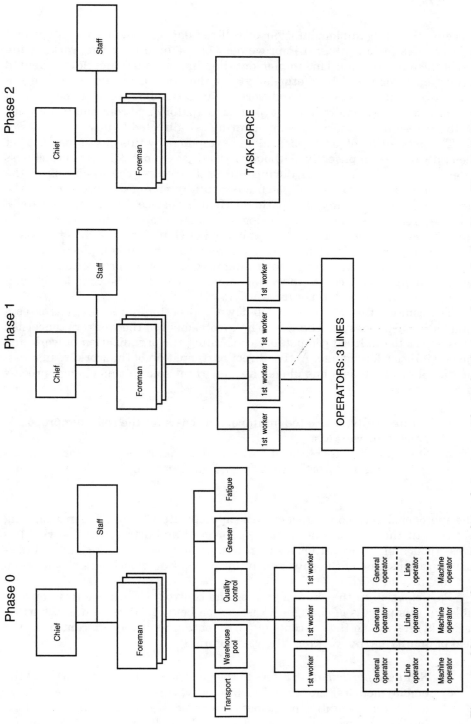

Figure 5. Movement from a complicated structure with simple jobs toward a simple structure with complex jobs.

Evaluation

It seems that the implementation of self-regulating teams creates optimal opportunities for an integral improvement of the quality of the working life and of the organization. This implementation implies a product flow–oriented production structure. The methodology for the structural and proactive improvement of the job structure and work organization has proved to be a useful tool for change, especially in creating a participatory and common framework for the redesigning of jobs by implementing self-directed teams.

The prevention of job stress–related symptoms by this design has not yet been fully proven empirically. Although in the case example the rate of sickness absenteeism was cut in half during the past 5 years, the diagnosis of the remaining sickness cases has not fundamentally changed. According to the figures from the company Occupational Health Service, however, the rate of sickness absenteeism due to psychological health problems has risen significantly in comparable plants, where this kind of change process has not taken place. So one can say that a relative improvement has taken place. Another explanation is that the intensive training program for all production workers caused a temporary increase in workload, which could not be completely compensated for by hiring temporary workers.

The combination of a mixed top-down and bottom-up strategy creates a solid basis for the desired changes. The involvement of the workers concerned gives access to qualified competence concerning the organization of work and the possibilities for change. Active direct participation of the workers in cross-functional design teams has played an important role in this change process in two ways:

1.   Strategically, it created an important basis for the redesign proposals among all workers.
2.   Qualitatively, it created detailed and adequate solutions for problems in the existing work situation and effective proposals for new situations.

The approach described here seems to be appropriate and effective in designing jobs that fit the demands of employees for good and attractive jobs with low stress risks and opportunities for learning, of employers for efficient and flexible operations, and of the government for prevention of sickness absenteeism and inability to work.

Participation in the change process and control at work are two key variables in this process of change. A distinction between three kinds of participation is relevant to the concepts of participation and workers control in the field of quality of the working life (see Figure 6):

1.   *Strategic participation* refers to the general conditions of work and the employment relationship. Traditionally, this is the area in which indirect, representative participation by unions and committees on safety, health, and well-being has occurred. It is the area of collective con-

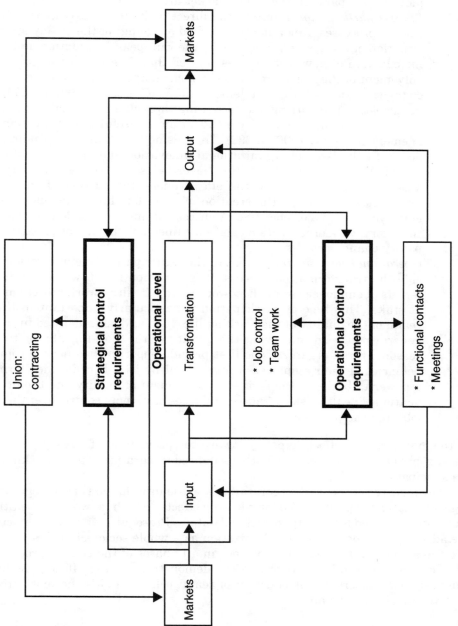

Figure 6. Participation and the transformation process.

tracting, with clauses on payment, working hours, shift systems, hazardous working conditions, and physical health risks. It is participation outside the transformation process, where the interests of employees as a party in the labor market are at stake.

2. *Process participation* refers to the direct or indirect participation in
    change processes, fundamentally aimed at changing the steady state
    situation of the system. A survey by the European Foundation on the
    introduction of new technologies showed that "there is little real in-
    volvement of the work force in technological and work organizational
    change outside of the implementation" (Cressey, 1990, p. 271).
    Participation is occurring and increasing through an informal and vol-
    untary form of involvement, dependent on its usefulness to the man-
    agement (Cressey, 1990, p. 292). There is no hint that these findings
    do not fit the issue of organizational innovation and improvement of
    the quality of the working life. Nevertheless, participation during
    a design phase is vital to the effectiveness and success of change
    processes, especially if the creation of room for the competencies of
    employees is a major objective. A successful implementation of a par-
    ticipatory work organization can be attained only by means of partici-
    patory change process.

3. *Operational participation* refers to the participation of employees in-
    side the transformation process. It is participation in which the in-
    terests of employees as healthy workers in a healthy work process are
    at stake. This type of participation is particularly important in the
    realm of the quality of the working life. It should be integrated in the
    general policy on improving the quality of the working life for two
    reasons. First, organizations that provide opportunities for the com-
    petencies of their employees contain healthy jobs. Second, they form
    a powerful basis for the further improvement of quality and the pre-
    vention of health risks because employees have more control over their
    jobs and the process.

In the long term, an effective policy toward the prevention of stress by redesigning jobs can be effective only with a balanced integration of all three kinds
of participation (see Figure 6).

The redesign of the work organization and the introduction of self-regulating teams can have positive and long-lasting effects on both (a) workers' health
and motivation and (b) the organizational output. Prerequisites for such effects
are adopting the concept of an organization as a whole sociotechnical system
and the active involvement of employees in all phases of the change process.

This case, like others (Terra, 1991), demonstrates these effects, as the
plant—5 years after the introduction of teamwork—remains the most productive site of the company.

References

Christis, J. (1989). *Work setting analysis*. Amsterdam: NIA.
Cressey, P. (1990). Participation and new technologies. In F. Butera, V. Dimartino, & E. Kohler

(Eds.), *Technological development and the improvement of living and working conditions: Options for the future* (pp. 253–303). London: Kogan Page Ltd.

de Sitter, L. U. (1981). *Op weg naar nieuwe kantoren en fabrieken* [A strategy for new offices and factories]. Deventer, the Netherlands: Kluwer.

de Sitter, L. U. (1988). *Kwaliteit van de arbeid. Het meten en beoordelen van de kwaliteit van werk* [Quality of jobs. The measurement and assessment of the quality of work]. Den Bosch, the Netherlands: Koers.

de Sitter, L. U. (1989). *Moderne sociotechniek* [Modern sociotechnics]. *Gedrag en Organisatie, 2,* 222–252.

Emery, F. E., & Trist, E. L. (1965). The causal texture of organizational environments. *Human Relations, 18*(3), 21–32.

Hackman, J. R., & Oldham, G. R. (1976). Development of the Job Diagnostic Survey: Test of a theory. *Organizational Behaviour and Human Performance, 16,* 250–279.

Hackman, J. R., & Oldham, G. R. (1980). *Work redesign.* Reading, MA: Addison-Wesley.

Karasek, R. A., Jr. (1979). Job demands, job decision latitude and mental strain: Implications for job redesign. *Administrative Science Quarterly, 24,* 285–308.

Karasek, R. A., Jr. (1989). Control in the workplace and its health-related aspects. In S. L. Sauter, J. J. Hurell, Jr., & C. L. Cooper (Eds.), *Job control and worker health* (pp. 129–161). New York: Wiley.

Karasek, R. A., Jr. (1990). Lower health risk with increased job control among white-collar workers. *Journal of Organizational Behaviour, 11,* 171–185.

Terra, N. (1988a). *Op weg naar beter werk* [A strategy to improve jobs]. Amsterdam: NIA.

Terra, N. (1988b). Ruimte voor nieuwe inhoud: Een reorganisatie met menselijke maat [Opportunities for new jobs: A change process with human dimensions]. *Gedrag en Organisatie, 1,* 72–90.

Terra, N. (1991). *Functies verbeteren in de Carrosseriebranche* [Improving jobs in the car body repair branch]. Amsterdam: NIA.

Terra, N. (1993). *Functieverbetering in de vleessector* [Improving jobs in the meat-processing industry]. Amsterdam: NIA.

18

Finnish Research in Organizational Development and Job Redesign

Kari Lindström

In this chapter, I discuss interventions focusing on job design and organizational development (OD) that were conducted in Finland during the 1980s and 1990s. Particular attention is paid to occupational health activities carried out by the Institute of Occupational Health. Other Finnish projects are also described briefly.

OD originally referred to human processual approaches. Job design and redesign have been classified among the sociotechnical or techno-structural approaches, which are closely related to the quality of working life (QWL) intervention as practiced in the United States in the 1970s and 1980s (e.g., Davies & Wacker, 1982; Faucheux, Amado, & Laurent, 1982; Karasek & Theorell, 1990). OD, however, is now seen as a general term for developing work and organizations (Beer & Walton, 1987). Within academic psychology, OD activities have often been related to organizational psychology, whereas QWL and the sociotechnical approach are related to work psychology.

Emphasis on Job Demands and Work Conditions

The emphasis of occupational and organizational psychology research performed in Finland clearly shifted at the beginning of the 1970s, as did the focus of OD interventions. Traditional OD activities, such as intragroup and interpersonal relation approaches and psychological personnel selection, were criticized by the labor unions in every northern European country. In the field of work psychology, health- and safety-oriented research in work psychology blossomed. The research work of Bertil Gardell in Sweden, dealing with production technology, alienation, and mental health, was one of the starting points for a new approach (Gardell, 1971). Kornhauser's study on the U.S. automobile industry (Kornhauser, 1965) and research on job demands and workers' health at the University of Michigan (Caplan, Cobb, French, Van Harrison, & Pinneau, 1975) were "model" projects. The traditional mental health and job satisfaction perspective shifted toward interaction between job demands and workers' health.

In the early 1970s, work conditions of various occupational groups were studied in Finland. At the same time, several practical job reorganization and redesign projects were carried out, wherein jobs were enriched and autonomous work groups were set up in order to increase productivity and reduce physical and mental stress (Kauppinen-Toropainen & Hänninen, 1981). These interventions can be classified under the sociotechnical approach or the QWL tradition. Traditional (OD) activities dealing with the human relations approach prevailed in the 1970s, but only some empirical studies were conducted. These included studies on the benefits of T-group training or sensitivity training among managers in governmental organizations (Miettinen, 1977) and the effects of OD training based on managerial grid (Tainio & Satalainen, 1984).

Theoretical Framework and Methodology

The survey approach was gradually supplemented around 1980 with survey feedback, intervention programs, and evaluation. Many studies also dealt with redesign and organizational change in connection with the implementation of new computer technology. In addition to industrial work, office and service work became targets of research. Before describing the organizational intervention programs, I will present a short overview of the theoretical framework and outcome measures used in this research.

The theoretical framework applied in the 1970s was based mainly on stress theory (e.g., Kagan & Levi, 1974; Lazarus & DeLongis 1983). Studies on the relationship between job demands and workers' health overlooked individual differences. Gradually, however, coping strategies, perceived control, and individual characteristics were recognized more as moderators or modifiers of job stressors. Furthermore, as an outcome variable, health was supplemented with the mastery of work. In intervention studies, organizational behavior has recently been added to this individual and health-oriented theoretical framework. Use of a systemic model to analyze organizations implies that an organization interacts with its environment to maintain a state of balance between internal arrangements and the environment (Weisbord, 1978). Interacting elements that can be used as bases for the diagnosis of organization for developmental work are goals/tasks, structure, inner social interaction, culture and values, work processes and methods, leadership, boundary location, and environment.

Tasks and jobs are seen to be determined by production and by technological, organizational, and individual needs (Davis & Wacker, 1982). Many of the elements incorporated into this systemic model are also QWL criteria, such as the following:

- physical environment (safety and health)
- compensation (pay, benefits)
- institutional rights and privileges (e.g., security, participation)
- job contents (variety of tasks, feedback, challenge, task identity, autonomy, use of skills)

- internal and external social relations
- learning and personal development

The impacts of OD and job design can be evaluated by means of process or output measures. Some examples of output measures, which are of course interrelated, include the following:

- organizational effectiveness (e.g., productivity and quality of production)
- well-being (e.g., health and affective well-being, such as subjective symptoms and job and life satisfaction)
- behavioral outcomes (e.g., competence, mastery, aspiration, psychological growth, and learning)

QWL interventions in the United States and Europe differ in that QWL interventions carried out in the United States have seldom included health outcomes (Karasek & Theorell, 1990).

Finnish Research on Working Life and Intervention Approaches in the 1980s and 1990s

Psychological research on working life and the interventions carried out in Finland over the past 15 years include both nationwide and local survey as well as survey feedback and other interventions. Most often, the criteria measures applied have dealt with health and well-being as well as competence and learning. These action programs have been highly dependent on organizational context and the theoretical background of the researcher. The following major approaches are currently applied in Finland:

- policy-making approach
- job redesign and OD as a means to promote workers' health
- cognitive approaches based on learning and optimizing workload

These approaches overlap in many ways, but they are classified according to their main focus.

Social Policy–Oriented Survey Approach

The Statistical Central Office of Finland conducted what is called the Wage Earners' Surveys, based on a random sample of Finnish wage earners, in 1977, 1984, and 1990. These surveys have been especially valuable in providing data on the psychological and social work demands and affective well-being at the national level. The latest survey in 1990 was based more on the concept of general well-being and the sociotechnical tradition. The survey results were used for policy making in the work environment arena (*Report of the Governmental Committee*, 1991). When compared against the previous surveys, the results of the latest survey indicated that QWL criteria of psychological job demands are now met better, and opportunities for learning and growth have improved. In contrast, however, the human relations problems and difficulties concerning affective well-being have increased (Kolu, 1991). A shorter version of the instrument applied in this particular survey is now used as a "barometer on work conditions." The barometer will be presented annually for the representative sample of Finnish wage earners.

Cognitive Approaches

Optimizing workload by means of mental training and job analysis. The Industrial Psychology Laboratory at the Helsinki University of Technology is conducting studies using methods of worker training and job analysis (Buhanist, 1989; Vartiainen, 1987). The case studies have dealt with the hierarchical development of mental training and the use of psychological job analysis methods for planning and job design. The studies focus on productivity, the outcomes of learning, and the optimization of mental workload. Attention is given also to activities involving personnel participation in redesigning their work, to collaboration among personnel, and to the effects of feedback on leadership behavior.

Developmental work research. One cognitive OD approach applied in Finland, called *developmental work research* is based on the activity theoretical model. It is characterized by the historical analysis of work and organization, by modeling and analyzing organizational functioning, and by studying the learning process longitudinally in order to discover contradictions that can be overcome and solved. The basic analysis model is a triangle containing the subject of the work, the work methods/tools, and the object/outcome. The method contains a participatory analysis of planning. The key concept is learning by expanding, which means that contradictions are the starting point for analyzing the process of learning and development. Instructional intervention also figures in the methodology. Little attention, however, is paid to individual goals and values, to social interaction, or to health and well-being. This method has been used in studies and interventions, for example, in manufacturing involving chemical or physical processes, in flexible manufacturing systems, and in health care settings (Engeström, 1987, 1990).

Job Redesign and OD to Promote Workers' Health

The following section describes six different intervention approaches in which survey feedback and process consultation are applied to promote the quality of working life, health, and well-being. These intervention approaches are carried out by the work psychologists at the Finnish Institute of Occupational Health in cooperation with the management, labor unions, and occupational health and safety representatives from the workplaces concerned.

Survey feedback interventions. The earliest interventions were structured on a survey feedback method for reducing occupational stress. Two studies were done in the health care sector, one dealing with psychiatric hospital personnel (Pöyhönen, 1987) and the other with child-care personnel and personnel from institutions for the mentally handicapped (Leppänen, 1984). Psychological job demands, health and well-being, and employees' suggestions for reducing stress were surveyed first. The personnel working at the institutions participated actively in both studies. The management, too, was involved in the study and in implementing the changes and improvements that were suggested. The results have been promising, but evaluation of the results is still lacking.

Union—researcher cooperation. In 1977, the Institute of Occupational Health and the Union of Commercial Workers started cooperation in order to improve the occupational health and safety of union members. At the outset, an extensive questionnaire was administered to all 9,500 union members. The physical work environment and psychological job demands were surveyed, as were health and well-being. On the basis of the results, various developmental activities were carried out, such as creation of a checklist for cashiers' work, training material on ways of supporting one's coworker, and in-depth surveys and studies dealing with ergonomics. The collaboration ended in 1989 with a questionnaire survey similar to the one carried out in the beginning (International Institute for Labour Studies, 1987).

Institutional support by occupational health service (OHS) personnel. Job redesign and organizational changes related to the implementation of advanced computer technology have been studied since the beginning of the 1980s. These studies usually started with survey feedback and continued with process consultation and evaluation.

The first example illustrates the institutional support by OHS in this context. Group-oriented support for the job redesign process following the transition to a new data system was carried out in an insurance company. Implementation of a new data system for life insurance policies was associated with a gradual shift toward comprehensive, expanded jobs. Staff members had been prepared for the job redesign process, but detailed plans as to how the new job designs would be implemented were lacking.

One case study dealt with a work group that was having major difficulties with the change. The OHS personnel and the research psychologist supported the group as it struggled with transitional difficulties, simultaneously encouraging the group to carry out job redesign. Special efforts were directed at decreasing neck and eye strain and mental stress when the work began piling up, and feedback and information were given about processes of change and about job redesign itself. Evaluation of the results was based on interviews, questionnaire surveys, and group discussions, all carried out before, during, and after the implementation phase. Attention was paid to measures of well-being, to positive job demands, and to productivity. The feelings of mastery and achievement were more positive, and the amount of routine manual tasks decreased among the intervention group more than among the control group, which had not received consultative support (Lindström, 1990).

In the same insurance company and also in a bank, the OHS personnel helped individuals encountering major difficulties associated with a change in visual display terminal (VDT) applications. This intervention included support for 30 patients consulting the OHS unit, owing to difficulties in coping with job demands. In the case of these patients, the intervention measures applied were job redesign, improvement of the work conditions, solving problems linked with intragroup relations, or promoting personal growth and learning. For each of the 30 patients, an individual action program was planned at the OHS. Implementation of the action program was followed continuously by OHS doctors or nurses. At the end of 1 to 2 years of follow-up, the patients' situations were evaluated. The situation was totally in order for 11 of the 30 patients and clearly better for 15 of them; only in 4 cases was the situation as poor as it had been in the beginning (Lindström, Pakkala, & Torstila, 1989).

Based on the experiences from these cases, a system for early rehabilitation was planned for people having difficulties in coping with job demands at company level. The rehabilitation system was based on collaboration between OHS personnel, personnel administration experts, and supervisors.

Increasing conceptual mastery of work. Optimization of workload and increasing productivity by improving workers' competence were the main objectives of an intervention study related to changes in computer technology in the paper industry. Before and after the intervention program, the workers filled out an Occupational Stress Questionnaire (OSQ; Elo, Leppänen, Lindström, & Ropponen, 1992), they were interviewed, and a diagnostic test of conceptual mastery of work was conducted. The problems in the production process itself and the operators' job stress were the primary targets of the study. In the intervention phase, the work groups in a paper factory analyzed the historical development of paper making up to the present phase of highly automated process operation. Analyzing the critical tasks in the work and modeling the production process, combined with training, improved the workers' conceptual mastery of the work process as well as their ability to function as a work group in problem situations. The workload could be optimized through greater mastery of work methods and tools. The quality and quantity of production also rose once the work was mastered further (Leppänen & Auvinen, 1989).

Joint management–union–research cooperation. A joint management–union–researcher approach to promote health and well-being was conducted in a big forest industry corporation employing about 10,000 persons. The initiative came from the company's OHS unit, which also assumed the main role for carrying out the questionnaire survey and feedback. The steering committee of the projects included representatives of the management, union, and the OHS unit, as well as the research group. The project started with a survey of perceived work conditions, work content and organization, cooperation, subjective symptoms, and job satisfaction. Each factory unit received feedback about its own survey results. The workers and the management were encouraged to cooperate in order to use the survey results for job redesign and health promotion. In addition, several specific intervention programs were conducted, such as workshops for improving supervisor–employee relations and communication in office work and for developing psychological service activities for OHS. At the end of the projects, an evaluation survey was carried out in those work units that had been actively involved with developmental work (n = 2,000). Changes both in health and well-being and in job demands were studied (Kalimo, 1990).

Process consultation in organizations under change. Process consultation to support organizational development and changes has been applied in two studies, one in the banking sector and the other in a general hospital. Both of these studies began with a survey and survey feedback.

The main aim of our intervention study in banking was to develop training and other management methods for change processes in one Finnish banking group. The study concentrated on the human and social aspects of change processes. Change processes in three case banks were followed and supported in order to get ecologically valid data for training programs.

One of the case banks, which employed 30 people, was undergoing major organizational change due to job redesign and reorganization following the appointment of a new bank manager. The role of the external consultant in the bank was to facilitate the human and social aspects of the job redesign and reorganization process, which was planned in great detail before the actual implementation. The consultant gave the supervisors and the employees feedback on the progress of the change and on group dynamics. Internal training and business consultants consulted with the manager and organized intergroup and intragroup training for the bank's employees. The evaluation at the end of the 2-year process showed that the change process had succeeded. In particular, the well-planned change process and the bank manager's involvement were critical elements. The difficulties that remained concerned intergroup relations and were caused partly by the management by results system that was being applied in the bank and partly by group dynamics (Lindström & Huuhtanen, 1993).

The projects to promote health and well-being in the general hospital were initiated by the OHS personnel. The project was guided by the hospital's executive management along with a representative of the employees, the OHS personnel, and the researchers. It started with a survey and individual interviews of the employees in 15 inpatient wards or outpatient units. The main problems, according to the survey, were lack of knowledge about the goals of the hospital as a whole, poor communication between the wards, and too little feedback from coworkers and supervisors. The needs for improvement were associated with the social work climate and cooperation, the external work conditions, services for the employees (e.g., OHS, day care for children), and management styles. After survey feedback, the main forms of consultation were the structuring of the development process and consulting with supervisors at the inpatient ward and unit level. The consultation at the work group or ward level dealt with communication, roles and tasks, decision making, problem solving, and management, according to the individual needs of each group (Kivimäki & Lindström, 1993). The follow-up 2 years later showed greater job satisfaction and better cooperation at the ward level.

The differences between the first and second survey may be due either to changes that occurred during the period or to the planned intervention.

Conclusions

The organizational intervention programs and job redesign efforts in the cases reviewed here were often initiated by OHS personnel or by management. The active involvement or participation of the OHS personnel in the intervention program itself has been minor.

Interventions started with the analysis of the situation in the organization concerned. Questionnaire surveys and feedback were used for this purpose. Based on job stress studies among various occupational groups, the Finnish Institute of Occupational Health has published a structured and standardized questionnaire, the OSQ, which was used in most of the intervention programs presented in this chapter. The OSQ is also meant for routine use by OHS personnel. In many cases, however, the survey results have given meager information for the planning of the intervention itself. The importance of the survey results has been in finding a consensus image of the problems and developmental needs. Furthermore, repeating the same survey after the intervention has revealed additional data necessary for drawing conclusions about the effects of the intervention. In the projects carried out in the paper industry (Leppänen & Auvinen, 1989), in hospitals (Kivimäki & Lindström, 1993), and in the insurance sector (Lindström, 1990), for instance, the planning of the intervention program has nevertheless gained more from group discussions at the worksite and from participatory analysis of work processes than from surveys.

The planning of most of the interventions mentioned was based on the joint efforts of the researcher/consultant and managers and employees. A broad consensus about the measures and goals is important in order to get as much involvement as possible among all interest groups. The realization of the plan, however, requires a clear-cut responsibility for the program. The supervisor or manager is usually the best possible person for assuming this responsibility because, in most cases, the measures applied in organizational intervention are a part of his or her basic tasks. The support of the top management is absolutely essential for each intervention project. The central role of supervisors was clearly apparent, for example, in the projects carried out in banking (Lindström & Huuhtanen, 1993), in the general hospital (Kivimäki & Lindström, 1993), and in the forest industry (Kalimo, 1990).

Evaluation of the effects of intervention programs proved to be very difficult. Measurement of job stressors, strain, and mastery of work before and after an intervention program gives only some hints about the impact an intervention may have had. Other simultaneous changes within the organization or in its surroundings may have a greater effect on the measurements afterward than the planned intervention itself. In addition, the questionnaire surveys and interviews reveal only a very narrow part of the planned changes or their effects. More objective data would be required, in particular, about the real changes in workers' health and in organizational effectiveness. Such data are lacking in many intervention studies. These criteria should have been taken into account already when the intervention program was being planned. Evaluation of the impact of an intervention requires analysis of the process itself, which in turn presupposes careful documentation during the entire intervention process. Outside evaluation is also needed. Especially in cases where the researcher and consultant is the same person, or when they are two people whose cooperation is close, objective outside evaluation is needed.

Inspection of the present and future trends in Finland reveals that various organizational development approaches based on different theoretical frameworks have come closer together. The health-oriented approaches have been supplemented by the organizational approach, which includes learning and growth as well as productivity as criteria. The scope of approaches based on cognitive learning have broadened to include either health and well-being or aspects of organizational behavior. A common departure point is to view the entire organization as an open systemic entity. Historical and value system analyses have introduced aspects of organizational culture.

In Finland's present economic recession, it is particularly important to create adaptive organizations with the capacity for innovation. An organization transformation (OT) framework has therefore been applied in order to promote cognitive changes and to build a new paradigm for organizations (Porras & Silvers, 1991). One recently applied approach has been the action research common in Norway; another is the conference method based on democratic dialogue. In the field of occupational health, an action program for developing work organizations called *healthy and productive work organization* continued from 1992 to 1996. Its main topics were:

- changes in work values and organizations
- organizational development interventions and methods
- management and leadership styles and their association with employee well-being
- work organization and health among health care personnel

The basic idea in this action program is that every development intervention measure should simultaneously take into account both health aspects and productivity or organizational effectiveness.

References

Beer, M., & Walton, A. E. (1987). Organization change and development. *Annual Review of Psychology, 38*, 339–367.

Buhanist, P. (1989). *Change and development of work and organisation: A case at the Central Statistical Office of Finland* (Report No. 113). Helsinki, Finland: University of Technology.

Caplan, R., Cobb, S., French, J. R. P., Jr., Van Harrison, R., & Pinneau, S. R., Jr. (1975). *Job demands and worker health* (Report No. 75-160). Washington, DC: National Institute for Occupational Safety and Health.

Davis, L. E., & Wacker, G. J. (1982). Job design. In G. Salvendy (Ed.), *Handbook of industrial engineering* (pp. 2.5.1–2.5.31). New York: Wiley.

Elo, A.-L., Leppänen, A., Lindström, K., & Ropponen, T. (1992). *OSQ—Occupational stress questionnaire: User's instructions* (Reviews No. 19). Helsinki: Institute of Occupational Health.

Engeström, Y. (1987). *Learning by expanding: An activity-theoretical approach to developmental research*. Helsinki, Finland: Orienta-Konsultit Oy.

Engeström, Y. (1990). *Learning, working and imagining*. Helsinki, Finland: Orieta-Konsultit Oy.

Faucheux, C., Amado, G., & Laurent, A. (1982). Organizational development and change. *Annual Review of Psychology, 33*, 343–370.

Gardell, B. (1971). *Produktionsteknik och arbetsglädje. En socialpsykologisk studie av industriellt arbete* [Production technology, alienation and mental health] (Meddelande No. 63). Stockholm: Personaladministrativa rådet. (In Swedish)

International Institute for Labour Studies. (1987). *From research to practice: A long road* (A report on co-operation between the union of commercial workers in Finland and the Finnish Institute of Occupational Health). Geneva, Switzerland: Author.

Kagan, A. R., & Levi, L. (1974). Health and environment—psychosocial stimuli: A review. *Society Science & Medicine, 8*, 225–241.

Kalimo, R. (1990, November). *Research–action program for mental well-being in an industrial corporation*. Paper presented in Work and Well-being: An Agenda for the '90s, a conference of the American Psychological Association in conjunction with The National Institute for Occupational Safety and Health, Washington, DC.

Karasek, R., & Theorell, T. (1990). *Healthy work. Stress, productivity, and the reconstruction of working life*. New York: Basic Books.

Kauppinen-Toropainen, K., & Hänninen, V. (1981). *Case studies on job reorganization and job redesign in Finland*. Helsinki, Finland: Institute of Occupational Health.

Kivimäki, M., & Lindström, K. (1993). *Jorvin sairaalan työyhteisö-projekti* [Organizational development in a general hospital] (Report from the Finnish Hospital Association). Report submitted for publication. (In Finnish)

Kolu, T. (1991). *Työelämän laatu 1977–1990* [Quality of work life in 1977–1990] (Research No. 188). Helsinki, Finland: Central Statistical Office. (In Finnish)

Kornhauser, A. (1965). *Mental health of the industrial worker*. New York: Wiley.

Lazarus, R. S., & DeLongis, A. (1983). Psychological stress and coping in aging. *American Psychologist, 38*, 245–254.

Leppänen, A. (1984). Reduction of stress by personnel at institutions for child care and for the mentally handicapped. In F. J. McGuigan, W. E. Sime, & J. MacDonald Wallace (Eds.), *Stress tension control 2*. New York: Plenum.

Leppänen, A., & Auvinen, E. (1989). Improvement of work and workers qualifications in a highly automated paper mill. In J. Ranta (Ed.), *Analysis, design and evaluation of man–machine systems 1988* (pp. 83–86). Oxford: Pergamon Press.

Lindström, K. (1990). Support of a working group during implementation of a new computer system and job redesign in a life insurance company. In S. Sauter, M. Dainoff, & M. Smith (Eds.), *Promoting health and productivity in the computerized office* (pp. 182–194). London: Taylor & Francis, Ltd.

Lindström, K., & Huuhtanen, P. (1993). *Managing organizational and social change processes in banks*. Paper presented at the Sixth European Congress on Work and Organizational Psychology, Alicante, Spain.

Lindström, K., Pakkala, K., & Torstila, I. (1989). Coping with technological change in banking and insurance. In M. J. Smith & G. Salvendy (Eds.), *Work with computers: Organizational, management, stress and health aspects* (pp. 256–263). Amsterdam: Elsevier.

Miettinen, A. (1977). *Organisaatio ja koulutustulosten pysyvyys* [Organization and maintenance of training results]. Unpublished doctoral dissertation, University of Helsinki, Finland. (In Finnish)

Porras, J. I., & Silvers, R. C. (1991). Organization development and transformation. *Annual Review of Psychology, 42*, 51–78.

Pöyhönen, T. (1987). Työ, toiminta stressitilanteissa ja mielenterveys—tutkimus psykiatrisen sairaalan henkilökunnasta [Work, coping with work stress, and mental health: A study among mental hospital personnel] (*Työ ja ihminen*, *1*, supplement 2). Helsinki, Finland: Finnish Institute of Occupational Health.

Report of the governmental committee on working conditions. (1991). (Komiteanmietintö 1991:37). Helsinki, Finland: Ministry of Labour.

Tainio, R., & Santalainen, T. (1984). Some evidence for cultural relativity of organization development programs. *Journal of Applied Behavioral Science*, *20*, 93–111.

Vartiainen, M. (1987). *The hierarchical development of mental training and training methods* (Report No. 100). Helsinki, Finland: Helsinki University of Technology.

Weisbord, M. K. (1978). *Organizational diagnosis: A workbook of theory and practice*. Reading, MA: Addison-Wesley.

19

Elder Care and the Changing Workforce

Andrew E. Scharlach

Elder care is rapidly emerging as an important human resources issue amid increasing evidence that employees' elder-care responsibilities can directly impact job performance, absenteeism, and turnover rates. Although only a small percentage of U.S. companies currently offer elder-care programs or benefits, it is predicted that employer-sponsored elder-care efforts will eventually be more common than child care, making it possible that elder care will be "the emerging employee benefit of the 1990s" (Friedman, 1986, p. 45).

Elder care is a mental health issue as well because of accumulating evidence that providing care for disabled elderly relatives is associated with increased rates of depression, somatic symptoms, psychotropic medication usage, and other stress-related physical and mental health problems. These mental health sequelae may be especially prevalent among the more than 40% of elder-care givers who also work full-time (American Association of Retired Persons [AARP], 1988; Stone, Cafferata, & Sange, 1987). For all of these reasons, elder care is becoming an important issue for psychologists to address.

This chapter begins with a review of the social and demographic changes that are making elder care a workforce issue. It then examines the prevalence and types of elder-care responsibilities faced by working Americans, and the impact of those responsibilities on employee mental health and job performance. Potential worksite elder-care programs and policies are then reviewed. Finally, the chapter considers how psychologists can most effectively become involved in preventing or treating mental health problems experienced by caregiving employees.

Background

A number of significant social and demographic trends have combined to produce ever-increasing numbers of working persons involved in caring for older relatives. Primary is the dramatic increase in the number of Americans aged 65 and older potentially in need of care. There currently are 32 million persons

Preparation of this chapter was supported in part by a grant from the Institute of Industrial Relations of the University of California.

aged 65 and older in the United States, up from only 3 million in 1900. By the year 2030, this figure is projected to grow to about 65 million older persons, or 21% of the American population (AARP, 1987b). Although most older people do not need care, the fastest growing segment of American society is the 85-and-older age group, almost half of whom require assistance with day-to-day activities (U.S. Senate Special Committee on Aging, 1985–1986).

These demographic processes are occurring at a time when dramatic changes in American families, including increased rates of divorce and geographical separation from kin, are likely to complicate families' efforts to provide care for their older members. Moreover, more than 70% of women aged 25 to 54 now are in the civilian labor force (Green & Epstein, 1988), as compared to only about 20% in 1900 (Foster, Siegel, & Jacobs, 1988). As a result, employees are experiencing increased elder-care responsibilities, while employers are seeking ways to maximize worker productivity and reduce potential work interference, due to current corporate efforts at downsizing as well as projections of a shrinking labor pool from which to draw new employees in the coming decades. These and other forces have combined to create increasing pressure for mental health professionals to work together with employers to develop appropriate programs and services to ease the strain experienced by working caregivers.

Prevalence of Elder Care in the Workforce

Most studies of elder care among employee groups have found that 20% to 30% of respondents currently provide assistance to older relatives, with some studies finding prevalence rates as high as 40% (Wagner, Neal, Gibeau, Scharlach, & Anastas, 1988). However, serious questions have been raised regarding the accuracy of these prevalence estimates, which have been based primarily on nonrepresentative samples with relatively low response rates (typically, 18% to 50%); such samples increase the risk of overestimating the actual prevalence of elder-care responsibilities among employees. Adjusting for response bias, actual prevalence rates in the U.S. labor force have been estimated to be approximately 6%, with rates for individual worksites probably ranging from less than 4% to more than 15% (Brice & Gorey, 1989).

Types of Elder-Care Responsibilities

The types of assistance that employees provide to older relatives range from occasional shopping trips to day-to-day, hands-on personal care. Studies of employee elder-care responsibilities indicate that caregiving employees provide an average of 6 to 10 hours of assistance per week, although at least 5% of caregivers give 35 hours or more of care each week, as much as a second full-time job (The Travelers, 1985). Approximately one third of caregiving employees receive no outside assistance in their efforts to care for their aged relative; about one half are assisted by family or friends; and the remaining

15% are assisted by a paid provider, such as a home care provider or home health aide (Scharlach, Lowe, & Schneider, 1991). Approximately 25% of employees with elder-care responsibilities provide assistance to two or more older persons (Scharlach & Fredriksen, 1993).

Impact on Employee Mental Health

Caring for an older person can create demands on an employee's personal and family resources that at times can be extremely stressful. Studies have found that 60% to 80% of employed caregivers report experiencing emotional strain as a result of their caregiving responsibilities, with more than 10% reporting "a great deal" of emotional strain (Scharlach & Fredriksen, 1993; Scharlach et al., 1991). A survey of employees at 33 companies in Portland, Oregon (Neal, Chapman, & Ingersoll-Dayton, 1987), for example, found that employees with elder-care responsibilities were more likely than other employees to experience stress regarding health, finances, family relationships, family health, and work. Stress and anxiety are apt to be particularly great for female employees and for those receiving lower than average salaries (*Fortune* Magazine and John Hancock Financial Services, 1989).

A number of recent studies have documented the significant mental health problems that can result from the demands of caring for a disabled relative. Gallagher and her colleagues (1989), for example, found that the incidence of depression among persons caring for a relative with Alzheimer's disease was four to ten times the rate of comparable community samples. A Duke University study found that caregivers used prescription drugs for depression, anxiety, and insomnia two to three times as often as a community sample (George & Gwyther, 1986). Moreover, some studies have documented increased alcohol use among caregivers (Walsh, Yoash-Gantz, Rinki, Koin, & Gallagher-Thompson, 1991).

An ongoing study of health and health behaviors among Northern California Kaiser Permanente Health Plan members aged 50 and older has found that caregivers were more likely to experience headaches, backaches, and other stress-related conditions than was a randomly selected group of noncaregivers (Scharlach, Runkle, Midanik, & Soghikian, 1994). A University of Bridgeport study (Creedon, 1987), moreover, found that employed caregivers were especially prone to depression, frequent anxiety, headaches, and weight changes and were more likely than other employees to be under a physician's care because of a chronic health condition (Creedon, 1987). However, caregivers have not generally been found to make greater use of medical or psychological services than do noncaregivers, after controlling for age, gender, and racial/ethnic differences between the two groups (Scharlach et al., 1994).

Caregiver stress is apt to be particularly high for persons caring for someone who is mentally ill. Although few studies have directly assessed the psychological functioning of the care recipient, it has been estimated that one third of caregivers are caring for someone who is agitated and who yells at the caregiver at times (U.S. House of Representatives Select Committee on

Aging, 1987). As a result, employees may arrive at work emotionally drained, may receive upsetting phone calls during the workday, and may return home to a barrage of complaints and emotional outbursts, all potentially contributing to higher levels of psychological distress and caregiver burnout (Crossman, London, & Barry, 1981).

It should be noted, however, that caring for an older person can have a salutary impact on mental health, as well. Many caregivers report an increased sense of self-worth and life satisfaction as a result of helping a loved one who is ill (Moss, Lawton, Dean, Goodman, & Schneider, 1989). Moreover, work can provide a much-needed break from all-encompassing elder-care responsibilities while affording opportunities for enhancing self-perceived self-efficacy, reducing feelings of hopelessness and helplessness, and obtaining social and emotional support (Neal, Chapman, Ingersoll-Dayton, & Emlen, 1993). Caregiving, in turn, has been reported to enhance job performance by promoting mature decision making and increasing employee sensitivity to the needs of customers and clients. For many caregivers, the salutary effects of combining work and caregiving may actually be perceived to exceed the deleterious effects (Scharlach, 1994). Thus, some studies (e.g., Giele, Mutschler, & Orodenker, 1987) have found that employed caregivers may actually experience less stress than do caregivers who are not employed.

Impact on Job Performance

Pressures associated with elder-care responsibilities can significantly affect job performance. Surveys by *Fortune* Magazine (*Fortune*, 1989) and the National Association of Area Agencies on Aging (Anastas, Gibeau, & Larson, 1987), for example, found that elder-care responsibilities interfered with the jobs of 77% of the caregiving employees polled. As a direct result of elder-care responsibilities, the average caregiving employee misses 3 to 5 hours of work each month (Scharlach & Boyd, 1989; Scharlach & Fredriksen, 1993), with some employees missing considerably more. Moreover, the demands of elder care force many employees to cut back on the number of hours they work, rearrange work schedules, forgo overtime work, or miss meetings or training sessions (Neal et al., 1987; Scharlach & Boyd, 1989; The Travelers, 1985; Wagner et al., 1988). Approximately 10% of caregivers report having to quit work, retire early, or take an extended leave of absence in order to provide care for an older relative (Stone et al., 1987).

Employees who have elder-care responsibilities report greater job stress and work–family conflict than do other employees (Neal et al., 1987; Scharlach & Boyd, 1989). It has been estimated that lost productivity resulting from the demands of caregiving costs the average company approximately $2,500 per year for each of its employees who has elder-care responsibilities (Scharlach et al., 1991), reflecting absenteeism; time off during business hours; missed overtime; impaired job performance because of stress and fatigue; and costs associated with job turnover, rehiring, and retraining.

Worksite Programs and Policies

The upsurge in elder-care interest has led a number of mental health professionals and senior service agencies to design programs specifically for employed persons. These providers often find the workplace to be a particularly effective site for efficiently reaching a large number of caregivers through brochures and other informational materials, lunchtime seminars, support groups, individual consultation, and referral to appropriate community resources. At the same time, workplace elder-care programs can be a mechanism for developing additional revenues and encouraging corporate contributions.

Worksite elder-care programs can be classified into six major categories: (a) informational programs, (b) resource and referral programs, (c) counseling and supportive services, (d) financial assistance, (e) direct caregiving services, and (f) family-oriented personnel policies. More detailed information on each of these types of programs is readily available from published resource materials (e.g., AARP, 1987a; Scharlach et al., 1991; Wagner, Creedon, Sasala, & Neal, 1989).

Informational Programs

Caregiver seminars, brown bag discussion groups, caregiver fairs, newsletters, videos, and other educational materials are among the most inexpensive and least complicated worksite efforts to assist employees with elder-care responsibilities. Programs such as these allow employees to share problems and concerns, identify community resources, and obtain information on specific elder-care issues. Moreover, informational programs often can be a first step in enabling employers to assess the need for other services while demonstrating concern for employees' family issues. The AARP has developed a Caregivers in the Workplace Program kit (AARP, 1987a), which includes a variety of informational materials that are useful for professionals and organizations interested in implementing informational programs for caregiving employees.

Resource and Referral Programs

Limited resource and referral information regarding local senior services is available from publicly supported Area Agencies on Aging in more than 650 communities nationwide, as well as through the U.S. Administration on Aging's Eldercare Locator (800-677-1116). However, the type of referral information needed by employees with elder-care concerns often requires more intensive consultation than many Area Agencies on Aging are equipped to provide. Persons seeking elder-care referrals, for example, may not know what services are available or which specific services are apt to be helpful in their particular situation. The referral process is complicated by the fact that at least 25% of employees live at a distance from the older person for whom they are caring (Scharlach et al., 1991). As a result, a growing number of employers contract with social service organizations or private elder-care specialists for elder-care resource and referral services. Moreover, the Communications Workers of America, the International Brotherhood of Electrical Workers, and a number of other labor unions have begun to include such resource and referral services in their contract negotiations.

Counseling and Support

Counseling and support services for employees with personal or family problems are usually offered through employee assistance programs (EAPs). Unfortunately, most EAP counselors have had little professional training regarding elder care or other family concerns, even though employees are now more likely to see an EAP counselor regarding family problems than for substance abuse problems. A survey of New York EAP professionals, for example, found that less than one fourth of respondents had ever attended a seminar or training program regarding elder care (Brice & Gorey, 1989). Because of the technical nature of adult dependent care, some companies—such as Hallmark and Marriott—contract with specialists to provide resource counseling for elder-care problems. In addition, some labor unions routinely provide counseling and support services to members who have personal or family problems (Molloy & Burmeister, 1989).

Financial Assistance

Elder care can be extremely expensive, averaging $20,000 to $30,000 per year for older persons who require long-term care. To help offset employee elder-care expenses, many companies offer financial assistance through dependent care assistance plans (DCAPs; Friedman, 1990). As authorized under Section 129 of the Internal Revenue Code, DCAPs allow employees to use before-tax dollars for dependent care expenses, with some employers also contributing additional dollars to augment available employee funds. However, DCAPs have been only sparsely used by caregiving employees, largely because of restrictive IRS regulations that require that care recipients be physically and financially dependent on employees and that employees be able to predict in advance their approximate annual caregiving expenses.

Direct Elder-Care Services

Most worksite elder-care programs are designed to provide information or support for caregiving employees, rather than to assist the impaired older person directly. However, some employers have developed services for older persons themselves, on the assumption that better meeting the needs of care recipients will reduce the strain and work interference experienced by their caregivers. Among the direct elder-care services that have been developed are elder-care centers, respite care, and case management, as well as grants and charitable contributions to support a wide variety of community-based services of potential benefit to employees and their older relatives.

One innovative example of an employer-sponsored elder-care program is the intergenerational day-care center at the corporate headquarters of Stride Rite Shoes in Cambridge, Massachusetts, operated in collaboration with Lesley College and Somerville-Cambridge Elder Services. The center serves older adults as well as children, affording opportunities for intergenerational activities. A number of labor unions, including the International Ladies' Garment Workers' Union (ILGWU), have established member support programs whereby volunteers provide companionship and respite care to assist fellow union members to continue to live independently (Barr, Johnson, & Warshaw, 1992). In addition, many major corporations make charitable contributions to senior services programs in their communities, thereby enhancing the network of services potentially available to employees and their older relatives. IBM, for example, has joined with more than 100 other businesses to create the American Business Collaboration for Dependent Care, which has committed more than $25 million to support innovative community elder-care and child-care services nationwide (American Business Collaboration for Quality Dependent Care information packet, 1993).

Family-Oriented Personnel Policies

Personnel policies responsive to employees' personal and family responsibilities often can be more helpful than specific elder-care programs because they provide employees with the flexibility to find individualized solutions that fit their particular caregiving situations. Of particular importance are flexible schedules, unpaid family leave, and family illness days or hours.

Flexible work schedules and flexible leave policies allow many employees to better meet the needs of their older relatives without neglecting their job responsibilities. Flexible work schedules, for example, are increasingly available; 50% of large companies surveyed by the Conference Board in 1988 reported that they offer flextime (Christensen, 1987). Surveys show that employees invariably desire opportunities for such flexibility. Moreover, flextime consistently has been found to reduce job turnover and enhance employee morale (Golembiewski & Proehl, 1980).

The Family and Medical Leave Act enacted in 1993 mandates that employers with 50 or more employees make available at least 12 weeks of leave per year for a variety of family-related reasons, including the birth or adoption of a child or the care of an ill parent. Although the leave can be unpaid, the employer is required to continue the employee's health benefits and guarantee a job when he or she returns to work. In addition, a number of states have family leave laws that are somewhat more extensive than the federal legislation. Connecticut, for example, provides state employees up to 24 consecutive weeks of leave time, with continued health insurance and the guarantee of a return to a comparable job and salary level.

Many companies also have flexible leave policies that allow workers the option of using their sick leave for other personal reasons such as caregiving. Having personal leave or release time available for emergencies—such as times when home care arrangements fall apart or the older care recipient is acutely ill, or for planned doctor visits—can be very helpful to employees. Some employers allow sick leave or personal absences to be broken up so that employees can leave work for a few hours to attend to the needs of an older relative without having to sacrifice an entire day of sick leave. Labor unions increasingly are playing an important role in advocating for such family-friendly personnel policies in negotiations over new collective bargaining agreements.

Implications for Psychologists

Industrial and organizational psychologists, as well as those specializing in clinical and community work with older persons, are in an advantageous position to develop interventions designed to prevent or treat mental health problems experienced by employed caregivers. Among the elder-care activities in which psychologists may wish to become involved are the following: (a) mental health services, including support groups, workshops, and clinical treatment of caregivers and their families; (b) needs assessments regarding the feasibility of developing elder-care programs and services; (c) evaluations of existing or proposed elder-care programs; and (d) community programs that support or enhance the availability of respite care and other needed services for disabled older persons. In addition, psychologists can play an important role in assisting organizations to develop family-friendly personnel policies and work–family structures.

Providing Mental Health Services

There is a pressing need for more comprehensive mental health services for caregivers, particularly in light of their documented vulnerability to depression and other psychological problems. However, serious questions have been raised regarding the ability of psychologists in general, and employee assistance professionals in particular, to respond effectively to the needs of employed caregivers (Scharlach et al., 1991).

A survey of employees at Transamerica Life Companies (Scharlach & Boyd, 1989), for example, found that more than 40% of the employees who had spoken to a psychologist or other employee assistance professional about their elder-care problems rated the contact as "not at all helpful." In a survey by the AARP (AARP and The Travelers Foundation, 1988), moreover, only 1% of caregiving employees found employee assistance professionals helpful with their elder-care concerns.

The primary limitation experienced by psychologists is a lack of knowledge about elder-care issues. For example, the majority of psychologists in EAP positions have little knowledge regarding the basic disorders of aging, the typical difficulties involved in caring for a disabled person, or the kinds of elder-care services available in their communities (Brice & Alegre, 1989). A study of employee assistance professionals in New York state, for example, found that 17% indicated no competence at all with regard to any of the 17 elder-care areas that were investigated (Brice & Gorey, 1989).

Psychologists require specialized training if they are to be responsive to the needs of employees with elder-care concerns. To date, less than one fourth of employee assistance professionals have ever attended a seminar or training program specifically concerned with elder-care issues in the workplace (Brice & Gorey, 1989). Nor do most existing psychology curricula include adequate content on aging, disability, or caregiving issues. As Brice and Alegre (1989) note, psychologists cannot be expected to possess information to which they have never been exposed.

Conducting Needs Assessments

Psychologists often have the combination of research skills and substantive knowledge required to assess the need for elder-care programs and services as well as the comparative feasibility of various options. Too often, employers select elder-care programs based on cost, convenience, or availability, rather than on a careful consideration of employee needs and employer goals. Yet, failure to adequately reflect employee needs and preferences has been shown to be one of the primary reasons why programs fail to meet their goals or are underutilized (Perry, 1982).

A properly conducted needs assessment is essential if elder-care programs are to meet most cost-effectively the needs of those employees who are most affected. However, most surveys conducted to date to investigate employee elder-care responsibilities have been hampered by poor response rates and nonrepresentative samples. Moreover, assessments of elder-care needs have gathered too much information regarding the characteristics of employees' elder-care situations and too little regarding the specific programs and services which, if implemented, would significantly reduce work interference and stress-related mental health problems.

Needs assessments can include employee surveys, focus groups, or individual interviews with employees or management. Whatever the form, the assessment process is itself an intervention; as such, it should be part of a carefully planned strategy for designing, promoting, and implementing an overall elder-care program. In so doing, the needs assessment can establish the foundation for a coherent and cost-effective approach to meeting the needs of employees with elder-care concerns.

Evaluating Elder-Care Programs

Although elder-care programs have many apparent benefits, virtually no evidence has been gathered to show that such programs actually result in desired outcomes such as reduced absenteeism, improved productivity, reduced caregiver burden, or better care for disabled older persons. The lack of adequate evaluation data, moreover, has made it difficult for companies to have a rational basis for deciding whether to modify or discontinue programs or program components that do not appear to achieve desired outcomes or do not seem to do so cost-effectively.

Most studies of program effectiveness conducted to date have simply asked participants whether or not the program was "helpful." Indicating that a program was "helpful," however, does not necessarily mean that it was effective in achieving desired objectives, such as relieving caregiver strain, reducing time lost from work, increasing productivity, or improving the amount or quality of care given. Retrospective self-reports, moreover, are notoriously unreliable and subject to unconscious distortion of the relevant facts by the individuals involved.

Future evaluation studies need to use measures that are as objective as practicable, include comparison groups and other controls over extraneous factors that can potentially influence intervention outcomes, and be guided by clearly articulated hypotheses that specify the particular outcomes likely to be observed in particular populations. For example, the hypothesis that resource and referral (R&R) services reduce caregiver strain by helping employees to access community elder-care services could be tested by assessing whether or not R&R users actually utilize community resources more often or more effectively than non-R&R users and whether those participants who make the most frequent or most appropriate use of community resources experience the greatest reduction in strain.

It is important to note that an elder-care intervention may produce effects that are desirable in some ways but not others. For example, it would not be surprising to find that an intervention designed to educate employees about community resources might result in reduced work time, at least over the short term, as employees take time during the workday to contact and use community resources about which they previously were unaware. Moreover, an intervention that helps employees find alternative sources of care for their older relatives may not necessarily achieve an employer's objectives (e.g., if it results in increased personal telephone use or increased worry) or benefit society at large (e.g., if it reduces the amount or quality of elder care older adults receive). It is likely, moreover, that some stress and strain are unavoidable if employees are to honor their commitments both to their families and to their jobs.

Meeting the Needs of Disabled Older Persons

Many of the difficulties experienced by employed caregivers result directly or indirectly from inadequacies in the existing system of long-term care in the United States and can be most cost-effectively resolved through improvements in the long-term care system rather than through particular employer-sponsored programs or benefits. Psychologists can help to develop needed community services (e.g., adult day care, quality home care, respite care) that can provide supportive assistance to older persons who have disabilities, reduce the incidence of mental health problems among older adults, and help alleviate the strain experienced by employees who have elder-care responsibilities.

Psychologists also can help develop collaborative efforts between employers and the public sector in order to prevent the inequity and inefficiency that can result from separate employer-sponsored and public-sponsored services for caregivers. Innovative public–private partnerships have been developed by the New York City Department for the Aging, the Metropolitan Chicago Coalition on Aging, the Los Angeles County Area Agency on Aging, and the Washington Business Group on Health (through the formation of coalitions between employers and community agencies in cities such as Boston, Hartford, Cleveland, and Jackson, MS). Psychologists also can play an important role by advocating for increased public funding for community-based, long-term care services, as well as tax code changes that facilitate the development and usefulness of employer-sponsored elder-care programs.

Conclusion

Elder care is an issue that transcends traditional boundaries between corporate America, the public sector, and psychological services. As a result, elder care provides exciting opportunities for psychologists and human resource professionals to work together in innovative ways to address the challenges associated with meeting the long-term care needs of an aging population.

References

American Association of Retired Persons. (1987a). *Caregivers in the work place program kit.* Washington, DC: Author.

American Association of Retired Persons. (1987b). *A profile of older Americans: 1987.* Washington, DC: Author.

American Association of Retired Persons and The Travelers Foundation. (1988). *A national study of caregivers: Final report.* Washington, DC: American Association of Retired Persons.

American Business Collaboration for Quality Dependent Care information packet. (1993). Boston: Work/Family Directions Development Corporation. (Available from Work/Family Directions, Inc., 930 Commonwealth Avenue, Boston, MA 02215-1274.)

Anastas, J. W., Gibeau, J. L., & Larson, P. J. (1987). *Breadwinners and caregivers: Supporting workers who care for elderly family members.* Final report submitted by the National Association of Area Agencies on Aging to the Administration on Aging (NAAAA; Grant #90AM158). (Available from NAAAA, 1112 16th Street, NW, Suite 100, Washington, DC 20036.)

Barr, J. K., Johnson, K. W., & Warshaw, L. J. (1992). Supporting the elderly: Workplace programs for employed citizens. *The Milbank Quarterly, 70,* 509–533.

Brice, G. C., & Alegre, M. R. (1989, July/August). Eldercare as an EAP concern. *EAP Digest,* 31–34.

Brice, G. C., & Gorey, K. M. (1989, November). *EAP coordinators' self-reported competence to handle care problems.* Paper presented at the annual meeting of the Gerontological Society of America, Minneapolis.

Christensen, K. E. (1987). *Flexible staffing and scheduling.* New York: The Conference Board.

Creedon, M. A. (1987). *Issues for an aging America: Employees and eldercare.* Bridgeport, CT: University of Bridgeport Center for the Study of Aging.

Crossman, L., London, C., & Barry, C. (1981). Older women caring for disabled spouses: A model for supportive services. *The Gerontologist, 21,* 464–470.

Fortune Magazine and John Hancock Financial Services. (1989). *Corporate and employee response to caring for the elderly: A national survey of U.S. companies and the workforce.* New York: *Fortune* Magazine.

Foster, C. D., Siegel, M. A., & Jacobs, N. R. (Eds.). (1988). *Women's changing roles.* Wylie, TX: Information Aids.

Friedman, D. E. (1986, June). Eldercare: The employee benefit of the 1990's? *Across the Board,* 45–51.

Friedman, D. E. (1990). Corporate responses to family needs. In D. G. Unger & M. B. Sussman (Eds.), *Families in community settings: Interdisciplinary perspectives* (pp. 77–98). New York: Haworth Press.

Gallagher, D., Rose, J., Rivera, P., Lovett, S., & Thompson, L. (1989). Prevalence of depression in family caregivers. *The Gerontologist, 29,* 449–456.

George, L. K., & Gwyther, L. P. (1986). Caregiver well-being: A multidimensional examination of family caregivers of demented adults. *The Gerontologist, 26,* 253–260.

Giele, J. Z., Mutschler, P. H., & Orodenker, S. Z. (1987). *Stress and burdens of caregiving for the frail elderly* (Working paper No. 36). Unpublished manuscript, Brandeis University, Florence Heller Graduate School, Waltham, MA.

Golembiewski, R. T., & Proehl, C. W. (1980). Public sector application of flexible work hours: A review of available experience. *Public Administration Review, 40,* 72–85.

Green, G. P., & Epstein, R. K. (Eds.). (1988). *Employment and earnings* [Vol. 35(2)]. Washington, DC: U.S. Department of Labor, Bureau of Labor Statistics.

Molloy, D., & Burmeister, L. (1989). Social workers in union-based programs. *Employee Assistance Quarterly, 5*(1), 37–51.

Moss, M. S., Lawton, M. P., Dean, J., Goodman, M., & Schneider, J. (1989). Satisfactions and burdens in caring for impaired elderly persons. *Journal of Gerontology, 44,* 181–189.

Neal, M. B., Chapman, N. J., & Ingersoll-Dayton, B. (1987, November). *Work and elder care: A survey of employees.* Paper presented at the annual scientific meeting of the Gerontological Society of America, Washington, DC.

Neal, M. B., Chapman, N. J., Ingersoll-Dayton, B., & Emlen, A. (1993). *Balancing work and caregiving.* Thousand Oaks, CA: Sage.

Perry, K. (1982). *Employers and child care: Establishing services through the workplace.* Washington, DC: U.S. Department of Labor, Women's Bureau.

Scharlach, A. (1994). Caregiving and employment: Competing or complementary roles? *The Gerontologist, 34,* 378–385.

Scharlach, A., & Boyd, S. (1989). Caregiving and employment: Results of an employee survey. *The Gerontologist, 29,* 382–387.

Scharlach, A., & Fredriksen, K. (1993). *Survey of caregiving employees for the University of California at Berkeley.* Berkeley, CA: Chancellor's Advisory Committee on Dependent Care, University of California at Berkeley.

Scharlach, A., Lowe, B., & Schneider, E. (1991). *Elder care and the workforce: Blueprint for action.* Lexington, MA: Lexington Books.

Scharlach, A. E., Runkle, C., Midanik, L., & Soghikian, K. (1994). Health conditions and service utilization of adults with elder care responsibilities. *Journal of Aging and Health, 6,* 336–352.

Stone, R. S., Cafferata, G. L., & Sangl, J. (1987). Caregivers of the frail elderly: A national profile. *The Gerontologist, 27,* 616–626.

The Travelers Companies. (1985). *The Travelers employee caregiver survey.* Hartford, CT: Author.

U.S. House of Representatives Select Committee on Aging. (1987). *Exploding the myths: Caregiving in America* (Comm. Pub. No. 99-611). Washington, DC: U.S. Government Printing Office.

U.S. Senate Special Committee on Aging in conjunction with the American Association of Retired Persons, the Federal Council on the Aging, and the Administration on Aging. (1985–1986). *Aging America: Trends and projections.* Washington, DC: U.S. Government Printing Office.

Wagner, D., Creedon, M., Sasala, J., & Neal, M. (1989). *Employees & eldercare: Designing effective responses for the workplace.* Bridgeport, CT: University of Bridgeport Center for the Study of Aging.

Wagner, D., Neal, M., Gibeau, J., Scharlach, A., & Anastas, J. (1988). *Eldercare and the working caregiver: An analysis of current research.* Unpublished manuscript (available from Donna Wagner, Center for the Study of Aging, University of Bridgeport, Bridgeport, CT 06601).

Walsh, W., Yoash-Gantz, R., Rinki, M., Koin, D., & Gallagher-Thompson, D. (1991, November). *The use of alcohol, exercise, smoking and psychotropic drugs among female caregivers.* Paper presented at the annual scientific meeting of the Gerontological Society of America, San Francisco, CA.

20

Interdependence and Personal Well-Being in a Training Environment

Janice R. W. Joplin, James Campbell Quick,
Debra L. Nelson, and Judy C. Turner

Social support in the work environment is a vital element in effective performance, both from organizational and individual viewpoints. From the organization's view, employees must have some degree of interaction to achieve goals, and the degree of interaction and supportive relationships required is dependent upon the characteristics of the job. The individual needs interaction with others to achieve organizational goals and sustain positive personal well-being. Supportive work relationships are an integral element in communicating vision and goals, clarifying values, and developing a team atmosphere. Reciprocally, visions, goals, clear values, and a team atmosphere can enhance supportive workplace relationships.

A sociological approach to social support in the work environment might focus upon the availability of others in the work environment in the form of work groups, physical proximity, formal or informal networks, or electronic connections. This approach would assume that, if others are available, interaction and support will occur at a level that will meet both organizational and individual needs. Availability of social support is a necessary, although not sufficient, condition for supportive relationships and personal well-being to occur. Organizations can work to increase the availability of social support in the workplace through interventions such as creating a common goal with group-level consequences, communicating the mission and goals of the organization, mentoring, team building, and targeting "at-risk" groups.

Our approach investigates an individual's orientation in interacting with other individuals in the work environment (both internal and external to the organization) and forming social supports that will (a) be conducive to personal welfare and the achievement of organizational goals and (b) affect whether the available social support is tapped. We consider an individual's personal well-being as central to performance in work settings, and we believe that interventions to increase social support will also enhance individual well-being.

We begin by discussing the theoretical basis of our approach to individual

The authors thank David Van Fleet, Jerry C. Wofford, and A. David Mangelsdorff for comments on an earlier draft, and Nancy Rowe for assistance with data analysis.

orientations in developing supportive relationships. Next, we present the findings of our longitudinal study of military officer trainees, conducted in the training environment. We then discuss the implications for workplace interventions.

Individual Orientations

Our approach is based on the ethological study of personality and resulting attachment theory, pioneered by Ainsworth and Bowlby (1991). Ainsworth and colleagues (1978) conducted research that classified three dominant patterns of attachment in children: secure, avoidant, and anxious–ambivalent. An *attachment figure* is one who provides protection and support, and one whom an individual spontaneously turns to and seeks out in distressing times. As research in this area has developed, evidence of continuation of the patterns of attachment and resulting individual orientations in seeking and forming human supports extends into adult years and across the life span (Hazan & Shaver, 1987; Kobak & Hazan, 1991; Kobak & Sceery, 1988; Weiss, 1982). Hazan and Shaver's (1990) empirical investigations suggest that attachments in adulthood are central to effectiveness and satisfaction in work activities.

The patterns of attachment that Ainsworth and colleagues (1978) identified have been labeled *interdependence* (secure or self-reliant), *counterdependence* (avoidant), and *overdependence* (anxious–ambivalent) in stress and management literature (Nelson, J. C. Quick, & Joplin, 1991; Quick, Nelson, & Quick, 1987). Each orientation may be seen as a dominant way of relating to others with whom an individual has a close relationship, whether working or personal. Our focus in this chapter is on relationships in the work environment. Thus, our discussion is centered on attachments in a work context. This does not negate the value of attachments in personal lives outside the work environment, which may be the primary social support available for many individuals. We do not contend that either personal or work relationships supersede each other, but that a healthy balance between the two is optimal.

The orientation of interdependence is characterized by a reciprocity and flexibility in relationships. It is based on an individual's secure knowledge that others will be available for assistance in stressful, anxiety-ridden situations. For adults, who have discretion as to the types of supportive relationships they form, interdependence will involve several high-quality supportive relationships across life arenas. A broad support system increases the likelihood of availability of others when needed, and likewise, offers the individual an opportunity to reciprocate and be available to others in a supportive manner. In a work context, interdependence would be characterized by close relationships with a variety of coworkers such as supervisors, subordinates, and peers, as well as professional colleagues and contacts outside an individual's primary organization or work setting.

Counterdependence and overdependence may be seen as tendencies that are not wholly interdependent, but rather encompass behaviors that rely upon engaging social support either too much (overdependence) or too little (counterdependence). Either orientation may have adverse effects upon the individual's long-term well-being.

Counterdependence occurs when an individual believes that no one will be available in situations of distress, and the individual is driven to be his or her own best support system. Although we believe that individuals are ultimately responsible for themselves, part of this responsibility is knowing where and how to receive the essential support for personal well-being and achieving organizational goals. Counterdependent individuals frequently overinvest in accomplishing work objectives alone, because they believe that no one else could do the job as well as they can. They may resist supportive overtures, thus eventually ensuring that others will not, in fact, be available in anxiety-provoking situations.

Overdependence is also undergirded by a belief that others may not be available when needed. However, the overdependent orientation is manifested when an individual seeks out and relies upon more supports than are necessary or appropriate for the situation. Overdependence frequently leads to an individual's relinquishing responsibility for personal well-being and leaving the achievement of organizational goals to others. By being overdependent on others, the individual may use a support to its capacity without reciprocating, and thus ultimately fulfill the fear that no one will be available when needed.

Health Consequences

Social isolation has been empirically shown to have an adverse impact upon health (House, Landis, & Umberson, 1988). We propose that attachment behavior, through the development of supportive relationships, is the mechanism that ameliorates the morbidity and mortality associated with social isolation. An individual's orientation in forming supportive relationships may affect personal well-being through his or her use of available supports in both work and personal contexts.

A psychobiological perspective is instructive in exploring the attachment orientation–personal well-being connection. Attachment is a behavioral system that activates when the individual is experiencing distress. It is manifested in proximity-seeking behaviors toward attachment figures, usually persons with whom the individual has regular interactions and close relationships.

Attachment provides biological homeostasis (Hofer, 1984, 1987), a form of steady state functioning critical to avoidance of strain under stress (Cannon, 1932). In close relationships where regular interaction occurs, individuals' biological functions such as appetite, sleep cycles, and hormone levels become synchronized. Mason (1959) found that individual members of B-52 bomber crews tended to show similar levels of adrenal cortical output while they worked closely together. Human interaction affects biological functions and well-being from both physiological and psychological perspectives.

To investigate the connections between individual orientation to forming supportive relationships and personal well-being, we studied a sample of military officer trainees that offers unique opportunities for insights. This adult population was temporarily suspended from availability for spontaneous contact with their regular support networks and were engaged in an intense program of training for new careers when we conducted our research.

Research in Individual Orientations to Social Support

In this section, we will describe (a) the sample and the nature of the training program in which the trainees are participating, (b) measures used in the research, and (c) results of the study. We will conclude with a discussion of unanswered questions and issues.

Military Officer Trainees

A longitudinal study of two cohorts of military officer trainees ($n_1 = 67$ and $n_2 = 70$) was conducted during their 14-week training period. The primary mission of this training program was to prepare trainees to serve as U.S. military officers. All officer trainees had to have a bachelor's degree as a prerequisite for entry into training, and age ranged up to 34 years. Leadership capabilities were continually scrutinized and evaluated throughout the program. During the first half of training, when trainees were considered in the lower class, all trainees served in followership positions. However, at the halfway point, trainees moved into the upper class and served in leadership positions, ranging from lower-level, single-task positions to Wing Commander, a position similar to a corporate president. In addition, students served on project action teams, and they had to work on an assigned project and present their findings to the commander for action.

The training curriculum consisted of 60 training days, although a trainee could be at the training facility for as many as 110 calendar days, depending on holidays, weekends, bad-weather days, or minor illness during the training period. All trainees had to meet excellent health and specific weight standards, based on one's gender and height, in order to complete the program. Exceeding the weight standard resulted in elimination from the program. Trainees found the program both physically and mentally demanding. Training was continuous from day one of arrival through 6 or 7 days of each week. Daily training schedules were extremely demanding, beginning at 0500 hours and ending with lights out at 2300. Students had to adhere to strict schedules throughout the day for formations, transit movements, meals, academics, physical fitness, and leadership activities. Trainees were constantly evaluated on personal appearance and conduct as well as on the application of principles of military discipline, customs, and courtesies.

One new trainee described the three most stressful aspects of training as (a) forced time management (too much to do in one day), (b) lack of rest, and (c) pressure to pass many measurements in a short time period. One senior trainee described the three most stressful aspects of the training program as (a) pace of the program, (b) fear of elimination for "whatever" reason, and (c) sometimes conflicting instructions or advice. Trainees had to meet rigorous physical *and* academic standards to pass the training program.

Physical fitness and *drill training* were one major component training time. Physical fitness was developed through organized conditioning classes, team sports events, and obstacle course training and was evaluated through nine tests administered to each trainee within the 60-day training period. Each test comprised five events: push-ups, sit-ups, long jump, pull-ups (men)/flexed-arm hang (women), and a 600-yard dash, with a four out of five pass ratio necessary to remain in training.

Academics were the second major portion of officer training. Five graded examinations were given, and trainees who exceeded two test failures were usually dismissed for military training deficiency. The core academic curriculum consisted of five major areas: (a) *leadership and management* (theory, motivation techniques, self-assessment, group dynamics, team building, individual behaviors, delegation, and followership; (b) *professional knowledge* (moral fortitude, maturity, ethics, and establishing proper social distance in professional relationships); (c) *communication skills* (briefings, military correspondence, and communication); (d) *health and fitness* (nutrition, morning runs, sports activities, and physical conditioning exercises; and (e) *defense studies* (service heritage and history, approaches to strategy, principles of war, doctrinal development, technology, and theorists).

Measures

The purpose of this longitudinal study was to assess interdependence and its relationship with personal well-being in military officer trainees during the 14-week training period. Four questions were of interest:

1. Do levels of interdependence remain stable over the course of intensive training when individuals are isolated from their normal support systems?
2. Is interdependence related to age and education?
3. Do those individuals who fail to complete training exhibit significantly higher levels of counterdependence or overdependence?
4. Is personal well-being over the course of the training a function of interdependence levels?

A measure of interdependence and established measures of health symptoms, along with demographics, were self-reported by the trainees. Attrition data was gathered from archival records, allowing access to reasons for each trainee's departure from training.

The Self-Reliance Inventory was developed as a self-report measure of a person's interpersonal attachment orientation. The first two versions of the inventory focused on the bipolar orientation to interdependent or counterdependent behavior (Quick, Nelson, & Quick, 1987, 1990). The revised inventory consisted of two subscales (Quick, Nelson, & Quick, 1991). One subscale focused on the orientation to interdependent or counterdependent behavior and is labeled Interdependence/C in the present study. The other subscale focused on the orientation to interdependent or overdependent behavior and is labeled Interdependence/O in the present study. A low score on both subscales indicates a higher degree of interdependence. This two-subscale version of the inventory consists of 20 items with a six-point Likert scale response format of 0 (strongly disagree), 1 (disagree), 2 (somewhat disagree), 3 (somewhat agree), 4 (agree), and 5 (strongly agree). The construct validity, internal consistency, and test–retest reliability of the two subscales have been reported earlier (Quick, Joplin, Nelson, & Quick, 1992).

Health symptoms have often been assessed through social, psychological, and physiological self-reports of well-being. In the present study, five measures of health symptoms were used. The General Health Questionnaire contains three 7-item, 4-point Likert scales to measure anxiety and insomnia, social dysfunction, and somatic symptoms (Goldberg & Hillier, 1979). An additional 26 items were used to measure psychological symptoms and physiological symptoms (Derogatis, 1977).

Self-report data for each trainee were matched over time using a unique four-digit code. Variables were measured at three different times during the training: Time 1 (t_1) measures were taken within the first few days of training, Time 2 (t_2) measures were taken at approximately 4 weeks into the 14-week training period, and Time 3 (t_3) measures were taken during the last week of training. The trainees initially totaled 146 in the two classes; however, usable data were collected at Time 1 for 137 trainees. A chi-square comparison of the two cohorts found no significant differences between the two, based on the demographic variables of age, education, or gender. Therefore, the cohorts were pooled into a single sample ($N = 137$) composed of 117 men and 20 women; 2 members were under age 20, 104 in their 20s, and 29 in their 30s; 127 members had bachelor's degrees, 8 had some graduate study, and 1 each had a master's and doctoral degree. Ninety-six percent of trainees were Caucasian, 1.6% were Hispanic, 1.6% were African American, and .8% were Asian. A total attrition (based on the initial 146 trainees) of 12.3% ($N_a = 18$) occurred in the two classes that constitute the sample, and the remaining 87.7% ($N_g = 126$) successfully graduated. Attrition is discussed in the Results section.

Results

The first analysis addresses the question of whether interdependence remains stable over the course of training. Table 1 presents the results of this analysis over the 14-week training period for the successful trainees who graduated ($N_g = 126$). Mean data for both of the interdependence subscales at each of the three measurement times during training, a comparison of the mean values, and the level of significance in the difference are given. A lower value on each of the interdependence subscales indicates greater levels of interdependent behavior.

The data indicate that the officer trainees maintained their initial counterdependence levels, as measured on the Interdependence/C subscale, during the course of training. Scores on the Interdependence/O subscale showed that

Table 1. Military Officer Candidate Results: ANOVA t Tests ($N_g = 126$)

Measure	Time 1	Time 2	Time 3	T_1-T_2		T_2-T_3		T_1-T_3	
				t	$p \leq$	t	$p \leq$	t	$p \leq$
Interdependence/C[a]	13.36[b]	13.78[b]	14.10[b]	1.06	.289	.79	.433	1.46	.147
	(4.60)[c]	(4.71)[c]	(4.89)[c]						
Interdependence/O[d]	14.03[b]	13.56[b]	13.31[b]	1.86	.065	1.57	.118	3.13	.002
	(3.80)[c]	(3.77)[c]	(3.45)[c]						

[a]Scale range 0 to 60; actual value range 0 to 27.
[b]Mean value.
[c]Standard deviation.
[d]Scale range 0 to 30; actual value range 4 to 23.

trainees became significantly less overdependent during the course of training. An explanation for this finding may be that candidates, faced with a novel situation at the beginning of training, were more highly dependent upon their peers than normal circumstances would have warranted and that the dependence decreased as the situation and training environment became more familiar. The initial measure was taken on the fourth or fifth days of training, after trainees had experienced the onset of "training reality." Without pre-training measures, it was not possible to determine whether the Time 1 measure is reflective of normal levels of overdependence or exacerbated levels due to introduction to training.

Comparative Analysis

Solomon, Noy, and Bar-On (1986) found age, education, and rank to be covariates helpful in explaining the risk exposure and vulnerability of military personnel to combat stress reactions. To investigate the question of whether age, education, and rank may be covariates helpful in explaining the development of interdependent behavior, we used the present sample of military officer trainees and a sample of "normal" basic military trainees from previous research (Quick, Joplin, Nelson, & Quick, 1991). A three-step comparative analysis was conducted. First, the groups were tested on the Interdependence/C and Interdependence/O subscales, age, and education. The officer trainees were significantly ($p < .0001$) more interdependent on both measures than their basic military trainee counterparts. The officer trainees were also found to be older (in their late 20s, versus just under 20 years old; $p < .0001$) and better educated (all with bachelor's, master's, or doctoral degrees, versus high school graduates with some college and a few with bachelor's degrees; $p < .0001$).

Second, a univariate F test and multivariate test (Wilks) were conducted within groups (officer trainees and basic military trainees) to determine if age or education explained portions of the interdependence variance within the groups. The results were not significant, suggesting that age and education did not explain within group variance.

Third, an ANCOVA was performed, with age and education as covariates, to examine differences between the officer trainees and the basic military trainees. The officer trainees were significantly more interdependent on both scales ($F = 3.10$, $p < .047$ for Interdependence/C, and $F = 5.30$, $p < .006$ for Interdependence/O). Taken together, these three analyses suggest that some of the difference in interdependence between the officer trainees and the basic military trainees is explained by age and education. Thus, age and education may contribute to the development of interdependent behavior. An alternate explanation may be that interdependent individuals are more likely to pursue higher levels of education.

Attrition Analysis

The attrition in this sample is 12.3%, with the normal being 12.7% per year over the past 10 years. A trainee may fail to graduate for one of five reasons. *Self-initiated elimination* occurs when a trainee withdraws from training because the culture shock is too great, the training is too rigorous, or for other possible personal reasons. *Lack of aptitude* attrition is initiated by the training commander, who closely observes his or her trainees and eliminates weak performers who do not demonstrate the aptitude for military leadership. *Military training deficiency* attrition results from unacceptable performance on academic tests during training. *Medical* attrition occurs due to injuries or poor health. Occasionally, attrition occurs for other reasons, such as prejudicial conduct, an honor violation, fraternization, or falsifications prior to entering training. Of the 18 cases of failure to graduate among officer trainees, 11 were self-initiated, 6 were for training deficiencies, and 1 was for an honor violation. Self-initiated elimination typically is the greatest component of attrition. It was 7.5% for this sample and is normally about 7% per class.

Our third analysis, an attrition analysis, compared those who failed to graduate with those who successfully graduated at the beginning of the training period. Using t tests, we found those who failed to graduate to be significantly ($t = 2.08$, $p < .04$) more counterdependent and less interdependent than their successful peers. In addition, they were found to have significantly higher levels of psychological symptoms ($t = 2.50$, $p < .02$), physiological symptoms ($t = 2.77$, $p < .007$), as well as anxiety and insomnia ($t = 2.42$, $p < .02$). This suggests that people who are too counterdependent may have difficulty forming the necessary social support systems in stressful circumstances to successfully manage those difficult times.

Well-Being and Interdependence

Our fourth question in this study was to assess the relationship of interdependence to levels of personal well-being over the course of the training period. Repeated measures MANOVAs were performed to address this question. The trainees' scores on the interdependence subscales at Time 1 were used as the basis for selecting groups to serve as the independent variable. Groups for each subscale were formed by splits at the third quartile (e.g., those low in counterdependence were in the lower three quartiles of the subscale, and those

Table 2. Repeated Measures MANOVAs: Interdependence/C Subscale ($N = 105$)

Well-Being	Interdependence/C subscale score	Means			F	p
		t_1	t_2	t_3		
Physiological	Low/C	10.65	7.12	5.34	4.55	.03
	High/C	12.28	10.93	8.50		
	Time				13.93	.0001
	Time × C/groups				1.20	.30
Psychological	Low/C	7.22	5.37	3.51	5.46	.02
	High/C	7.56	7.20	6.16	13.43	.0001
	Time × C/groups				2.66	.07
Somatic	Low/C	12.21	12.04	11.90	1.65	.20
	High/C	13.45	13.81	12.09		
	Time				1.50	.20
	Time × C/groups				.96	.40
Anxiety & insomnia	Low/C	16.47	14.13	12.42	7.29	.01
	High/C	17.94	16.05	14.26		
	Time				41.76	.0001
	Time × C/groups				.19	.80
Social dys- function	Low/C	13.64	12.76	12.41	13.13	.0005
	High/C	15.09	14.15	13.78		
	Time				8.09	.0005
	Time × C/groups				.007	.99

high in counterdependence scored in the top quartile). The psychological, physiological, somatic, anxiety and insomnia, and social dysfunction measures over the three time periods each served as the repeated measures dependent variable. The results are shown in Tables 2 (Interdependence/C) and 3 (Interdependence/O).

The results show that there were significant time effects for all health measures except somatic symptoms, for which there were no significant findings with either the counterdependent or overdependent groupings. As shown in Tables 2 and 3, health improved significantly for the trainees over the course of the training period.

The high counterdependence group was significantly higher on psychological ($F = 5.46$, $p < .02$), physiological ($F = 4.55$, $p < .03$), anxiety and insomnia ($F = 7.29$, $p < .01$), and social dysfunction ($F = 13.13$, $p < .0005$) symptoms than those in the low counterdependence group. It is interesting to note that the most significant differences were on the anxiety and insomnia and the social dysfunction scales. The patterns of the two groups' gains on the health measures did not significantly differ (i.e., there was no interaction effect).

The only significant group effect found when trainees were grouped by overdependence scores was on the anxiety and insomnia measure. Those who were high in overdependence reported significantly more anxiety and insomnia ($F = 4.60, p < .03$) on average than the low overdependent group. No significant interaction effects were found; therefore, the patterns of the groups' health gains were not significantly different over the training period.

Table 3. Repeated Measures MANOVAs: Interdependence/O Subscale ($N = 105$)

Well-Being	Interdependence/O subscale score	Means			F	p
		t_1	t_2	t_3		
Physiological	Low/O	11.03	7.55	5.88	.90	.30
	High/O	11.45	9.47	7.19		
	Time				17.37	.0001
	Time × O/groups				.64	.50
Psychological	Low/O	7.11	5.69	4.01	1.18	.30
	High/O	7.80	6.30	4.83		
	Time				20.88	.0001
	Time × O/group				.05	.95
Somatic	Low/O	12.57	12.51	11.90	.05	.80
	High/O	12.30	12.25	12.00		
	Time				.56	.60
	Time × O/groups				.09	.90
Anxiety & insomnia	Low/O	16.53	14.13	12.42	4.60	.03
	High/O	17.57	15.53	13.91		
	Time				48.49	.0001
	Time × O/groups				.17	.80
Social dysfunction	Low/O	13.95	13.04	12.69	.99	.30
	High/O	14.27	13.43	13.13		
	Time				8.23	.0005
	Time × O/groups				.02	.98

Trainees who were high in overdependence at Time 1 were not significantly different from trainees who were low in overdependence on health measures, except on anxiety and insomnia. Given that overdependence for the group as a whole significantly decreased over the training period, this would indicate that individuals who entered training with high levels of overdependence also carried significantly higher levels of anxiety and insomnia throughout training.

Trainees who were initially higher in counterdependence did not experience health gains commensurate with those who were lower in counterdependence, with the most significant adverse effects being in psychological, physiological, anxiety and insomnia, and social dysfunction areas. Thus, the orientation toward counterdependence and social isolation seems to lead to poorer health and retention rates in training.

Issues to Be Addressed

There are two issues that remain to be addressed. First, this study has not established either what is normal nor what is healthy with regard to interdependence. Further research with other groups will make it possible to establish norms without great difficulty. It will be more difficult to establish healthy, at-risk, and unhealthy markers on these interdependence scales.

Second, the best strategies for nurturing interdependent behavior in the adult years have not been established. Some elements of the training program, both cognitive and physical, may contribute to enhanced interdependence. Future research should address this developmental issue.

Organizational Actions for Promoting Interdependence

Interdependence is an orientation and individual strategy for forming relationships that encourage health and well-being, and there are actions that organizations can take to promote and sustain interdependent behavior in work settings. Encouraging individuals to develop interdependence, targeting specific groups for interventions, and designing organizational systems that help sustain interdependence are proactive means by which organizations can promote member health and well-being.

Developing Interdependence

In examining the experience of military officer trainees, there are lessons that emerge that can be used by all types of organizations. Much of the training used a team approach. Trainees participated in project action teams and team sports activities and received instruction in team building and group dynamics. The team approach is proliferating in U.S. organizations, and team-building interventions are ideal vehicles for encouraging interdependence.

The Cadillac division of General Motors used the team concept to design its new models. Teams consisting of engineers, managers, and assemblers worked together to improve the quality of Cadillac cars, and one result was the Malcolm Baldrige National Quality Award (Grettenberger, 1992). Interdependence is a behavioral strategy that is crucial for effective teamwork, and organizations that utilize the team concept can stress the value of relationships among team members that are reciprocal in terms of support and secure in terms of availability.

Interdependence is a characteristic of cohesive teams and groups. Actions that encourage cohesiveness can therefore be effective also in encouraging interdependent behavior. Creating a sense of common goals and a common fate is one way to foster cohesiveness, and this is a strategy exemplified by the military in its officer training. Organizations can do this as well by creating cohorts of new employees and supporting the development of shared goals within the cohort. Mutual goals that can be achieved only through teamwork will support the development of interdependence.

Within the teams, members should have opportunities to exercise both follower and leader functions. This strategy helps members realize that the leader–follower exchange is one characterized by interdependence. It also discourages empire building and potential turf wars, both of which can discourage interdependent behavior. By engaging in roles both as leaders and as followers, individuals can identify their overdependent or counterdependent tendencies and learn that neither behavioral strategy is an effective one for a teamwork culture.

Mentoring is another avenue through which organizations can encourage interdependence. Many companies support formal mentoring relationships, but in most organizations, mentoring relationships develop in informal ways. Mentors can provide support to protégés in many forms: (a) information on the political climate of the organization, (b) modeling of appropriate behavior, and (c) emotional support during stressful times. Mentors should serve as models of interdependent behavior. Individuals should be encouraged to seek out mentors, and experienced employees should be encouraged to serve as mentors.

Newcomer socialization is a natural process that lends itself to the development of interdependence among employees. Newcomers should be introduced to reliable support figures early in their socialization, and they should be encouraged to develop mutually supportive relationships with other newcomers. Providing opportunities for newcomers to socialize informally with experienced organization members gives newcomers a wider range of opportunities to develop their own relationships with senior colleagues.

All organization members can benefit from careful introspection and self-diagnosis of their own tendencies in forming relationships with others. The organization should encourage interdependence as the valued strategy and should also help employees develop support networks within the organization. In addition, employees should be encouraged to join interorganizational networks and professional societies to broaden their support networks.

Focal Groups for Workplace Interventions

Interventions that encourage interdependence at work are beneficial to all employees, but there are particular individuals and groups that can be targeted because of special needs. Newcomers, as we discussed earlier, need guidance for developing support networks. It is important that interdependent behavior among newcomers be nurtured and reinforced.

Another targeted group is organizational members involved in change. Mergers and acquisitions, downsizing, and restructuring can result in drastic alterations in the interpersonal relationships within the organization. Disruptions in supportive relationships may leave employees lacking the support they need to sustain their performance and health. Employees should be encouraged to examine and revamp their support networks and to develop a wide range of interdependent relationships that can help them weather the changes at work. Layoff survivors, for example, may retreat to a counterdependent or overdependent strategy because of the loss of secure relationships. These individuals need to be reminded to reach out for support and to be an available source of support for others.

There are particular jobs that are at risk for the development of counterdependent or overdependent behaviors. Physically or geographically isolated employees may find it difficult to sustain interdependent relationships. Salespersons with hectic travel schedules, individuals who work via telecommuting, and expatriate workers all need to be encouraged to develop support networks and to periodically review and revise their networks as conditions change.

Sustaining Interdependent Behavior at Work

Promoting interdependent behavior by team building, mentoring, and newcomer socialization is but half of the task of encouraging interdependence. The organization's vision, mission, goals, and values must work in concert to deliver the message that teamwork is a key element in the organization's culture. Organizations, if they hope to encourage employees to sustain interdependent behavior, must take actions to consistently communicate that such behavior is valued and that it will be rewarded. Reward systems must recognize and reinforce interdependent behavior at work, especially teamwork. Cooperative group rewards in which individuals are compensated for successful group performance promote interdependence among members. Seeking help from others should be a valued behavior and should be rewarded as a sign of knowing one's limits. Mentoring and advising newcomers should be rewarded, and individuals who are so involved should be carefully selected. They should be models of interdependent behavior. Tangible rewards for supportive behavior should be provided, and performance appraisal systems should include interdependent behaviors as part of the evaluation criteria.

Many organizations engage in health promotion and wellness activities. Given that supportive relationships are essential for health and well-being, education concerning the health benefits of interdependent relationships and ways to develop social support networks are important inclusions in health promotion efforts. Wellness activities that are group-oriented provide another avenue for helping organization members enlarge their support networks.

Conversely, counterdependent behavior should be discouraged. In the military trainee study, counterdependence and the resulting social isolation were related to poorer health. Counterdependence may be the natural tendency for some employees. Training that points out the adverse effects of counterdependence in terms of well-being and teaches interdependent behaviors is important. Practicing interdependent behaviors in team settings will help counterdependent individuals overcome their fears, doubts, and anxieties. Because interdependence is not the natural tendency for these individuals, they should be encouraged gently and reinforced for their efforts to become more interdependent.

Top management support is essential if interdependent behavior is to be sustained. Top management teams must display interdependent behavior and a commitment to reward and promote those employees who do likewise. As U.S. organizations move toward the team approach and empowerment of work teams, the behavioral strategy of interdependence and resulting reciprocally supportive relationships can help ensure the success of these approaches.

References

Ainsworth, M. D. S., Blehar, M. C., Waters, E., & Wall, S. (1978). *Patterns of attachment: A psychological analysis of the strange situation*. Hillsdale, NJ: Erlbaum.

Ainsworth, M. D. S., & Bowlby, J. (1991). An ethological approach to personality. *American Psychologist, 46*(4), 333–341.

Cannon, W. B. (1932). *The Wisdom of the Body*. New York: Norton.

Derogatis, L. (1977). *SCL-90-R Administration*. Baltimore: Clinical Psychometric Research.

Goldberg, D. P., & Hillier, V. F. (1979). A scaled version of the General Health Questionnaire. *Psychological Medicine, 9*, 139–145.

Grettenberger, J. O. (1992). *America's greatness—Past, present, or future?* Arlington, TX: College of Business Administration, University of Texas at Arlington.

Hazan, C., & Shaver, P. (1987). Romantic love conceptualized as an attachment process. *Journal of Personality and Social Psychology, 52*, 511–524.

Hazan, C., & Shaver, P. (1990). Love and work: An attachment–theoretical perspective. *Journal of Personality and Social Psychology, 59*, 270–280.

Hofer, M. (1984). Relationships as regulators: A psychobiologic perspective of bereavement. *Psychosomatic Medicine, 46*(3), 183–197.

Hofer, M. (1987). Early social relationships: A psychobiologist's view. *Child Development, 58*, 633–647.

House, J. S., Landis, K. R., & Umberson, D. (1988). Social relationships and health. *Science, 241*, 540–545.

Kobak, R., & Hazan, C. (1991). Accommodating working models in marital relationships: The role of attachment security and communication. *Journal of Personality and Social Psychology, 60*, 861–869.

Kobak, R., & Sceery, A. (1988). Attachment in late adolescence: Working models, affect regulation, and representations of self and others. *Child Development, 59*, 135–146.

Mason, J. (1959). Psychological influences on the pituitary adrenal–cortical system. *Recent Programs Hormone Research, 15*, 345–389.

Nelson, D. L., Quick, J. C., & Joplin, J. R. (1991). Psychological contracting and newcomer socialization: An attachment theory foundation. *Journal of Social Behavior and Personality (Special Stress Issue), 6*, 55–72.

Quick, J. C., Joplin, J. R., Nelson, D. L., & Quick, J. D. (1991, September). *Self-reliance for stress and combat*. Paper presented at the 8th Combat Stress Conference, U.S. Army Health Services Command, Fort Sam Houston, TX.

Quick, J. C., Joplin, J. R., Nelson, D. L., & Quick, J. D. (1992). Behavioral responses to anxiety: Self-reliance, counterdependence, and overdependence. *Anxiety, Stress, and Coping, 5*, 41–54.

Quick, J. C., Nelson, D. L., & Quick, J. D. (1987). Successful executives: How independent? *Academy of Management Executives, 1*(2), 139–146.

Quick, J. C., Nelson, D. L., & Quick, J. D. (1990). *Stress and challenge and the top: The paradox of the successful executive*. Chichester, England: Wiley.

Quick, J. C., Nelson, D. L., & Quick, J. D. (1991). The self-reliance inventory. In J. W. Pfeiffer (Ed.), *The 1991 annual: Developing human resources* (pp. 149–161). San Diego: University Associates.

Solomon, Z., Noy, S., & Bar-On, R. (1986). Who is at high risk of combat stress reaction syndrome? In N. A. Milgram (Ed.), *Stress and coping in time of war: Generalizations from the Israeli experience* (pp. 78–83). New York: Brunner/Mazel.

Weiss, R. S. (1982). Attachment in adult life. In C. M. Parks & J. Stevenson-Hinde (Eds.), *The place of attachment in human behavior* (pp. 171–184). New York: Basic Books.

21

Interventions for Building Healthy Organizations: Suggestions From the Stress Research Literature

Daniel C. Ganster

The belief that stress, and in particular, work stress, is a causal agent in physical and mental disorders, as well as organizational outcomes such as absenteeism and reduced productivity, has gained widespread acceptance. In particular, claims for "gradual mental stress," a workers' compensation term that refers to the cumulative emotional effects of exposure to primarily psychosocial demands at work, accounted for 11% of all occupational disease claims in the period 1981–1982 (National Council on Compensation Insurance, 1985). The general notion that prolonged exposure to "stressful" job demands can lead to a variety of pathological outcomes receives tantalizing support from a broad literature in behavioral medicine and epidemiology. Close inspection of the research investigating specific work-related factors, however, fails to produce a satisfying picture of how, or even whether, certain work experiences lead to physical or mental disorders.

Kasl (1986) has been an eloquent critic of this literature. Writing from a perspective of occupational epidemiology, Kasl has articulated better than anyone the methodological criteria that must be satisfied in order to reach conclusions about whether objective occupational exposures (e.g., to high levels of workload) are causally involved in the etiology of disease (e.g., coronary heart disease). In his view, existing research designs do not approximate closely enough this set of criteria to allow us to make causal inferences. Whereas Kasl's emphasis has been mostly on *how* work stress is studied, Brief and Atieh (1987) have questioned *what* is studied. Brief and Atieh concluded that the correlational evidence does not convincingly demonstrate that commonly measured work stresses (e.g., role conflict and ambiguity) are even strongly related to measures of subjective well-being outside of the work sphere, much less causally implicated. Their recommendation was that attention be shifted to particular types of stresses, specifically those related to economic issues, rather than the role stresses that have been so ubiquitous in this literature.

Whether work stress really costs the economy billions of dollars is debatable. Less debatable is the significant investment that the academic community continues to make in studying the issue. A perusal of this literature uncovered more than 300 published articles in just the past 10 years dealing specifically with work and stress. Such writings appear in the academic journals of a diverse array of fields, including psychology, sociology, engineering, public health, epidemiology, management, criminal justice, and law. Articles in the popular press and the trade journals contribute hundreds more to this figure. In addition, there are a number of review articles and books that cover various aspects of this literature (see, e.g., Ganster & Schaubroeck, 1991).

In this chapter, my primary aim is to provide a brief overview of the approaches that organizations might adopt in order to improve the well-being of their members. A second aim is to examine how these approaches might also reduce costs and boost the return on investment. This latter question has received much less attention than the employee well-being issue, but it has great implications for the organizational support of programs that might otherwise be seen as addressing "just employee well-being." This chapter is guided by the research literature, and I will focus mostly on issues that have received specific empirical attention in the organizational or health education literatures. There are many ways to classify the various approaches that organizations can take to reduce the effects of stress. I have rather arbitrarily chosen a structure in which to discuss this literature that is based on the variables most often addressed in the work stress research literature.

The first approach consists of worksite stress management and health promotion programs, and I provide a brief review of their impacts. The other approaches I have classified under the headings of (a) job redesign, (b) social support and supervision, and (c) role clarification. These approaches have generally not been the targets of actual interventions evaluated in any scientific way, although there are a few exceptions. They have, however, been the topics of much research in the organizational arena, and this research points to their viability as approaches for improving employee well-being.

Worksite Stress Management and Health Promotion

The general intent of programs in this category is to help individuals cope with demands that they face at the worksite or elsewhere. The interventions that are used vary widely but can be roughly grouped into (a) those that attempt to train individuals to better deal with work or general life stresses and (b) those that attempt to improve employees' general health. The latter type does not usually focus on work-related stressors but rather targets specific health-promoting behavior regimens such as smoking cessation, hypertension control, or weight reduction.

The first category, stress management interventions, has been the subject of much empirical evaluation. Early reviews of this literature (Murphy, 1988) cited the lack of experimental control in most evaluations of these interventions. Later studies (Murphy, 1988), however, gradually became more rigorous in their evaluation designs. Most of these studies (Murphy, 1988) have evaluated some program of stress management training. This training is usually delivered to groups of employees at the worksite and sometimes during work hours. Program content varies considerably but most often includes some attention to cognitive reappraisal, relaxation, exercise, and biofeedback. More recently, Murphy (1988) has discussed the potential of Employee Assistance Programs (EAPs) to provide counseling services to those suffering the consequences of high levels of work stress. Research evaluating these programs has been thoroughly reviewed (Murphy, 1988). This research suggests several conclusions:

1. Well-designed stress management training programs can produce relatively short-term changes in measures of psychological distress (i.e., anxiety, depression, and irritation), muscle tension, blood pressure and heart rate, and stress hormones.
2. There has been too little long-term follow-up of these interventions to conclude that the successful interventions have a permanent impact. Most evidence points to a deterioration of effects that implies the need for periodic booster sessions.
3. There has been little in the way of assessing the effects of stress management training programs on organizational outcomes such as absenteeism, tardiness, sick days, accidents, or productivity. Thus, it is difficult to estimate the financial impact of these interventions on the sponsoring organization.
4. Results from individual counseling or psychotherapy suggest stronger and more long-lasting effects on individual well-being and even sickness absence (Allison, Cooper, & Reynolds, 1989).

Stress management training programs, with their emphasis on training individuals to better cope with the stressors faced in the workplace, have been criticized on the grounds that they misattribute the responsibility for stress management (Ganster, Mayes, Sime, & Tharp, 1982). Because no attempt is made to reduce exposures to stressful job conditions, it can be argued that these programs put the responsibility for managing stress on the individual, who is expected to develop a better tolerance for noxious organizational conditions. Ganster and colleagues (1982) have argued that the best deployment of these training programs might be as supplements to organizational change efforts that *do* attempt to remove organizational stressors or in cases where stress exposures cannot be altered.

In addition to programs designed to train individuals to better cope with job stressors, many companies have adopted broader wellness programs that address a range of health-related behaviors. Some examples of these are the STAYWELL program developed by Control Data and the Live for Life program at Johnson & Johnson. These are broad health promotion programs that attempt to lower employee health risks through exercise, hypertension control, weight control, smoking cessation, as well as stress management. Reviews of these programs often report positive effects on the targeted outcomes. Fitness programs, in particular, have been shown to be effective in producing a broad range of desirable outcomes. Well-designed and administered programs are effective in improving the fitness levels of their participants. In addition, there is some evidence that fitness programs can reduce organizational health care costs (Shephard, Corey, Renzland, & Cox, 1982), improve self-concept, and reduce absenteeism and turnover (Belles, Norvell, & Slater, 1988).

There is also some evidence that physical fitness levels can moderate the effects of exposure to life and work stressors. For example, Csanadi (1981) observed that psychological disorders were related to both life and work stressors only among law enforcement officers who did not regularly engage in aerobic exercise. Although such evidence is strongly supportive of exercise programs, there is still the possibility that uncontrolled differences between exercisers and nonexercisers might account for some of the differences in outcomes. Also detracting from the generally positive review of exercise programs are the reports from several investigators that the relationship between exercise and psychological well-being is nonexistent or very small (Jex, Spector, Gudanowski, & Newman, 1991).

Overall, the evidence strongly favors adherence to consistent aerobic exercise regimens for improving individual health. However, evaluators have been less effective in demonstrating the cost–benefit ratio of these programs to the sponsoring organization. In addition, some have raised the issue that, despite the positive impact that wellness programs might have on individuals, it has not been convincingly demonstrated that the workplace is necessarily the ideal or most efficient site for the coordination and delivery of such programs (Kasl, 1986).

Job Redesign

Rather than put the responsibility for stress management on the individual employee, exposure to stressful work conditions might be reduced by the appropriate redesign of the work itself. Work redesign has long been advocated in the organizational behavior literature as a method of improving worker morale, motivation, and performance. More recently, attention has been directed at the health consequences of work design. Most of this attention has been inspired and informed by Karasek's (1979) model of job decision latitude. In its basic form, the model specifies two broad constructs that can vary independently in the work environment. Job *demands* are defined as psychological stressors such as requirements for working fast and hard, having a great deal to do, not having enough time, and having conflicting demands. It must be stressed that these are psychological demands and not physical ones. Thus, a fast and hectic work pace may impose physical requirements that lead to fatigue, but the stress-related outcomes predicted by the model are related to the psychological effects of this workload (e.g., the anxiety associated with the need to maintain the work pace and the associated consequences of failing to complete the work). Job *decision latitude* comprises two components: (a) the worker's authority to make decisions on the job (decision authority) and (b) the variety of skills used by the worker on the job (skill discretion). Operationally, these two components are combined into one measure of decision latitude, or control.

The first major hypothesis of the model is that "strain," which is a stressful condition that leads to mental and physical health problems, occurs when jobs are simultaneously high in demands and low in control. This hypothesis rests on the reasoning that high demands produce a state of arousal in the worker that would normally be reflected in such responses as heart rate or adrenaline excretion. When there is a constraint on the responses of the worker, as would occur under conditions of low control, the arousal cannot be appropriately channeled into a coping response and thus produces an even larger physiological reaction that persists for a longer time. The second hypothesis is that positive outcomes (e.g., motivation, learning, and healthful regeneration) occur when an individual occupies an "active" job, that is, one that has both a high level of psychological demands and a high level of control.

Although there seems to be a growing consensus that worker control is important for health and well-being (Sauter, Hurrell, & Cooper, 1989) and that the demands–control model provides a useful vehicle for studying control, two broad criticisms of the model remain. First, job decision latitude (control) combines a number of theoretically distinct constructs, and these are apparent in the operationalizations of researchers. For example, control measures have included such diverse indicators as (a) dealing with customers and the public (Haynes, LaCroix, & Lippin, 1987), repetitious or monotonous work (Haynes et al., 1987; Karasek, 1979), educational requirements of the job (Karasek, 1979), skill utilization (Sauter, 1989), and possibilities for ongoing education as part of the job (Johnson & Hall, 1988).

Such a broad inclusion threatens to make the control construct virtually indistinguishable from the more traditional conceptualization of stress as the imbalance between individual capabilities and environmental demands. Kasl (1989) and Sauter and Hurrell (1989) question what has been learned theoretically or practically by the model if control remains such a broadly conceived construct. Second, it is not always clear what is meant by the "joint effects" of demands and control. Karasek's (1979, 1989) discussion of the construct clearly reflects an interactive meaning, but how this translates into a statistical modeling of the interaction has been debated (Ganster & Fusilier, 1989; Kasl, 1989). These critics have concluded that the epidemiological evidence seems to support mostly an additive model of demands and control rather than an interactive one. Karasek (1989) has countered that the interaction formulation endorsed by the critics is too restrictive, and that indeed, job demands will have a different impact, depending on the decision latitude of the worker.

Tests of the model have been of two types. The most extensive efforts and generally the ones most supportive of the model have been large-scale epidemiological analyses that rely on occupational-level assessments of the independent variables (demands and control). These have been both cross-sectional and longitudinal studies. The other methodology consists of cross-sectional studies that relate, at the individual level of analysis, self-reports of demands and control to various stress-related outcomes. The epidemiological studies focus on coronary heart disease and associated risk factors (e.g., blood pressure), whereas the self-report studies generally focus on self-reported disorders (usually of an affective nature). Lately, a few of the individual-level studies have used either physiological outcomes such as catecholamine excretion (Ganster & Mayes, 1988) or behaviorally based outcomes such as sick days (Dwyer & Ganster, 1991).

Overall, support for an interactive demands–control model is mixed. The early studies (Alfredsson, 1985; Karasek, 1979; Karasek, Baker, Marxer, Ahlbom, & Theorell, 1981) were generally reported to be supportive of the model, but on closer examination, this evidence is difficult to interpret. For one thing, there is little evidence of a statistical interaction between demands and control variables that fits the predictions of the model. Second, a variety of other confounding factors—including both individual risk factors and other job characteristics such as physical exertion—potentially come into play in explaining the results of any given study. In addition, some of the later studies have failed to find any supportive results (Pieper, LaCroix, & Karasek, 1989; Reed, LaCroix, Karasek, Miller, & MacLean, 1989). As a whole, then, the large-scale, occupation-based studies using diagnosis of coronary disease or associated risk factors as criteria fail to provide convincing support for the model. The evidence from the individual-level studies is also mixed.

The job demands–job decision latitude model, despite its lack of clear-cut empirical support, will likely continue to exert a major influence on the field of occupational stress. A variety of methodological limitations have been discussed by reviewers of the model (Ganster, 1989; Kasl, 1989) as potential alternative explanations for supportive findings. However, many of these methodological issues might have also conspired against the theory. For example, just as ecological correlations (from the occupation-level studies) can lead to spurious inferences about the effects of individual-level variables, so can they also mask true effects. Aggregating individual responses to the occupation level is a very crude procedure that eliminates a great deal of true variability existing within occupations, thus making it very difficult to detect effects. Similarly, imprecision in the operationalization of the job decision latitude construct can mask real effects by incorporating irrelevant dimensions and neglecting relevant ones. Several authors have also suggested typologies that might lend more precision to the measurement of the control construct (Ganster, 1989; McLaney & Hurrell, 1988).

The demands–control model of job stress provides an appealing theoretical basis for organizational stress practitioners. First, it has a natural kinship with other organizational theories, particularly in the area of task design, with its concern for worker autonomy and utilization of skills. Second, the central proposition of the theory draws support from much basic experimental evidence in psychology that demonstrates the importance of personal control in explaining reactions to stress (Miller, 1979). Third, the theoretical mediation process involving chronic neuroendocrine and cardiovascular overarousal is a plausible explanation for the development of morbidity. Finally, the theory suggests a practical approach toward alleviating the detrimental effects of job demands that is not predicted to reduce productivity. In fact, the theory predicts that interventions increasing worker decision latitude can increase productivity through the enhanced learning and motivation that is expected to follow. Thus, despite the lack of uniform empirical support for the model, we recommend that organizational researchers continue to devise better tests of it.

The evidence is certainly strong enough to warrant the experimentation with job redesign interventions to improve employee well-being. Unfortunately, there are almost no evaluations of interventions in the workplace that are based on such job redesign models. Jackson's (1983) experiment found beneficial psychological health effects from a program that increased employee participation. Autonomous work groups are another means for implementing change in the nature of work and increasing worker control, but it has not been demonstrated that such approaches will produce measurable benefits in terms of employee health or organizational effectiveness. A large-scale quasi-experiment by Wall, Kemp, Jackson, and Clegg (1986) evaluated the outcomes from an autonomous work groups intervention. Although they found quite substantial effects on employees' intrinsic job satisfaction, the intervention showed no benefits in terms of work motivation or performance. Moreover, turnover actually increased as a result of the intervention. In summary, work redesign has a strong theoretical basis to recommend it as an approach for enhancing employee well-being. However, the translation of theory and basic research into effective interventions is proving to be a challenging task. Nevertheless, such interventions warrant careful and rigorous evaluation in large-scale organizational settings.

Another factor that merits consideration is the possibility that jobs high in decision latitude and other forms of complexity might not be healthy for all individuals. The idea that there are individual differences that moderate reactions to job characteristics has been investigated for a long time. Recent laboratory research, however, has found that Type A personalities respond with adverse reactions to certain characteristics of enriched jobs. This may have two important implications for job design recommendations. If increasing job complexity by enriching jobs is advocated on the grounds that this improves quality of work life, then any adverse health consequences stemming from enrichment need to be seriously considered. In addition, Barley and Knight (1992) suggested that stressor–strain correlations observed in job stress research are misleading because individuals are taught by organizations and the broader society to experience certain job characteristics as stressful. In a meta-analysis of hyperreactivity studies, perceptual–motor challenges were found to elicit the greatest cardiovascular lability among Type As (Harbin, 1989). A field study conducted by Campion and Thayer (1985) observed that perceptual–motor challenges characterized psychologically complex jobs. In fact, laboratory studies have found that increased task complexity is associated with higher levels of physiological arousal (Taylor, 1981).

For these reasons, one might hypothesize that Type A incumbents of complex jobs would more frequently manifest Type A behavior and thus suffer its health consequences to a greater extent than would Type A workers in less complex jobs or than Type Bs in general. This plausible interaction between Type A and job complexity led Schaubroeck, Ganster, and Kemmerer (1994) to hypothesize that Type A workers in complex jobs would suffer greater degrees of cardiovascular disorder than would Type As in less complex jobs, and greater levels than would Type Bs in complex jobs. They obtained interview measures of Type A behavior pattern and psychological and objective indexes of job complexity from a sample of 251 police and fire department personnel with sound cardiovascular health. They collected complete follow-up data on work satisfaction and cardiovascular health 7 years later from individuals who remained with the organization. They found that Type A behavior pattern predicted cardiovascular disorder over the time and that the relationships between the complexity measures and cardiovascular disorder were positive among Type As, whereas they were negative among Type Bs. Of further interest, they found that job complexity was related to ill health over time for Type As, and yet these jobs were found to be more satisfying than unenriched jobs in both the Type A and the Type B groups. These results therefore question the conclusion that job design factors that workers find pleasing necessarily improve the quality of work life, a premise that permeates the job design literature. Such findings reinforce the need to conduct careful evaluation studies of job design interventions that use measures of employee health as well as attitudinal measures. They also suggest that Type A and perhaps other personality factors need to be considered when these interventions are conducted.

Social Support and Leadership

The social support buffering hypothesis has been prevalent in the work stress literature almost since its inception. In their classic monograph, Kahn, Wolfe, Quinn, Snoek, and Rosenthal (1964) suggested that the quality of interpersonal relationships at work, or social climate, might temper a worker's response to role stress. However, the evidence of a social support buffering effect with regard to work stressors is decidedly mixed. In their review, Ganster and Victor (1988) found that there are more cases of no buffering or "opposite buffering" reported in the work stress literature than there are in support of the buffering hypothesis.

Despite the lack of support for the buffering hypothesis itself, however, there is much evidence that suggests that social support can play a significant role in enhancing the level of employee well-being. For example, Haynes and Feinleib (1980) reported that female clerical workers with unsupportive supervisors were much more likely to develop coronary heart disease than those with supportive ones. Matthews, Cottington, Talbott, Kuller, and Siegel (1987) found that the presence of supportive foremen and coworkers in male factory workers was negatively associated with diastolic blood pressure. In general, then, the evidence is very consistent in showing that social support in the workplace is associated with a range of psychological and physiological benefits. Unfortunately, there is simply a lack of evaluation research that shows how or if social support can be augmented in work settings and whether it would have the positive impact on well-being that the basic research literature suggests. Clearly, this is an area that has great promise, because the underlying evidence supporting the benefits of social support is very strong. Furthermore, social support is a factor that lends itself to incorporation into leadership and supervisory training programs.

Finally, the adoption of self-managed work team structures by many organizations also suggests that there are many opportunities to develop coworker support mechanisms as part of ongoing restructuring interventions. What is needed is for the intervention specialists who are facilitating team interventions to work with evaluation researchers so that it can be shown that social support variables do indeed increase the well-being of employees.

Closely associated with the social support construct is leadership or supervisory behavior. Worker reports indicate that supervisors' excessive demands and personal insensitivity are viewed as among the more critical daily hassles that interfere with workers' performance and create strain (Lazarus, 1981). As noted by Sutherland and Cooper (1988) in their review of the job stress literature, "Inconsiderate behavior on the part of the supervisor appears to contribute significantly to feelings of job pressure . . . and close supervision and rigid performance monitoring can be stressful" (p. 17). In fact, recently publicized litigation has extracted damages from companies on the charge that a supervisor in their employ was instrumental in the deterioration of a subordinate's health (Sand, 1990). It is therefore surprising that no research has sought to determine whether there are individual differences among supervisors that correspond to their undesirable behavior and which are in turn associated with important work unit outcomes.

The Type A supervisor would seem likely to create a stressful milieu for his or her subordinates. Levinson's (1978) concept of the abrasive manager, taken from anecdotal accounts, depicts an individual consistent with the Type A profile: condescending and critical of subordinates, obsessed with control and achievement, hurried, and impatient. As Levinson suggests, the abrasive person's drive and normally high intelligence may make him or her a valued employee, but maintaining a cooperative relationship with him or her may be difficult; as a superior, he or she may create an inordinate amount of stress for subordinates. Similarly, Jenkins (1979) described the Type A individual as egocentric, self-centered, abrasive, aggressive, and a poor listener. Studies of marital relationships reinforce this speculation. Type As and their spouses report more marital strain and conflict than do Type Bs and their spouses (Haynes, Feinleib, Levine, Scotch, & Kannel, 1978).

One would expect a hurried, impatient, driven, competitive, control-oriented supervisor to demonstrate a lack of consideration, to give subordinates little opportunity for discretion or initiative, and to fail to consult with them on work unit decisions. Rosenman (1986) also notes that Type As tend to develop and concurrently maintain an excessive number of ambiguously defined goals. Hence, one would expect subordinates to be given vague performance goals, and there might be an enhanced potential for the supervisor to relay incongruent role expectations to subordinates. Subordinates might also avoid attempting to increase their personal autonomy or seeking to clarify goals or role obligations in the expectation that such initiatives would lead to heated conflicts with the Type A supervisor. Nominal control over the work situation and lack of leader consideration and role clarification can be expected to lead to distress (i.e., health symptoms and psychological strain) and dissatisfaction with supervision (Ganster & Fusilier, 1989; Jackson & Schuler, 1985).

This evidence led Ganster, Schaubroeck, Sime, and Mayes (1991) to hypothesize that Type A leaders would have more distressed subordinates than Type B leaders. For similar reasons, they also examined trait negative affectivity (NA) and assessed the effects that both types of leaders had in terms of work group satisfaction, health, and performance. Contrary to what they predicted, Type A leaders had higher performing work groups than did Type Bs, but their subordinates reported higher levels of irritation, depression, and physical symptoms. High NA leaders had lower performing work groups and less satisfied subordinates than did low NA leaders. Thus, it appears that certain leader traits can be predictive of the well-being of work groups, and organizations might be advised to incorporate such measures in their hiring practices or use such personality measures as part of supervisory training and development programs.

Role Clarification

Some of the earliest writings on job stress (Kahn et al., 1964) highlighted the constructs of role ambiguity and role conflict. These variables have been among the most frequently studied in the work stress literature, and hundreds of studies have linked them to attitudinal, behavioral, and health outcomes (Jackson & Schuler, 1985). Although some have questioned the potency of these role stresses in explaining meaningful measures of employee well-being (Brief & Atieh, 1987), they continue to occupy the attention of stress researchers and figure prominently in recommendations concerning the improvement of working conditions (Murphy, 1988). In discussing the human and legal consequences of role stressors, Kahn (1987) noted that "the implicit assumption is that these characteristics of work roles reflect managerial decisions and choices, and that choices leading to less stressful role characteristics are feasible. Indeed, it is the argument of stress avoidability and management choice that makes these stressors subject to legal action and compensation payments . . . ." (p. 315). Bennis (1966) posed a provocative question in drawing implications from Kahn and colleagues' (1964) study: "What would happen . . . if we trained people to understand their role space more fully so that they could gain clarity in their work relationships through reducing excess conflict and ambiguity?" (p. 195). Role clarity and consensus is often viewed as essential for effective individual performance, and hence an intervention aimed at increasing it should be doubly attractive to practitioners. Despite the ubiquity of these constructs in the basic research literature, however, experimental tests of interventions that attempt to reduce them are very few.

Neuman, Edwards, and Raju (1989) conducted a meta-analysis of various organizational development interventions, but no role clarification studies were identified. I am aware of only three studies that evaluated interventions in this category. Dayal and Thomas (1968) described how a role clarification intervention, by anecdotal accounts, promoted employee communication in managing stressful demands in a case study of an engineering company. In a quasi-experimental design in which supervisors in a Canadian social services agency were trained in role emphasis, and efforts were made to reduce stressors by "promoting clear, consistent, and positive feedback; clarifying rules, policies, and roles," qualitative data indicated that the program was successful in reducing burnout among newly hired staffers (Burke, 1987, pp. 38–39). Finally, Quick (1979) tested a supervisor–subordinate interactive goal setting intervention in an insurance company. This intervention included much of the mutually investigative aspects of the role-making process typically attributed to role clarification. Significant decreases in role stressors, psychological strain, and absenteeism were observed to follow the training in the process. As Quick noted, however, there was little control of threats to internal validity.

Given the compelling theoretical reasons for implementing role clarification programs and the paucity of interpretable research regarding their efficacy, my colleagues and I recently set out to rigorously test an intervention whose aim was to reduce role ambiguity in the business services department of a large university (Schaubroeck, Ganster, Sime, & Ditman, 1993). We spent about a year and a half conducting in-depth interviews and group meetings and administered questionnaires throughout the organization in order to jointly (i.e., with managers and employee representation groups) arrive at a diagnosis of the high levels of felt stress. We then collaborated with employee teams to develop an intervention whose primary goal was to reduce the high levels of perceived role ambiguity. Using a responsibility charting approach, we started with the management team, ensuring that their roles and coordination of their functions was negotiated to a consensus. Then managers were randomly assigned to either (a) a "waterfall" condition, in which we helped them negotiate and clarify roles with each of their subordinates, or (b) a wait-control group. A professional consultant was hired to implement the intervention. In addition, the research team participated in all phases of the intervention and assessed the treatment delivery throughout the months of the intervention.

Our evaluation data were collected 6 months after the intervention had been fully implemented but before the control group was brought in for training. Based on these data, the intervention was clearly successful in reducing perceptions of role ambiguity, the primary target of the process. It also improved satisfaction with supervision. The stress outcome data were disappointing, however. The intervention had no measurable effect on subjective psychological strain, physical symptoms, or lost time due to illness. Although this is only one particular method of reducing role ambiguity, the intervention appeared to be well designed and implemented, because it clearly affected the processes it was designed to change. I believe that it points out the difficulty of demonstrating the impact of stress reduction interventions in ongoing organizational settings. The findings further emphasize the need to continue to develop and carefully evaluate interventions that are based on the underlying empirical findings in occupational stress research.

Conclusions

Despite a voluminous literature on the effects of various organizational conditions on the well-being of workers, there remain few examples of carefully controlled evaluations of interventions that aim to change the reputed underlying causes of stress and strain. The absence of such studies should not be taken to imply that too little is known to confidently recommend to managers that they undertake such interventions, however. The basic research provides a strong foundation and points to the types of interventions that would seem to have the most potential in improving employee well-being. There is much to be done, however, if organizational practitioners are to take these urgings seriously. It is one thing to conclude that role ambiguity is likely a cause of stress-related problems, but it is a far more difficult matter to design an intervention that effectively reduces role ambiguity and that becomes part of the ongoing management practice in the organization. Similar challenges exist with designing interventions addressing other factors that are known to affect well-being, such as control and social support. Unless interventions are rigorously evaluated, moreover, and results can be demonstrated for "hard" outcomes such as employee health care costs, it will be a difficult accomplishment to convince managers that they should invest in such interventions. This challenge presents an ideal opportunity for collaborative efforts between organizational development specialists, who are expert in the practical issues of diagnosis and intervention, and researchers who have the expertise to design evaluation studies. To me, this challenge presents more than an opportunity; it is a necessity if real progress is to be achieved in building healthier workplaces.

References

Alfredsson, L. (1985). Myocardial infarction and environment. Use of registers in epidemiology. *Acta Medica Scandinavia, 13*(Suppl. 698), 3–24.

Allison, T., Cooper, C. L., & Reynolds, P. (1989). Stress counseling in the workplace: The Post Office experience. *The Psychologist, 2*, 384–388.

Barley, S. R., & Knight, D. B. (1992). Toward a cultural theory of stress complaints. In *Research in Organizational Behavior, 14*, 1–48.

Belles, D., Norvell, N., & Slater, S. (1988). *The psychological benefits of Nautilus weight training in law enforcement personnel.* Unpublished manuscript, University of Florida, Gainesville.

Bennis, W. G. (1966). *Changing organizations.* New York: McGraw-Hill.

Brief, A., & Atieh, J. (1987). Studying job stress: Are we making mountains out of molehills? *Journal of Occupational Behaviour, 8*, 115–126.

Burke, R. J. (1987). Issues and implications for health care delivery systems. In J. C. Quick, R. S. Bhagat, J. E. Dalton, & J. D. Quick (Eds.), *Work stress: Health care systems in the workplace* (pp. 27–49). New York: Praeger.

Campion, M. A., & Thayer, P. W. (1985). Development and field evaluation of an interdisciplinary measure of job design. *Journal of Applied Psychology, 70*, 29–43.

Csanadi, S. B. (1981). *Physical activity and stressor–strain relationships in law enforcement.* Unpublished doctoral dissertation, University of South Florida, Tampa.

Dayal, I., & Thomas, J. M. (1968). Operation KPE: Developing a new organization. *Journal of Applied Behavioral Science, 4*, 473–506.

Dwyer, D. J., & Ganster, D. C. (1991). The effects of job demands and control on employee attendance and satisfaction. *Journal of Organizational Behavior, 12*, 595–608.

Ganster, D. C. (1989). Improving measures of worker control in job stress research. In J. J. Hurrell, L. R. Murphy, S. L. Sauter, & C. L. Cooper (Eds.), *Occupational stress: Issues and developments in research* (pp. 88–99). London: Taylor & Francis.

Ganster, D. C., & Fusilier, M. R. (1989). Control in the workplace. In C. L. Cooper & I. T. Robertson (Eds.), *International review of industrial and organizational psychology 1989* (pp. 235–280). Chichester, England: Wiley.

Ganster, D. C., & Mayes, B. T. (1988, August). A field test of the interactive effects of job demands and control on worker well-being. Paper presented at the annual meeting of the Academy of Management, Anaheim, CA.

Ganster, D. C., Mayes, B. T., Sime, W. E., & Tharp, G. D. (1982). Managing organizational stress: A field experiment. *Journal of Applied Psychology, 67*, 533–542.

Ganster, D., & Schaubroeck, J. (1991). Work stress and employee health. *Journal of Management, 17*, 235–271.

Ganster, D. C., Schaubroeck, J., Sime, W., & Mayes, B. T. (1991, August). *Unhealthy leader dispositions, work group strain, and performance.* Paper presented at the annual meeting of the Academy of Management, San Francisco.

Ganster, D. C., & Victor, B. (1988). The impact of social support on mental and physical health. *British Journal of Medical Psychology, 61*, 17–36.

Harbin, T. J. (1989). The relationship between Type A behavior pattern and physiological responsivity: A quantitative review. *Psychophysiology, 26*, 110–119.

Haynes, S. G., & Feinleib, M. (1980). Women, work, and coronary heart disease: Prospective findings from the Framingham heart study. *American Journal of Public Health, 70*, 133–141.

Haynes, S. G., Feinleib, M., Levine, S., Scotch, N., & Kannel, W. B. (1978). The relationship of psychosocial factors to coronary heart disease in the Framingham study II: Prevalence of heart disease. *American Journal of Epidemiology, 107*, 384–402.

Haynes, S. G., LaCroix, A. Z., & Lippin, T. (1987). The effect of high job demands and low control on the health of employed women. In J. C. Quick, R. S. Bhagat, J. E. Dalton, & J. D. Quick (Eds.), *Work stress: Health care systems in the workplace* (pp. 93–101). New York: Praeger.

Jackson, S. E. (1983). Participation in decision making as a strategy for reducing job-related strain. *Journal of Applied Psychology, 68*, 3–19.

Jackson, S. E., & Schuler, R. S. (1985). A meta-analysis and conceptual critique of research on role ambiguity and role conflict in work settings. *Organizational Behavior and Human Decision Processes, 36*, 16–78.

Jenkins, C. D. (1979). The coronary-prone personality. In W. D. Gentry & R. B. Williams (Eds.), *Psychological aspects of myocardial infarction and coronary care* (pp. 34–52). St. Louis: Mosby.

Jex, S. M., Spector, P. E., Gudanowski, D. M., & Newman, R. A. (1991). Relations between exercise and employee responses to work stressors: A summary of two studies. *Journal of Social Behavior and Personality, 6*, 425–443.

Johnson, J. V., & Hall, E. (1988). Job strain, workplace social support, and cardiovascular disease: A cross-sectional study of a random sample of the Swedish working population. *American Journal of Public Health, 78*, 1336–1342.

Kahn, R. (1987). Work stress in the 1980's: Research and practice. In J. C. Quick, R. S. Bhagat, J. E. Dalton, & J. D. Quick (Eds.), *Work stress: Health care systems in the workplace* (pp. 311–320). New York: Praeger.

Kahn, R., Wolfe, D., Quinn, R., Snoek, J., & Rosenthal, R. (1964). *Organizational stress: Studies in role conflict and ambiguity.* New York: Wiley.

Karasek, R. (1979). Job demands, job decision latitude, and mental strain: Implications for job redesign. *Administrative Science Quarterly, 24*, 285–306.

Karasek, R. (1989). Control in the workplace and its health-related aspects. In S. L. Sauter, J. J. Hurrell, & C. L. Cooper (Eds.), *Job control and worker health* (pp. 129–159). Chichester, England: Wiley.

Karasek, R., Baker, D., Marxer, F., Ahlbom, A., & Theorell, T. (1981). Job decision latitude, job demands, and cardiovascular disease: A prospective study of Swedish men. *American Journal of Public Health, 71*, 694–705.

Kasl, S. (1986). Stress and disease in the workplace: A methodological commentary on the accumulated evidence. In M. F. Cataldo & T. J. Coates (Eds.), *Health and industry: A behavioral medicine perspective* (pp. 52–85). New York: Wiley.

Kasl, S. (1989). An epidemiological perspective on the role of control in health. In S. L. Sauter, J. J. Hurrell, & C. L. Cooper (Eds.), *Job control and worker health* (pp. 161–190). Chichester, England: Wiley.

Lazarus, R. S. (1981, July). Little hassles can be hazardous to health. *Psychology Today*, 58–62.

Levinson, D. J. (1978, May/June). The abrasive personality. *Harvard Business Review, 56*, 86–94.

Matthews, K. A., Cottington, E. M., Talbott, E., Kuller, L. H., & Siegel, J. M. (1987). Stressful work conditions and diastolic blood pressure among blue collar factory workers. *American Journal of Epidemiology, 126*, 280–291.

McLaney, M., & Hurrell, J. J. (1988). Control, stress, and job satisfaction. *Work and Stress, 2*, 217–224.

Miller, S. M. (1979). Controllability and human stress: Method, evidence, and theory. *Behavior Research and Therapy, 17*, 287–304.

Murphy, L. R. (1988). Workplace interventions for stress reduction and prevention. In C. L. Cooper & R. Payne (Eds.), *Causes and consequences of stress at work* (pp. 88–114). Chichester, England: Wiley.

National Council on Compensation Insurance. (1985). *Emotional stress in the workplace: New legal rights in the eighties*. New York: Author.

Neuman, J. E., Edwards, J. E., & Raju, N. S. (1989). Organizational development interventions: A meta-analysis of their effects on satisfaction and other attitudes. *Personnel Psychology, 42*, 461–489.

Pieper, C., LaCroix, A., & Karasek, R. (1989). The relation of psychosocial dimensions of work with coronary heart disease risk factors: A meta-analysis of five United States data bases. *American Journal of Epidemiology, 129*, 483–494.

Quick, J. C. (1979). Dyadic goal setting and role stress: A field study. *Academy of Management Journal, 22*, 241–252.

Reed, D., LaCroix, A., Karasek, R., Miller, D., & MacLean, C. (1989). Occupational strain and the incidence of coronary heart disease. *American Journal of Epidemiology, 129*, 495–502.

Rosenman, R. (1986). Current and past history of Type A behavior pattern. In T. Schmidt, T. M. Dembroski, & G. Blumchen (Eds.), *Biological and psychological factors in cardiovascular disease*. New York: Springer-Verlag.

Sand, R. H. (1990). OSHA preemption of state criminal prosecutions, fetal protection, and workers' compensation for emotional stress. *Employee Relations Law Journal, 15*, 441–447.

Sauter, S. L. (1989). NIOSH studies of control and worker well-being: Moderating effects of job control on health complaints in office work. In S. L. Sauter, J. J. Hurrell, & C. L. Cooper (Eds.), *Job control and worker health* (pp. 91–96). Chichester, England: Wiley.

Sauter, S. L., & Hurrell, J. J. (1989). Introduction. In S. L. Sauter, J. J. Hurrell, & C. L. Cooper (Eds.), *Job control and worker health* (pp. xiii–xx). Chichester, England: Wiley.

Sauter, S. L., Hurrell, J. J., Jr., & Cooper, C. L. (Eds.). (1989). *Job control and worker health*. Chichester, England: Wiley.

Schaubroeck, J., Ganster, D., & Kemmerer, B. (1994). Job complexity, "Type A" behavior, and cardiovascular disorder: A prospective study. *Academy of Management Journal, 37*, 426–439.

Schaubroeck, J., Ganster, D. C., Sime, W., & Dittman, D. (1993). A field experiment testing supervisory role clarification. *Personnel Psychology, 46*, 1–25.

Shephard, R. J., Corey, P., Renzland, P., & Cox, M. (1982). The influence of an employee fitness and life modification program upon medical care costs. *Canadian Journal of Public Health, 73*, 259–263.

Sutherland, V. J., & Cooper, C. L. (1988). Sources of work stress. In J. J. Hurrell, L. R. Murphy, S. L. Sauter, & C. L. Cooper (Eds.), *Occupational stress: Issues and developments in research*. New York: Taylor & Francis.

Taylor, M. S. (1981). The motivational effects of task challenge. *Organizational Behavior and Human Performance, 27*, 255–278.

Wall, T. D., Kemp, N. J., Jackson, P. R., & Clegg, C. W. (1986). An outcome evaluation of autonomous work groups: A longitudinal field experiment. *Academy of Management Journal, 29*, 280–304.

22

Courses on Work Stress: A Growing Market, But What About Their Quality?

Irene L. D. Houtman and Michiel A. J. Kompier

In the Netherlands, work stress is clearly seen as a major health and safety issue, especially by the Dutch Ministry of Social Affairs and Employment (de Gier, Kompier, Smulders, & Draaisma, 1993). The Dutch government developed a broad legal framework with respect to both the physical and psychosocial work environment: the Working Environment Act, which is discussed later. Its Ministry of Social Affairs and Employment also developed a stress program aimed at the prevention of work stress, the development of instruments for stress monitoring, the identification of risk groups, information transfer, and so on.

At the request of the Ministry of Social Affairs and Employment and as a part of its stress program, Houtman and colleagues (Houtman, Dam, van Hessen, van den Heuvel, & Kompier, 1992) carried out a study to inventory, characterize, and assess the quality of courses on work stress, offered on the "open market," in the Netherlands. In this chapter, we will describe the study in detail. First, however, we will introduce a conceptual framework for stress prevention and intervention as well as discuss the background of the Working Environment Act and then proceed to analyze the results of the study in this context.

Stress Prevention and Intervention

Stress programs at the worksite can be classified into (a) those directed at changing corporate characteristics at the work environment that are stressful for employees and (b) those directed at changing employees, that is, teaching employees stress management or stress reduction skills (Leroy, Green, Mullen, & Foshee, 1984). Examples of the first approach are job design to improve working conditions, and increasing workers' control, for example, through

The authors wish to thank J. Dam, P. van Hessen, and S. van den Heuvel for their contribution to the study reported.

This research was granted by the Dutch Ministry of Social Affairs and Employment.

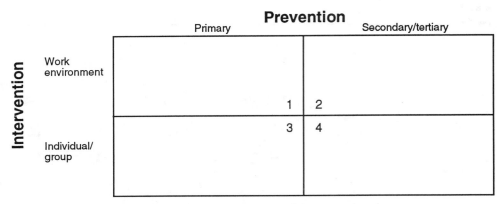

Figure 1. A framework for stress prevention and intervention.

employee participation in decision making. Those programs that attempt to reduce the strains evoked by stressors and those that aim to alter the resistance to stress on the part of the employee are examples of the second approach (Kahn & Byosiere, 1990).

As to stress prevention and intervention, another important distinction can be made, that between primary prevention on the one hand and secondary and tertiary prevention on the other. Primary prevention concerns interventions aimed at eliminating, reducing, or altering stressors in the working situation. Secondary prevention concerns approaches designed to prevent employees who already show signs of stress from getting sick and to increase their coping capacity. Tertiary prevention concerns treatment directed at those employees who show strong stress reactions, and rehabilitation after sickness absenteeism.

By combining those two main axes—changing work versus changing the employee and eliminating risks versus preventing conditions from becoming worse—a conceptual framework can be developed that indicates four types of prevention and intervention possibilities (see Figure 1).

Examples of first quadrant interventions are: (a) changing job content, such as by job enrichment; (b) increasing workers' control and participation; (c) changing work and resting schedules; (d) career development activities; (e) team building; and (f) social supports efforts within the organization.

Examples of second quadrant interventions are comparable measures, directed at those employees who already show signs of stress, such as special work schedules for older employees or workers recovering from a heart attack. Examples of third quadrant interventions are (a) personnel selection and (b) preemployment medical examination, health promotion, and wellness programs, such as corporate fitness and relaxation training programs. Measures from the fourth quadrant are often directed at individual employees with serious stress-related problems: (a) rehabilitation after sick leave, (b) posttraumatic stress assistant programs (e.g., for bank employees, police officers, or firefighters), and (c) response- or symptom-directed approaches such as relaxation techniques and psychotherapy.

The Dutch Working Environment Act

The Dutch Working Environment Act was enacted by parliament in 1980, but 10 years passed before it was fully implemented. This act aims at increasing the level of safety in the workplace and improving both the mental and physical health and the well-being of employees. This Act applies to all employed persons, both in the private and the public sectors, and in companies of all sizes. As to the language regarding the psychosocial aspects of the working situation—the well-being clause of this legislation—it is stated that:

- The employees should have the possibility to organize their own work in accordance with their own professional qualifications.
- The employees should have sufficient opportunity to determine their own work pace.
- Each employee has the right to be informed about the purpose and the results of his or her work.
- The employees should have sufficient opportunity to keep in contact with their colleagues.
- The workplace should be laid out in accordance with modern ergonomic principles.
- Monotonous and repetitive jobs should be avoided.
- Differences between the workers' personal characteristics, such as age, gender, physical and mental constitution, work experience, skills, and knowledge of the working language, should be taken into account.
- The safety and health hazards must, to the extent that is practicable, be prevented at the source.

It is stated in this law that the employer is responsible for the work environment. Employees also have a certain responsibility for their own safety and health, and they are obliged to cooperate on health and safety matters with their managers (Bayens & Prins, 1990).

It is clear that, in terms of the framework presented in Figure 1, this Act puts primacy on the first quadrant, that is, prevention at the source.

Courses: Education and Training

Information dissemination, education, and training can provide top-level management, middle management, first-line supervisors, and employees on the shop floor with basic knowledge and skills on each of the four types of prevention and intervention. Adequate monitoring is a *conditio sine qua non* for effective stress prevention and intervention. Education and training can also be directed to monitoring stressful situations and stress reactions. Worker education is needed, in particular regarding work and nonwork risk factors, recognition of individual signs, and organizational manifestations of stress and strain (Sauter, Murphy, & Hurrell, 1990). It is very important that top management recognize work stress as a major organizational issue and that it be willing to place resolution of it on the company's agenda. Courses on work stress can play an important role in management education as well. The study that we will now discuss was undertaken to (a) make an inventory of courses on work stress that were offered on the Dutch "market" of education and training and (b) assess their quality according to specific criteria.

Methods

Research Procedure

In the study (Houtman et al., 1992) to investigate courses on work stress, several efforts were undertaken to track them down:

1. *consulting experts* in the field of work, stress, and health, chosen from either an experimental/ergonomical, clinical, or organizational perspective;
2. *consulting institutions* that were known or assumed to have surveys on relevant courses; and
3. *advertising in relevant journals* in the field of work and health, human resource management, and education in practice.

Institutions were contacted in the period from October 1990 to February 1991. A course offered by the training institutions was selected for study when:

- it was still being offered;
- written information about the course was available (in brochures, curricula, etc.);
- its objective was to have the participants *learn* something (i.e., gain knowledge, insights, or skills);
- it was about work stress, that is, one or more of the following key words were present in the title or in the objectives formulated for the course: (work) *stress*; *mental, multiple*, or *psychological job demands*; *coping* or *stress management*; *relaxation* or *assertiveness training* (in relation to stress); (prevention of) *strain and burnout*;
- it was given on more than one occasion.

After selecting courses on work stress on the basis of these criteria, a questionnaire was sent to the training institutions, in which they were asked to provide information by which the courses could be characterized and assessed. The questionnaire was used as a framework for a telephone interview in which the training institutions were asked to elaborate on several of the questions.

Criteria for Characterization and Assessment

For characterization and quality assessment of the courses on work stress, both educational models (Earl, 1987; van Gelder as cited in Smuling, Brants, & Pilot, 1982) and stress models (Kompier & Marcelissen, 1990) were used.

Characterization of the course took place based on the following criteria:

- general characteristics (e.g., course length, costs, number of participants, number of times the course has been offered, year in which the course was first offered)
- objectives
- target groups
- course content
- method and form of teaching and teaching material(s)
- assessment of participants
- course evaluation

Assessment of the courses was based on whether the course objectives were described explicitly.

Furthermore, a course can contribute to stress management only when:

- it links up with the stress problems of the participants. This was operationalized by asking not only *if* this linkage was obtained in the course but especially *how* this was obtained (e.g., if instruments were used to identify stressors in the work situation, which instruments were used, and to what extent these instruments might influence the design of the course);
- it is structurally evaluated. Training institutions were asked how the course evaluation took place, if an evaluation report was written, and what was done with the evaluation results (e.g., if, in case of in-company training, the evaluation results were made available to the company).

Results

Participation of Training Institutions

The research procedure described resulted in a first contact with 50 training institutions. After selection according to the aforementioned criteria, 24 training institutions, offering a total of 28 courses, became participants in the study. Those training institutions were excluded that (a) did not provide written material (16 cases, a number of which appeared not to offer any courses on work stress; (b) did not offer courses about work stress as operationalized (5 cases); (c) did not offer actual courses but rather advice or project management services (2 cases); or (d) offered only a "study meeting" of one day (no regular course was offered; 2 cases). One training institution that initially agreed to

Table 1. General Information About the Courses

Characteristic	Mean	Range
Length of course (in hours)	21	3 to 49
Costs (in U.S. dollars per hour, per participant)	27	9 to 51
Number of participants		
minimum	9	5 to 12
maximum	17	8 to 100
Number of times the course is offered (per year)	14	0 to 100

Note. $N = 28$.

participate and sent written information about its course appeared to have no time to participate later on.

General Information About the Courses

The results suggest that the number of courses offered on the open market is growing fast. The "oldest" course was started in 1980. Three of the courses in the sample of the present study were about to make their debut in 1991. The number of courses offered in the period from 1989 to January 1991 is twice that of courses started in the period from 1980 to 1989. With the design of the present study, however, it is impossible to correct for the number of courses that have been offered for some time but have stopped since 1980, and for ephemerons. Almost half of the courses were *always* offered as in-company courses (46%), whereas 43% of the courses were *optionally* offered in-company.

In Table 1, some general information about the courses on work stress is provided. The large differences in the participation costs are shown: The costs per hour per person differed from 9 to 51 U.S. dollars. The length of the course differed from 3 to 49 hours.

Objectives

The courses could not be characterized very well with respect to objectives, nor to target groups or to course content. Although all training institutions formulated global objectives, for only 5 courses (18%) were these made specific into observable behavior and skills or assessable knowledge and insights that the participants were meant to acquire. When asked to set priorities in different types of objectives, the accent appeared to be on psychosocial and problem-solving skills (see Table 2). For 14% to 25% of the courses, however, no priorities were set by the training institutions (Houtman et al., 1992).

Target Groups

It appeared that most courses were directed at the management and the employees on the shop floor. When courses were directed at the employees, the

Table 2. Percentage of Courses for Which Several Types of Objectives Have High Priority

Type of objective	% of courses with high priority
Knowledge	21
Insights	61
Psychosocial skills	50
Problem-solving skills	54
Psychomotor skills[a]	11

Note. $N = 28$.

[a]Psychomotor skills refer to learning to manage stress by way of relaxation or exercise.

objective in 64% of the courses was to have them learn to handle their own stress. When the management was considered a target group, the objective was to teach managers to handle their own stress (71%) or to handle stress at a group level (i.e., the work stress to which their subordinates are exposed; 61%). Courses were less often directed at experts in the field of work and health or human resource management (32%) and representatives of employees (19%). Most courses were directed at more than one target group; only 5 courses (18%) were directed at just one target group. Four of these were directed at employees. All combinations of target groups for a course on work stress were mentioned in the responses.

Course Content

With respect to the course content, often no choices were made explicit. Most frequently, all possible topics for a course on work stress that were mentioned in the questionnaire were stated as part of course content. When the institutions were asked to assign priorities to the possible topics of the course,

Table 3. Percentage of Courses Addressing a Specific Course Content

Course content	High priority	Addressed but no priority	Not addressed
Directed at the individual			
Knowledge	21	64	4
Emotional skills	18	36	21
Rational thinking skills	39	39	11
Assertiveness	18	46	21
Time management	14	43	39
Relaxation	21	43	39
Fitness training	4	36	57
Directed at the work situation			
Job content	21	39	39
Work environment	14	39	43
Terms of employment	4	28	64
Social relations at work	7	36	50

Note. $N = 28$.

aspects concerning the individual were mentioned much more frequently as having high priority as compared to aspects concerning the work situation (see Table 3). The work situation was addressed, however, in a number of cases, but in most cases, this was explicitly *not* an aspect to be addressed in the course. No trend could be detected indicating that it was the more recent courses in particular that paid attention to the work situation.

In all courses, a linkage was said to be made between the stress problems of the participants and the objectives and contents of the course. In most cases, this was done by way of an orientation in the company (78%) or an individual intake (43%). In most courses, it remained unclear *how* the orientation or intake took place and *how* these were of influence to the course objectives and contents. In only 6 courses (21%) were instruments used to analyze the stress problems.

Teaching Materials and Participant Assessment

All courses used textbooks prepared by the company administering the course, and in 43% of the cases, published books and articles were used as well. In 10 courses (36%), the gain in knowledge, insights, or skills of the participants was assessed. Most of these assessments were said to be diagnostic in nature and had no further consequences for the participant. During most courses, the assessment was made by observing the individual and giving him or her feedback. Two courses also used multiple choice and open questions in the assessment. In several courses, the participants were said to be assessed during an apparently evaluative conversation, usually at the end of the course.

Course Evaluation

All training institutions evaluate their courses, one way or the other. For only about 50% of the courses, however, was an evaluation performed in a structured way. Most evaluations took place during conversations at the end of the course (79%). An evaluation report was written in only 46% of the courses. The evaluation was not always available for the person or company that paid for the course (only 36%).

Conclusions and Discussion

The present study suggests that courses on work stress constitute a growing market. Apart from courses on work stress, many courses on related subjects (e.g., human resource management) or simple advice on how to handle work stress appear to be offered. Other authors also have commented on this "flood of practitioner activity in the field of stress reduction and stress management" (Kahn & Byosiere, 1990, p. 572). Today, stress management seems to have become a booming market and an industry in itself. This market has been characterized by Martin (1992) as a market in which the most widespread demand is quick, low-cost training that quiets employees' complaints, if not their stress.

Characterizing the courses on work stress did not, however, appear to be an easy task. Most training institutions did not specify their objectives explicitly and did not make a choice for specific target groups and course content. The written material about the courses often was not very informative about these aspects. Even when explicitly asked, training institutions did not or could not specify exactly what the course should achieve, for which individuals, or pertaining to what topics on work, stress, and health. In cases where priorities were set with respect to course content, most often, aspects related to the individual (both the manager and the executive) were addressed, and less often, aspects related to the work situation.

Because the courses were difficult to characterize, the quality assessment of the courses was difficult. Although all courses were said to have made the linkage with the stress problems, specific to the participant, often the way by which this linkage was achieved remained unclear. Due to the fact that the evaluation of the course was often unstructured and oral, an evaluation report was not often written, and the evaluation was not always available to the person or company that ordered or required the course, we concluded that the quality of the courses was in question.

One of the reasons for the inability to characterize the courses on work stress might be that many institutions delivered or optionally delivered in-company training in which the course was explicitly directed at managing stress problems in a specific company. Training might then be directed to risk factors or risk groups to be identified in that company. In such a case, the need to be explicit about objectives, target groups, and content of the course, however, was subordinated to the need of being explicit about the way in which in-company risk factors and risk groups were identified and, consequently, specific objectives, target groups, course content, and perhaps even other measures were chosen for stress management. Many training institutions appeared to be not very explicit about the latter, either. Only few training institutions used instruments such as questionnaires, structured observational techniques, and the like to identify risk factors (and risk groups) that might (re)direct course objectives and content.

Placed against the framework for stress prevention and intervention (see Figure 1), it is clear that the emphasis was merely on changing the person (quadrants 3 and 4). There was no trend that the more recent courses paid more attention to the work situation. This might have been expected as a result of the Dutch Working Environment Act, which places emphasis on prevention at the source (quadrant 1 in Figure 1). As to the Dutch situation, this finding is in line with previous research from Marcelissen and colleagues (1988), who studied the amount and nature of preventive stress management programs in 14 Dutch companies, and with a recent study by Kamphuis and colleagues (1992). Most programs proved to be directed at the individual employee, and there were very few preventive programs that directly addressed stressors in the workplace.

Kahn and Byosiere (1990) extended this finding to the field of stress reduction and stress management in general, concluding that "advice or service for dealing with organizational stress emphasize methods intended to increase host resistance rather than to decrease the imposition of stress on individuals" (p. 572) and that "this activity (stress reduction and stress management) has been little informed by current research" (p. 572). Quick and Quick (1984) earlier arrived at the same conclusion: "There are virtually no studies which have examined the impact of the stressor-directed methods upon the consequences of distress" (pp. 275ff). Conclusions like these have stimulated the Dutch government to grant several national demonstration projects directed at stress reduction, reduced absenteeism, improved work quality, and a healthy work environment. In these projects, along the guidelines of the Working Environment Act, an integrated action program has been carried out combining measures from the four quadrants represented in Figure 1.

Recommendations

Recommendations on the basis of the results of the present study are the following:

1. Training institutions should pay more attention to monitoring and changing the work situation (e.g., demands, control, social support) and less to teaching individuals how to cope with stressors and stress symptoms. Stress is a broader issue than health promotion, and stress training must go beyond teaching "coping" or "tips to live by." The suggestion that stress can be adequately dealt with by coping makes stress trivial and blames the victims by implying that it is their responses to reality that are inadequate instead of aspects of that reality itself (Martin, 1992). More courses should be directed at reducing the presence of stressors at work instead of merely reducing the effects of stress. This strategy links up with the legal framework for stress prevention, provided by the Working Environment Act and also by the recent European Framework Directive on Health and Safety at Work. The emphasis in work stress courses should be more on how to manage stress in a structural, that is, stepwise way. This can be done by introducing instruments to signal and identify stress symptoms and stress risks in the work situation ("surveillance"). These instruments—checklists; interviews; questionnaires; and analyses of productivity, sickness absenteeism, and accidents (Kompier & Marcelissen, 1990)—may, for example, identify the presence of job demands such as the pace of work, monotony, conflicting task demands, stressors related to the working environment, terms of employment, and social relations at work, as well as lack of control possibilities with respect to these stressors. This can be done also by teaching managers or employees basic principles of action research, job redesign, and worker participation and by discussing successful examples of healthy work environments.

2. Training institutions should offer better information. They should be more explicit either about their choice of objectives, target groups, and course content or about the way risk factors and risk groups are identified and what that means for the course content.

3. The identification of stress risks and symptoms of stress should be structured with reliable and valid instruments (Kompier & Marcelissen, 1990).

4. Training institutions should evaluate in a structured way. These reports should be open to participants or the company that paid for the course. For evaluation of the effects of the course, the same instruments could be used that were used for the identification of stress risks.

5. Work stress courses should be directed at homogenous risk groups such as police officers, city bus drivers, nurses, and banking personnel. In this way, participants who face the same types of stressors would be selected. The work-related character of stress symptoms (e.g., sickness absenteeism, sleeplessness, headaches, fatigue) could be more easily and adequately understood. It often is an eye-opener for employees to learn that their stress symptoms are not so much signs of individual dysfunctioning or weakness but are rather—as often is the case—of a more collective nature, merely reflecting dysfunctional working situations. Effective coping mechanisms (e.g., time management, learning to set priorities, learning to say "No") can then more easily be discussed and taught. Also, the participants can be trained to develop a stepwise approach for preventive action ("action learning," Martin, 1992), for instance, discussions with coworkers and the course teachers. Such a plan could be directed at one individual ("Which steps am I about to make after I have finished this course in order to improve my working situation and to reduce the effects of stress?") or group directed ("Which steps do my colleagues and I have to make in order to make our working situation less stress provoking?"). There is a need for such training, especially among blue-collar workers. There is hardly a tradition, in corporate organizations or in labor organizations, for blue-collar education on stressors at the workplace.

6. Work stress courses should be directed toward persons with a specific role and responsibility in stress prevention and intervention: top and middle management, employees' representatives (e.g., unions), and occupational health professionals (e.g., occupational physicians, personnel department staff). The specific informational and training needs of these parties can vary according to their role and responsibilities but should encompass (a) recognition of work stress as an occupational health problem as well as an organizational problem, (b) understanding and monitoring of work and nonwork risk factors, (c) recognition and monitoring of individual signs and organizational manifestations of work stress, (d) reduction of stressful working conditions and personal risks, and (e) treatment of psychological disorders (Sauter et al., 1990).

Historically, the training of occupational physicians, labor inspectors, and ergonomists has disproportionally concentrated on physical and chemical hazards in the worksite rather than psychosocial hazards of work. Training and courses should provide these professionals with the tools for prevention and intervention. Training could also provide these persons with basic knowledge and experience with respect to principles of organizational change and participatory approaches based on the active commitment of several parties in the organization.

Companies and individuals looking for a course should not expect too much of a single course. For maximum effectiveness, stress training should be presented in the context of visible and institutionalized efforts—optimally, an explicit program—for stress abatement (Martin, 1992). They also should bear in mind that the choice of an intervention strategy in order to reduce work stress cannot be made without adequate monitoring of stress risks and symptoms of stress. Monitoring means systematically searching for risk factors and risk groups. Stress monitoring and stress prevention is primarily the responsibility of the employer. Often, it is stimulated by trade unions, representatives of employees, or occupational health professionals.

A successful approach chooses priorities based on (a) the impact of the risk, (b) the number of people at risk, (c) the possibility to attack the problem at the source (primary prevention), (d) the chance of success with the specific measure, (e) the amount of support in the organization, and (f) costs and benefits (Kompier & Marcelissen, 1990). Often, measures will be combined from all four quadrants shown in Figure 1. Courses on work stress *can* be an important part of such a program. For such a course to be successful, it should be integrated in a broader program, aiming at healthy work environments in healthy organizations. Without such an integration, there is a major risk that an "automatic" choice for a course on work stress will be the wrong medicine.

References

Bayens, G., & Prins, R. (1990). *The Labour Inspectorate and the quality of working life in the Netherlands*. The Hague, the Netherlands: Ministry of Social Affairs and Employment.

de Gier, H. G., Kompier, M. A. J., Smulders, P. G. W., & Draaisma, D. (1993). *Regulations, policies and practice on the prevention of work stress and the improvement of well-being at work: A comparative study in five European countries*. Leiden, the Netherlands: TNO Institute of Preventive Health Care.

Earl, T. (1987). *Cursusontwikkeling: kunst en vaardigheid* [Course development: Art and skill]. Almere, the Netherlands: Versluys.

Houtman, I. L. D., Dam, J., van Hessen, P., van den Heuvel, S., & Kompier, M. A. J. (1992). *Inventarisatie en evaluatie van cursussen op het gebied van werkstress* [Inventory and assessment of courses on work stress]. The Hague, the Netherlands: Ministry of Social Affairs and Employment.

Kahn, R. L., & Byosiere, P. (1990). Stress in organizations. In R. A. Dunnette & M. B. Hough (Eds.), *Handbook of industrial and organizational psychology* (2nd ed., pp. 571–650). Palo Alto, CA: Consulting Psychologists Press.

Kamphuis, P. L., ter Huurne, A. G., & van Poppel, J. W. M. J. (1992). *Evaluatie handboek werkstress* [Evaluation handbook of work stress]. Tilburg, the Netherlands: Institut voor Sociaal-weten-schappelijk onderzoek (IVA).

Kompier, M. A. J., & Marcelissen, F. H. G. (1990). *Handboek werkstress* [Handbook of work stress]. Amsterdam: NIA.

Leroy, K. R., Green, L. W., Mullen, K. D., & Foshee, V. (1984). Assessing the effects of health promotion in worksites: A review of the stress program evaluations. *Health Education Quarterly, 11*(4), 379–401.

Marcelissen, F. H. G., Madsen, M., & Schlatman, M. (1988). *Werkstress, voorkomen en bestrijden* [Work stress, prevention, and reduction]. The Hague, the Netherlands: Ministry of Social Affairs and Employment.

Martin, E. V. (1992). Designing stress training. In J. C. Quick, L. R. Murphy, & J. J. Hurrell, Jr. (Eds.), *Stress and well-being at work: Assessments and interventions for occupational mental health* (pp. 207–224). Washington, DC: American Psychological Association.

Quick, J. C., & Quick, J. D. (1984). *Organizational stress and preventive management.* New York: McGraw-Hill.

Sauter, S. L., Murphy, L. R., & Hurrell, J. J., Jr. (1990). Prevention of work-related psychological disorders: A national strategy proposed by the National Institute for Occupational Safety and Health (NIOSH). *American Psychologist, 45*(10), 1146–1158.

Smuling, E. B., Brants, J., & Pilot, A. (Eds.). (1982). *Orientatie op leren en onderwijzen* [Orientation to learning and education]. Utrecht, the Netherlands: Het Spectrum (AULA-808).

POLICY AND LEGISLATION

Introduction

The chapters in this section provide an overview of macro-level policy and legislative approaches to controlling job stress. Such approaches are controversial and have engendered considerable debate among the scientific, insurance, and legal communities. In the first chapter, Kohler Moran, Wolff, and Green provide a history of workers' compensation for occupational stress in the United States. Contending that the workers' compensation system in the United States is "out of control," they provide case examples of how companies have collaborated with an insurance carrier to reduce human and financial losses associated with workplace stress. Elisburg, in the second chapter, describes the complex challenges mental health experts face in dealing with workers' compensation issues. The third chapter, by Wiggins, makes the case for filling an important gap in the research literature: developing a diagnostic system for stress-related disorders. In the fourth chapter, Biersner provides an in-depth discussion of the process and potential for standards for occupational stress being developed under the U.S. Occupational Safety and Health Act of 1970. In the final chapter, de Gier traces legislative strategies in the area of occupational safety and health in Europe and makes recommendations for change.

Workers' Compensation and Occupational Stress: Gaining Control

Stacey Kohler Moran, Shelly C. Wolff, and James E. Green

There is a direct relationship between employer practices, disability management, and workers' compensation claim experience. Combating what many deem to be a "system out of control," some employers, in partnership with insurance companies, are taking control of their workers' compensation costs. This partnership has shown that effectively managing employer practices significantly reduces human and financial loss, resulting in a "win–win" situation for both employees and employers.

We begin this chapter with a synopsis of the forces shaping the present workers' compensation system. We then demonstrate a model under which employer initiatives can be used to control skyrocketing workers' compensation costs. Finally, we present data that show how this approach has helped employers gain control of the occupational stress factors that serve as the foundation of their workers' compensation costs.

The Workers' Compensation System: What Went Wrong?

Nearly 100 years ago, lawmakers established the workers' compensation system as a "no-fault system" to compensate injured employees. The system represented a trade-off: Employees would receive medical and lost-wage benefits for any injury incurred within the course and scope of employment. In return, employees forfeited the right to sue their employers for negligence.

For the majority of employees, the workers' compensation system works reasonably well. Statistics show that approximately 90% of injured employees return to work within 6 months (Wolff, 1990). However, those same statistics show that 25% of injured employees receive 75% of the benefits paid. This smaller group, many of whom miss more than 6 months of work, devour billions of dollars in resources annually. These costs continue to escalate, leading many to believe that workers' compensation is in crisis.

We would like to express our sincere thanks to Tim Fletcher and John Kamp for comments and suggestions on earlier versions of this chapter and to Cindy Wettschreck for help with the graphics.

The trends leading to this crisis are escalation of costs, an expanded definition of compensable work-related injuries, well-intended reform efforts with limited impact, and a system that has evolved from no fault to tort. We discuss each of these trends in more detail.

Escalation of Costs

Workers' compensation costs are soaring at a staggering rate—claim costs have more than doubled in the past 5 years (Berkowitz, 1990). The impact on a corporation's payroll can range from 3% to 6% (Schwartz, Watson, Galvin, & Lipoff, 1989) and up to 40% for some industry groups. Nationwide, workers' compensation costs range from $50 to $70 billion annually (National Council on Compensation Insurance [NCCI], 1991).

Although the reasons for this increase are many, the prime motivator continues to be unabating health care costs. In 1993, for example, the United States spent $884 billion on health care (The Universal Almanac, 1995). As a percentage of the gross national product (GNP), the United States spends more on health care than do other industrialized countries. In 1991, for example, the United States spent 13.2% of its GNP on health care, whereas Canada spent 10.0%, Germany, 8.5%, and the United Kingdom, 6.6% (U.S. Department of Health and Human Services, National Center for Health Statistics, 1991). Some attribute the high costs to the research dollars needed to develop new technologies, others attribute the costs to the privatization of health care, and still others theorize that until enough of the costs are shared with the patient and payer, costs will continue skyward. The workers' compensation system has felt the impact—its costs represent 5% of the total health care dollars spent in the United States, resulting in a phenomenal drain on an employer's resources (NCCI, 1991).

The Expanded Definition of Work-Related Injury

Over the years, the definition of *work related* in the compensation system has expanded considerably to include many illnesses not historically considered as such. Examples include cardiac disease, occupational stress with no physical injury, AIDS, cancer, and video display terminal (VDT) illness. Today, these illnesses consume a greater share of the cost burden. Additionally, because workers' compensation is the last type of insurance not mandating copayments, health care providers have begun shifting health-related medical problems into the workers' compensation arena. By doing so, providers circumvent "caps," or maximum annual costs, paid by health insurance.

Key to the expanding definition of *worker-related injury* has been the advent of occupational stress claims. Hurrell (cited in Bureau of National Affairs, Inc., 1992) defined work-related stress as "diseases of adaptation," which result in stress reactions ranging from anxiety to major depression. Among the states, California leads in compensable work stress claims: Seventeen percent of all lost time claims are due to mental stress (California

Workers Compensation Institute, 1990). Currently, several states accept mental stress as an industrial injury, whereas others have strong case laws clearly requiring that to be work related, injuries must have both physical and mental components. Several other states have inconsistent case law. Given this muddled picture, some employers are recognizing occupational-related stress factors as liabilities needing to be controlled.

Reform Efforts

Nationally, the dozens of efforts to reform and improve workers' compensation have had limited impact (NCCI, 1990). Some examples include the introduction of rehabilitation services, medical fee schedules, alternative legal methods for dispute management, and structured settlements. Each of these efforts focus on systems or professionals beyond the employee and employer. Rehabilitation firms were originally set up to function as a neutral party representing both employee and employer interests. In many states, rehabilitation activities are closely monitored by a state agency that sometimes delays expedient high-quality services. State medical fee schedules include only select medical services and therefore result in only a partial solution to the skyrocketing medical costs in workers' compensation. Once a claim becomes litigated, alternative dispute resolutions or structured settlements can help contain costs. However, the intent of the system was to remove workers' compensation from the legal environment.

The latest reform effort focuses on managed care as a means to control spiraling costs. Managed care, a combination of control strategies that review the quantity and quality of medical care provided to patients, have in some pilot programs decreased lost-wage claims by as much as 75% (Minnesota Department of Labor and Industry, 1992). Although at first glance impressive, managed care ignores the employee as a possible solution to the problem. One of the best ways to maximize efficiency and cost savings is through a comprehensive, integrated disability management program (discussed later in the Gaining Control Model section).

No Fault to Tort

The final trend leading to the workers' compensation crisis has been the degeneration of the workers' compensation system from no fault to tort. As mentioned previously, the workers' compensation system as originally constituted represented a trade-off: Employees were given wage loss and medical benefits for all work-related injuries in exchange for the right to bring negligence suits against their employers. This protection of employers from such negligence suits is called *the exclusive remedy doctrine.*

Legislative and case law changes, however, have made it much easier for an employee to directly sue his or her employer. One recent example is the July 1992 enactment of the Americans with Disabilities Act (ADA), which allows employees the right to sue employers directly for alleged employment discrimination. If an employee is not offered a modified job after being injured, he or she can bring suit for not complying with the ADA. The ADA requires employers to review reasonable accommodation possibilities with all employees who have had a disability. This should actually help employers save in workers' compensation costs by mandating this important return to work strategy. Unfortunately, the ADA represents the deterioration of the exclusive remedy doctrine. More significant and disturbing, it demonstrates how adversarial the workers' compensation has become.

The Root Cause of the Problem

Workers' compensation represents a tangled web frequently involving multiple professionals and systems operating under the cover of an adversarial environment. Figure 1 depicts a typical workers' compensation claim, in which the injured individual is bombarded by a number of people often asking for similar information but pursuing conflicting goals. The physician wants to keep the employee off work to maximize healing, whereas the employer wants to get the employee back to work in a light-duty or work-hardening capacity as quickly as possible. Added to the mix is the employee's attorney, who views the system's goal as one of maximizing the permanency settlement, which often entails extended recovery periods and testing.

Left in the middle is the injured employee, who, faced with these conflicting demands, feels confused and stressed. He or she may begin to wonder who to trust and believe, especially when given the seemingly conflicting information provided by second opinions and independent medical examinations. Given this, it is easy to see how some claims involving simple injuries can quickly become complex and, if poorly handled, evolve into cases of permanent total disability. The following example illustrates this scenario.

Isidro Rodriguez (not his real name), a 31-year-old employee at a Chicago-based regional bridge construction company, was a Mexican immigrant who had been in this country for 8 years. While unloading cement, Isidro caught his dominant hand between a wheelbarrow and a piece of equipment. A traumatic amputation of his ring finger resulted. Surgery to reattach the finger proved unsuccessful. During the estimated 6 weeks of recovery, Isidro developed psychological complications because of the disfigurement, and eventually he developed reflex sympathetic dystrophy, a complicated and difficult-to-treat pain cycle with accompanying physical symptomatology.

Despite extensive psychological and physical treatment, Isidro was still out of work 3 years after the accident. At this point, Isidro continued to seek treatment and remained totally disabled, according to his doctor. Because of the lack of medical progress, the length of time off work, and lack of transferable skills into a less physically demanding job, it was unlikely Isidro would ever return to work. This claim then became defined as a permanent total disability claim with guaranteed lifetime medical and wage loss benefits. The original estimate of $11,000 for the claim had escalated to an estimated $1.3 million under Illinois workers' compensation law.

What went wrong? No single entity should be blamed; rather, the entire

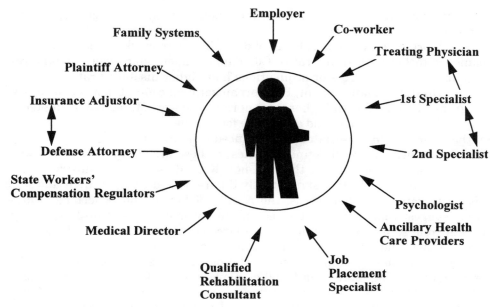

Figure 1. Workers' compensation web.

system should be indicted. The medical team failed to recognize early symptoms of delayed recovery and significant psychological stress reaction to the disfigurement. The employer ignored the cultural issues that would complicate Isidro's recovery and had few procedures in place to effectively manage the employee and his injury. Finally, the employer abandoned the claim to its insurance carrier, who proved unsuccessful in getting control of it. How much influence can employers have over this process? As we suggest in the next section, employers are critically important.

Employer Research

Researchers know that employer practices and policies affect both the frequency and severity of claims. In 1989, researchers at Columbia University Graduate School of Business conducted an extensive study aimed at identifying organizational characteristics that would best predict the number of lost-time days due to occupational (and nonoccupational) illnesses and injuries. Using a combination of research review, case studies, and data gathered from 77 companies employing approximately 700,000 workers, they found that four human resource policy variables were directly related to the frequency and length of disability (Lewin & Schecter, 1991):

1. Employee participation: Employee involvement programs such as information sharing, scope of involvement in decision making, and the availability of profit sharing with employees were associated with fewer claims.

2. Conflict resolution: Disability rates were lower when effective avenues

for conflict resolution were available and when mechanisms existed for airing conflict openly.

3. Workforce experience: Rates of disability were markedly lower in companies with lower turnover rates. Companies undergoing severe layoffs, reorganizations, or mergers or acquisitions had higher disability rates.

4. Disability management: High organizational commitment to disability programs correlated with higher rates of return to work. Effective lifting techniques, health promotion, and assistance for disabled employees were also part of the interventions associated with reduced disability rates.

Companies with well-defined policies in these areas experienced a lower rate of disability than those that did not. Regardless of the industry, these four organizational factors significantly differentiated between high and low disability rates. In other words, the results of Lewin and Schecter's (1991) study suggest that any industry seeking to lower its rates of disability may benefit from scrutinizing its human resource policies on these four factors.

Another study underscores the control that employers can have over disability and ultimately employee stress claims. Sponsored by the State of Michigan and including more than 5,000 employers, Habeck, Leahy, Hunt, Chan, and Welch (1991) reviewed the workers' compensation results by identifying the factors that differentiate the best and worst organizations within each industry (Standard Industrial Classification [SIC] code) group. The findings substantiate the Columbia study discussed earlier in which management practices largely influenced disability results.

The Habeck et al. (1991) study showed two key findings: First, the worst organizations had at least 10 times as many claims as the best in each industry group. Second, the cause for high disability rates were related mainly to internal company practices and policies over which an employer has control. This is particularly enlightening given that the study compared similar industries operating under the same state workers' compensation statute.

The research also showed that low-loss organizations were strongly committed to safety and accident prevention; had a progressive disability prevention and management program; and maintained a positive management and culture. High-loss organizations had less active safety, health, and disability programs; showed a greater likelihood of poor labor–management relations; displayed a controlling management style; devoted limited management to employee communications; and had a record of high employee turnover.

As the results of these studies indicate, workers' compensation costs and associated occupational stress can be managed through integrated employer-driven initiatives. In fact, although some of the cost drivers were external to employers, the most important determinants were within the organization itself and its management practices.

Gaining Control: Individuals, Employers, and the Socioeconomic Environment

Three main factors influence the outcome of workers' compensation claim costs and associated occupational stress: the individual, the employer and work

environment, and the socioeconomic environment. These three systems interact with one another to ultimately influence a claim's outcome. A detailed look
at each level illustrates how this multilevel approach to managing occupational
stress can benefit both employer and employee.

Individuals

Each individual brings to the work environment a unique set of skills, motivations, and interests. Because of this, loss control strategies must not only
be built as a set of best practices but allow the employer flexibility to respond
to the unique needs each disability situation presents. Management practices
must be applied consistently to maximize effectiveness and ensure that all
employees are treated fairly.

Bigos et al. (1991) conducted a study that showed just how important
psychological factors can be in claim experience. Their prospective study demonstrated that an employee's motivation and work perceptions significantly
affected the outcome of claim activity. The study of 3,020 aircraft employees
identified risk factors for reporting back pain at work. Results show that
employees who "hardly ever" enjoyed their job were 2.5 times more likely to
report a back injury than were employees who "almost always" enjoyed their
job. Therefore, understanding each employee's psychological makeup and perceptual reaction to his or her job is just as important, and sometimes more
important, than knowing the specific physical diagnosis and treatment.

The complexity of the workers' compensation system can cause an injured
employee to feel overwhelmed and powerless. When employees do not get the
information they need or begin to mistrust individuals in the system, they will
often go outside the work environment to get answers. Frequently, the only
known source is an attorney. When this happens, the cost of the claim usually
doubles (NCCI, 1992). For this reason, employers must focus their programs
on minimizing employee confusion and maximizing the support and information given to employees.

Employers

Employers can leverage their relationship with employees through a structured disability management program to ensure that employees get the most
effective medical treatment for a quick return to work. The frontline supervisor
is the most influential key to any program's success. Well-trained supervisors
who learn to deal effectively with an accident before and after it occurs can
make a significant difference in a claim. Too often, frontline supervisors cause
the process to fall apart right from the beginning. A common example illustrates this: An employee sustains an injury and reports it immediately to his
or her supervisor. The supervisor may say, "There goes my safety program,"
leading the employee to feel angry and alienated. Already, an adversarial tone
between employer and employee has been set.

Supervisors not only affect subordinate job performance but also employee burnout. The results of two recent studies show that employees who had a supportive supervisor reported a significantly lower rate of burnout (Kohler & Kamp, 1992; Northwestern National Life Insurance Company, 1992). Supervisors can have a major effect on reducing employee stress by empowering employees and reducing overtime requirements. Supportive supervisors who delegate control over the job give employees the ability to take action to solve problems. The St. Paul Fire and Marine Insurance Company study (Kohler & Kamp, 1992) showed that employees with supportive supervisors reported lower absenteeism, lower rates of burnout, work units that emphasized quality, and higher productivity, and the company adjusted well to change.

The Northwestern National Life Insurance Company (1992) research also found that companies who complied with the following suggestions had higher morale and productivity plus lower employee illness and turnover than companies that did not: (a) allow employees to talk freely with one another, (b) reduce personal conflicts on the job, (c) give employees adequate control over how they do their work, (d) ensure adequate staffing and expense budgets, (e) talk openly with employees, (f) support employees' efforts, (g) provide competitive personal leave and vacation benefits, (h) maintain current levels of employee benefits, (i) reduce the amount of red tape for employees, and (j) recognize and reward employees for their accomplishments and contributions.

Employers who maintain a positive working relationship with their employees, train supervisors well on all aspects of managing disability, and keep employee disability management a corporate priority will be the most successful. They will also achieve a return on investment for their most important corporate asset: employees.

The Socioeconomic Environment

Once a claim reaches this level, the cost of the claim becomes significant. The system outside the immediate individual and employer environment can be, and often does, increase costs and confusion. These outside systems include the legal community, government regulators, and laws that cause delays and confusion for both employee and employer. In addition, conflicting opinions from health care providers, rehabilitation professionals, and the psychological community can also cause alienation, confusion, and added costs to the workers' compensation process.

Unless an employer has practices in place to engender trust with its employees, claim costs will escalate, irrespective of injury severity. The system factors, once pushed out into a legal interpretative environment, create multilevel confusion for all parties, causing the employee to be a victim of the process.

We know from research and experience that the most effective way to control workers' compensation costs is through integrated employer-driven initiatives. Next, we take a historical look at loss control strategies and present case examples of how some companies have successfully joined with their insurance carrier for a creative approach to controlling their losses.

Comprehensive Loss Control Strategies

Historically, loss control efforts focused primarily on the physical working environment, for example, by ensuring that machinery was safety guarded and in proper working condition. Even when equipment was inspected and tagged as safe, however, injuries still occurred.

Loss control strategies were then expanded to include training in job procedures. By arming employees with effective procedures for completing their work, such as proper lifting techniques and defensive driving, loss control specialists sought to reduce the number of accidents, injuries, and errors. However, experience has taught us that even well-trained employees working in safe environments can still be involved in a loss. Thus, to truly succeed, loss control strategies must become more comprehensive.

The missing link between these traditional safety approaches and losses is the *human factor*. The notion is that "things don't cause losses—people do." The human element in losses includes, for example, not following procedures, risk taking, preoccupation or distraction, alcohol or drug impairment, fatigue, and poor communication.

The St. Paul Fire and Marine Insurance Company has a department dedicated solely to studying and consulting in the third side of this risk management triangle, the human factor. The model guiding much of our work includes three general categories of human risk factors: *workplace stressors*, *personal stressors*, and *lifestyle risks*. The amount of *strain* employees feel is a function of their perceptions and reactions to the risk factors in these three general categories. High employee strain, in turn, leads to *losses*, both for the employee and his or her organization.

To assist organizations in managing the human element in loss, St. Paul Fire and Marine Insurance Company developed an employee survey, the Human Factors Inventory (HFI).[1] The HFI is a 130-item perception and attitude survey that employees complete anonymously. Items are grouped into 15 scales that assess work stress, personal stress, lifestyle practices, employee strain, and organizational losses. Survey responses are sent to St. Paul Fire and Marine for analysis, interpretation, and recommendations. Item- and scale-level results overall, as well as for work groups or job classifications, are presented in a client report. Further description of the HFI scales is provided in Table 1. Thus, the HFI is a comprehensive employee survey that assesses both on-the-job and off-the-job human risk factors that affect employee well-being and organizational performance.

Hundreds of organizations have used the HFI over the past 10 years. As the following examples demonstrate, scores on the HFI do relate to a company's actual workers' compensation claim experience. Higher (i.e., more unfavorable) HFI scores are associated with worse claim experience.

---

[1] For information on revisions to the HFI, write to Human Factors Services, St. Paul Fire and Marine Insurance Co., 385 Washington St., MC 505E, St. Paul, MN 55102-1396.

Table 1. Human Factors Inventory (HFI) Scale Categories and Scale Definitions

Scale categories	Scale definitions
Work stressors	
Workload	Level of job demands
Challenge	The amount of stimulation and challenge employees get from their job
Supervision	Quality of guidance and support provided by supervisors
Working relations	Quality of employees' relations with coworkers and customers
Personnel practices	Perceived adequacy and fairness of pay, benefits, promotions, and so on
Organizational culture	Level of communication, flexibility, and employee input
Personal life stressors	The one HFI scale in this category inquires about various personal problems an employee may have experienced over the past year (e.g., relationships, illness or death of a loved one, dependent care, and finances)
Lifestyle risks	
Stress management	Stress management skills such as time management strategies and relaxation practices
Health practices	Employee lifestyle behaviors (e.g., exercise, smoking, diet) that affect health
Substance use	Drinking and drug use behavior at and away from work
Employee strain	
Job satisfaction	Employees' overall job satisfaction and desire to stay
Stress emotions	Amount of tension, worry, fatigue, etc., that employees feel at work
Physical health	Amount of stress-related health symptoms that employees report
Organizational losses	
Department performance	Perceptions of department productivity, safety, quality, and customer satisfaction
Employee conduct	Employee respect for company rules and property

Case example: copy machine company. The first example involves a nationwide copy machine distributor headquartered in the Northeast. The company surveyed 22 of its locations with the HFI in 1992. For our study, we looked only at those locations with an employee participation rate of at least 60%, which reduced our sample to 18 locations. Three of these locations each had three or more claims totaling $30,000 or more ("high-claim experience"). By contrast, 15 locations had a "low-claim experience" of two or fewer claims totaling less than $2,000. In all cases, the high-claim locations had more unfavorable HFI scale scores. The 13-percentile-point difference between the two groups on their overall HFI score was associated with a marked difference in frequency and severity of workers' compensation claims.

Similar to the research sponsored by the State of Michigan, this example demonstrates that organizational and employee-related factors differentiate organizations (or locations of one organization) with high- and low-loss claim experience. Identifying high-risk locations of a company, or high-risk areas (e.g., work overload) within one location, is only the first step in managing human risks. Success in preventing losses requires efforts directed at managing and reducing these risks. The next case study illustrates how an organization successfully acted on its HFI results to reduce its workers' compensation costs.

Case example: transfer and storage company. Six locations of a southern storage and transfer company completed the HFI. Several areas of high risk were identified, including high levels of personal life problems, employee counterproductivity, low morale, alcohol and drug use, and problems caused by excessive VDT use. In response, the company launched multiple programs aimed specifically at these risk areas. They shared HFI results with all employees, began holding regular meetings to communicate important information to employees, and sought employee input in work processes, safety, and other issues. The company implemented a more thorough, formal hiring process, installed video glare screens to reduce eye strain, and offered workshops on VDT and other work stress issues. A second administration of the HFI 2 years later showed the results of the company's efforts. Not only did HFI scores decrease significantly, but the company also realized a 55% decrease in workers' compensation claims and an 88% reduction in driving accidents.

Finally, we take an in-depth look at one company that implemented many innovative employee-focused strategies resulting in a significant reduction of the frequency and severity of their workers' compensation losses.

An In-Depth Look: Justin Industries, Inc.

Justin Industries, Inc., is a diversified manufacturing company based in Fort Worth, Texas. The company employs approximately 4,600 people who are involved in the manufacture of western footwear and building materials. The company's manufacturing facilities are located in seven states and are scattered in approximately 40 cities.

In the late 1980s, Justin, like many other employers, was experiencing a rapid increase in the cost of on-the-job injuries. From 1987 through 1990, the company's cost for worker-related injuries more than doubled even though the company had ceased operations in one of its most hazardous building materials industries. It was clear that steps had to be taken to gain control of this serious problem.

The company recognized that an employee who was injured on the job was affected beyond the physical nature of the injury. The injury also disrupted the employee's emotional and personal life away from the job. Production employees' work lives are highly predictable. They are told when to come to work, when to go home, when to take breaks, and sometimes when they can take a vacation. Their personal lives often become bound by the restrictions created by this regimentation. Along with predictability, this lifestyle promotes stability and comfort. An employee who is disabled, even temporarily, finds this predictability disrupted. Whereas before the injury the employee would almost always know where and what he or she would be doing at any given day and time, the employee now finds himself or herself in the midst of uncertainty.

The family of the injured worker is similarly affected. The spouse wonders if the injured worker's job is secure. The couple wonder who will pay the medical bills and who will provide the income necessary to support the family. They may even wonder if the injured worker will ever return to work. Children are sometimes confused by the presence of the parent at home during working hours. They also may harbor concerns about the family's financial condition. All of these issues create stress and uncertainty for the injured worker.

One factor that was obvious from a review of Justin's injury claims was that more and more employees were represented by counsel as their claims were processed through the various industrial accident boards. It was estimated that approximately 90% of the "compensable" claims had attorney involvement. The company believed that addressing the full range of issues facing an injured worker might reduce the need for the worker to seek advice from parties extraneous to the employee disability system. Procedures were developed to allow the company to immediately take the lead in controlling any employee injury.

Among the first steps taken was to require the injured worker's supervisor to provide transportation to and from the clinic and to stay with the employee while waiting for treatment. Supervisors were instructed to speak directly with the treating physician to make certain that accurate information had been provided regarding the nature of the employee's injuries and the working conditions at the workplace. The supervisor also was instructed to take responsibility for getting prescription drug orders filled and to make certain that the employee fully understood how and when to take the medication. Every effort is taken to define limitations placed on the injured worker and to identify a job the employee can perform within those limitations.

Immediately after medical treatment is completed, both the employee and the supervisor are expected to complete a report describing the accident, the nature of the injuries, and any measures that could be taken to prevent a recurrence of the accident. The employee's report of on-the-job injury is intended to make the injured worker a part of the accident investigation process, thus making the employee accept some responsibility for his or her own involvement in the accident. The report form also contains a declaration, signed by the employee, that the information provided is correct and accurate.

These reports, along with the employer's first report of injury, are immediately transmitted to a company claims coordinator, whose job is to monitor the claim on a daily basis until the employee is released to return to work without limitations. The claims coordinator makes contact with the injured worker as soon as possible. It is the claims coordinator's responsibility to provide accurate and timely information to the employee regarding his or her injury, the workers' compensation process, and the involvement of the insurance company and to address any other questions or concerns expressed by

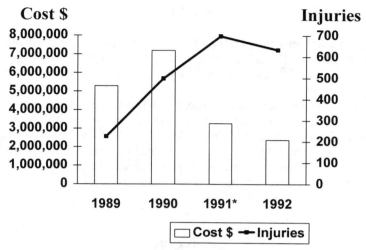

Figure 2. Justin Industries, Inc. *$p < .05$.

the employee. The claims coordinator sends a letter to the injured worker's residence explaining the steps that will occur as the claim proceeds and provides the employee with a toll-free phone number to call in the event the employee or his or her family have any questions. It is the stated goal of the claims coordinator program that no injured worker or a member of his or her family should go to bed at night with any unanswered questions regarding the injury, the treatment, or the job.

Claims coordinators also work closely with the injured worker's plant manager to identify alternative work assignments within the employee's limitations. The claim coordinator also works with the insurance company's claims adjuster to make certain that disability payments are processed promptly and the treating physician defines limitations, coordinates rehabilitation, and sets follow-up appointments. The goal of this process is to remove as much stress from the employee as possible and to facilitate a quick return to work.

Justin's beginning-to-end claims control program has produced dramatic results. The number of lost-time accidents has been reduced, as has the average number of lost-time days per accident. Attorney involvement has dropped from an estimated 90% to approximately 11%. And the cost of employee injuries has gone from $7.2 million in 1990 to $2.4 million in 1992 (see Figure 2).

Without a doubt, Justin has benefited from the reform legislation that went into effect January 1, 1991, in Texas. However, the company has experienced similar results in the other states in which it operates. The Justin program is not unique or new. It is a composite of cost-containment programs that has been implemented by various employers all over the United States. It has been successful because it has the commitment of top management and local plant managers alike. It has been effective because the focus is not on cost but on the employee.

Conclusions

The workers' compensation system, in its current form, is clearly out of control. Fragmented reform efforts have proved to be ineffective. In addition, employers have historically looked externally for solutions to their workers' compensation problems.

Current research and companies' practical experience demonstrate the significant amount of influence employers can have on the system. The case examples presented in this chapter demonstrate how some companies have teamed up with an insurance carrier to reduce their human and financial losses. Employers who cultivate strong management practices focused on the employee have created a win–win situation reducing employee stress and workers' compensation costs.

References

Berkowitz, M. (1990). Should rehabilitation be mandatory in workers' compensation programs? *Journal of Disability Policy Studies, 1,* 63–80.

Bigos, S. J., Battie, M. C., Spengler, D. M., Fisher, L. D., Fordyce, W. E., Hansson, T. H., Nachemson, A. L., & Wortley, M. D. (1991). A prospective study of work perceptions and psychosocial factors affecting the report of back injury. *Spine, 1,* 1–7.

Bureau of National Affairs, Inc. (1992, April 13). *Job-related stress blamed for many workplace injuries.* Washington, DC: Author.

California Workers Compensation Institute Bulletin. (1990, November 15). San Francisco, CA: Author.

Habeck, R. H., Leahy, M. J., Hunt, H. A., Chan, R., & Welch, E. M. (1991). Employer factors related to workers' compensation claims and disability management. *Rehabilitation Counseling Bulletin, 34,* 210–227.

Kohler, S., & Kamp, J. (1992). *American workers under pressure* (Tech. Rep.). St. Paul, MN: St. Paul Fire and Marine Insurance Company.

Lewin, D., & Schecter, S. (1991). Four factors lower disability rates. *Personnel Journal, 3,* 99–103.

Minnesota Department of Labor and Industry. (1992). *Managed care pilot.* Unpublished report, State of Minnesota. (Write to Minnesota Dept. of Labor and Industry, 443 Lafayette Rd., St. Paul, MN 55101.)

National Council on Compensation Insurance. (1990, December). Cost containment. *Digest, 4,* 24–49.

National Council on Compensation Insurance. (1991). *Issues report, 1991.* Boca Raton, FL: Author.

National Council on Compensation Insurance. (1992). *Workers compensation claim characteristics* (Exhibit VIII-A). Boca Raton, FL: Author.

Northwestern National Life Insurance Company. (1992). *Employee burnout: Causes and cures* (Part 1/Employee stress levels). Minneapolis, MN: Employee Benefits Division.

Schwartz, G. E., Watson, S. D., Galvin, D. E., & Lipoff, S. (1989). *The disability management sourcebook.* Washington, DC: Washington Business Group on Health/Institute for Rehabilitation and Disability Management.

The Universal Almanac. (1995). Kansas City, MO: Universal Press Syndicate Company, Andrews and McNeel.

U.S. Department of Health and Human Services, National Center for Health Statistics. (1992). *Health United States, 1992.* (Out of print. For access through a depository library, call 301-436-8500.)

Wolff, S. C. (1990). *Return to work: A human factors guide.* Minneapolis, MN: St. Paul Fire and Marine Insurance Company.

24

Workers' Compensation Issues for Psychologists: The Workers' Point of View

Donald Elisburg

> Stress on the job is not a new phenomenon, but for as long as most people can remember it was not considered a management problem. Not anymore. Employers worldwide are beginning to take job stress seriously because it's costing them money, according to a new report by the International Labor Organization [ILO]. Stress, says the United Nations agency, has become the disease of the modern workplace. "Stress has become one of the most serious health issues of the 20th century—a problem not just for individuals in terms of physical and mental disability, but for employers and governments who have started to assess the financial damage," the ILO said in its new Work Labor Report. (Swoboda, 1993)

Most discussions of workers' compensation stress claims focus on the costs to employers and the increasing tension in attempting to handle stress as a compensable illness. The insurance industry and employer organizations argue that stress-related claims severely undercut the existing workers' compensation system and raise costs prohibitively. The point is usually made with alarm by statements such as "judges and juries are not the only parties struggling to cope with the tremendous proliferation in cases, bizarre theories for recovery, and questionable claims of disability . . . . [or] somehow, it seems, the original purpose of the compensation system got waylaid and turned on its head" (Bisbing, 1992). To be more blunt, others have stated that, "the flood gates have now been unleashed and employee stress-related workers' compensation injuries have skyrocketed in frequency and costs" (Green, Kohler, & Wolff, 1992). That the system does not handle stress claims well is also well documented.

However, why the system is not helping workers is not as well understood. Rarely, is it mentioned that workers are often people with potential claims who also have serious problems in dealing with a generally ill-prepared workers' compensation system. It must be understood that coping with newly emerging workplace illnesses, such as those determined to be stress related, is a problem that affects employers, industry, the compensation system, and workers.

Any substantive discussion of this field must begin with the knowledge

369

that the charge that most stress-related claims are fraudulent efforts by malingerers to receive workers' compensation is simply not true. If this were true, the enormous amount of work being done on dealing with stress in the workplace by organizations such as the American Psychological Association and the National Institute of Occupational Safety and Health would be channeled in other directions.

The real social and economic burden that employees have to face has little to do with the workers' compensation system. What needs to be done is to change the public's perception that an illness caused by mental stress in the workplace is real, not imagined, and that it comes from an increasingly pressure-oriented workplace. The acceptance of a stress-related illness caused by mental pressure in the workplace is only the first step for the worker.

The current interpretations of law generally work against the worker who is attempting to establish a work-related stress illness, particularly in situations in which the claim is that mental stress led to the mental illness, both with respect to identifying the condition and establishing that it is work related. Therefore, it is important to understand the workers' compensation system as it affects the medical and expert issues facing stress in the workplace.

Claims for stress-related illnesses have to meet a number of institutional hurdles, including the identification of the illness, whether it was caused by the job, and, in many states, whether such stress claims are directly related to a workplace injury. A number of issues surround the determination of the existence of a stress-related illness. Even if the condition is established, whether the illness is job related becomes a major concern, particularly with on- and off-the-job contributing factors. Finally, there is the remaining question of the degree of impairment and the extent to which the condition affects the worker's wage-earning capacity. These are complex and rapidly changing issues within the workers' compensation system.

Overview of the Issues

As early as 6 years ago, there was a paucity of cases, articles, and learned commentary on the subject of stress. In fact, one state workers' compensation commissioner stated emphatically that his state did not have any problems with stress cases. There were few newspaper articles and few scholarly works written on workers' compensation stress claims. By 1990, however, things changed, and many were writing about it (Elisburg, 1990). The issue of workplace stress remains a popular topic in the press; many magazines and newspapers still have stories about it.

Several years ago, the *Wall Street Journal* ran an article titled "Law: Fearful of Future, Plaintiffs Are Suing Firms for What Hasn't Happened Yet" (Marcus, 1990). This article dealt with the fear of what could happen in the future and the distress from current events such as a near-miss airplane crash. The case before the Supreme Court involved mental distress suffered aboard an Eastern Airlines flight in which the engines malfunctioned and shut down. As the plane lost altitude, the passengers were told there might be a crash landing in the ocean. However, the crew restarted one of the engines and the plane returned safely to an airport. The case was one of personal injury against the airline. Suppose, however, that one of the passengers was on a business trip and filed for a workers' compensation claim on the basis of the mental distress suffered during the trip. Would that case receive favorable treatment (Marcus, 1990)?

An even more relevant article appeared in the *Wall Street Journal* on November 6, 1990. Titled "Fear and Stress in the Office Take Toll," Boyle (1990) described the problems that workers are having in the "fast lane" of business:

- An advertising salesman screamed so loudly when he argued with his boss that he punctured a lung.
- An office receptionist suffered stress-induced vomiting to the point of having to quit her job.
- A Wall Street broker under treatment for hypertension was so certain that his death was imminent that he refused to take his children to the park for fear they would be abandoned when he died.
- "Human resource managers, as well as doctors, psychologists and pollsters, agree that workplace stress is way up. Layoffs—and the pervasive fear of dismissal—are jangling nerves" (Boyle, 1990, p. B1).

The list is endless. Recent major news, magazine articles, and stories on workers' compensation stress issues now even relate to actual cases.

A story by Lauerman (1992) in the *Chicago Tribune Magazine* had the same kinds of examples cited earlier, and it was estimated that workplace stress is now a $200 billion a year drain on the economy. Lauerman (1992) provided an example of an Illinois workers' compensation law and a specific case:

> A teacher . . . burns out over a period of 30 years in inner-city schools and has a real psychological problem. And the Board of Education's doctors and her own doctors say it is a real disability, a real injury that keeps that teacher from going back into a class room ever again. But in Illinois that case is not compensable. Since it is a gradual accident, a repetitive thing over time that produces the disability, Illinois has held that it's not an accident that arises out of and in the course of one's employment. So Illinois is very employer-oriented in the mental-mental category of cases. (p. 18)

Cases in other jurisdictions have been settled in other ways:

- A Colorado court held that a woman who claimed that she suffered mental stress resulting in temporary total disability caused by implementation of a smoking ban at her workplace could not recover workers' compensation ("Employee Traumatized by Smoking Ban," 1992).
- In New Jersey, firefighters and rescue personnel were given extensive counseling as a result of the stress caused at a gasoline truck accident

in which the driver died before the area could be made safe enough to permit rescuers access to the trapped driver (Nordheimer, 1992).

- *The Washington Post* ran an article about a woman in Florida who successfully filed a stress claim that she was unable to work with Blacks because of a mugging experience (Booth, 1992).[1]

In many respects, these stories are not new. The question is not whether there is more stress in the workplace, or whether such stress leads to illness, but how such stress-related illnesses are treated under the workers' compensation system.

This subject has captured the attention of those who study and write about workers' compensation developments. Some writers have developed a "Chicken Little approach," with stress being considered the approaching ruin of the workers' compensation system. Others, such as Burton (1988), have taken a more balanced view of the process and, analyzing the cases, have determined that the sky has not yet fallen.

There has always been stress-related illness in the workplace. It has been only recently that such illnesses have been recognized as compensable by the workers' compensation system. Stress claims may be a form of taxing the employer for non–work-related problems, but, if employers are to pay, they want to pay only for their responsibility. This is viewed as another social security payment but to a different fund, and that is why there is such resistance to these claims. The primary issue is always discussed in terms of dollars and reducing the financial burden on the employer. The health and well-being of the worker is always secondary.

The Workers' Compensation System

Although lawyers have their own language, psychologists and other medical professionals also have theirs. These professionals rarely communicate with each other effectively, and that is why it is useful to briefly review the workers' compensation approach to disability.

The basic purpose of the workers' compensation system is to provide continued income and medical care to workers injured on the job. Historically, it is considered to be a no-fault system that provides certain benefits in lieu of the common law tort suit situation in which various defenses could leave an injured worker with no economic support and a burden on society (Rosenblum, 1973).

In the United States, there are several disability systems in addition to the approximately 54 state, federal, and territorial workers' compensation systems (*Workers' Compensation and Unemployment Insurance*, 1993). Most notable is the social security disability system, which covers nonworkplace injuries and illness. The workers' compensation system has always worked better for traumatic injuries because the system is based on the concept of

---

[1]This case was later settled. Although the plaintiff received a payment of $500,000, the lawyers received $450,000 in fees and the plaintiff received $50,000 in damages.

benefits for a work-related injury that is caused in the course of employment. It is obvious that occupational diseases complicate the system. Some develop over many years with many different employers. Others may involve exposures that take place outside of the workplace. For decades the workers' compensation systems in the 50 states were extremely restrictive in defining injury so as to exclude occupational disease and to be restrictive on any determination of work relatedness to limit the liability of employers for the disability benefits.

In many other countries, the disability system is integrated so that regardless of whether an individual is injured or made ill on or off the job, the benefits were close or identical (Englund, 1991). Other countries have national health care of some kind, so the payment of medical costs is across the entire system rather than on a particular employer.

Despite the fact that benefits in many states are low, the overall workers' compensation system pays better for a work-related injury than does the social security disability system. Therein lies the problem and one of the main reasons for the tremendous amount of litigation in the United States. For the most part, litigation occurs regardless of whether the injury or illness is work related (i.e., arising out of and in the course of employment as the first step). The difference in outcomes frequently can be the difference between an income level that closely approximates what the worker earned before the injury versus a social security disability payment that could drop the worker and the worker's family so far down the economic scale as to be eligible for a Dickensonian porridge kitchen.

The second problem with the system is the determination of the degree of disability, because the level of economic benefit when there is less than total disability is a percentage of the worker's wage-earning capacity. Obviously, a 40% disability has far more economic clout than does a 10% disability. Thus, the workers' compensation system, under the law, requires the accommodation of medical experts. Consequently, the psychologist is asked to deal with the problems brought about by stress in the workplace in several different ways: (a) What is the determination of the particular condition of the worker? (b) What are the factors that led to the development of the condition? (c) Are those factors consistent with the legal requirements showing that they were caused by the employment? (This is very important because it is the key to having the employer pay.) (d) What is the degree of disability? (e) What can be done to rehabilitate and return the employee to work?

Elements of Workplace Stress

Although most state laws permit mental stress claims, many are also so restrictive that they do not permit claims involving the normal employment process. Others insist that the worker must show some sudden stimulus, or if it is a cumulative stress, the worker must show that such stress is unusual. Some states still require that an injury be shown to establish the stress claim. Consequently, to establish a compensable claim, workers must follow a strict claims development process if a claim is to be successful. The burden of proof is on the worker to define the stress-related condition and to establish whether the illness is work related.

Mental Problems Caused by Physical Injury

There has been relatively little resistance to the compensability of physical injury that leads to mental illness. The concept of payment for this type of traumatic injury is well established, as is the obligation to pay for all of the consequences of that injury, including development of mental problems. This is not to say that the problems of proof of the illness and the relationship of the illness to the traumatic injury do not present difficulties; however, once the case is made for the relationship, the laws accept the result.

Physical Injury Due to Mental Problems

The compensability of mental illness that leads to physical disability also is relatively accepted. Again, the central thesis is the payment for the physical injury as long as it can be shown to be work related.

Mental Injury Caused by Mental Problems

Identifying stress-related illness, particularly a mental illness due to mental activity, is still difficult in workers' compensation law. There appear to be four categories of how states treat mental–mental cases, although some states are not consistent and let the particular facts decide a case.

1. Mental injury produced by mental stimulus is compensable even if the stress is gradual and not unusual compared with that of ordinary life or employment. (The cases in this classification still seem to require some abnormal situation that caused the disorder and fairly clear demonstration that the workplace can be identified as the source of the disorder.)
2. A mental–mental case is compensable even if the stimulus is gradual, but only if the stress is unusual (e.g., routine fear of job loss is not enough).
3. A mental–mental case is compensable, but only if the stimulus is sudden.
4. A mental–mental case is never compensable, unless there is some physical component in the injury (Burton, 1988).

Problems That Lead to Workplace Stress

How is it decided which of these newly discovered stressful activities will receive payment for disability? As a no-fault system, the determination of work-relatedness has been fairly conservative. This occurs because the employer assumes a large obligation with no ability to defend the fault once a claim is determined to be work related. With few exceptions, it does not matter that the employee was careless and responsible for the injury. If it happened at work, the employee gets paid. Thus, the fringe activities, events outside of the workplace, and, of course, anything concerning illness, has always required more complex proof of causation.

What is work related and what is ordinary disease of life—or even what is work and home related—remains highly controversial. As described earlier, the development of a stress claim requires overcoming several obstacles. Before it can be determined whether the condition is "work related," whether the diagnosed condition is an illness that warrants any compensation must be determined.

Employers are extremely reluctant to acknowledge that working conditions can lead to a work-related mental problem. Indeed, case law is not sympathetic to workers who try to claim compensation because the "boss was too tough" or "the work was too hard." The mental–mental compensation cases work best when the claimant can show that some unusual and not acceptable work practice or supervisor behavior contributed to the mental problem. There is much latitude to this type of claim, and the problems of proof are extremely difficult.

The legal requirements of proving mental stress claims also are frequently difficult to establish, and it is the medical profession that must find a way to make clear what is acceptable and not acceptable job-related stress. The workers' compensation system does not work in a vacuum, nor can it handle extreme theories. To the extent that there are widely varied medical theories on work-related stress causation, there will be uncertain claims situations.

Unfortunately, the experts writing about the problem may feed the result as the adjudicators search the literature for the "correct" results. See, for example, a recent anthology by DeCarlo and Minkowitz (1989). They wrote,

> Numerous commentators have suggested that well-intentioned psychiatrists cannot even answer the most fundamental question of whether a patient suffers from a mental disability, let alone evaluate the source or extent of that disability with the more probable than not level of certainty generally required by the law. Studies have suggested that psychiatrists have a greater tendency to err by diagnosing sickness in healthy people than by diagnosing good health in sick people. This tendency may come into play particularly in a workers' compensation claim where a psychiatrist will, understandably, be reluctant to label an apparently healthy claimant as a malingerer. Other studies have concluded that two psychiatrists, examining the same patient, will concur in choosing between the four possible diagnoses of psychosis, neurosis, personality disorder, and normality only between one-third and one-half of the time. Finally, the diagnostic standards used by psychiatrists have been criticized as too vague and unreliable to be the basis for legal judgements. (DeCarlo & Minkowitz, 1989, p. 288)[2]

---

[2] Reprinted with permission.

They continued,

> Of course, these problems may not indict psychiatry as a form of treatment; there may be no harm in treating the well along with the sick. But in light of the recognized fine line between the legal extremes of malingering and disabling neurosis, and the fact that psychiatry has not advanced to the point where it is an exact science in the same sense that physical medicine is an exact science, it is not surprising that the courts have taken a cautious attitude toward mental-mental claims. (DeCarlo & Minkowitz, 1989, p. 288)[3]

This is not a statement from 1889 but from 1989, and it was not written by fringe commentators but by highly respected and influential experts in the workers' compensation field. Although they did not write for the majority, they clearly were attempting to instill in the decision makers' minds sufficient doubt about the viability of mental–mental claims to limit the acceptance of such claims by the workers' compensation system.

Once the worker establishes the development of some form of legitimate mental problem from various stress activities in the workplace, it must be shown what kind of events can be related to the stress problem that has been diagnosed. This is the most critical of the analyses that the professional will have to undertake. It also will require that the individual be able to defend against the argument that the stress illness is related to everything else but the workplace activities.

Stress-related issues began with heart attack or stroke from events at work, usually based on extra hours, miserable working conditions, and similar arguments. This is still difficult to prove because of the view that such events develop over such a long time and that one's entire life is a contributor, not just the job. There are now a number of new technologies that have led to stress claims, and the fairly simple diagnosis of heart attack and stroke have expanded to all kinds of mental conditions, ranging from the easily diagnosed to the exotic.

Some of the workplace activities that now stimulate stress-related claims include using VDTs or electronic monitoring; noise; overtime; fear of economics; sexual harassment; other discrimination; violence and fear of violence for oneself; posttraumatic stress syndrome from violence done to others, such as postal workers who have experienced mass homicides by angry coworkers, homicides in fast-food restaurants, and fire and police employees who must sometimes stand by and watch people die; and combat fatigue stemming from civilian jobs such as air traffic controller burnout (Abramsky, 1992; Lauerman, 1992; National Institute of Occupational Safety and Health, 1992).

There also are a number of other workplace or near-workplace activities or events that are more difficult to prove. For example, the earlier-cited case of the woman who became afraid of Black people as a result of a mugging confronts the system with some basic civil rights questions. If the employer is required under law to hire without discrimination, there will be minority group members in the workplace. If so, the fear espoused in this claim may just be

---

[3] Reprinted with permission.

considered an ordinary problem of life in the workplace and not unusual enough to warrant any disability consideration.

What are some of the limitations of the system regarding stress claims? It is difficult to establish a case that involves normal personnel actions or even nasty supervisors. If the stress is involving such personnel matters as poor performance, bad attendance, or generally unacceptable work habits, a claim would be difficult to establish. Other personnel practices such as failure to promote, failure to grant a pay raise or an appropriate pay raise, poor relations with coworkers or customers, and misconduct or discipline do not lend themselves to a workers' compensation claim, absent an unusual or extreme situation that takes the matter out of the "normal" workplace relationship. In short, the workers' compensation system requires a worker to tolerate the customary and usual requirements of the job and the stresses that go with them. Normal employment issues, no matter how tough, generally do not get paid compensation (Burton, 1988).

As a practical matter, the psychologist generally will be asked to participate as an expert in the evaluation of the claim either for the plaintiff, the employer, or sometimes as an independent. In each case, the technique and methodology will be about the same. Most of the literature on the subject advises the professional to be serious about the investigation of the claim and to examine all of the employment and medical records that are available. This includes looking at the job conditions, interviews and depositions of the claimant and other witnesses, and any other inquiry that will help the expert to form an opinion.

Professionals must remember that when asked to undertake the diagnosis of the stress problem, the relationship to the workplace, the degree of disability, or issues surrounding rehabilitation, all must be considered. It will be necessary to relate the findings to the fourth edition of the *Diagnostic and Statistical Manual of Mental Disorders* and, in the event that it becomes a question of degree of disability, the *AMA Guidelines to Impairment* (Abramsky, 1992; Bisbing, 1991).

The most difficult task will be the determination of the percentage of disability, because that is probably one of the most subjective of a highly subjective series of diagnoses. Much of what the expert is asked to do is difficult because the law requires the expert to state with certainty that which is not certain. This is true when the judgment is whether the diagnosed condition is work related, particularly when the question is how much the working conditions contributed to the condition. The question arises again when the expert is asked to determine whether the disability is full or partial, temporary, or permanent. Clearly, the most trying decision will be when the expert is asked to make a determination of permanent partial disability and then to explain the percentage of the partial disability.

Summary

Stress in today's workplace is a serious area of concern. Although the ideal is to address the problem and work on prevention, it also is important to have a fair system that helps those who legitimately become ill or injured on the job. Therefore, the role of the medical professional is critical in working through the process of identifying and treating the disability.

Mental health experts must consider the following about workers' compensation and stress cases: First, these experts must understand that the workers' compensation system is special and complex. It is the experts who will have to learn how to deal within the system because the system will not change for them. Second, the workers' compensation system is designed not just to compensate for a workplace disability but to provide an opportunity for medical treatment and rehabilitation that will allow the employee to return to work. For mental conditions, it may be important to establish treatment and therapy that helps employees back to work. Third, under the Americans with Disabilities Act, there also is a significant incentive for the employer to find a job for the worker receiving compensation. Changing some of the physical requirements of the job is difficult. Changing the factors that led to the stress conditions will be no less daunting. Finally, the acceptance of mental–mental conditions is subject to a rigorous examination of the facts of each case, and the potential expert is "fair game" for this process.

References

Abramsky, M. F. (1992, July). Work traumas and psychological damage. *Trial*, pp. 48–52.

Bisbing, S. B. (1991, November). *Challenging the psychological injury claim in workers' compensation cases: Defense theories and strategies.* Paper presented at the Defense Research Institute's seminar on employers' liability and workers' compensation, New York.

Bisbing, S. B. (1992, November). *The psychological injury claim in workers' compensation: Unraveling one of industry's most vexing challenges.* Abstracts presented at the meeting of the American Psychological Association and the National Institute of Occupational Safety and Health, Washington, DC.

Booth, W. (1992, August 13). Phobia about blacks brings workers' compensation award. *Washington Post*, p. A3.

Boyle, T. F. (1990, November 6). Fear and stress in the office take toll. *Wall Street Journal*, p. B1.

Burton, J., Jr. (Ed.). (1988, February). The compensability of workplace stress. *John Burton's Workers' Compensation Monitor*, pp. 12–23.

DeCarlo, D. T., & Minkowitz, M. (1989). *Workers' compensation insurance and law practice: The next generation.* Fort Washington, PA: LRP Publications.

Elisburg, D. (1990, November). *Stress related illness and the workers' compensation system from the workers' perspective.* Paper presented at the meeting of the American Psychological Association and the National Institute of Occupational Safety and Health, Washington, DC.

Employee traumatized by smoking ban could not recover for mental stress under the Colorado comp act. (1992, July). *Workplace Injury Reporter*, pp. 69–70.

Englund, A. (1991, October). *U.S. need for data: Relevance and importance of international experience.* Paper presented at the Center to Protect Workers' Rights Conference, Washington, DC.

Green, J. E., Kohler, S. S., & Wolff, S. C. (1992, November). *Workers' compensation and employee stress: Gaining control.* Abstracts presented at the meeting of the American Psychological Association and the National Institute of Occupational Safety and Health, Washington, DC.

Lauerman, C. (1992, July 12). The duress of success: Stress makes for even harder days at the office. *Chicago Tribune Magazine*, p. 18.

Marcus, A. D. (1990, July 11). Law: Fearful of future, plaintiffs are suing firms for what hasn't happened yet. *Wall Street Journal*, p. B1.

National Institute of Occupational Safety and Health. (1992, July). *Health hazard evaluation report: VDTs* (HETA 89-299-2230). Washington, DC: U.S. Department of Health and Human Services, Public Health Service.

Nordheimer, J. (1992, August 11). After a tragedy, helping rescuers walk away. *New York Times*, p. A7.

Rosenblum, M. (Ed.). (1973). *Compendium on workmen's compensation*. National Commission on State Workmen's Compensation Laws. Washington, DC: U.S. Government Printing Office.

Swoboda, F. (1993, March 28). Employers recognizing what stress costs them, U.N. report suggests. *Washington Post*, p. H2.

Workers' compensation and unemployment insurance under state laws. (1993). (Publication No. R-36-0393-15). Washington, DC: AFL-CIO.

25

Appraising Occupational Stress–Related Disorders

Jack G. Wiggins, Jr.

Psychologists now accept that work and well-being are inextricably linked. However, neither conventional wisdom nor formal diagnostic processes have been quick to reflect this acceptance. In the 1940s, conventional wisdom held that psychotherapy was beneficial for the young and affluent, whereas the simple resolution of work issues—with concomitant mental recovery and prevention of relapse in treatment—was seldom given therapeutic value. Twenty years later, the link between work and well-being was begrudgingly recognized in a formal way when parity was established between psychological conditions and physical disabilities in the Vocational Rehabilitation Act of 1973.

Given that people spend the majority of their waking hours working, even slow acceptance of the importance of work to well-being is heartening. Even more encouraging is the fact that research studies and practical explorations are paving the way for formal measures of work-related disorders. In the remainder of this chapter, I explore how formal classification has lagged behind the understanding and acceptance of work-related disorders.

Work-related stress disorders have increased to epidemic proportions according to the results of separate studies by the Northwestern National Life Insurance Company (1991) and the St. Paul Fire and Marine Insurance Company (1991). In 1991, Northwestern National Life reported that 25% of their sample had multiple stress-related illnesses compared with 13% reported on a similar but different sample in 1985. Forty-six percent of these workers felt highly stressed compared with 20% of the 1985 sample. Only 20% of the employees reported that their employers had supportive work and family policies, whereas 40% felt that their employer did not have supportive work and family policies.

Barnett, Marshall, and Pleck (1992) studied psychological distress and the job, marriage, and parent role quality of 300 men in two-income families. They found that those with positive home lives had fewer job-related symptoms of distress. Also, in 1992, Kohler reported a study of 28,000 employees conducted over a 3-year period. She concluded that the relationship between the effect

---

As the 100th president of the American Psychological Association, Dr. Wiggins pronounced psychology at work as the central theme of his centennial-year presidency.

of work on home life and home life on work showed that

> the two frequently create a compounding effect that, if not checked, can lead to a downward spiral of mistakes and accidents on the job and reduced quality of life for the employee. . . . Problems at work can have a more negative effect on both work and home life than problems at home. Contrary to what might be expected, problems in an employee's personal life due to his/her job led to burnout, work performance problems and health problems much more frequently than did the most potent, truly personal problems such as death of a family member or relationship problems. (Kohler, 1992a)

Classification of Work-Related Stress Disorders

The profound interactions among work, family, and health are not clearly recognized in the current diagnostic classification systems. Work-related stress disorders are classified as minor adjustment reactions or V code qualifiers and are not identified separately as major stressors in either the *Diagnostic and Statistical Manual of Mental Disorders* (*DSM*) system of the American Psychiatric Association or in the *International Classification of Diseases* of the World Health Organization. Thus, disorders of workers resulting from occupational stress are stigmatized by defining them as psychiatric conditions rather than normal psychological reactions to environmental pressures.

Psychiatric diagnosis has largely focused on the biological basis of behavior and a psychosocial model of repeated ineffective behaviors and reaction patterns beginning in early childhood. In the revised third edition and the fourth edition of the *DSM*, the diagnosis of mental disorder is weighted toward biological signs and symptoms. Adjustment reactions due to current stressors are discounted as being less disabling than biological factors. Supporters of the biopsychosocial model of mental disorders have tried to create a legal basis of reimbursement for services favoring supposedly biologically based conditions, such as schizophrenia or bipolar depression. This bias against stress-induced disorders is also prevalent in workers' compensation plans. Many, if not most, state workers' compensation plans divide claims into physical and mental. Disabilities due to physical injury are compensable, whereas mental claims must be the result of some physical injury to be compensable. Thus, the stress-induced disorder, a mental–mental claim, is not compensable except under unusual circumstances, which have been subject to prolonged legal battle. Although there is a growing body of legal evidence that mental–mental or stress-induced conditions should be compensated, the current workers' compensation standards generally require mental distress to be the result of physical injury. Furthermore, the worker must then be stigmatized as experiencing a psychiatric condition. This bias against psychological conditions ignores the fact that most episodes of mental disorders are precipitated by environmental or situational stressors.

Although there are exciting advances from studies of the genetic basis of behavior, the best estimate of the genetic or biological determination of behavior is one third or less, according to meta-analyses conducted by Plomin

(1990) and Gatz, Pederson, Plomin, Nesselroade, and McClaren (1991). Thus, two thirds of human adjustment is primarily due to environmental factors.

Measures of behavioral influences in the health field by Cummings and VandenBos (1981) showed "that when all barriers to physical health care are removed, the system becomes overloaded with 60% or more of physician visits by patients manifesting somatized emotional distress." Shapiro and Morris (1978) provided data that 60% of visits to physicians were by patients who had nothing physically wrong with them. When medical visits by patients whose physical illnesses were stress related were added, the total approaches a staggering 80–90%.

What is needed is a psychological classification system that neither stigmatizes the worker nor unfairly blames work conditions. It must be descriptive of the psychological functions involved rather than the signs and symptoms of disease. A psychological diagnostic system must account for the effects of both work and family on the mental and physical health as well as disabilities of individuals. The *International Classification of Impairments, Disabilities and Handicaps* (*ICIDH*) has specific codes for dysfunctions in family and work (World Health Organization, 1980). It is currently under revision for use in North America and can serve as a basis for a psychological diagnostic system.[1] A fresh look at work stressors and classification of their attendant disorders are also needed.

Definition of Occupational Stress–Related Disorders

Psychological reactions to occupational stress require a reappraisal of the work environment that must be clearly distinguished from worker deficiencies due to biological defects, unfortunate early childhood experiences, or both. Occupational stress–related disorders can be best understood using a psychological trauma paradigm. Psychological trauma may be defined as an excess of stimulation that overwhelms the individual's resources for coping with this arousal reaction. Stimulation can be caused by external sources or be internally generated. It is the total effect of excitation, both situationally and cumulatively, that produces the overload condition known as *stress*. An occupational stress–related disorder may be defined as a traumatic situation in which the demands of work exceed the worker's capacities to fulfill and maintain the requirements of the job with existing job resources and under current work conditions. Thus, occupational stress–related disorders can be a function of heavy work demands of the job, work environment, interpersonal conflicts, poor or hazardous work conditions, or worker–job dissonance.

---

[1]Because the concept of "family" is considered a personal or private matter protected by civil liberties, it is not as available for study, measurement, and classification as are work-related behaviors. A task force of the Division of Family Psychology of the American Psychological Association headed by Florence Kaslow is drafting a classification system specifically for family problems.

Worker–Job Dissonance as Occupational Stress

The exposition of psychological traumatic effects from work follows a commonsense explanation of work pressure overload. Still, it must be asked, What about complaints of mental distress and other work-related complaints in which paradoxically the work is not that demanding or the level of performance is well within the repertoire of skills of the individual? Can the psychological trauma definition of stress explain worker reaction when the response resources are equal to or even exceed the pressure of the stimulus?

The traditional conception of worker stress is that of the conflict (dissonance) between supervisor and supervisee, or human versus machine, or corporation versus worker. Although these sources of dissonance are undoubtedly correct, they do not account for the stress of jobs that place a premium on response and do not inherently appear to be overstimulating or demanding. There are two examples that have little to do with one another yet establish similar psychological reaction patterns: "piecework" jobs and commission sales jobs. By placing the economic incentive on the response, appropriate stimulation must be supplied by internally generated motives of the worker, including desire, ambition, vision, and greed, rather than externally induced supervision and direction. Thus, these jobs are likely to produce burnout when internal motivations are insufficient to keep up with response demands. Such jobs require a high degree of self-regulation and personal consistency. Under these conditions, employees are vulnerable to increased quotas or reduced compensation and are likely to experience periods of burnout, anxiety, or depression.

There are four classes of worker–job dissonance that can account for much of "occupational" stress: (a) The worker does not want to do the job; (b) a mismatch between the worker and the job; (c) jobs that require sustained high motivation of the worker for success (already mentioned); and (d) the worker heavily identified with the job who is threatened by minor job changes.

These four conflictual scenarios precipitate psychological dissonance at work and are actually examples of internally generated overstimulation perceived by the individual as work stressors. It is easy to dismiss the psychological reactions to work stressors as being employee problems so that the corporation has little responsibility for inadvertently inducing worker stress. Worker stress claims, either through workers' compensation or health insurance claims, are frustrating to corporations, unions, workers, and workers' families. Each party looks to blame the other. This often results in an adversarial situation and is dealt with as a costly legal problem, rather than as an intrinsic psychological issue of work.

The proposed definition of occupational stress–related disorders can adequately account for psychological reactions to work when it is recalled that the stimulation is the combined effect of both the internally generated and the external stimulation. Thus, controlling or measuring the external events alone does not fully account for the pressures a person experiences on a job. Some examples are useful to illustrate internally generated stress reactions even in an apparently benign work environment.

Probably the simplest circumstance of internally generated job pressure occurs when the person does not want to do the job. It is not that the work is so difficult. It is the preconceived attitudes of the individual about performing the work requirements that create dissonance, frustration, and stress. Reasons for such work dissonance are many. Perhaps the individual is not used to working or is not trained to perform tasks for others, or the work ethic has low status compared with other activities available to the individual (e.g., socializing, athletics, use of drugs, etc.). Perhaps the status of a particular job classification (e.g., working in a fast-food restaurant) is out of keeping with the family lifestyle. This can create dissonance or work stress, and even job refusal.

Personal motivation versus job status conflict is only one of a myriad of reasons for job dissonance. Low pay, length of hours, time of day of work, and inside versus outside jobs are some of the factors that can produce job dissatisfaction and job stress based on personal choices of an employee. Other personal objections, too numerous to list here, create stressful working conditions from the view of the employee. These internally generated objections may be sufficient in and of themselves to result in stress overload, even though the objectives of work are manifest and the work environment appears to be satisfactory.

Even if the job requirements, status, pay, and other objective job characteristics are seemingly satisfactory, dissonance can still occur. Although workers can adapt to a certain amount of dissonance over time, this is not always the case. Sometimes, workers adjust to the job at the expense of developing physical and psychological stress patterns, whereby they attempt to control their work environment by special bodily reactions, such as gritting teeth, creating temporomandibular joint pain.

Some workers' compensation claims come from employees who have been on their jobs 6 months or less. It is tempting to dismiss these complaints as malingering. However, a substantial number of these stress claims are the result of mismatches between worker expectations and work assignments. If this dissonance explanation of stress is applicable, then a disproportionate number of "new hires" and younger workers who cannot exercise their job preferences will be represented among these individuals who are miscast in their work roles. It is likely that workers who identify heavily with their jobs will be the ones most affected by changes in the work environment. Thus, the loyal employee with many years of service who has few options for other employment will be the one most likely to experience job stress from pending changes at work. Retirement stress reaction may be anticipated by increased injury and illness disability claims among older employees.

A Work-Related Psychological Diagnostic System

To study the stressful effects of the environment, I propose that a work-related psychological diagnostic system (WRPDS) be developed. A new nomenclature of behavior will be needed to identify work stressors leading to psychological disturbances.

Because work is subject to public scrutiny, human responses to work stress are measurable and can be made manageable. A WRPDS need not take long to develop. It would have significant utility in assessing mental stress claims in workers' compensation. The U.S. Department of Labor's workers' compensation program could serve as a useful laboratory to study and test the value of a WRPDS.

Another positive contribution of a WRPDS would be to destigmatize worker stress. This could enable workers not only to accept stress reduction consultation but to actively seek it. This would promote early work-related interventions as a primary means of modifying worker stress. Furthermore, by using a WRPDS, business and labor would have a common language to deal with job stress, which should facilitate mutual understanding in dealing with work stressors. Using the stress overload psychological trauma formula, work stressors of a given job would take into account both environmental and psychological pressures and would make mental stress more measurable. A WRPDS has a great deal to offer in conflict resolution, understanding the meaning of work, and the selection of workers and matching workers with their jobs. A WRPDS would include the commonsense explanation of stress overload and the stimulation from psychological dissonance with work. It is through the understanding and alleviation of psychological dissonance that corporations, unions, and workers can make work more meaningful and rewarding.

In conclusion, some of the implications I see in the psychological dissonance theory of work stress are as follows:

1. Business can meet its corporate goals with a psychologically and physically healthy workforce by maintaining a psychologically sound work environment.
2. The potentials for mutual enhancement of corporate and worker goals depend on recognition of matching job functions with the purposiveness of workers rather than by merely establishing corporate goals from the top.
3. Worker stress due to work dissonance is likely to be improperly classified as a psychiatric disorder rather than a work-related response that can be corrected by identifying the work-related stressors.
4. If psychological reactions to work-related stressors are misunderstood as psychiatric disorders, corporations will be saddled with excessively high health and injury costs.
5. Excessively high health and injury costs will reduce profitability and wages that will divert economic growth into welfare expansion, workers' compensation claims, and inflated insurance premiums.
6. To the extent worker stress is due to externally stimulated work stressors or work-induced psychological dissonance, a new work-related psychological diagnostic system must be developed.

References

Barnett, R. C., Marshall, N. L., & Pleck, J. M. (1992). Men's multiple roles and their relationship to men's psychological distress. *Journal of Marriage and the Family*, *54*, 358–367.

Cummings, N. A., & VandenBos, G. R. (1981). The twenty year Kaiser-Permanente experience with psychotherapy and medical utilization: Implications for national health policy and national health insurance. *Health Policy Quarterly*, *1*, 159–174.

Gatz, M., Pederson, N. L., Plomin, R., Nesselroade, J. R., & McClaren, G. E. (1991). The importance of shared genes and shared environment for symptoms of depression in older adults. *Journal of Abnormal Psychology*, *101*, 701–708.

Kohler, S. (1992a, October 13). *American workers under pressure* [News release]. St. Paul, MN: St. Paul Fire and Marine Insurance Company.

Kohler, S. (1992b). *The St. Paul Fire and Marine Insurance Company study*. St. Paul, MN: St. Paul Fire and Marine Insurance Company.

Northwestern National Life survey of working Americans on workplace stress. (1991). Minneapolis, MN: Northwestern National Life Insurance Company.

Plomin, R. (1990). The role of inheritance in behavior. *Science*, *248*, 183–188.

Shapiro, A. K., & Morris, L. A. (1978). The placebo effect in medical and psychological therapies. In S. L. Garfield & A. E. Bergin (Eds.), *Handbook of psychotherapy and behavior change: An empirical analysis* (2nd ed.). New York: Wiley.

World Health Organization. (1980). *International classification of impairments, disabilities, and handicaps*. Geneva, Switzerland: Author.

26

Developing an Occupational Stress Standard: Rule-Making Pitfalls

Robert J. Biersner

The Occupational Safety and Health Act of 1970 provides for research on occupational stress (OS), but it contains no explicit mandate to publish regulations controlling this source of psychological stress. An OS standard will therefore depend on documentation of OS incidents using reporting vehicles such as workers' compensation claims and the injury-and-illness logs required by the Occupational Safety and Health Administration (OSHA) to be completed by employers. These logs, however, must be revised to accommodate the reporting of work-related psychological stress. This documentation can be used to support an OS standard by (a) identifying the sources and effects of OS; (b) demonstrating, at an acceptable level of reliability and validity, the efficacy and feasibility of recommended prevention (vice treatment) procedures; and (c) delineating the costs and benefits of these procedures. This documentation will be necessary to configure a proposed standard, defend this proposal through a rigorous comment-and-hearing period, and compose a final standard that will withstand subsequent legal challenge. To ease this effort, a number of discrete standards addressing well-researched OS conditions (e.g., shift work, video display terminal [VDT]-induced stress, workplace violence) may be preferable to a single, generic standard; additionally, prevention procedures should be defined in terms of risk-prevention objectives instead of highly elaborate, prescriptive language. In this chapter I describe how occupational health standards are developed, and I discuss some of the challenges associated with that process.

The origins of occupational safety and health rule making have been lost in antiquity. The bible, however, records that Moses issued an occupational safety and health regulation, admonishing the Israelites to build parapets on the roofs of houses to prevent workers from falling (Mintz, 1984). Modern laws preventing occupational injuries and illnesses were instituted during the Industrial Revolution. The Health and Morals of Apprentices Act was the first such law; this act was passed by the British Parliament in 1802 to regulate the hours of work and schooling, and the sanitary and ventilation conditions, to which children working in cotton mills were exposed (Bokat & Thompson,

This chapter represents the author's views, interpretations, and opinions, and no endorsement of this chapter by the Department of Labor is intended or should be construed.

1988). In the United States, occupational safety and health regulations were enacted initially by the states, with Pennsylvania instituting mine inspections in 1869 and Massachusetts enacting a factory inspection statute in 1877 (Bokat & Thompson, 1988). More than 20 years ago, a comprehensive national statute regulating occupational safety and health was enacted: the Occupational Safety and Health Act of 1970. This act emphasizes prevention of occupational accidents, unlike workers' compensation statutes that regulate treatment of occupational illness and injuries. Under the act, OSHA, which is located within the Department of Labor (DOL), has the authority to develop and enforce occupational standards.

The Act and Occupational Stress

The Occupational Safety and Health Act discusses OS in terms of psychological stress, but it does so largely in a research context, failing to directly acknowledge psychological stress as a major source of occupational morbidity. Listed are sections of the act dealing with psychological stress (assuming that the terms *stress* and *functional capacity* imply psychological stress).

Section (2)(b)(5). Provides for occupational safety and health research, specifically identifying "psychological factors" involved in occupational safety and health problems.

Section (2)(b)(7). Medical criteria must be used to prevent "diminished . . . functional capacity . . . as a result of . . . work."

Section (20)(a)(4). Directs the secretary of the Department of Health and Human Services (DHHS) to "conduct research into the motivational and behavioral factors relating to . . . occupational safety and health."

Section (20)(a)(7). Requires the secretary of DHHS to conduct and publish annual, industrywide studies relating "chronic or low-level exposure to industrial materials, processes, and stresses on the potential for illness, disease, or loss of functional capacity in aging adults." (The phrase "aging adults" refers to determining the effects of continuous exposures to hazards over the work span [i.e., 45 years].)

Under the act, responsibility for conducting occupational safety and health research has been assigned to the director of the National Institute for Occupational Safety and Health (NIOSH), who acts on behalf of the secretary of the DHHS.

The initial standards developed by OSHA emphasized accidents associated principally with the *structural configuration of the workplace* (e.g., inadequate ventilation of industrial chemicals, poor guarding of production equipment). Chemical exposure effects and acute traumatic accidents had been assessed extensively by occupational safety and health professionals prior to passage of the act and therefore could be corrected directly by publishing standards based on available toxicological and engineering knowledge.

Beginning in the 1980s, the *functional configuration of the job* (also known as "job design") was recognized as a major source of occupational morbidity. Job-design accidents, resulting from the manner in which a job is performed, did not have the extensive research history noted earlier for accidents related to the structural configuration of the workplace and therefore were not addressed by OSHA's early standards.

Cumulative trauma disorders (CTDs) were among the first injuries to be identified as being induced by faulty job design. CTDs occur as a result of repetitious movement of a specific body part, often accompanied by musculoskeletal overloading and working at awkward or severe angles; lower back disorders and carpal tunnel syndrome are two CTDs commonly experienced by workers. In the mid-1980s, a rapid growth in the number of CTDs documented on OSHA 200 logs (the standard form used by industry to report occupational illnesses and injuries) and a commensurate rise in the number of ergonomic violations identified by OSHA compliance officers (COs) performing occupational safety and health inspections of workplaces, culminated in an announcement by the secretary of labor in 1990 that OSHA would initiate rule making for an ergonomics standard. The final ergonomics standard will not only prevent CTDs, but provide COs with objective criteria to use in assessing ergonomic hazards and issuing citations for violations of safe ergonomic working conditions prescribed under the standard. Ergonomic hazard citations now are issued under Section (5)(a)(1) of the act, known as the "general duty clause," which authorizes OSHA COs to cite employers who fail to provide workers with "employment and a place of employment which are free from recognized hazards that are causing or are likely to cause death or serious physical harm." Typically, COs identify hazards through inspection of OSHA 200 logs retained by employers or through a written request by employees or employee representatives (e.g., union agents). The final rule likely will reduce litigation resulting from enforcement that is based on the general duty clause, in defense of which employers often claim that the hazard is not generally recognized within the industry or that the prevention measures adopted conform to those measures used generally by the industry.

The development of an ergonomics standard described earlier has important implications for OS. If OS is to achieve recognition comparable to ergonomic hazards, psychologists must engage in an intensive training program among occupational safety and health practitioners, management, and labor to improve recognition and diagnosis of the disorder and ensure the disorder is documented on OSHA 200 logs in a retrievable form. (Currently, OS is classified under the "all other occupational illnesses" category on the OSHA 200 log; Bureau of Labor Statistics, 1986.) Proper documentation of OS using OSHA 200 logs and other data (e.g., workers' compensation files, Social Security claims, hospital and clinic admission records) will allow precise identification of occupational conditions involved in stress disorders, formulation of dose–response relationships, and evaluation of preventive methodologies. Without proper documentation of OS events, causative conditions, and successful interventions, OSHA COs will be reluctant to cite OS violations under the general duty clause, and development of a standard will be impeded.

Some question remains, however, whether the general duty clause could be used legally by COs to cite an OS hazard. Note that the hazard cited must result in *physical* harm; at best, this test could be met only if research or epidemiological data demonstrate (and the professional occupational safety and health community recognizes) that the physiological and biochemical effects of OS (e.g., elevated blood pressure and heart rate, muscle tension) result in end-stage conditions such as cardiovascular and neuromuscular disorders.

In the following discussion I include a generic description of the process by which most successful occupational safety and health standards are developed into enforceable instruments; this process is presented in the temporal sequence typical of most standards. The process consists of two major parts: the rule-making procedure and legal challenges. The part on the rule-making procedure describes several stages required by federal statute and case law to provide the public with notice of an impending standard and an opportunity to provide data and opinions that can be used by OSHA in composing a final standard. Legal challenges consist of several tests that previous standards have failed to meet; these tests are based on judicial interpretations of statutory language enacted by the U.S. Congress to protect the rule-making procedure from bias and to ensure that final standards meet specific criteria (e.g., protect against significant hazards, are feasible both technologically and economically). After describing each stage in the rule-making procedure and each of the legal criteria established by federal courts, I present a brief summary of the specific implications for an OS standard. This discussion should expedite development of a successful OS standard by avoiding pitfalls that have delayed or invalidated previous standards-development efforts.

The Rule-Making Procedure

The rule-making procedure progresses through four stages: petitioning, advance notice of proposed rule making or request for information, proposed standards, and final standards.

Petitioning for a Standard

Generic description. Many sources can recommend, in writing, that the secretary of labor or OSHA develop a standard. Typical sources are national labor unions, professional groups (e.g., private standards organizations, professional occupational safety and health societies), other government agencies (especially NIOSH), OSHA (e.g., advisory committees, recommendations from the OSHA staff), the U.S. Congress, and even the federal courts.

Although OSHA has not developed formal criteria for use in determining whether to accept recommendations for standards development, it has compiled several criteria for assigning priorities to standards under development that may serve as a guide to the rationale used by OSHA in making decisions regarding standards recommendations. OSHA, as the respondent in *National Congress of Hispanic American Citizens v. Marshall* (1979), submitted to the D.C. Circuit Court a list of these criteria separately for health and safety standards; the court endorsed these criteria via nonbinding language in its subsequent opinion. The health standards criteria endorsed by the court included (a) severity of the unregulated hazards (defined by OSHA as the most important criterion); (b) the number of workers exposed to these hazards; (c) the existence of research on hazard identification and methods of hazard control; (d) recommendations of NIOSH; (e) petitions requesting that standards be developed to prevent identified hazards; and (f) court decisions and other factors affecting the enforceability of a standard.

Similar criteria have been defined for safety standards, including (a) the number of workers exposed to specified hazards; (b) accident rates for these hazards; (c) the nature and severity of the hazards (although undefined, the term *nature* likely refers to the extent to which the hazardous work is amenable to modification); (d) the need for classification, simplification, and revision to improve the compliance and enforceability of an existing standard; (e) revisions to previous work practices; (f) decisions of federal courts and the Occupational Safety and Health Review Commission (OSHRC) that affect the enforceability of existing standards (the OSHRC is the panel that reviews decisions rendered by administrative law judges regarding OSHA citations); (g) the availability of other information relevant to hazard identification and hazard-control methods; (h) recommendations of NIOSH and DOL–OSHA advisory committees; and (i) petitions requesting that standards be developed to prevent the hazards.

Implications for an OS standard. Information accompanying a petition requesting an OS standard must be specific and extensive if approval is to be granted. The OS hazard must be identified with some degree of specificity, and the incidence of the disorder should be defined on a national scale if possible (e.g., using valid epidemiological data). Methods of controlling OS should be delineated, data demonstrating the effectiveness of these interventions should be included (e.g., reduced incidence, improved production outcomes), and implementation and recurring costs should be provided if available. If the professional occupational safety and health community (including OSHA COs) remains unsophisticated about OS, petition requests will likely come from scientific groups (e.g., NIOSH, professional psychological research organizations) or standards-development groups heavily dependent on scientific advice (e.g., the American National Standards Institute).

Advance Notice of Proposed Rule Making or Request for Information

Generic description. If existing information is sufficient to convince OSHA that a new or revised standard is needed, feasible and effective technologies exist to control the hazard, costs of implementing controls can be estimated with some degree of accuracy, and a standard can be developed within existing legal and statutory constraints, this preliminary stage may be bypassed. If some of this information is missing, OSHA may obtain this information from the interested parties by publishing an advanced notice of proposed rule making (ANPR) or a request for information (RFI) in the *Federal Register*. The public has a specific period in which to respond (normally 6 months), after which OSHA analyzes these responses and decides whether to proceed with developing the standard.

Implications for an OS standard. Should an incomplete petition requesting an OS standard be submitted to and accepted by OSHA, organizations having scientific data on OS must, when responding to an ANPR or RFI, be prepared to assemble and submit these data expediently and in a comprehensible form to OSHA.

Proposed Standards

Generic description. This stage conforms to the provisions of the Administrative Procedures Act of 1946 (5 U.S.C., Sections 551–559, 1988) and Section (6)(b) of the Occupational Safety and Health Act; it is designed to provide the public with notice of standards that have been formulated by the executive branch of the federal government and with a reasonable opportunity to comment (either in writing or at an informal hearing) on proposed standards prior to final enactment. The proposal stage provides those parties likely to be subject to a final rule (e.g., workers and industry) with notice and rationale regarding the scope of coverage (e.g., the number of workers and types of industries to be covered), the specific types of hazards to be controlled and, if appropriate, the maximum level and duration of hazard exposure, the proposed methods and techniques to be used in controlling the hazards, the expected effectiveness of these controls, and costs associated with implementing the proposed hazard controls. This information should be reasonably specific and accurate; options can be presented as long as the final standard remains within the scope of the variables and parameters defined by these options.

On publication of the proposed rule, the public has at least 30 days (usually 90 days) in which to provide written comments and other documentation regarding the proposal. These comments then are assembled in order of receipt by OSHA in a file (referred to as a "docket") that is open to the public. If any member of the public objects to the proposed rule, requests a public hearing, and this request meets the requirements of OSHA's regulations on rule making ("Rules of Procedure," 1994), such a hearing must be convened. OSHA also has the authority to convene a hearing without such a request. The dates and locations of the hearings are announced in the *Federal Register* at least 60 days in advance to allow for adequate preparation. Parties whose testimony at a hearing is expected to exceed 10–15 min must notify OSHA in advance and provide OSHA with written copies of this testimony and any supporting documentation prior to the hearing; this procedure ensures that testimony is relevant to the issues identified in the earlier *Federal Register* announcement and that adequate time is allotted for testimony. Copies of this written testimony and supporting documentation are placed in the docket by OSHA so that other parties can prepare questions to be asked at the hearings. OSHA also provides copies of testimony to be presented by expert witnesses who testify for it.

An administrative law judge (ALJ) presides over the hearing to maintain the predetermined schedule established for oral testimony and to ensure that questioning of witnesses is orderly and complies with prescribed time limits. A transcription is made of the proceedings and placed in the docket after the hearings. The ALJ usually keeps the record open for at least 30 days to receive additional comments and information, and at least 60 days to receive legal briefs, submitted in response to testimony and information provided at the hearings. The record then is certified and closed by the ALJ, and OSHA reviews this information and determines the extent to which the proposed standard should be revised in developing a final standard.

Implications for an OS standard. During this stage, the framework of the final standard is established, and no additional data or information normally can be submitted to the closed record. Supporters and opponents of an OS standard must be prepared to testify on behalf of their position and to provide the latest research documents substantiating this position. Although the hearing is informal, they will be interrogated by other witnesses, lawyers, and perhaps by the OSHA staff and the ALJ conducting the hearing. Clarity, organization, and a rational defense of factual material will enhance the possibility that this material will be incorporated into the final standard. Ambiguous responses and failures to address information deficiencies or conflicts leaves to others (e.g., OSHA) the task of resolving these issues and controlling the manner in which these issues are represented in the final standard.

Final Standards

Generic description. As noted earlier, the final standard must conform to the framework established by the proposed rule; the final standard must be based solely on information contained in the rule-making record. The final standard consists typically of a lengthy preamble, followed by the regulatory text. The preamble usually is composed of the following items: (a) identification and characterization of the hazard being regulated; (b) the regulatory history (i.e., key events prior to, and during, the hearing); (c) a summary of documentation and comments contained in the record, including a summary of major issues (e.g., morbidity data, workforce risk, technical feasibility of hazard-control methodologies, and an analysis of the economic effects of implementing the hazard-control technology); (d) a section-by-section explanation of the standard, including OSHA's rationale for determining the scope of coverage and selecting specific risk profiles and hazard-control options; and (e) a discussion of the standard's compliance with appropriate legislative and executive branch requirements (e.g., presidentially mandated regulatory analyses, environmental effects of the standard, economic effects on small business).

Although Section (6)(b) of the act requires that a standard be published in the *Federal Register* within 60 days of a hearing, or within 60 days after publication of a proposed standard if no hearing is convened, courts have held that these time requirements are not binding if delays resulted from good-faith considerations (e.g., redirecting OSHA staff to developing higher priority standards; see *National Congress of Hispanic American Citizens v. Marshall*, 1979). Recently, several years elapsed between completion of hearings and publication of final standards; these delays result largely from the extensive and complicated records that have developed in response to the proposals and the limited number of OSHA staff available to review and compile the findings into final standards. Additional delays occur if OSHA chooses to postpone the effective date of the final rule on the basis of feasibility or other considerations or if administrative stays are imposed in response to petitions from interested parties.

Implications for an OS standard. The preamble presents the rationale for the final standard, including the hazards (i.e., stress variables or conditions) to be controlled, the interventions or techniques to be used in controlling these hazards, and the economic and technical feasibility of implementing these controls. Therefore, the preamble relies heavily on information supplied by interested parties at the ANPR or RFI and proposed rule stages. In essence, interested parties must be prepared to provide the information identified in Items A–D in the first paragraph of this section. Also, interested parties should recognize that several years may elapse, even after the intense and time-consuming efforts involved in addressing the proposed standard, before the final standard is promulgated.

Legal Challenges

The act provides that any party subject to a standard (e.g., workers who are, or should be, protected under the standard, or an industry that must comply with the standard) may challenge that standard by filing a petition in a federal appellate court of appropriate jurisdiction prior to the 60th day (i.e., within 59 days; see *AFL-CIO v. OSHA*, 1990) after the standard is "promulgated" (i.e., published in the *Federal Register*; see, e.g., *United Technologies Corp. v. OSHA*, 1987). Reviewing courts may stay a standard temporarily, in whole or in part, prior to rendering a final decision; the final decision also may stay or vacate a standard in whole or in part. Stays prohibit OSHA from enforcing the pertinent parts of a standard until these issues are resolved. If a standard is vacated entirely, OSHA must repeat the rule-making process in compliance with the court's ruling should OSHA decide to reissue the standard.

Legal challenges usually involve several issues: notice, ex parte communications and bias of the decision maker, and the factual basis of a standard (i.e., substantial evidence, significant risk, material impairment, and feasibility).

Notice

Generic description. Notice issues arise when a party claims the rule-making procedure failed to define an important variable or parameter sufficiently to allow knowledgeable comment (e.g., the workforce or industry subject to the standard was not identified adequately, durations or other exposure limits lacked precision, hazard-control options were not discussed fully). Although courts have held that key variables and parameters must be identified, OSHA has been granted much leeway regarding the specificity with which these variables and parameters are defined, holding that adequate notice is provided if OSHA selects from among variables or a range of parameters identified nominally in a public document published prior to the final standard (e.g., noting that a final exposure limit may be lower than the proposed limit; see *United Steelworkers of America, AFL-CIO-CLC v. Marshall*, 1980).

Implications for an OS standard. Although notice claims are rare, those who are dissatisfied with the variables and parameters defined in a final OS standard may challenge the standard if reasonable notice and discussion were not provided regarding this information. The risk in taking such action, however, is that the standard may be voided in whole or in part, thereby delaying even further the protection provided by the original standard.

Ex Parte Communications and Biased Decision Making

Generic description. Ex parte communication claims assert that OSHA decisions regarding the final standard are founded on information obtained from "outside" parties (i.e., a party not considered integral with the OSHA staff) and not documented in the public record; cases claiming biased decision making contend that OSHA–DOL officials involved in approving a final standard were biased in favor of specific options. In general, these legal challenges have been unsuccessful.

With regard to ex parte communication challenges, federal courts have ruled that OSHA can receive summaries and analyses of information contained in the public record from consultants hired by OSHA, provided these work products are placed in the docket prior to publication of a standard (see *United Steelworkers of America, AFL-CIO-CLC v. Marshall*, 1980). In this regard, consultants are treated by the courts as OSHA employees. Case law regarding the informal rule making of other federal regulatory agencies indicates that OSHA can discuss prepublished versions of standards with interested parties, including other executive branch agencies (e.g., the Office of Management and Budget); only oral and written information and data obtained by OSHA during these discussions that result in substantive revisions to the prepublished standard must be made part of the public record (and in a timely fashion so that other interested parties may submit comments to OSHA regarding these revisions; see *Sierra Club v. Costle*, 1981).

Claims of biased decision making likely will be sustained only if key policy officials involved in approving a final standard express bias publicly prior to taking approval action and do so with remarks and conduct so extreme as to indicate an inability to weigh contrary information fairly (see *United Steelworkers of America, AFL-CIO-CLC v. Marshall*, 1980).

Implications for an OS standard. Claims of ex parte communication and biased decision making often arise when development of a standard has been contentious (i.e., parties who support or oppose a standard suspect each other of exercising undue influence on those responsible for developing or approving the standard). Advocating for a standard with members of the legislative branch and senior policymakers in the executive branch is acceptable; however, parties interested in an OS standard should take care not to provide information that may be used in formulating the eventual standard to OSHA staff involved in writing the standard outside the public forums prescribed by law. Of course, if evidence of undue influence is found, OSHA should be notified at once; if OSHA fails to take appropriate action, the final standard may be challenged on this basis if necessary.

Substantial Evidence

Generic description. The act provides that federal courts reviewing evidence submitted by OSHA in support of a final rule should do so using the "substantial evidence" test as the standard of review (see *Industrial Union Department, AFL-CIO v. Hodgson*, 1974). To satisfy this test, such decisions must be rational. In *American Textile Manufacturers Institute, Inc. v. Donovan* (1981), the U.S. Supreme Court, referring to an earlier case, stated "we have defined substantial evidence as 'such relevant evidence as a reasonable mind might accept as adequate to support a conclusion.'" Where possible, OSHA decisions should be founded on definitive data; if, however, the data are ambiguous, conflicting, or missing, OSHA has the discretion to resolve these problems based on OSHA policy judgments, including erring in favor of worker protection. Addressing the scientific basis of OSHA's decisions, the U.S. Supreme Court in *Industrial Union Department, AFL-CIO v. American Petroleum Institute* (1980) stated that "OSHA is not required to support its [decisions] . . . with anything approaching scientific certainty." In this same case, the Supreme Court also deferred to OSHA's policy with regard to interpreting problematic scientific data, finding that "so long as [OSHA's decisions] are supported by a body of reputable scientific thought, the Agency is free to use conservative assumptions in interpreting the data, . . . risking error on the side of over-protection rather than under-protection."

Implications for an OS standard. An OS standard based on thorough research that resolves conflicting and ambiguous data, and reduces the likelihood of missing data, will probably withstand the rigors of scrutiny during public hearings and comment, as well as judicial review. The following data should be provided in formulating an OS standard: (a) identification of the sources and effects of occupational stress, preferably in terms of dose–response relationships (to allow for balancing between control procedures and costs if necessary); (b) demonstration, at an acceptable level of validity, of the efficacy of recommended control procedures, emphasizing preventive instead of treatment interventions; and (c) documentation of costs, including the cost of treatment, lost productivity, and hiring replacement workers, as well as the cost of control and training procedures.

Significant Risk

Generic description. In *Industrial Union Department, AFL-CIO v. American Petroleum Institute* (1980), the U.S. Supreme Court held that OSHA "is required to make a threshold finding that a place of employment is unsafe—in the sense that significant risks are present and can be eliminated or lessened by a change in practices." The Supreme Court gave OSHA the discretion to determine the probability level that would constitute "significant risk" over a 45-year work span but stated in nonbinding language that an elevated risk of one in a billion likely would not be significant, whereas an enhanced risk of one in 1,000 could reasonably be interpreted as significant. Although the term *significant risk* does not appear in the act, the Supreme Court nevertheless interpreted the act as requiring that significance of risk be expressed in terms of statistical probabilities derived from objective data.

Implications for an OS standard. This legal test merely states that the standard should not exceed the existing data. If the research on which an OS standard is based is thorough and expressed in valid statistical terms, this legal test should be easily satisfied.

Material Impairment

Generic description. This term appears in the first sentence of Section (6)(b)(5) of the act and, as such, is applied principally to health standards. (Note that health standards address only toxic materials [i.e., chemicals] and harmful physical agents; by implication, other occupational disorders, including OS, would be covered under safety standards.) With OSHA's emphasis on serious work-related disorders, the assumption has been that this term refers to the severity with which a physical function is impaired as a result of exposure to toxic chemicals and harmful physical agents (Rothstein, 1983). This interpretation is consistent with the general duty clause, which requires that every employer provide a workplace that will not cause "death or serious physical harm" to workers. The limited case law on this issue, however, indicates that material impairment need not be evidenced by frank illness. In *United Steelworkers of America v. AFL-CIO-CLC* (1980), the court held that the term applied to "subclinical effects . . . that lie on a continuum shared with overt disease." Therefore, a standard that must demonstrate material impairment may be based on precursor effects that have not yet developed into end-stage disease or illness.

Implications for an OS standard. This test may not apply to an OS standard because the act mentions this test only in association with standards addressing toxic chemicals and harmful physical agents (i.e., Section [6][b][5] standards). Nevertheless, OSHA would be reluctant to develop a standard for which prevention of material impairment, whether physical or psychological, could not be demonstrated. In this regard, OSHA likely would adopt one of the paradigms used to adjudicate OS claims under various workers' compensation

systems (i.e., the disorder may have a physical source with mental consequences, a mental source with physical consequences, or a mental source with
mental consequences; see National Council on Compensation Insurance, 1985,
for a detailed review of these paradigms). If the material impairment test is
found to apply to an OS standard (i.e., the standard is covered by Section
[6][b][5]), then the standard would have to demonstrate that a significant
relationship exists between OS effects and measurable workplace conditions
and that this relationship evidences substantial reliability and validity. These
OS effects, however, may consist of indexes of fully developed mental or physical illnesses as long as these indexes have been found to be related reliably
and validly to the end-stage conditions.

Feasibility

Generic description. Every OSHA standard must demonstrate technological and economic feasibility. As noted earlier, OSHA's judgments of technological feasibility are based on a thorough discussion of facts contained in the
record, with conflicts among these data resolved in a rational manner that
may rely on well-articulated policy judgments.

The Occupational Safety and Health Act of 1970 requires that health
standards provide protection "to the extent feasible," a provision that has been
interpreted by federal appellate courts to imply both technological and economic feasibility (e.g., *Industrial Union Department, AFL-CIO v. Hodgson*,
1974). Technological and economic feasibility are closely intertwined, with
sophisticated hazard-control technology (i.e., engineering controls) requiring
large outlays of capital. In reviewing OSHA's technological feasibility data,
the courts generally have applied the same substantial evidence criterion used
for determining risk and exposure limits (e.g., *AFL-CIO v. OSHA*, 1992).
Additionally, courts have permitted OSHA to apply hazard-control technology
across industrial sectors in a progressive or "technology-forcing" fashion (see,
e.g., *United Steelworkers of America, AFL-CIO-CLC v. Marshall*, 1980).

Regarding health standards, the U.S. Supreme Court ruled in *American
Textile Manufacturers Institute, Inc. v. Donovan* (1981) that the legislative
history of the act, as well as similar congressional statutes enacted prior to
the act that expressly included cost–benefit analysis requirements, indicated
that Congress did not intend that cost–benefit analysis be applied to health
standards. The Supreme Court stated that OSHA's economic analysis was
appropriate provided that the "long-term profitability and competitiveness" of
industrial sectors was maintained.

Two federal appellate courts have ruled on economic feasibility tests applicable to safety standards. In *National Grain and Feed Association, Inc. v.
OSHA* (1989), the U.S. Court of Appeals for the Fifth Circuit ruled that the
economic feasibility test for safety standards under the act was "an intermediate one between the feasibility mandate [for health standards] and a strict
cost–benefit analysis." In a later response to this court, OSHA justified the
standard using a cost-effectiveness analysis (i.e., attaining the protective ef-

fects at the least cost), which the court endorsed (see *National Grain and Feed Association, Inc. v. OSHA*, 1990).

In *International Union, United Automobile, Aerospace and Agricultural Implement Workers of America, UAW v. OSHA* (1994), the U.S. Court of Appeals for the District of Columbia Circuit accepted a safety standard demonstrated by OSHA to bear a reasonable relationship between costs and benefits. In doing so, the court accepted OSHA's premise that Section (3)(8) of the act requires OSHA to provide a high degree of safety protection to employees; however, the court held that the economic feasibility of this degree of safety protection can "deviate only modestly from the stringency required . . . for health standards."

These two federal appellate courts appear to be contending that an appropriate economic feasibility test for safety standards must constrain the protection provided by OSHA in a manner similar to the economic feasibility test applied to health standards; a variety of cost–benefit analyses, in which OSHA demonstrates a reasonable relationship between the economic burden imposed by the standard and the deaths and injuries prevented, would be acceptable to these courts. Future cases, perhaps at the U.S. Supreme Court level, will be necessary to clarify and resolve this issue.

Implications for an OS standard. Despite prevailing wisdom, and identification of job-induced emotional disorders as illnesses by the Bureau of Labor Statistics (1986), an OS standard may not fit the definition of a health standard under the act; therefore, OS, by implication, most likely will be defined as a safety hazard. As a consequence, an OS standard should conform to the economic feasibility test for safety standards that has been defined recently by federal appellate courts; this definition includes a variety of cost–benefit analyses. To meet this test, valid and reliable cost data should be obtained for (a) prescribed interventions, including associated training and record keeping; (b) productivity enhancements or reductions; and (c) treatment and hospitalization savings.

Conclusions

To ease the standards-development effort and to gain the confidence of the occupational safety and health community, the best strategy may be to develop a number of discrete standards addressing well-researched stress conditions with measurable physiological and biochemical (i.e., functional) consequences rather than promoting a broad, generic OS standard covering variable workplace conditions. Generic standards are complex, lengthy, and involve years of effort and still may not withstand judicial scrutiny, whereas discrete standards are more manageable than generic standards and permit a timely demonstration of efficacy. Note that the average period required to develop an OSHA standard (from the ANPR–RFI–proposal stages to publication of the final rule) is now more than 4 years, not including delays resulting from legal challenges. Candidate topics for OS standards include extended or rapidly rotating shift work, psychological stress associated with VDT operations, and workplace violence. These topics are supported by extensive research and address serious workplace problems.

Implementation of performance-based standards may reduce the standards-development effort while permitting flexibility with regard to control procedures. Performance-based standards, which are preferred under the act, define risk prevention objectives, allowing management to identify the most appropriate hazard-control procedures and technologies for accomplishing these objectives. Typical standards define hazard control in elaborate detail and are referred to as "specification standards." The intervention flexibility permitted under performance-based standards, however, makes these standards more difficult for OSHA to enforce than the more prescriptive specification standards (i.e., management resorts to many of the same defenses used to avert citations issued under the general duty clause).

For the past several years, subcommittees of both houses of the U.S. Congress responsible for overseeing OSHA's statutory authority have been trying to revise the Occupational Safety and Health Act. This legislation is referred to as the Comprehensive Occupational Safety and Health Reform Act (see Bureau of National Affairs, Inc., 1992, for a description of proposed reforms). These reforms have major implications for OSHA's rule-making authority and, consequently, the American workplace. Nevertheless, this legislation has never reached the floor of either house. With the recent shift in majority parties in Congress, the future of the reform act remains uncertain.

References

Administrative Procedures Act of 1946, 5 U.S.C., sections 551–559 (1988).

AFL-CIO v. OSHA, 905 F.2d 1568 (D.C. Cir. 1990).

AFL-CIO v. OSHA, 965 F.2d 962 (11th Cir. 1992).

American Textile Manufacturers Institute, Inc. v. Donovan, 452 U.S. 490 (1981).

Bokat, S. A., & Thompson, H. A. (Eds.). (1988). *Occupational safety and health law*. Washington, DC: Bureau of National Affairs, Inc.

Bureau of Labor Statistics. (1986). *Recordkeeping guidelines for occupational injuries and illnesses*. Washington, DC: U.S. Government Printing Office.

Bureau of National Affairs, Inc. (1992, June 24). Special report: The Comprehensive Occupational Safety and Health Reform Act (S 1622, HR 3160). *Occupational Safety and Health Reporter*, pp. 156–160.

Industrial Union Department, AFL-CIO v. Hodgson, 499 F.2d 467 (D.C. Cir. 1974).

Industrial Union Department, AFL-CIO v. American Petroleum Institute, 448 U.S. 607 (1980).

International Union, United Automobile, Aerospace and Agricultural Implement Workers of America, UAW v. OSHA, No. 89-1559 (D.C. Cir. Oct. 21, 1994).

Mintz, B. J. (1984). *OSHA: History, law, and policy*. Washington, DC: Bureau of National Affairs, Inc.

National Congress of Hispanic American Citizens v. Marshall, 626 F.2d 882 (D.C. Cir. 1979).

National Council on Compensation Insurance. (1985). *Emotional stress in the workplace: New legal rights in the eighties*. New York: Author.

National Grain and Feed Association, Inc. v. OSHA, 866 F.2d 717 (5th Cir. 1989).

National Grain and Feed Association, Inc. v. OSHA, 903 F.2d 308 (5th Cir. 1990).

Occupational Safety and Health Act of 1970, 29 U.S.C., sections 651–678 (1988).

Rothstein, M. A. (1983). *Occupational safety and health law* (2nd ed.). St. Paul, MN: West Publishing.

Rules of Procedure for Promulgating, Modifying, or Revoking Occupational Safety and Health
    Standards, 29 C.F.R., Pt. 1911 (1994).
Sierra Club v. Costle, 657 F.2d 298 (D.C. Cir. 1981).
United Steelworkers of America, AFL-CIO-CLC v. Marshall, 647 F.2d 1189 (D.C. Cir. 1980).
United Technologies Corp. v. OSHA, 836 F.2d 52 (2nd Cir. 1987).

27

Occupational Welfare in the European Community: Past, Present, and Future

Erik de Gier

In Western Europe, occupational health policies are going through a period of transition, characterized by laws at the European level for the protection of health, safety, and well-being at work and increased employer attention to human resource policies. There is tension between the legalistic strategy of the public authorities (including the European Union [EU]) and the human resources policies of private companies. The outcome of this tension is not obvious yet, but it is foreseeable that the interaction of both types of policies will foster a new type of labor policy in EU countries, that is, a policy in which a coupling of social and economic goals (i.e., labor protection and care for product quality and development) seems real at both the national and company levels.

To get an idea about the future, this chapter will reconstruct the development of postwar policy reforms in health and safety at work in Western European countries and inside the EU. The terms *occupational welfare, labor policy*, and *social policy* are alternately used for matters regarding health, safety, and well-being at work.

The first section explores the health and safety reforms of the 1970s, during which time concepts such as the improvement of the quality of working life, or humanization of work, became popular among policymakers as well as managers. The second section, The Europeanization of Public Labor Policy During the 1980s, focuses on the evolution of the EU initiatives directed at health and safety of workers, which began in the 1980s. The EU took over the former initiatives for reforming health and safety legislation at the national level. The final section, The Future of Labor Policy in Europe, brings together the various parts of the chapter and speculates on developments in occupational health and welfare during the remaining years of this century.

Reforms of Labor Policy in European Industrial States During the 1970s

Traditionally, the state has been an important leading actor in Western European countries with respect to the introduction and development of occupational health and safety measures for workers in enterprises. The first legal measures date back to the final quarter of the last century. Next to social security laws, for example, sickness benefits, unemployment benefits, and health expenses, labor protection laws stand as the fundaments of the 20th-century welfare states (Hepple, 1986). The central hallmark of health and safety legislation was the employers' primary responsibility for the consequences of occupational injuries and illnesses; the employee was seen as a victim who needed protection. Three basic kinds of labor protection laws evolved. The first dealt with the protection of child labor and labor of women, the second type concerned the regulation of work time, and the third concerned provisions for worker compensation for occupational illness and injury. After a rapid initial development at the end of the 19th century and the first two decades of the 20th century, legal labor protection became less focal.

Further extension legislation came to a standstill in the 1930s, when public attention increasingly focused on the development of social insurance for workers (de Swaan, 1988). An explanation for this development can be found in the economic and social crisis of the 1930s (i.e., the worldwide Great Depression) and the desperation caused by World War II, but these were not the only reasons. New ideas about public economic policies stressed the importance of stimulating the demand side of the economy. Keynesianism was partly responsible for the shift of public attention from labor protection to the introduction of social security, and this development lasted until the mid-1970s.

Also significant at this time was the emergence of doubts about the lasting efficacy of Keynesian socioeconomic policies. The relatively high levels of public expenditures were perceived as burdensome, and renewed attention was focused on prevention as a contributor to decreased public expenditures. A third reason deals with sociocultural developments. After years of ongoing income growth and a general increase in wealth, other needs of citizens, such as the possible contribution of work to self-realization, became manifest. In this respect, the low attraction of much paid work was recognized. This was thought to be reflected by an increase in the number of work accidents, sickness absenteeism, and disability and by increased difficulty attracting workers to jobs with relatively poor working conditions. In summary, there were several urgent reasons to reexamine the efficacy of the existing laws regarding health and safety at work.

In several countries, action was taken to assess and reform legislation. One of the most interesting countries in this period was the United Kingdom. In 1970, a State Committee on Health and Safety was appointed. This committee, named after its chairman, Lord Robens, evaluated the British regulatory system against the background of the large number of workplace injuries and illnesses. Important conclusions from the Robens report were the following:

- The regulatory system in Britain did not prevent a large number of workers' being killed and injured each year in industry.
- Much of the existing law was obscure and unintelligible to those whose actions it was intended to influence.
- The various inspection bodies had overlapping jurisdictions.

- There was one main cause for accidents and ill health: apathy at all levels among employers and workers (de Gier, 1991a).

Based on these conclusions, the Robens Committee offered some far-reaching proposals, such as (a) increasing awareness and responsibility of employers and employees on matters concerning safety and health, (b) a more unified enforcement system, (c) less state regulation, and (d) a single, comprehensive framework legislation, supplemented by a series of controls and assisted by voluntary standards and more flexible codes of practice. These proposals were adopted by the government, the trade unions, and employer organizations and resulted in the Health and Safety at Work Act (HSWA) in 1974. The developments in the United Kingdom would serve as a model for what was going to happen in other European countries. Apart from the United Kingdom, new legislation was introduced in the following other EU countries (Social Europe, 1990): Denmark, 1975 (Working Environment Act); the Netherlands, 1980 (Working Environment Act); Greece, 1985 (Health and Safety of Workers Act); and Ireland, 1989 (Safety, Health and Welfare at Work Act). Furthermore, partial extension of existing legislation took place in Spain (1974), France (1976), Belgium (1978), Germany (1978), and Italy (1978). Although additional changes continued until about 1990, the momentum of the legal reforms was greatest between 1974 and 1980, in the direct aftermath of the peak of the European welfare state development.

The following six points summarize this important period of social policy reforms:

1. There was a broadening of objectives of the traditional legislation. Next to mainly technical safety matters, more attention was directed toward personal and collective health and well-being at work.
2. Most countries abstained from the habit of regulating through detailed prescriptions. Instead, a decision was made to formulate general regulations (i.e., framework legislation) through which it was possible to adapt existing legislation in a faster and more flexible way, thus preventing rapid technical obsolescence.
3. A fundamental choice was made to regard health and safety at work as a joint responsibility for the employer *and* the worker.
4. The principle of self-regulation at the enterprise level was reappraised. In the new framework legislation, various obligations stimulate the employer to organize self-regulative policies with regard to working conditions inside the company.
5. Adaptations in the predominant enforcement practices were introduced. Next to the traditional penal enforcement strategy, new strategies directed at guidance and support of the (self-regulative) parties at the enterprise level came to the fore.
6. The reforms were directed at making more transparent and simple the complex labor protection laws.

In Table 1, an overall picture is given for five EU countries. This table

Table 1. Legal Changes in Health and Safety in Five EU Countries During the 1970s

Legal change	NL	F	FRG	UK	DK
Broadening scope	+	+	+	+	+
Framework legislation	+	−	−/+	+	+
Worker participation	+	+	+	+	+
Self-regulation	+/−	−	+/−	+	+
Supportive enforcement	+	−	+/−	+	+
Simplification	+	−	−	+	+

Note. NL = the Netherlands; F = France; FRG = Federal Republic of Germany; UK = United Kingdom; DK = Denmark; + = the presence of the legal change; +/− = some aspect of the legal change is present; − = the legal change is absent.

clearly shows that after a long period of years, health and safety were fully reinstated in the political agenda during the 1970s. This was not an accidental development, and, until today, health and safety have remained high in the political agenda, albeit in an adjusted way. In particular, the EU has become the new pacesetter.

The Europeanization of Public Labor Policy During the 1980s

Since the first treaties, the EU paid attention to working conditions. In article 6 of the 1952 ECSC-Treaty, for example, it was stated that the Community had the right to contribute to the improvement of working conditions by means of harmonization of national regulations. A comparable statement was made in the 1952 Euratom-Treaty, as well as in the 1957 Treaty of Rome (articles 117 and 118). The first real effort dates back to 1960. In that year, a legally binding directive was adopted with respect to the classification and labeling of dangerous substances. In 1978, the First Action Program on health and safety at work was launched, followed by new Action Programs in 1984 and 1988. A Fourth Action Program is being run for the period 1993–1998. Formulating Action Programs and successive initiatives for directives is the common way of policy making in the health and safety field at the EU level. Up to 1985, relatively little happened at the EU level, compared with initiatives on working conditions at the national level about a decade earlier.

The year 1985, however, was a turning point. In 1985, the EU decided to introduce the so-called New Approach, which was directed at realizing a free economic market without trade barriers, beginning in January 1993. The New Approach implied the adoption of an extension of the Treaty of Rome and became the Single European Act (SEA) of 1987. Hallmarks of the SEA were the following:

1. A simpler procedure for decision making about economic and social directives, including health and safety, was in place. From that moment, the Council of Ministers, which makes the final decision about

the introduction of new directives, no longer needs a full majority but a qualified majority.

2. Directives were henceforth to be stated in general terms instead of in detailed terms, which simplified the decision-making process.

3. More powers were given to the European Parliament (EP). The EP gained more influence in the decision-making process of the European Commission (the executive body of the EU) and the Council of Ministers. Through this measure, some of the democratic deficit inside the EU was solved.

The adoption of the SEA was followed by the Third Action Program in 1988, which has resulted in the introduction of some 20 new directives in the field of health and safety. Crucial in this respect was the introduction in 1989 of the "framework directive on health and safety at work" based on article 118A SEA on the one hand and the introduction of the machinery directive based on article 100A SEA on the other. In particular, the framework directive formed the basis of a number of specific social directives on health and safety (e.g., personal protective equipment, work with visual display units, and handling of heavy loads involving risk of back injury).

The content of the 1989 framework directive is stated in general terms and bears a lot of similarities to the new framework laws in countries such as the United Kingdom, Denmark, and the Netherlands. This directive can be seen as a sort of European "work environment act." Apart from general employer and employee obligations, this directive contains specific employer obligations regarding the quality of the job content, well-being of workers at work, medical examination and other in-company services, training, information, and worker participation. However, the norms in this directive (and all the other directives based on the social policy article 118A) are only *minimum requirements*. The separate Member States retain the right to organize its health and safety legislation at higher standards than those prescribed by the EU. This right is complicated to some extent by the fact that directives based on the economic policy article 100A, like the machinery directive, prescribe fixed (maximum) requirements. In such a conflict, the 100A directives prevail over 118A directives.

The main objective of 100A directives is preventing (and meeting) economical and technical trade barriers between Member States inside the EU. Therefore, these directives, often referred to as product safety directives, are related to the safety and health of workers, although they are primarily aimed at the economic performance of the EU.

According to article 100A, SEA product safety directives must take "as a base, a high level of protection." This relates to the need of relatively high standards of protection all over the EU. Since the introduction of the New Approach, directives based on article 100A are stated in general terms, and further specification of the general standards are delegated to the European normalization institutes, CEN (European Standardization Committee) and CENELEC (European Committee for Electrotechnical Standardization). Directives based on article 118A are the worker protective directives and lay down minimum requirements with regard to health and safety matters; separate Member States have the freedom to demand higher standards. In this case, CEN and CENELEC play no formal role.

The ultimate goal of transposing directives into national regulatory systems is the harmonization of legislation in the EU. The instrument of the directive has been developed for this specific purpose. A directive has binding force in relation to the result to be achieved for each Member State to which it is addressed, but, at the same time, it leaves the Member States free to choose the form and methods for implementing it (Kapteyn & Verlooren Van Themaat, 1989). Although the EU until now (for reasons of enforceability and equal treatment) preferred national implementation by means of parliamentary legislation, the formal circumscription of the term directive leaves the Member States some maneuvering room in the implementation process. Recent empirical research has shown that this is indeed the case. A research project was carried out in 1991 in five Member States and examined the way these countries actually implement EU directives, specifically, the framework directive (de Gier, 1991b). This study found that there were at least three different implementation models in the EU. Two countries (France and the Federal Republic of Germany) were formal implementers and used parliamentary laws to implement the directive. Two other countries (the United Kingdom and Denmark) preferred to implement via secondary legislation (i.e., rules and orders) and nonbinding (quasi-) legislation. The Netherlands took a position between these groups and used all three forms of implementation. The variety in ways of implementing the EU directives reflected differences in administrative systems and systems of industrial relations between Member States (Slomp, 1990).

In summary, the EU has taken over the initiative from the separate Member States in making rules on health and safety at work. To a large extent, the EU has taken into account the previous developments in the Member States in giving a central role to the framework directive in the further harmonization of EU rules on health and safety. It is uncertain whether this development will continue undisturbed in the years to come.

The Future of Labor Policy in Europe

After the introduction of the SEA in 1987, a further addition of the Treaty of Rome was formulated in 1991, and the Treaty of Maastricht was adopted in 1993. An important part of this treaty is the "Social Protocol," which contains further extensions on safety and health. For example, the Social Protocol involves a widening of competencies combined with increased flexibility of the decision-making process with regard to European social policy. Also, organized labor at the European level will become more important in the making and administration of European social policy. From the outset, the European social partners will be involved in developing European labor law—not only health and safety legislation, but also other matters such as the politically sensitive question of the introduction of European work councils. Finally, the European

Employer and Trade Union Organizations have, under certain conditions, the right to make European-wide collective agreements. These could take various forms such as enterprise agreements, sectorial agreements, multisectorial agreements, and multiregional agreements.

The Treaty of Maastricht, for the very first time in the history of the EU, explicitly links the political decision-making process with the national and supranational bargaining circuits. How the Treaty and the Social Protocol will actually function in the near future is uncertain.

There have been some problems with adopting the Treaty of Maastricht. The most important problem was that the United Kingdom opted out of the Social Protocol, a problem not totally unexpected. Already in 1989, the United Kingdom did not sign the European Social Charter (a sort of nonlegal complement of the SEA in the social field). Part of the problem was the perceived lack of national influence on activities at the EU level. Some countries experience EU policies as too arrogant and top-down—oriented, leaving little maneuvering room for the Member States. This situation triggered a debate on two issues: (a) transparency (i.e., openness vs. bureaucracy) of EU policies and (b) subsidiarity (i.e., greater efficiency of solving problems at the lowest possible level). Thus, if certain rules on health and safety could be better made at a sectorial or national level, the EU has to refrain from rule making.

At the moment, the outcome of the debate on subsidiarity is unclear. However, one may expect that it will have some far-reaching consequences for the future of EU efforts and in the field of working conditions. It may, for example, be expected that the high speed of introducing new directives, since the coming into force of the SEA in 1986, will substantially slow down for a while. At the same time, a partial shift of attention will take place from introducing and implementing new directives to the enforcement of the new European rules in the Member States. Until now, the EU hardly paid attention to this practical side of the implementation process. Apart from this, one may wonder if the renewed evolution of attention to working conditions in Europe since the 1970s has not reached a second turning point. Therefore, it is necessary to take a closer look at actual developments in working conditions since then.

Beginning in the 1970s, much effort has been put into improving the quality of working life in Western European countries. I have described the important wave of national statutory reforms from the mid-1970s to the beginning of the 1980s, and new EU initiatives at the supranational level. As a result of these new rules, one might expect that the quality of work life and working conditions has been improved in the EU. If not, there is probably something seriously wrong with the new regulatory framework. There are several ways to measure effects of new rules and policies. One is to monitor the developments in working conditions at the workplace level; another is to monitor select indicators, such as the level of sickness absenteeism or occupational disability. The problem with these methods is that they have not been widely and systematically applied, either in most European countries or at the EU level.

National data collected in varied ways and at various moments are the best sources of information available. Thus, for example, in the Netherlands, we know that from the mid-1970s to the early 1990s there has occurred a shift in attention from physical constraints to time pressure and psychosocial risk factors (e.g., monotonous work and lack of promotion prospects [Houtman, Bloemhoff, Kompier, & Marcelissen, 1991]). At the same time, the level of sickness absenteeism has remained constant at a high level of about 10% of the active working population, and the number of disabled workers steadily increased from less than 100,000 workers in 1967 to nearly 1 million workers in 1992. Based solely on these figures, one might conclude that the Dutch Working Environment Act is not very efficient. However, the situation is much more complex. The development of these Dutch figures reflects more the difficult labor market than the quality of working life. After studying the disability figures over a long time span, Rein and Freeman concluded that the Dutch labor force has been shrinking substantially for several decades because of permanent productivity gains (Rein & Freeman, 1988).

To obtain insight into the efficacy of legislative reforms in Europe, a monitoring system has to be developed at the EU level. One of the European institutions, the European Foundation for the Improvement of Living and Working Conditions, in Dublin, took the first step and published the results of the First European Survey on the Work Environment 1991–1992 (European Foundation for the Improvement of Living and Working Conditions,[1] 1992). The project was carried out during the spring of 1991 among a representative sample of 12,500 workers in the EU, about 1,000 workers per country.

The results indicated that more than 30% of the interviewed workers experienced health risks, and there were large differences among the Member States. Thus, Spain had the highest score (62%), followed by Greece (44%) and Luxembourg (34%). The Netherlands (15%) and Belgium (18%) had the lowest scores. In the survey, a distinction was made between physical/chemical constraints and organizational constraints. Physical/chemical constraints included noise, bad weather, postures, dangerous substances and materials, and premises. Organizational constraints included working times, night work, deadlines, computer equipment, time pressure, repetitive work, autonomy, information, training, and support. High scores on organizational constraints were found with respect to lack of autonomy on task (38%), work rhythm (35%), rate-related income (26%), repetitive short cycles (23%), high time pressure (20%), and long working hours per week (23%). Low scores were found for night work (5%) and lack of training (9%). With respect to physical/chemical constraints, low scores were found for inadequate premises, inadequate equipment, and painful working positions (between 15.2% and 18%).

Men, more than women, experience problems with physical/chemical constraints. For organizational constraints, however, women complain about time pressure and repetitive short cycles, whereas men have many complaints about long working hours, work with computers, and lack of autonomy. Workers under age 25 complain about air pollution, handling dangerous substances, and painful working positions. Workers age 55 or older report extremes of

[1]The European Foundation for the Improvement of Living and Working Conditions is an autonomous body, established by a regulation of the EU Council of Ministers on May 26, 1975.

weather, painful positions, heavy loads, and inadequate equipment. Regarding organizational constraints, younger workers (under age 25) mainly report repetitive short cycles, lack of autonomy, and nonprovision of training. Between 24 and 40 years of age, the predominant complaints concern time pressure and work with computers; over 55 years of age, the complaints concern long working hours, rate-related income, nonprovision of information, and nonprovision of support. The age category that is better off is the category ages 40 to 45. This group complains only about long working hours.

The overall picture of the EU makes it possible to distinguish between three groups of countries. The first group (Belgium, Denmark, Great Britain, the former Federal Republic of Germany, Luxembourg, and the Netherlands) possess a good infrastructure (i.e., the availability of professional services, research, consultancy, and training facilities, etc.), and the main constraints are not physical/chemical, but organizational. The second group of countries (Greece, Portugal, and Spain), on the other hand, report more physical/chemical than organizational constraints and, apart from this, long working hours and great time pressure. The last group of nations (France, Italy, Ireland, and the former German Democratic Republic) take a middle position.

Although this is the first such survey ever carried out in the EU, and therefore its significance is limited, it clearly illustrates the quality of working life inside the EU and highlights substantial differences among countries. It is impossible to determine to what extent these differences are caused by the new EU rules. New surveys at different time points are needed. At the same time, the finding that the northern Member States experience less physical and more organizational constraints than the southern Member States indicates that legislation alone does not totally explain the quality of working life in the EU.

I stated earlier that the postwar legal reforms in the field of health and safety started in the heyday of the Western welfare state. National governments still believed strongly in the beneficiaries of legislation, but this belief started to crumble under the influence of Reaganism and Thatcherism. Nevertheless, in a number of European countries, new legislation about working conditions was fully realized (see Table 1). Concessions in the direction of the new supply-side paradigm (i.e., deregulation and privatization) did not go further than special attention to self-regulation of the parties involved at the enterprise level. From the mid-1980s, the EU had a stronger position with respect to product safety as well as health and safety policies. Because of that, supply-side principles became more visible (Baldwin & Daintith, 1992). The New Approach of the EU focused on economic policy, that is, introducing a free economic market in the EU before 1993. Social policy was, and still is, derived from this economic policy. Yet, as has been described, the EU social policy is overwhelmingly based on a legislative strategy. In this respect, it still can be defined as Keynesian-inspired and a logical continuation of the national reforms during the 1970s and first half of the 1980s.

Apart from the legislative evolution, there were a number of developments at the enterprise level. The paradigm shift from Keynesian, demand-side economic policies to supply-side policies implied the introduction of "structural adjustment" of the national and international economy as a new issue (Organization for Economic Co-operation and Development [OECD], 1989). By structural adjustment was meant a reappraisal of free market principles in the economy through flexibilization, deregulation, privatization, and adjustment of economic structures. Next to the OECD, the International Monetary Fund (IMF) also stimulated structural adjustment. Structural adjustment as a policy objective was introduced at an important moment in the history of Western capitalism (Piore & Sabel, 1984). The predominant way of production at the time, mass production, was no longer sufficiently competitive on the world market; consumer preferences also had changed fundamentally. Instead, there arose a growing need for flexible specialization. Flexible specialization is "a strategy of permanent innovation: accommodation to ceaseless change rather than an effort to control it" (Piore & Sabel, 1984, p. 17). The shift from mass production to flexible specialization also had tremendous consequences for the quality of work in enterprises, especially in countries with well-developed industries, such as the northern Member States of the EU. The difference in the prevalence of physical and organizational constraints among northern and southern Member States can be explained by the ongoing flexibilization process.

The evolution to flexible specialization went together with a decrease of the importance of manufacturing and an increase in service work. Also, the nature of work changed: The number of routine jobs went down in favor of in-person services and symbolic–analytic services (Reich, 1992). In-person services, like routine jobs, also entail simple and repetitive tasks, but these services (e.g., janitors, taxi drivers, hotel workers, house cleaners, hairdressers, security guards) must be provided person-to-person. Symbolic–analytic services include all the problem-solving, problem-identifying, and strategic-brokering activities, such as bankers, lawyers, design engineers, software engineers, public relations executives, and researchers.

Another related development is the ongoing transformation of big corporations into smaller networks of core organizations and suppliers, caused in part by the influence of the global economy (Peters, 1992; Porter, 1985, 1990). Generally speaking, this trend weakens the position of labor because it undermines the traditional power position of trade unions at the enterprise level and contributes to the flexibilization of collective and individual labor contracts (van Liemt, 1992). The category of workers that gains most from this development are the symbolic–analysts, whereas negative effects on the content of jobs are expected in the category of routine jobs and in-person services.

In a growing number of cases, enterprises are introducing new production concepts, such as "just-in-time production" and "lean" production, which include a redesign of individual tasks into autonomous working groups. Autonomous groups combine formerly fragmented tasks such as manufacturing, planning, maintenance, and quality control (Womack, Jones, & Roos, 1991). Introduction of new production concepts usually takes shape in the context of corporate human resources management, in which the application of human capital plays a key role. It is therefore highly competitive with public labor policy. An important question in this respect is whether the increasing worker demands in autonomous working groups will cause serious stress problems. Research findings in Sweden and the United States show an increase of stress-related physical and mental health problems among workers in jobs where the work demands outpace the decision latitude needed to successfully complete the job (Karasek & Theorell, 1990).

In summary, despite important legal reforms during the past two decades at the national and EU level, recent European survey research still shows the presence of physical, chemical, and organizational constraints in the working environment. Because of this, the efficacy of the new legal regulations can be questioned. If, on the other hand, developments at the supply side of the globalizing economy are taken into account, one may state that far-reaching changes are taking place that, in principle, are difficult to tackle with legal worker protection rules.

Conclusion

The main conclusion to be drawn from this chapter is that there is a serious gap between the legal efforts of the EU on the one hand and the actual developments with respect to the working environment at the enterprise and workplace level on the other hand. After two decades of restructuring the existing legal worker protection legislation in Member States and, subsequently, the EU, serious doubts may be raised about the efficacy of the legal strategy, even as far as minimum requirements are concerned. This particular strategy is gradually overhauled by actual developments in the economy, such as the paradigm shift in economic policy from Keynesian welfare economics to supply-side economics, the tendency to structural adjustment, the restructuring of manufacturing, and the ongoing shift from manufacturing to services.

Another critical factor is the increased significance of the economic orientation of EU policies after the introduction of the SEA. From that moment, more obviously than before, economic objectives of the EU have prevailed over social objectives. In this sense, the EU strategy directed at realizing a single market without trade barriers may be valued as a neoliberal structural adjustment policy. This implies that EU rules primarily have to facilitate the free market economy inside the EU. What is urgently needed is the organization of a strong counterbalance of labor against management at the enterprise and sectorial levels regarding health and safety. Trade unions, for example, can no longer rely uniquely on legal strategies.

The impact of legal reforms on health and safety in the years to come will be limited, and trade unions will need to strive for closer coalitions with the EU. In this respect, the Social Protocol of the Maastricht Treaty can be helpful. This protocol stimulates and endorses the opportunity to strive for European-wide collective agreements between labor and capital. If, in that case, employer organizations and trade unions do not succeed in making a European collective agreement, the EU might take initiatives for new directives and a further juridification of the health and safety field. It is my expectation that this will be a "big stick" for both parties. The result probably will be a new sort of labor policy characterized by less reliance on the traditional legalistic welfare state approach, and more accent on responsibilities and self-regulation of the parties (i.e., management, trade unions, and workers) at the enterprise level. Apart from this, the nature of social policy at the enterprise and sectorial levels will be an efficient mixture of economic and social motives.

References

Baldwin, R., & Daintith, T. (1992). *Harmonization and hazard: Regulating the workplace health and safety in the European Community*. London: Graham & Trotman.

de Gier, E. (1991a). The future of occupational welfare in the Netherlands and the UK. In G. Room (Ed.), *Towards a European welfare state?* (pp. 235–251). Bristol, England: School for Advanced Urban Studies.

de Gier, E. (1991b). *Implementation of EC directives on working conditions and product safety: Possibilities and limitations*. Amsterdam: Hugo Sinzheimer Institute.

de Swaan, A. (1988). *In care of the state*. Oxford, England: Polity.

Health and safety at work in the European Community [Special issue]. (1990). *Social Europe*, *3*(2), 5–89.

Hepple, B. (Ed). (1986). *The making of labour law in Europe: A comparative study of nine countries up to 1945*. London: Mansell.

Houtman, I. L. D., Bloemhoff, A., Kompier, M. A. J., & Marcelissen, F. H. G. (1991). *Werkstress risico's in bedrijf en beroep. Secundaire analyse van leefsituatie-onderzoeksgegevens van 1977, 1983 en 1986* [Work stress rises in trade and profession. Secondary analysis of life situation research findings of 1977]. The Hague, the Netherlands: Ministry of Social Affairs and Employment.

Kapteyn, P. J. G., & Verlooren Van Themaat, P. (1989). *Introduction to the law of the European Communities after the coming into force of the Single European Act*. Boston: Kluwer.

Karasek, R., & Theorell, T. (1990). *Healthy work: Stress, productivity and the reconstruction of working life*. New York: Basic Books.

Organization for Economic Co-operation and Development. (1989). *Economies in transition: Structural adjustment in OECD countries*. Paris: Author.

Paoli, P. (1992). *First European survey on the work environment*. Dublin, Ireland: European Foundation for the Improvement of Living and Working Conditions.

Peters, T. (1992). *Liberation management: Necessary disorganization for the nanosecond nineties*. New York: Knopf.

Piore, M. J., & Sabel, C. F. (1984). *The second industrial divide: Possibilities for prosperity*. New York: Basic Books.

Porter, M. (1985). *Competitive advantage: Creating and sustaining superior performance*. New York: Free Press.

Porter, M. (1990). *The competitive advantage of nations*. New York: Macmillan.

Reich, R. B. (1992). *The work of nations: Preparing ourselves for 21st century capitalism*. New York: Vintage.

Rein, M., & Freeman, R. (1988). *The Dutch choice: A plea for social policy complementary to work*. The Hague, the Netherlands: Harmonisatie Raad Welzijnsbeleid.

Slomp, H. (1990). *Labor relations in Europe: A history of issues and developments*. New York: Greenwood.

van Liemt, G. (1992). Economic globalization: Labour options and business strategies in high labour cost countries. *International Labour Review*, *131*(4–5), 453–470.

Womack, J. P., Jones, D. T., & Roos, D. (1991). *The machine that changed the world: The story of lean production*. New York: Harper Perennial.

Author Index

Numbers in italics refer to listings in reference sections.

Subject Index

Accidents
  associated with workplace structural config-
    uration, 390
  job-design, 390–391
Administrative Procedures Act of 1946, 394
Aggression. *See also* Violence
  definition, 22
  individuals with mental retardation, 45–46
Agoraphobia, spouse-assisted treatment, 142
Americans with Disabilities Act, 357–358
Anger
  definition, 22
  as motivation for aggressive behavior, 22
Anger Inventory, 49, 52
Anger management, 21–29
  conceptualization, 24
  healthy, 22–23
  ineffective, 28
  Rochester training module, 23–27
    results, 27
    statistical analyses, 26–27
    study design, 25–26
  stress inoculation training, 23
  studies, 23
  training programs, organizational barriers,
    23
Anxiety
  counterdependence and, 317
  overdependence and, 317–318
Area Agencies on Aging, 299
ASA, 266
Assaulted staff action program, 199–211
  assaults, 205–206
  clinical care, 206–207
  crisis intervention, 203–204, 208
  critical incident stress debriefing, 204–205
  decline in violence, 210
  functions, 203–205
  gender differences, 207
  hospital costs, 207–208
  methodological issues, 210–211
  patient assaults, 209–210
  philosophy, 201
  psychological trauma, 200–201, 208–209
  rationale, 201–202
  reductions in assaults, 207
  setting, 205
  specialized services, 205
  staff victim's support group, 204
  structure, 202–203

  victims who declined, 207
  victims who participated, 206–207
Attachment
  biological homeostasis, 311
  patterns, 310
Attachment figures, 310

Biased decision making, 397–398
Blue-collar employees
  blood pressure, 12–13
  Job In General scale, 15–16
  learning measure, 11–12, 17
  measures, 8–9
  outcome measures, 12–17
  procedure, 10
  reaction measure, 10–11, 16–17
  sample, 8
  SCL-90-R, 13–14
  State-Trait Anxiety Inventory, 14–15
  stress management, 7–19
Brief Symptom Index, 190

Cardiovascular disease, incidence in firefighters, 185
Career development, stress, 227
Caregivers. *See* Elder care
Caregivers in the workplace program,
  299
Caregiver Support Program, 93–106
  content, 95–96
  effectiveness of "train-the-trainer" ap-
    proach, 101–103
  impact, 104–105
  learning processes, 96–97
  measures, 98, 100–101
  participation, 101
  sample, recruitment and data collection,
    97–99
  transfer of training, 97
Catharsis, critical incident stress debriefing,
  179
Cognitive functioning, measurement, stress
  management intervention, 34–35
Conflict management, training, 46
Construct validity, worksite health promotion, 84
Control, escape, and symptom management
  coping scales, 113

429

About the Editors

Lawrence R. Murphy is a research psychologist with the National Institute for Occupational Safety and Health (NIOSH) and an adjunct associate professor of psychology at Xavier University in Cincinnati, Ohio. He received his MA and PhD degrees from DePaul University, Chicago, Illinois, and postdoctoral training at the Institute for Psychosomatic & Psychiatric Research, Michael Reese Medical Center, Chicago. He has published many articles in the area of occupational stress and stress management and has coedited several books, including *Stress Management in Work Settings* (with T. Schoenborn; 1989) and *Stress and Well-Being at Work: Assessments and Interventions for Occupational Mental Health* (with J. C. Quick & J. J. Hurrell, Jr.; 1992). His research interests are job stress assessment, stress management interventions, and worker compliance with universal precautions to prevent HIV/AIDS exposure in occupational settings.

Joseph J. Hurrell, Jr., is a Supervisory Research Epidemiologist with NIOSH and an adjunct professor of psychology at Xavier University in Cincinnati, Ohio. He received his PhD in psychology from Miami University. His primary research interests lie in the relationship between occupational stress and health, and he has published numerous articles and edited four books on this subject. He is currently associate editor of the *Journal of Occupational Health Psychology*.

Steven L. Sauter is Chief of the Applied Psychology and Ergonomics Branch at NIOSH and an adjunct professor of human factors engineering at the University of Cincinnati. His research interests focus on occupational stress and ergonomics, with a special emphasis on office and computer work. He is an Associate Editor of the *Journal of Occupational Health Psychology* and has prepared numerous articles and books on psychosocial aspects of occupational health.

Gwendolyn Puryear Keita is the Associate Executive Director of the Public Interest Directorate and Director of the Women's Programs Office of the American Psychological Association. Dr. Keita received her PhD in psychology from Howard University. Her primary research interests are the health and well-being of women and ethnic minorities, including issues of women and ethnic minorities in the workplace, psychosocial and behavioral factors in women's health, violence against women, women and depression, mental health issues of women and ethnic minorities, and occupational stress and health. She has published numerous articles in these areas.